Building the Data Warehouse, Fourth Edition

Building the Data Warehouse, Fourth Edition

W. H. Inmon

Wiley Publishing, Inc.

Building the Data Warehouse, Fourth Edition
Published by
Wiley Publishing, Inc.
10475 Crosspoint Boulevard
Indianapolis, IN 46256
www.wiley.com

For general information on our other products and services or to obtain technical support, please contact our Customer Care Department within the U.S. at (800) 762-2974, outside the U.S. at (317) 572-3993 or fax (317) 572-4002.

Wiley also publishes its books in a variety of electronic formats. Some content that appears in print may not be available in electronic books.

ISBN-13: 978-0-7645-9944-6
ISBN-10: 0-7645-9944-5

Manufactured in the United States of America

10 9 8 7 6 5 4 3

4B/SS/QZ/QV/IN

Credits

Executive Editor
Robert Elliott

Development Editor
Kevin Shafer

Production Editor
Pamela Hanley

Copy Editor
Kathi Duggan

Editorial Manager
Mary Beth Wakefield

Production Manager
Tim Tate

Vice President & Executive Group Publisher
Richard Swadley

Vice President and Publisher
Joseph B. Wikert

Project Coordinator
Erin Smith

Graphics and Production Specialists
Jonelle Burns
Kelly Emkow
Carrie A. Foster
Joyce Haughey
Jennifer Heleine
Stephanie D. Jumper

Quality Control Technician
Leeann Harney

Proofreading and Indexing
TECHBOOKS Production Services

To Jeanne Friedman and Kevin Gould — friends for all times.

About the Author

Bill Inmon, the father of the data warehouse concept, has written 40 books on data management, data warehouse, design review, and management of data processing. Bill has had his books translated into Russian, German, French, Japanese, Portuguese, Chinese, Korean, and Dutch. Bill has published more than 250 articles in many trade journals. Bill founded and took public Prism Solutions. His latest company — Pine Cone Systems — builds software for the management of the data warehouse/data mart environment. Bill holds two software patents. Articles, white papers, presentations, and much more material can be found on his Web site, www.billinmon.com.

Contents

Preface   **xix**

Acknowledgments   **xxvii**

Chapter 1   **Evolution of Decision Support Systems**   **1**

The Evolution   2

    The Advent of DASD   4

    PC/4GL Technology   4

    Enter the Extract Program   5

    The Spider Web   6

Problems with the Naturally Evolving Architecture   7

    Lack of Data Credibility   7

    Problems with Productivity   9

    From Data to Information   12

    A Change in Approach   14

    The Architected Environment   16

    Data Integration in the Architected Environment   18

    Who Is the User?   20

The Development Life Cycle   20

Patterns of Hardware Utilization   22

Setting the Stage for Re-engineering   23

Monitoring the Data Warehouse Environment   25

Summary   28

Chapter 2   **The Data Warehouse Environment**   **29**

The Structure of the Data Warehouse   33

Subject Orientation   34

Day 1 to Day *n* Phenomenon   39

Granularity   41
   The Benefits of Granularity   42
   An Example of Granularity   43
   Dual Levels of Granularity   46
Exploration and Data Mining   50
Living Sample Database   50
Partitioning as a Design Approach   53
   Partitioning of Data   53
Structuring Data in the Data Warehouse   56
Auditing and the Data Warehouse   61
Data Homogeneity and Heterogeneity   61
Purging Warehouse Data   64
Reporting and the Architected Environment   64
The Operational Window of Opportunity   65
Incorrect Data in the Data Warehouse   67
Summary   69

Chapter 3   The Data Warehouse and Design   71
Beginning with Operational Data   71
Process and Data Models and the Architected Environment   78
The Data Warehouse and Data Models   79
   The Data Warehouse Data Model   81
   The Midlevel Data Model   84
   The Physical Data Model   88
The Data Model and Iterative Development   91
Normalization and Denormalization   94
   Snapshots in the Data Warehouse   100
Metadata   102
   Managing Reference Tables in a Data Warehouse   103
Cyclicity of Data — The Wrinkle of Time   105
Complexity of Transformation and Integration   108
Triggering the Data Warehouse Record   112
   Events   112
   Components of the Snapshot   113
   Some Examples   113
Profile Records   114
Managing Volume   115
Creating Multiple Profile Records   117
Going from the Data Warehouse to the
  Operational Environment   117
Direct Operational Access of Data Warehouse Data   118
Indirect Access of Data Warehouse Data   119
   An Airline Commission Calculation System   119
   A Retail Personalization System   121
   Credit Scoring   123
Indirect Use of Data Warehouse Data   125

	Star Joins	126
	Supporting the ODS	133
	Requirements and the Zachman Framework	134
	Summary	136
Chapter 4	**Granularity in the Data Warehouse**	**139**
	Raw Estimates	140
	Input to the Planning Process	141
	Data in Overflow	142
	Overflow Storage	144
	What the Levels of Granularity Will Be	147
	Some Feedback Loop Techniques	148
	Levels of Granularity — Banking Environment	150
	Feeding the Data Marts	157
	Summary	157
Chapter 5	**The Data Warehouse and Technology**	**159**
	Managing Large Amounts of Data	159
	Managing Multiple Media	161
	Indexing and Monitoring Data	162
	Interfaces to Many Technologies	162
	Programmer or Designer Control of Data Placement	163
	Parallel Storage and Management of Data	164
	Metadata Management	165
	Language Interface	166
	Efficient Loading of Data	166
	Efficient Index Utilization	168
	Compaction of Data	169
	Compound Keys	169
	Variable-Length Data	169
	Lock Management	171
	Index-Only Processing	171
	Fast Restore	171
	Other Technological Features	172
	DBMS Types and the Data Warehouse	172
	Changing DBMS Technology	174
	Multidimensional DBMS and the Data Warehouse	175
	Data Warehousing across Multiple Storage Media	182
	The Role of Metadata in the Data Warehouse Environment	182
	Context and Content	185
	Three Types of Contextual Information	186
	Capturing and Managing Contextual Information	187
	Looking at the Past	187
	Refreshing the Data Warehouse	188
	Testing	190
	Summary	191

Chapter 6   **The Distributed Data Warehouse**   **193**
Types of Distributed Data Warehouses   193
  Local and Global Data Warehouses   194
    The Local Data Warehouse   197
    The Global Data Warehouse   198
    Intersection of Global and Local Data   201
    Redundancy   206
    Access of Local and Global Data   207
  The Technologically Distributed Data Warehouse   211
  The Independently Evolving Distributed Data Warehouse   213
The Nature of the Development Efforts   213
  Completely Unrelated Warehouses   215
Distributed Data Warehouse Development   217
  Coordinating Development across Distributed Locations   218
  The Corporate Data Model — Distributed   219
  Metadata in the Distributed Warehouse   223
Building the Warehouse on Multiple Levels   223
Multiple Groups Building the Current Level of Detail   226
  Different Requirements at Different Levels   228
  Other Types of Detailed Data   232
  Metadata   234
Multiple Platforms for Common Detail Data   235
Summary   236

Chapter 7   **Executive Information Systems and the Data Warehouse**   **239**
EIS — The Promise   240
A Simple Example   240
Drill-Down Analysis   243
Supporting the Drill-Down Process   245
The Data Warehouse as a Basis for EIS   247
Where to Turn   248
Event Mapping   251
Detailed Data and EIS   253
Keeping Only Summary Data in the EIS   254
Summary   255

Chapter 8   **External Data and the Data Warehouse**   **257**
External Data in the Data Warehouse   260
Metadata and External Data   261
Storing External Data   263
Different Components of External Data   264
Modeling and External Data   265
Secondary Reports   266
Archiving External Data   267
Comparing Internal Data to External Data   267
Summary   268

Chapter 9   **Migration to the Architected Environment**   **269**
    A Migration Plan   270
    The Feedback Loop   278
    Strategic Considerations   280
    Methodology and Migration   283
    A Data-Driven Development Methodology   283
        Data-Driven Methodology   286
        System Development Life Cycles   286
        A Philosophical Observation   286
    Summary   287

Chapter 10   **The Data Warehouse and the Web**   **289**
    Supporting the eBusiness Environment   299
    Moving Data from the Web to the Data Warehouse   300
    Moving Data from the Data Warehouse to the Web   301
    Web Support   302
    Summary   302

Chapter 11   **Unstructured Data and the Data Warehouse**   **305**
    Integrating the Two Worlds   307
        Text — The Common Link   308
        A Fundamental Mismatch   310
        Matching Text across the Environments   310
        A Probabilistic Match   311
        Matching All the Information   312
    A Themed Match   313
        Industrially Recognized Themes   313
        Naturally Occurring Themes   316
        Linkage through Themes and Themed Words 317
        Linkage through Abstraction and Metadata 318
    A Two-Tiered Data Warehouse   320
        Dividing the Unstructured Data Warehouse 321
        Documents in the Unstructured Data Warehouse 322
        Visualizing Unstructured Data   323
    A Self-Organizing Map (SOM)   324
        The Unstructured Data Warehouse   325
        Volumes of Data and the Unstructured Data Warehouse 326
    Fitting the Two Environments Together   327
    Summary   330

Chapter 12   **The Really Large Data Warehouse**   **331**
    Why the Rapid Growth?   332
    The Impact of Large Volumes of Data   333
        Basic Data-Management Activities   334
        The Cost of Storage   335
        The Real Costs of Storage   336
        The Usage Pattern of Data in the Face of Large Volumes 336

A Simple Calculation   337
Two Classes of Data   338
Implications of Separating Data into Two Classes   339
Disk Storage in the Face of Data Separation   340
   Near-Line Storage   341
   Access Speed and Disk Storage   342
   Archival Storage   343
   Implications of Transparency   345
Moving Data from One Environment to Another   346
   The CMSM Approach   347
   A Data Warehouse Usage Monitor   348
   The Extension of the Data Warehouse
     across Different Storage Media   349
Inverting the Data Warehouse   350
Total Cost   351
Maximum Capacity   352
Summary   354

Chapter 13 **The Relational and the Multidimensional Models
as a Basis for Database Design** **357**
The Relational Model   357
The Multidimensional Model   360
Snowflake Structures   361
Differences between the Models   362
   The Roots of the Differences   363
   Reshaping Relational Data   364
   Indirect Access and Direct Access of Data   365
   Servicing Future Unknown Needs   366
   Servicing the Need to Change Gracefully   367
Independent Data Marts   370
Building Independent Data Marts   371
Summary   375

Chapter 14 **Data Warehouse Advanced Topics** **377**
End-User Requirements and the Data Warehouse   377
   The Data Warehouse and the Data Model   378
   The Relational Foundation   378
   The Data Warehouse and Statistical Processing 379
Resource Contention in the Data Warehouse   380
   The Exploration Warehouse   380
   The Data Mining Warehouse   382
   Freezing the Exploration Warehouse   383
   External Data and the Exploration Warehouse   384
Data Marts and Data Warehouses in the Same Processor   384
The Life Cycle of Data   386
   Mapping the Life Cycle to the Data Warehouse Environment 387
Testing and the Data Warehouse   388

Tracing the Flow of Data through the Data Warehouse   390
    Data Velocity in the Data Warehouse   391
    "Pushing" and "Pulling" Data   393
Data Warehouse and the Web-Based eBusiness Environment   393
    The Interface between the Two Environments   394
    The Granularity Manager   394
    Profile Records   396
    The ODS, Profile Records, and Performance   397
The Financial Data Warehouse   397
The System of Record   399
A Brief History of Architecture — Evolving
  to the Corporate Information Factory   402
    Evolving from the CIF   404
    Obstacles   406
CIF — Into the Future   406
    Analytics   406
    ERP/SAP   407
    Unstructured Data   408
    Volumes of Data   409
Summary   410

**Chapter 15   Cost-Justification and Return on Investment
        for a Data Warehouse   413**
Copying the Competition   413
The Macro Level of Cost-Justification   414
A Micro Level Cost-Justification   415
Information from the Legacy Environment   418
    The Cost of New Information   419
    Gathering Information with a Data Warehouse   419
    Comparing the Costs   420
    Building the Data Warehouse   420
    A Complete Picture   421
    Information Frustration   422
The Time Value of Data   422
    The Speed of Information   423
Integrated Information   424
    The Value of Historical Data   425
    Historical Data and CRM   426
Summary   426

Chapter 16   The Data Warehouse and the ODS   429
Complementary Structures   430
    Updates in the ODS   430
    Historical Data and the ODS   431
    Profile Records   432
Different Classes of ODS   434
Database Design — A Hybrid Approach   435

Drawn to Proportion   436
Transaction Integrity in the ODS   437
Time Slicing the ODS Day   438
Multiple ODS   439
ODS and the Web Environment   439
An Example of an ODS   440
Summary   441

Chapter 17   Corporate Information Compliance and
**   Data Warehousing**   **443**
Two Basic Activities   445
Financial Compliance   446
    The "What"   447
    The "Why"   449
Auditing Corporate Communications   452
Summary   454

Chapter 18   The End-User Community   **457**
The Farmer   458
The Explorer   458
The Miner   459
The Tourist   459
The Community   459
Different Types of Data   460
Cost-Justification and ROI Analysis   461
Summary   462

Chapter 19   Data Warehouse Design Review Checklist   **463**
When to Do a Design Review   464
Who Should Be in the Design Review?   465
What Should the Agenda Be?   465
The Results   465
Administering the Review   466
A Typical Data Warehouse Design Review   466
Summary   488

Glossary   **489**

References   **507**
Articles   507
Books   510
White Papers   512

Index   **517**

Preface for the Second Edition

Databases and database theory have been around for a long time. Early renditions of databases centered around a single database serving every purpose known to the information processing community—from transaction to batch processing to analytical processing. In most cases, the primary focus of the early database systems was operational—usually transactional—processing. In recent years, a more sophisticated notion of the database has emerged—one that serves operational needs and another that serves informational or analytical needs. To some extent, this more enlightened notion of the database is due to the advent of PCs, 4GL technology, and the empowerment of the end user.

The split of operational and informational databases occurs for many reasons:

- The data serving operational needs is physically different data from that serving informational or analytic needs.

- The supporting technology for operational processing is fundamentally different from the technology used to support informational or analytical needs.

- The user community for operational data is different from the one served by informational or analytical data.

- The processing characteristics for the operational environment and the informational environment are fundamentally different.

Because of these reasons (and many more), the modern way to build systems is to separate the operational from the informational or analytical processing and data.

This book is about the analytical [or the decision support systems (DSS)] environment and the structuring of data in that environment. The focus of the book is on what is termed the "data warehouse" (or "information warehouse"), which is at the heart of informational, DSS processing.

The discussions in this book are geared to the manager and the developer. Where appropriate, some level of discussion will be at the technical level. But, for the most part, the book is about issues and techniques. This book is meant to serve as a guideline for the designer and the developer.

When the first edition of Building the Data Warehouse was printed, the database theorists scoffed at the notion of the data warehouse. One theoretician stated that data warehousing set back the information technology industry 20 years. Another stated that the founder of data warehousing should not be allowed to speak in public. And yet another academic proclaimed that data warehousing was nothing new and that the world of academia had known about data warehousing all along although there were no books, no articles, no classes, no seminars, no conferences, no presentations, no references, no papers, and no use of the terms or concepts in existence in academia at that time.

When the second edition of the book appeared, the world was mad for anything of the Internet. In order to be successful it had to be "e" something— e-business, e-commerce, e-tailing, and so forth. One venture capitalist was known to say, "Why do we need a data warehouse when we have the Internet?"

But data warehousing has surpassed the database theoreticians who wanted to put all data in a single database. Data warehousing survived the dot.com disaster brought on by the short-sighted venture capitalists. In an age when technology in general is spurned by Wall Street and Main Street, data warehousing has never been more alive or stronger. There are conferences, seminars, books, articles, consulting, and the like. But mostly there are companies doing data warehousing, and making the discovery that, unlike the overhyped New Economy, the data warehouse actually delivers, even though Silicon Valley is still in a state of denial.

Preface for the Third Edition

The third edition of this book heralds a newer and even stronger day for data warehousing. Today data warehousing is not a theory but a fact of life. New technology is right around the corner to support some of the more exotic needs of a data warehouse. Corporations are running major pieces of their business on data warehouses. The cost of information has dropped dramatically because of data warehouses. Managers at long last have a viable solution to the ugliness of the legacy systems environment. For the first time, a corporate "memory" of historical information is available. Integration of data across the corporation is a real possibility, in most cases for the first time. Corporations are learning how to go from data to information to competitive advantage. In short, data warehousing has unlocked a world of possibility.

One confusing aspect of data warehousing is that it is an architecture, not a technology. This frustrates the technician and the venture capitalist alike because these people want to buy something in a nice clean box. But data warehousing simply does not lend itself to being "boxed up." The difference between an architecture and a technology is like the difference between Santa Fe, New Mexico, and adobe bricks. If you drive the streets of Santa Fe you know you are there and nowhere else. Each home, each office building, each restaurant has a distinctive look that says "This is Santa Fe." The look and style that makes Santa Fe distinctive are the architecture. Now, that architecture is made up of such things as adobe bricks and exposed beams. There is a whole art to the making of adobe bricks and exposed beams. And it is certainly true that you could not have Santa Fe architecture without having adobe bricks and exposed beams. But adobe bricks and exposed beams by themselves do not make an architecture. They are independent technologies. For example, you have adobe bricks throughout the Southwest and the rest of the world that are not Santa Fe architecture.

Thus it is with architecture and technology, and with data warehousing and databases and other technology. There is the architecture, then there is the underlying technology, and they are two very different things. Unquestionably, there is a relationship between data warehousing and database technology, but they are most certainly not the same. Data warehousing requires the support of many different kinds of technology.

With the third edition of this book, we now know what works and what does not. When the first edition was written, there was some experience with developing and using warehouses, but truthfully, there was not the broad base of experience that exists today. For example, today we know with certainty the following:

- Data warehouses are built under a different development methodology than applications. Not keeping this in mind is a recipe for disaster.

- Data warehouses are fundamentally different from data marts. The two do not mix—they are like oil and water.

- Data warehouses deliver on their promise, unlike many overhyped technologies that simply faded away.

- Data warehouses attract huge amounts of data, to the point that entirely new approaches to the management of large amounts of data are required.

But perhaps the most intriguing thing that has been learned about data warehousing is that data warehouses form a foundation for many other forms of processing. The granular data found in the data warehouse can be reshaped and reused. If there is any immutable and profound truth about data warehouses, it is that data warehouses provide an ideal foundation for many other forms of information processing. There are a whole host of reasons why this foundation is so important:

- There is a single version of the truth.
- Data can be reconciled if necessary.
- Data is immediately available for new, unknown uses.

And, finally, data warehousing has lowered the cost of information in the organization. With data warehousing, data is inexpensive to get to and fast to access.

Databases and database theory have been around for a long time. Early renditions of databases centered around a single database serving every purpose known to the information processing community—from transaction to batch processing to analytical processing. In most cases, the primary focus of the early database systems was operational—usually transactional—processing. In recent years, a more sophisticated notion of the database has emerged—one that serves operational needs and another that serves informational or analytical needs. To some extent, this more enlightened notion of the database is due to the advent of PCs, 4GL technology, and the empowerment of the end user. The split of operational and informational databases occurs for many reasons:

- The data serving operational needs is physically different data from that serving informational or analytic needs.
- The supporting technology for operational processing is fundamentally different from the technology used to support informational or analytical needs.
- The user community for operational data is different from the one served by informational or analytical data.
- The processing characteristics for the operational environment and the informational environment are fundamentally different.

For these reasons (and many more), the modern way to build systems is to separate the operational from the informational or analytical processing and data.

This book is about the analytical or the DSS environment and the structuring of data in that environment. The focus of the book is on what is termed the data warehouse (or information warehouse), which is at the heart of informational, DSS processing.

What is analytical, informational processing? It is processing that serves the needs of management in the decision-making process. Often known as DSS processing, analytical processing looks across broad vistas of data to detect trends. Instead of looking at one or two records of data (as is the case in operational processing), when the DSS analyst does analytical processing, many records are accessed.

It is rare for the DSS analyst to update data. In operational systems, data is constantly being updated at the individual record level. In analytical processing, records are constantly being accessed, and their contents are gathered for analysis, but little or no alteration of individual records occurs.

In analytical processing, the response time requirements are greatly relaxed compared to those of traditional operational processing. Analytical response time is measured from 30 minutes to 24 hours. Response times measured in this range for operational processing would be an unmitigated disaster.

The network that serves the analytical community is much smaller than the one that serves the operational community. Usually there are far fewer users of the analytical network than of the operational network.

Unlike the technology that serves the analytical environment, operational environment technology must concern itself with data and transaction locking, contention for data, deadlock, and so on.

There are, then, many major differences between the operational environment and the analytical environment. This book is about the analytical, DSS environment and addresses the following issues:

- Granularity of data
- Partitioning of data
- Meta data
- Lack of credibility of data
- Integration of DSS data
- The time basis of DSS data
- Identifying the source of DSS data-the system of record
- Migration and methodology

This book is for developers, managers, designers, data administrators, database administrators, and others who are building systems in a modern data processing environment. In addition, students of information processing will find this book useful. Where appropriate, some discussions will be more technical. But, for the most part, the book is about issues and techniques, and it is meant to serve as a guideline for the designer and the developer.

This book is the first in a series of books relating to data warehouse. The next book in the series is Using the Data Warehouse (Wiley, 1994). Using the Data Warehouse addresses the issues that arise once you have built the data warehouse. In addition, Using the Data Warehouse introduces the concept of a larger architecture and the notion of an operational data store (ODS). An operational data store is a similar architectural construct to the data warehouse, except the ODS applies only to operational systems, not informational systems. The third book in the series is Building the Operational Data Store (Wiley, 1999), which addresses the issues of what an ODS is and how an ODS is built.

The next book in the series is Corporate Information Factory, Third Edition (Wiley, 2002). This book addresses the larger framework of which the data warehouse is the center. In many regards the CIF book and the DW book are companions. The CIF book provides the larger picture and the DW book provides a more focused discussion. Another related book is Exploration Warehousing (Wiley, 2000). This book addresses a specialized kind of processing-pattern analysis using statistical techniques on data found in the data warehouse.

Building the Data Warehouse, however, is the cornerstone of all the related books. The data warehouse forms the foundation of all other forms of DSS processing.

There is perhaps no more eloquent testimony to the advances made by data warehousing and the corporate information factory than the References at the back of this book. When the first edition was published, there were no other books, no white papers, and only a handful of articles that could be referenced. In this third edition, there are many books, articles, and white papers that are mentioned. Indeed the references only start to explore some of the more important works.

Preface for the Fourth Edition

In the beginning was a theory of database that held that all data should be held in a common source. It was easy to see how this notion came about. Prior to database, there were master files. These master files resided on sequential media and were built for every application that came along. There was absolutely no integration among master files. Thus, the idea of integrating data into a single source — a database — held great appeal.

It was into this mindset that data warehouse was born. Data warehousing was an intellectual threat to those who subscribed to conventional database theory because data warehousing suggested that there ought to be different kinds of databases. And the thought that there should be different kinds of databases was not accepted by the database theoreticians.

Today, data warehousing has achieved the status of conventional wisdom. For a variety of reasons, data warehousing is just what you do. Recently a survey showed that corporate spending on data warehouse and business intelligence surpassed spending on transactional processing and OLTP, something unthinkable a few years back.

The day of data warehouse maturity has arrived.

It is appropriate, then, that the Fourth Edition of the book that began the data warehousing phenomenon has been written.

In addition to the time-honored concepts of data warehousing, this edition contains the data warehouse basics. But it also contains many topics current to today's information infrastructure.

Following are some of the more important new topics in this edition:

- Compliance (dealing with Sarbanes Oxley, HIPAA, Basel II, and more)
- Near line storage (extending the data warehouse to infinity)
- Multi dimensional database design
- Unstructured data
- End users (who they are and what their needs are)
- ODS and the data warehouse

In addition to having new topics, this edition reflects that larger architecture that surrounds a data warehouse.

Technology has grown up with data warehousing. In the early days of data warehousing, 50 GB to 100 GB of data was considered a large warehouse. Today, some data warehouses are in the petabyte range. Other technology includes advances made in multi-dimensional technology — in data marts and star joins. Yet other technology advances have occurred in the storage of data on storage media other than disk storage.

In short, technology advances have made possible the technological achievements of today. Without modern technology, there would be no data warehouse.

This book is for architects and system designers. The end user may find this book useful as an explanation of what data warehousing is all about. And managers and students will also find this book to be useful.

Acknowledgments

The following people have influenced—directly and indirectly—the material found in this book. The author is grateful for the long-term relationships that have been formed and for the experiences that have provided a basis for learning.

Guy Hildebrand, a partner like no other

Lynn Inmon, a wife and helpmate like no other

Ryan Sousa, a free thinker for the times

Jim Shank and Nick Johnson, without whom there would be nothing

Ron Powell and Shawn Rogers, friends and inspirations for all times

Joyce Norris Montanari, Intelligent Solutions, an inspiration throughout the ages

John Zachman, Zachman International, a friend and a world class architect

Dan Meers, BillInmon.com, a real visionary and a real friend

Cheryl Estep, independent consultant, who was there at the beginning

Claudia Imhoff, Intelligent Solutions

Jon Geiger, Intelligent Solutions

John Ladley, Meta Group

Bob Terdeman, EMC Corporation

Lowell Fryman, independent consultant

David Fender, SAS Japan

Jim Davis, SAS

Peter Grendel, SAP

Allen Houpt, CA

Building the Data Warehouse, Fourth Edition

Evolution of Decision Support Systems

We are told that the hieroglyphics in Egypt are primarily the work of an accountant declaring how much grain is owed the Pharaoh. Some of the streets in Rome were laid out by civil engineers more than 2,000 years ago. Examination of bones found in archeological excavations in Chile shows that medicine — in, at least, a rudimentary form — was practiced as far back as 10,000 years ago. Other professions have roots that can be traced to antiquity. From this perspective, the profession and practice of information systems and processing are certainly immature, because they have existed only since the early 1960s.

Information processing shows this immaturity in many ways, such as its tendency to dwell on detail. There is the notion that if we get the details right, the end result will somehow take care of itself, and we will achieve success. It's like saying that if we know how to lay concrete, how to drill, and how to install nuts and bolts, we don't have to worry about the shape or the use of the bridge we are building. Such an attitude would drive a professionally mature civil engineer crazy. Getting all the details right does not necessarily equate success.

The data warehouse requires an architecture that begins by looking at the whole and then works down to the particulars. Certainly, details are important throughout the data warehouse. But details are important only when viewed in a broader context.

The story of the data warehouse begins with the evolution of information and decision support systems. This broad view of how it was that data warehousing evolved enables valuable insight.

The Evolution

The origins of data warehousing and *decision support systems (DSS)* processing hark back to the very early days of computers and information systems. It is interesting that DSS processing developed out of a long and complex evolution of information technology. Its evolution continues today.

Figure 1-1 shows the evolution of information processing from the early 1960s through 1980. In the early 1960s, the world of computation consisted of creating individual applications that were run using master files. The applications featured reports and programs, usually built in an early language such as Fortran or COBOL. Punched cards and paper tape were common. The master files of the day were housed on magnetic tape. The magnetic tapes were good for storing a large volume of data cheaply, but the drawback was that they had to be accessed sequentially. In a given pass of a magnetic tape file, where 100 percent of the records have to be accessed, typically only 5 percent or fewer of the records are actually needed. In addition, accessing an entire tape file may take as long as 20 to 30 minutes, depending on the data on the file and the processing that is done.

Around the mid-1960s, the growth of master files and magnetic tape exploded. And with that growth came huge amounts of redundant data. The proliferation of master files and redundant data presented some very insidious problems:

- The need to synchronize data upon update
- The complexity of maintaining programs
- The complexity of developing new programs
- The need for extensive amounts of hardware to support all the master files

In short order, the problems of master files — problems inherent to the medium itself — became stifling.

It is interesting to speculate what the world of information processing would look like if the only medium for storing data had been the magnetic tape. If there had never been anything to store bulk data on other than magnetic tape files, the world would have never had large, fast reservations systems, ATM systems, and the like. Indeed, the ability to store and manage data on new kinds of media opened up the way for a more powerful type of processing that brought the technician and the businessperson together as never before.

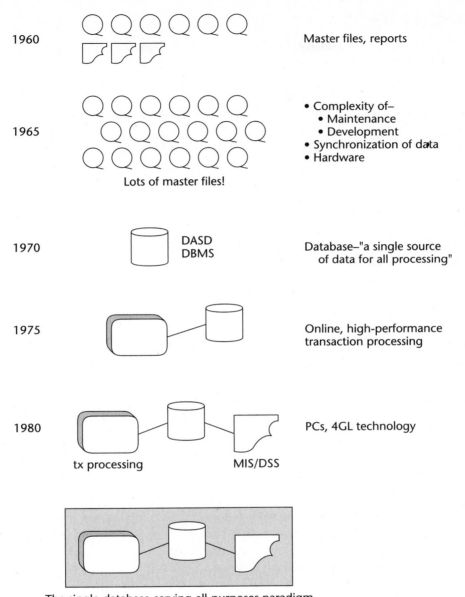

1960 — Master files, reports

1965 — Lots of master files!
- Complexity of–
  - Maintenance
  - Development
- Synchronization of data
- Hardware

1970 — DASD DBMS — Database–"a single source of data for all processing"

1975 — Online, high-performance transaction processing

1980 — tx processing — MIS/DSS — PCs, 4GL technology

The single-database-serving-all-purposes paradigm

Figure 1-1   The early evolutionary stages of the architected environment.

The Advent of DASD

By 1970, the day of a new technology for the storage and access of data had dawned. The 1970s saw the advent of disk storage, or the *direct access storage device (DASD)*. Disk storage was fundamentally different from magnetic tape storage in that data could be accessed directly on a DASD. There was no need to go through records 1, 2, 3, . . . n to get to record $n + 1$. Once the address of record $n + 1$ was known, it was a simple matter to go to record $n + 1$ directly. Furthermore, the time required to go to record $n + 1$ was significantly less than the time required to scan a tape. In fact, the time to locate a record on a DASD could be measured in milliseconds.

With the DASD came a new type of system software known as a *database management system (DBMS)*. The purpose of the DBMS was to make it easy for the programmer to store and access data on a DASD. In addition, the DBMS took care of such tasks as storing data on a DASD, indexing data, and so forth. With the DASD and DBMS came a technological solution to the problems of master files. And with the DBMS came the notion of a "database." In looking at the mess that was created by master files and the masses of redundant data aggregated on them, it is no wonder that in the 1970s, a database was defined as a single source of data for all processing.

By the mid-1970s, *online transaction processing (OLTP)* made even faster access to data possible, opening whole new vistas for business and processing. The computer could now be used for tasks not previously possible, including driving reservations systems, bank teller systems, manufacturing control systems, and the like. Had the world remained in a magnetic-tape-file state, most of the systems that we take for granted today would not have been possible.

PC/4GL Technology

By the 1980s, more new technologies, such as PCs and *fourth-generation languages (4GLs)*, began to surface. The end user began to assume a role previously unfathomed — directly controlling data and systems — a role previously reserved for the professional data processor. With PCs and 4GL technology came the notion that more could be done with data than simply processing online transactions. A *Management Information System (MIS)*, as it was called in the early days, could also be implemented. Today known as DSS, MIS was processing used to drive management decisions. Previously, data and technology were used exclusively to drive detailed operational decisions. No single database could serve both operational transaction processing and analytical processing at the same time. The single-database paradigm was previously shown in Figure 1-1.

Enter the Extract Program

Shortly after the advent of massive OLTP systems, an innocuous program for "extract" processing began to appear (see Figure 1-2).

The *extract program* is the simplest of all programs. It rummages through a file or database, uses some criteria for selecting data, and, on finding qualified data, transports the data to another file or database.

The extract program became very popular for at least two reasons:

■ Because extract processing can move data out of the way of high-performance online processing, there is no conflict in terms of performance when the data needs to be analyzed en masse.

■ When data is moved out of the operational, transaction-processing domain with an extract program, a shift in control of the data occurs. The end user then owns the data once he or she takes control of it. For these (and probably a host of other) reasons, extract processing was soon found everywhere.

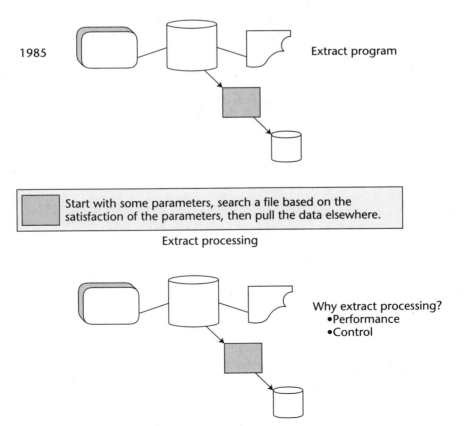

Figure 1-2   The nature of extract processing.

The Spider Web

As illustrated in Figure 1-3, a "spider web" of extract processing began to form. First, there were extracts; then there were extracts of extracts; then extracts of extracts of extracts; and so forth. It was not unusual for a large company to perform as many as 45,000 extracts per day.

This pattern of out-of-control extract processing across the organization became so commonplace that it was given its own name — the "naturally evolving architecture" — which occurs when an organization handles the whole process of hardware and software architecture with a laissez-faire attitude. The larger and more mature the organization, the worse the problems of the naturally evolving architecture become.

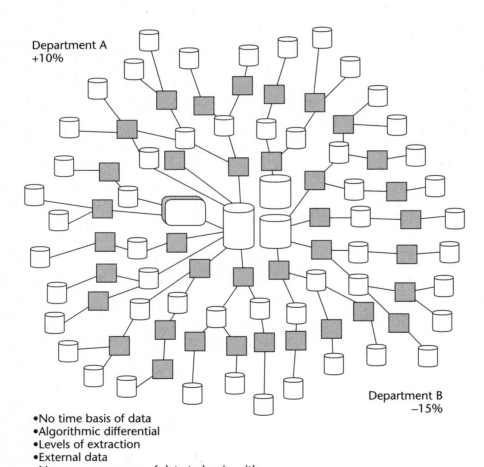

Department A
+10%

Department B
−15%

- No time basis of data
- Algorithmic differential
- Levels of extraction
- External data
- No common source of data to begin with

Figure 1-3 Lack of data credibility in the naturally evolving architecture.

Problems with the Naturally Evolving Architecture

The naturally evolving architecture presents many challenges, such as:

- Data credibility
- Productivity
- Inability to transform data into information

Lack of Data Credibility

The lack of data credibility was illustrated in Figure 1-3. Say two departments are delivering a report to management — one department claims that activity is down 15 percent, the other says that activity is up 10 percent. Not only are the two departments not in sync with each other, they are off by very large margins. In addition, trying to reconcile the different information from the different departments is difficult. Unless very careful documentation has been done, reconciliation is, for all practical purposes, impossible.

When management receives the conflicting reports, it is forced to make decisions based on politics and personalities because neither source is more or less credible. This is an example of the crisis of data credibility in the naturally evolving architecture.

This crisis is widespread and predictable. Why? As it was depicted in Figure 1-3, there are five reasons:

- No time basis of data
- The algorithmic differential of data
- The levels of extraction
- The problem of external data
- No common source of data from the beginning

The first reason for the predictability of the crisis is that there is no time basis for the data. Figure 1-4 shows such a time discrepancy. One department has extracted its data for analysis on a Sunday evening, and the other department extracted on a Wednesday afternoon. Is there any reason to believe that analysis done on one sample of data taken on one day will be the same as the analysis for a sample of data taken on another day? Of course not. Data is always changing within the corporation. Any correlation between analyzed sets of data that are taken at different points in time is only coincidental.

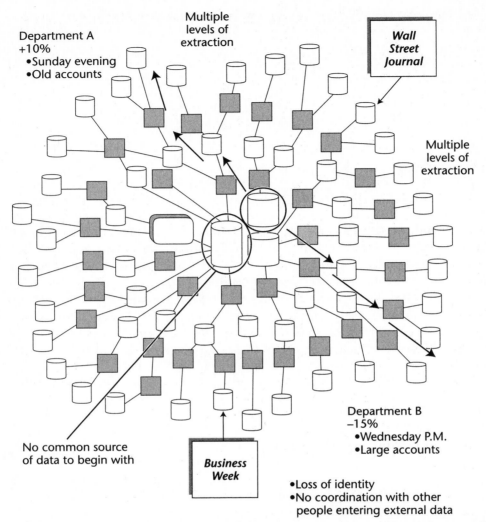

Figure 1-4 The reasons for the predictability of the crisis in data credibility in the naturally evolving architecture.

The second reason is the algorithmic differential. For example, one department has chosen to analyze all old accounts. Another department has chosen to analyze all large accounts. Is there any necessary correlation between the characteristics of customers who have old accounts and customers who have large accounts? Probably not. So why should a very different result surprise anyone?

The third reason is one that merely magnifies the first two reasons. Every time a new extraction is done, the probabilities of a discrepancy arise because of the timing or the algorithmic differential. And it is not unusual for a corporation to have eight or nine levels of extraction being done from the time the data enters the corporation's system to the time analysis is prepared for management. There are extracts, extracts of extracts, extracts of extracts of extracts, and so on. Each new level of extraction exaggerates the other problems that occur.

The fourth reason for the lack of credibility is the problem posed by external data. With today's technologies at the PC level, it is very easy to bring in data from outside sources. For example, Figure 1-4 showed one analyst bringing data into the mainstream of analysis from the *Wall Street Journal*, and another analyst bringing data in from *Business Week*. However, when the analyst brings data in, he or she strips the external data of its identity. Because the origin of the data is not captured, it becomes generic data that could have come from any source.

Furthermore, the analyst who brings in data from the *Wall Street Journal* knows nothing about the data being entered from *Business Week*, and vice versa. No wonder, then, that external data contributes to the lack of credibility of data in the naturally evolving architecture.

The last contributing factor to the lack of credibility is that often there is no common source of data to begin with. Analysis for department A originates from file XYZ. Analysis for department B originates from database ABC. There is no synchronization or sharing of data whatsoever between file XYZ and database ABC.

Given these reasons, it is no small wonder that there is a crisis of credibility brewing in every organization that allows its legacy of hardware, software, and data to evolve naturally into the spider web.

Problems with Productivity

Data credibility is not the only major problem with the naturally evolving architecture. Productivity is also abysmal, especially when there is a need to analyze data across the organization.

Consider an organization that has been in business for a while and has built up a large collection of data, as shown in the top of Figure 1-5.

Management wants to produce a corporate report, using the many files and collections of data that have accumulated over the years. The designer assigned the task decides that three things must be done to produce the corporate report:

- Locate and analyze the data for the report.
- Compile the data for the report.
- Get programmer/analyst resources to accomplish these two tasks.

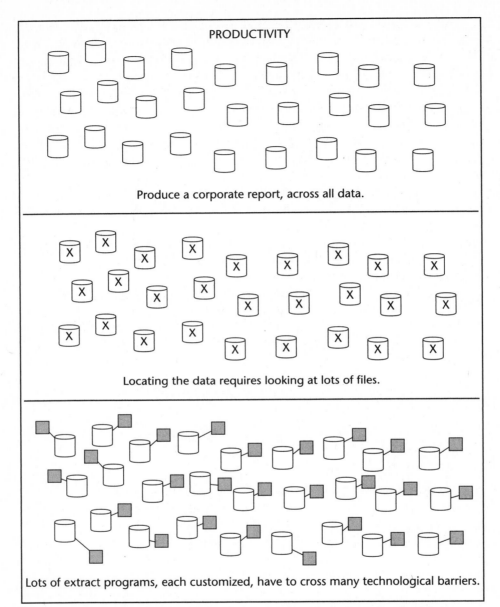

Figure 1-5   The naturally evolving architecture is not conducive to productivity.

In order to locate the data, many files and layouts of data must be analyzed. Some files use the *Virtual Storage Access Method (VSAM)*, some use the *Information Management System (IMS)*, some use *Adabas*, some use the *Integrated Database Management System (IDMS)*. Different skill sets are required in order to access data across the enterprise. Furthermore, there are complicating factors. For example, two files might have an element called BALANCE, but the two elements are very different. In another case, one database might have a file known as CURRBAL, and another collection of data might have a file called INVLEVEL that happens to represent the same information as CURRBAL. Having to go through every piece of data — not just by name but by definition and calculation — is a very tedious process. But if the corporate report is to be produced, this exercise must be done properly. Unless data is analyzed and "rationalized," the report will end up mixing apples and oranges, creating yet another level of confusion.

The next task for producing the report is to compile the data once it is located. The program that must be written to get data from its many sources should be simple. It is complicated, though, by the following facts:

- Lots of programs have to be written.
- Each program must be customized.
- The programs cross every technology that the company uses.

In short, even though the report-generation program should be simple to write, retrieving the data for the report is tedious.

In a corporation facing exactly the problems described, an analyst recently estimated a very long time to accomplish the tasks, as shown in Figure 1-6.

If the designer had asked for only two or three man-months of resources, then generating the report might not have required much management attention. But when an analyst requisitions many resources, management must consider the request with all the other requests for resources and must prioritize the requests.

Creating the reports using a large amount of resources wouldn't be bad if there were a one-time penalty to be paid. In other words, if the first corporate report generated required a large amount of resources, and if all succeeding reports could build on the first report, then it might be worthwhile to pay the price for generating the first report. But that is not the case.

Unless future corporate reporting requirements are known in advance and are factored into building the first corporate report, each new corporate report will probably require the same large overhead. In other words, it is unlikely that the first corporate report will be adequate for future corporate reporting requirements.

Productivity, then, in the corporate environment is a major issue in the face of the naturally evolving architecture and its legacy systems. Simply stated, when using the spider web of legacy systems, information is expensive to access and takes a long time to create.

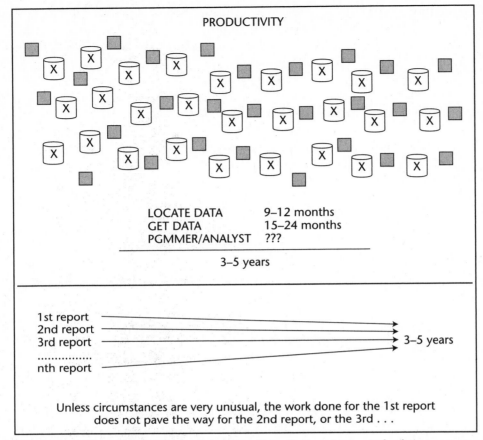

Figure 1-6 When the first report is being written, the requirements for future reports are not known.

From Data to Information

As if productivity and credibility were not problems enough, there is another major fault of the naturally evolving architecture — the inability to go from data to information. At first glance, the notion of going from data to information seems to be an ethereal concept with little substance. But that is not the case at all.

Consider the following request for information, typical in a banking environment: "How has account activity differed this year from each of the past five years?"

Figure 1-7 shows the request for information.

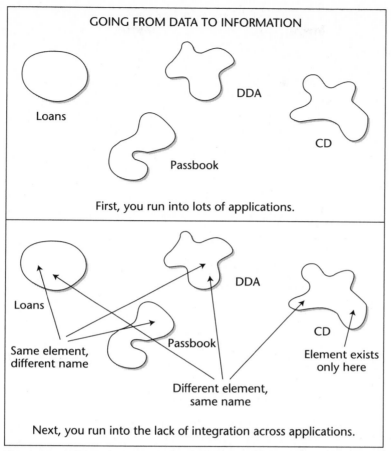

Figure 1-7 "How has account activity been different this year from each of the past five years for the financial institution?"

The first thing the DSS analyst discovers in trying to satisfy the request for information is that going to existing systems for the necessary data is the worst thing to do. The DSS analyst will have to deal with lots of unintegrated non-integrated legacy applications. For example, a bank may have separate savings, loan, direct-deposit, and trust applications. However, trying to draw information from them on a regular basis is nearly impossible because the applications were never constructed with integration in mind, and they are no easier for the DSS analyst to decipher than they are for anyone else.

But integration is not the only difficulty the analyst meets in trying to satisfy an informational request. A second major obstacle is that there is not enough historical data stored in the applications to meet the needs of the DSS request.

Figure 1-8 shows that the loan department has up to two years' worth of data, passbook processing has up to one year of data, DDA applications have up to 30 days of data, and CD processing has up to 18 months of data. The applications were built to service the needs of current balance processing. They were never designed to hold the historical data needed for DSS analysis. It is no wonder, then, that going to existing systems for DSS analysis is a poor choice. But where else is there to go?

The systems found in the naturally evolving architecture are simply inadequate for supporting information needs. They lack integration and there is a discrepancy between the time horizon (or parameter of time) needed for analytical processing and the available time horizon that exists in the applications.

A Change in Approach

The status quo of the naturally evolving architecture, where most shops began, simply is not robust enough to meet the future needs. What is needed is something much larger — a change in architectures. That is where the architected data warehouse comes in.

There are fundamentally two kinds of data at the heart of an "architected" environment — *primitive data* and *derived data*. Figure 1-9 shows some of the major differences between primitive and derived data.

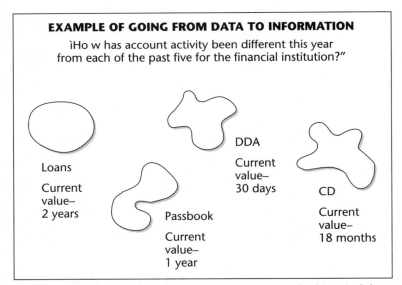

Figure 1-8   Existing applications simply do not have the historical data required to convert data into information.

A CHANGE IN APPROACHES

PRIMITIVE DATA/OPERATIONAL DATA	DERIVED DATA/DSS DATA
• Application-oriented	• Subject-oriented
• Detailed	• Summarized, otherwise refined
• Accurate, as of the moment of access	• Represents values over time, snapshots
• Serves the clerical community	• Serves the managerial community
• Can be updated	• Is not updated
• Run repetitively	• Run heuristically
• Requirements for processing understood *a priori*	• Requirements for processing not understood *a priori*
• Compatible with the SDLC	• Completely different life cycle
• Performance-sensitive	• Performance relaxed
• Accessed a unit at a time	• Accessed a set at a time
• Transaction-driven	• Analysis-driven
• Control of update a major concern in terms of ownership	• Control of update no issue
• High availability	• Relaxed availability
• Managed in its entirety	• Managed by subsets
• Nonredundancy	• Redundancy is a fact of life
• Static structure; variable contents	• Flexible structure
• Small amount of data used in a process	• Large amount of data used in a process
• Supports day-to-day operations	• Supports managerial needs
• High probability of access	• Low, modest probability of access

Figure 1-9 Differences between primitive and derived data.

Following are some other differences between the two.

■ Primitive data is detailed data used to run the day-to-day operations of the company. Derived data has been summarized or otherwise calculated to meet the needs of the management of the company.

■ Primitive data can be updated. Derived data can be recalculated but cannot be directly updated.

■ Primitive data is primarily current-value data. Derived data is often historical data.

■ Primitive data is operated on by repetitive procedures. Derived data is operated on by heuristic, nonrepetitive programs and procedures.

■ Operational data is primitive; DSS data is derived.

■ Primitive data supports the clerical function. Derived data supports the managerial function.

It is a wonder that the information processing community ever thought that both primitive and derived data would fit and peacefully coexist in a single database. In fact, primitive data and derived data are so different that they do not reside in the same database or even the same environment.

The Architected Environment

The natural extension of the split in data caused by the difference between primitive and derived data is shown in Figure 1-10.

There are four levels of data in the architected environment — the *operational level*, the *atomic* (or the *data warehouse*) *level*, the *departmental* (or the *data mart*) level, and the *individual level*. These different levels of data are the basis of a larger architecture called the *corporate information factory (CIF)*. The operational level of data holds application-oriented primitive data only and primarily serves the high-performance transaction-processing community. The data-warehouse level of data holds integrated, historical primitive data that cannot be updated. In addition, some derived data is found there. The departmental or data mart level of data contains derived data almost exclusively. The departmental or data mart level of data is shaped by end-user requirements into a form specifically suited to the needs of the department. And the individual level of data is where much heuristic analysis is done.

The different levels of data form a higher set of architectural entities. These entities constitute the corporate information factory, and they are described in more detail in my book, *The Corporate Information Factory, Second Edition* (Hoboken, N.J.: Wiley, 2002).

Some people believe the architected environment generates too much redundant data. Though it is not obvious at first glance, this is not the case at all. Instead, it is the spider web environment that generates the gross amounts of data redundancy.

LEVELS OF THE ARCHITECTURE

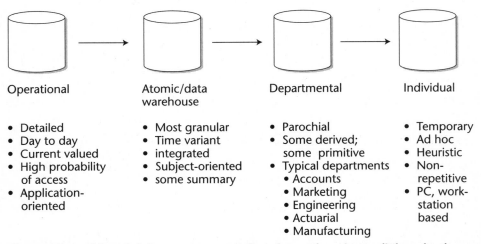

Operational	Atomic/data warehouse	Departmental	Individual

• Detailed
• Day to day
• Current valued
• High probability of access
• Application-oriented
	• Most granular
	• Time variant
	• integrated
	• Subject-oriented
	• some summary
		• Parochial
		• Some derived; some primitive
		• Typical departments
		  • Accounts
		  • Marketing
		  • Engineering
		  • Actuarial
		  • Manufacturing
			• Temporary
			• Ad hoc
			• Heuristic
			• Non-repetitive
			• PC, work-station based

Figure 1-10   Although it is not apparent at first glance, there is very little redundancy of data across the architected environment.

Consider the simple example of data throughout the architecture, shown in Figure 1-11. At the operational level there is a record for a customer, J Jones. The operational-level record contains current-value data that can be updated at a moment's notice and shows the customer's current status. Of course, if the information for J Jones changes, the operational-level record will be changed to reflect the correct data.

The data warehouse environment contains several records for J Jones, which show the history of information about J Jones. For example, the data warehouse would be searched to discover where J Jones lived last year. There is no overlap between the records in the operational environment, where current information is found, and the data warehouse environment, where historical information is found. If there is a change of address for J Jones, then a new record will be created in the data warehouse, reflecting the from and to dates that J Jones lived at the previous address. Note that the records in the data warehouse do not overlap. Also note that there is some element of time associated with each record in the data warehouse.

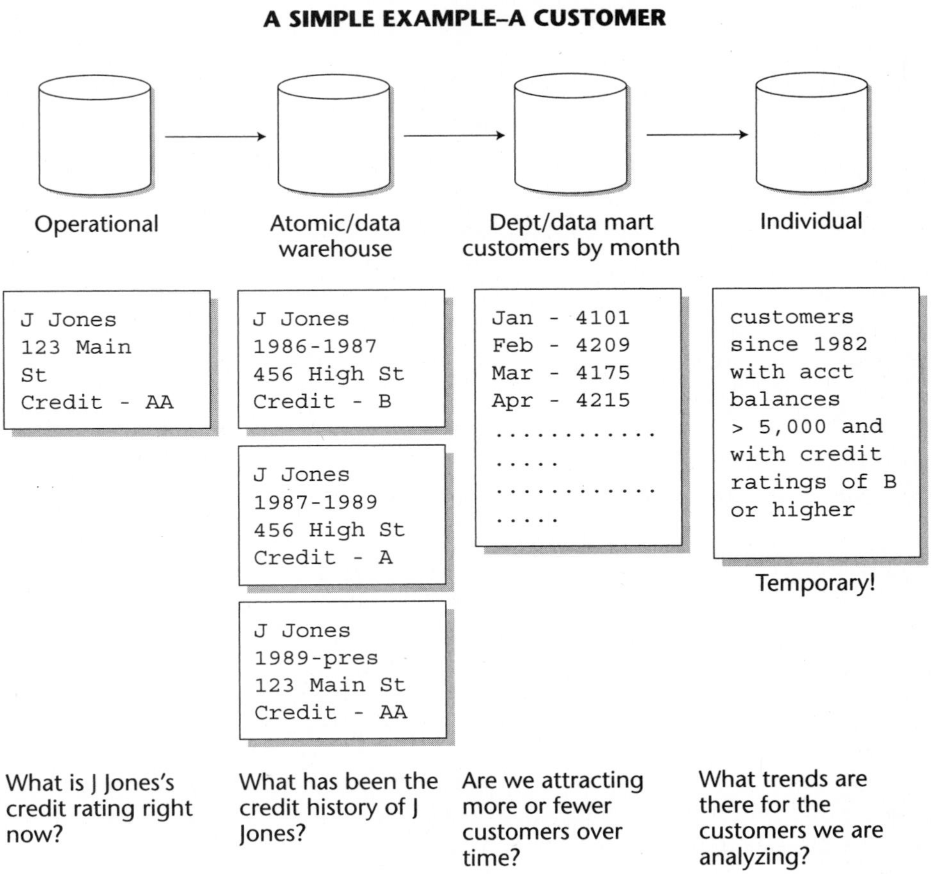

A SIMPLE EXAMPLE–A CUSTOMER

Operational	Atomic/data warehouse	Dept/data mart customers by month	Individual
J Jones 123 Main St Credit - AA	J Jones 1986-1987 456 High St Credit - B	Jan - 4101 Feb - 4209 Mar - 4175 Apr - 4215	customers since 1982 with acct balances > 5,000 and with credit ratings of B or higher
	J Jones 1987-1989 456 High St Credit - A		Temporary!
	J Jones 1989-pres 123 Main St Credit - AA		
What is J Jones's credit rating right now?	What has been the credit history of J Jones?	Are we attracting more or fewer customers over time?	What trends are there for the customers we are analyzing?

Figure 1-11 The kinds of queries for which the different levels of data can be used.

The departmental environment — sometimes called the *data mart level*, the *OLAP level*, or the *multidimensional DBMS level* — contains information useful to the different parochial departments of a company. There is a marketing departmental database, an accounting departmental database, an actuarial departmental database, and so forth. The data warehouse is the source of all departmental data. While data in the data mart certainly relates to data found in the operational level or the data warehouse, the data found in the departmental or data mart environment is fundamentally different from the data found in the data warehouse environment, because data mart data is denormalized, summarized, and shaped by the operating requirements of a single department.

Typical of data at the departmental or data mart level is a monthly customer file. In the file is a list of all customers by category. J Jones is tallied into this summary each month, along with many other customers. It is a stretch to consider the tallying of information to be redundant.

The final level of data is the individual level. Individual data is usually temporary and small. Much heuristic analysis is done at the individual level. As a rule, the individual levels of data are supported by the PC. Executive information systems (EIS) processing typically runs on the individual levels.

Data Integration in the Architected Environment

One important aspect of the architected environment that was not shown in Figure 1-11 is the integration of data that occurs across the architecture. As data passes from the operational environment to the data warehouse environment, it is integrated, as shown in Figure 1-12.

There is no point in bringing data over from the operational environment into the data warehouse environment without integrating it. If the data arrives at the data warehouse in an unintegrated state, it cannot be used to support a corporate view of data. And a corporate view of data is one of the essences of the architected environment.

In every environment, the unintegrated operational data is complex and difficult to deal with. This is simply a fact of life. And the task of getting your hands dirty with the process of integration is never pleasant. To achieve the real benefits of a data warehouse, though, it is necessary to undergo this painful, complex, and time-consuming exercise. *Extract/transform/load (ETL)* software can automate much of this tedious process. In addition, this process of integration has to be done only once. But, in any case, it is mandatory that data flowing into the data warehouse be integrated, not merely tossed — whole cloth — into the data warehouse from the operational environment.

A SIMPLE EXAMPLE–A CUSTOMER

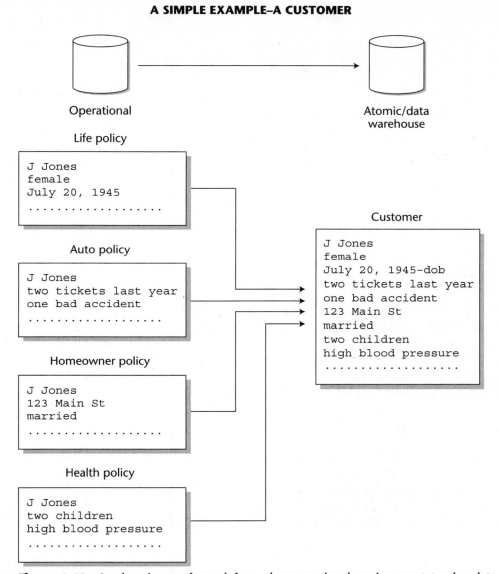

Figure 1-12 As data is transformed from the operational environment to the data warehouse environment, it is also integrated.

Who Is the User?

Much about the data warehouse or DSS environment is fundamentally different from the operational environment. When developers and designers who have spent their entire careers in the operational environment first encounter the data warehouse or DSS environment, they often feel ill at ease. To help them appreciate why there is such a difference from the world they have known, they should understand a little bit about the different users of the data warehouse.

The data-warehouse user — also called the *DSS analyst* — is a businessperson first and foremost, and a technician second. The primary job of the DSS analyst is to define and discover information used in corporate decision-making.

It is important to peer inside the head of the DSS analyst and view how he or she perceives the use of the data warehouse. The DSS analyst has a mindset of "Give me what I say I want, and then I can tell you what I really want." In other words, the DSS analyst operates in a mode of discovery. Only on seeing a report or seeing a screen can the DSS analyst begin to explore the possibilities for DSS. The DSS analyst often says, "Ah! Now that I see what the possibilities are, I can tell you what I really want to see. But until I know what the possibilities are I cannot describe to you what I want."

The attitude of the DSS analyst is important for the following reasons:

- It is legitimate. This is simply how DSS analysts think and how they conduct their business.

- It is pervasive. DSS analysts around the world think like this.

- It has a profound effect on the way the data warehouse is developed and on how systems using the data warehouse are developed.

The classical *system development life cycle (SDLC)* does not work in the world of the DSS analyst. The SDLC assumes that requirements are known (or are able to be known) at the start of design, or at least that the requirements can be discovered. In the world of the DSS analyst, though, new requirements usually are the last thing to be discovered in the DSS development life cycle. The DSS analyst starts with existing requirements, but factoring in new requirements is almost an impossibility. A very different development life cycle is associated with the data warehouse.

The Development Life Cycle

We have seen how operational data is usually application-oriented and, as a consequence, is unintegrated, whereas data warehouse data must be integrated. Other major differences also exist between the operational level of data and processing, and the data warehouse level of data and processing. The underlying development life cycles of these systems can be a profound concern, as shown in Figure 1-13.

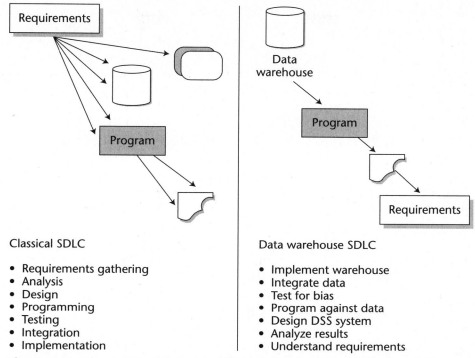

Figure 1-13   The system development life cycle for the data warehouse environment is almost exactly the opposite of the classical SDLC.

Figure 1-13 shows that the operational environment is supported by the classical systems development life cycle (the SDLC). The SDLC is often called the "waterfall" development approach because the different activities are specified and one activity — upon its completion — spills down into the next activity and triggers its start.

The development of the data warehouse operates under a very different life cycle, sometimes called the CLDS (the reverse of the SDLC). The classical SDLC is driven by requirements. In order to build systems, you must first understand the requirements. Then you go into stages of design and development. The CLDS is almost exactly the reverse. The CLDS starts with data. Once the data is in hand, it is integrated and then tested to see what bias there is to the data, if any. Programs are then written against the data. The results of the programs are analyzed, and finally the requirements of the system are understood. Once the requirements are understood, adjustments are made to the design of the system, and the cycle starts all over again for a different set of data. Because of the constant resetting of the development life cycle for different types of data, the CLDS development approach is usually called a "spiral" development methodology.

The CLDS is a classic data-driven development life cycle, while the SDLC is a classic requirements-driven development life cycle. Trying to apply inappropriate tools and techniques of development results only in waste and confusion. For example, the *Computer Aided Software Engineering (CASE)* world is dominated by requirements-driven analysis. Trying to apply CASE tools and techniques to the world of the data warehouse is not advisable, and vice versa.

Patterns of Hardware Utilization

Yet another major difference between the operational and the data warehouse environments is the pattern of hardware utilization that occurs in each environment. Figure 1-14 illustrates this.

The left side of Figure 1-14 shows the classic pattern of hardware utilization for operational processing. There are peaks and valleys in operational processing, but ultimately there is a relatively static and predictable pattern of hardware utilization.

There is an essentially different pattern of hardware utilization in the data warehouse environment (shown on the right side of the figure) — a binary pattern of utilization. Either the hardware is being utilized fully or not at all. It is not useful to calculate a mean percentage of utilization for the data warehouse environment. Even calculating the moments when the data warehouse is heavily used is not particularly useful or enlightening.

This fundamental difference is one more reason why trying to mix the two environments on the same machine at the same time does not work. You can optimize your machine either for operational processing or for data warehouse processing, but you cannot do both at the same time on the same piece of equipment.

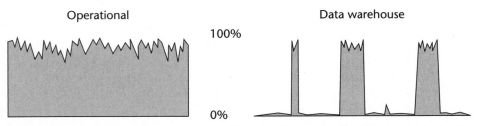

Figure 1-14   The different patterns of hardware utilization in the different environments.

Setting the Stage for Re-engineering

Although indirect, there is a very beneficial side effect of going from the production environment to the architected, data warehouse environment. Figure 1-15 shows the progression.

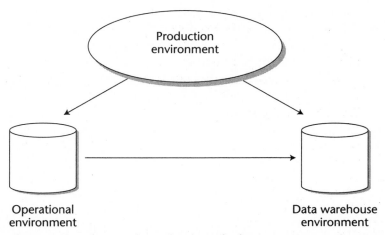

Figure 1-15 The transformation from the legacy systems environment to the architected, data warehouse–centered environment.

In Figure 1-15, a transformation is made in the production environment. The first effect is the removal of the bulk of data — mostly archival — from the production environment. The removal of massive volumes of data has a beneficial effect in various ways. The production environment is easier to:

- Correct
- Restructure
- Monitor
- Index

In short, the mere removal of a significant volume of data makes the production environment a much more malleable one.

Another important effect of the separation of the operational and the data warehouse environments is the removal of informational processing from the production environment. Informational processing occurs in the form of reports, screens, extracts, and so forth. The very nature of information processing is constant change. Business conditions change, the organization changes, management changes, accounting practices change, and so on. Each of these changes has an effect on summary and informational processing. When informational processing is included in the production, legacy environment, maintenance seems to be eternal. But much of what is called maintenance in the production environment is actually informational processing going through the normal cycle of changes. By moving most informational processing off to the data warehouse, the maintenance burden in the production environment is greatly alleviated. Figure 1-16 shows the effect of removing volumes of data and informational processing from the production environment.

Once the production environment undergoes the changes associated with transformation to the data warehouse-centered, architected environment, the production environment is primed for re-engineering because:

- It is smaller.
- It is simpler.
- It is focused.

In summary, the single most important step a company can take to make its efforts in re-engineering successful is to first go to the data warehouse environment.

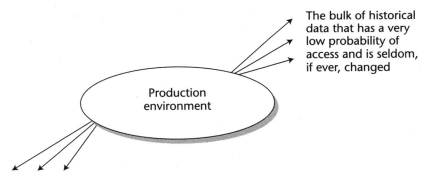

The bulk of historical data that has a very low probability of access and is seldom, if ever, changed

Production environment

Informational, analytical requirements that show up as eternal maintenance

Figure 1-16   Removing unneeded data and information requirements from the production environment — the effects of going to the data warehouse environment.

Monitoring the Data Warehouse Environment

Once the data warehouse is built, it must be maintained. A major component of maintaining the data warehouse is managing performance, which begins by monitoring the data warehouse environment.

Two operating components are monitored on a regular basis: the data residing in the data warehouse and the usage of the data. Monitoring the usage of the data in the data warehouse environment is essential to effectively manage the data warehouse. Some of the important results that are achieved by monitoring this data include the following:

- Identifying what growth is occurring, where the growth is occurring, and at what rate the growth is occurring
- Identifying what data is being used
- Calculating what response time the end user is getting
- Determining who is actually using the data warehouse
- Specifying how much of the data warehouse end users are using
- Pinpointing when the data warehouse is being used
- Recognizing how much of the data warehouse is being used
- Examining the level of usage of the data warehouse

If the data architect does not know the answer to these questions, he or she can't effectively manage the data warehouse environment on an ongoing basis.

As an example of the usefulness of monitoring the data warehouse, consider the importance of knowing what data is being used inside the data warehouse. The nature of a data warehouse is constant growth. History is constantly being added to the warehouse. Summarizations are constantly being added. New extract streams are being created. And the storage and processing technology on which the data warehouse resides can be expensive. At some point, questions arise such as, "Why is all of this data being accumulated? Is there really anyone using all of this?" Whether there is any legitimate user of the data warehouse, there certainly is a growing cost to the data warehouse as data is put into it during its normal operation.

As long as the data architect has no way to monitor usage of the data inside the warehouse, there is no choice but to continually buy new computer resources — more storage, more processors, and so forth. When the data architect can monitor activity and usage in the data warehouse, he or she can determine which data is not being used. It is then possible, and sensible, to move unused data to less-expensive media. This is a very real and immediate payback to monitoring data and activity.

The data profiles that can be created during the data-monitoring process include the following:

- A catalog of all tables in the warehouse
- A profile of the contents of those tables
- A profile of the growth of the tables in the data warehouse
- A catalog of the indexes available for entry to the tables
- A catalog of the summary tables and the sources for the summary

The need to monitor activity in the data warehouse is illustrated by the following questions:

- What data is being accessed?
  - When?
  - By whom?
  - How frequently?
  - At what level of detail?
- What is the response time for the request?
- At what point in the day is the request submitted?
- How big was the request?
- Was the request terminated, or did it end naturally?

Response time in the DSS environment is quite different from response time in the OLTP environment. In the OLTP environment, response time is almost always mission critical. The business starts to suffer immediately when response time turns bad in OLTP. In the DSS environment, there is no such relationship. Response time in the DSS data warehouse environment is always relaxed. There is no mission-critical nature to response time in DSS. Accordingly, response time in the DSS data warehouse environment is measured in minutes and hours and, in some cases, in terms of days.

Just because response time is relaxed in the DSS data warehouse environment does not mean that response time is not important. In the DSS data warehouse environment, the end user does development iteratively. This means that the next level of investigation of any iterative development depends on the results attained by the current analysis. If the end user does an iterative analysis and the turnaround time is only 10 minutes, he or she will be much more productive than if turnaround time is 24 hours. There is, then, a very important relationship between response time and productivity in the DSS environment. Just because response time in the DSS environment is not mission-critical does not mean that it is not important.

The ability to measure response time in the DSS environment is the first step toward being able to manage it. For this reason alone, monitoring DSS activity is an important procedure.

One of the issues of response time measurement in the DSS environment is the question, "What is being measured?" In an OLTP environment, it is clear what is being measured. A request is sent, serviced, and returned to the end user. In the OLTP environment, the measurement of response time is from the moment of submission to the moment of return. But the DSS data warehouse environment varies from the OLTP environment in that there is no clear time for measuring the return of data. In the DSS data warehouse environment, often a lot of data is returned as a result of a query. Some of the data is returned at one moment, and other data is returned later. Defining the moment of return of data for the data warehouse environment is no easy matter. One interpretation is the moment of the first return of data; another interpretation is the last return of data. And there are many other possibilities for the measurement of response time; the DSS data warehouse activity monitor must be able to provide many different interpretations.

One of the fundamental issues of using a monitor on the data warehouse environment is where to do the monitoring. One place the monitoring can be done is at the end-user terminal, which is convenient — many machine cycles are free here and the impact on system-wide performance is minimal. To monitor the system at the end-user terminal level implies that each terminal that will be monitored will require its own administration. In a world where there are as many as 10,000 terminals in a single DSS network, trying to administer the monitoring of each terminal is nearly impossible.

The alternative is to do the monitoring of the DSS system at the server level. After the query has been formulated and passed to the server that manages the data warehouse, the monitoring of activity can occur. Undoubtedly, administration of the monitor is much easier here. But there is a very good possibility that a system-wide performance penalty will be incurred. Because the monitor is using resources at the server, the impact on performance is felt throughout the DSS data warehouse environment. The placement of the monitor is an important issue that must be thought out carefully. The trade-off is between ease of administration and minimization of performance requirements.

One of the most powerful uses of a monitor is to be able to compare today's results against an "average" day. When unusual system conditions occur, it is often useful to ask, "How different is today from the average day?" In many cases, it will be seen that the variations in performance are not nearly as bad as imagined. But in order to make such a comparison, there needs to be an average-day profile, which contains the standard important measures that describe a day in the DSS environment. Once the current day is measured, it can then be compared to the average-day profile.

Of course, the average day changes over time, and it makes sense to track these changes periodically so that long-term system trends can be measured.

Summary

This chapter has discussed the origins of the data warehouse and the larger architecture into which the data warehouse fits. The architecture has evolved throughout the history of the different stages of information processing. There are four levels of data and processing in the architecture — the operational level, the data warehouse level, the departmental or data mart level, and the individual level.

The data warehouse is built from the application data found in the operational environment. The application data is integrated as it passes into the data warehouse. The act of integrating data is always a complex and tedious task. Data flows from the data warehouse into the departmental or data mart environment. Data in the departmental or data mart environment is shaped by the unique processing requirements of the department.

The data warehouse is developed under a completely different development approach than that used for classical application systems. Classically, applications have been developed by a life cycle known as the SDLC. The data warehouse is developed under an approach called the *spiral development methodology*. The spiral development approach mandates that small parts of the data warehouse be developed to completion, and then other small parts of the warehouse be developed in an iterative approach.

The users of the data warehouse environment have a completely different approach to using the system. Unlike operational users who have a straightforward approach to defining their requirements, the data warehouse user operates in a mindset of discovery. The end user of the data warehouse says, "Give me what I say I want, and then I can tell you what I really want."

CHAPTER 2

The Data Warehouse Environment

The data warehouse is the heart of the architected environment, and is the foundation of all DSS processing. The job of the DSS analyst in the data warehouse environment is immeasurably easier than the job of the analyst in the classical legacy environment because there is a single integrated source of data to draw from (the data warehouse), because the granular data in the data warehouse is easily accessible, and because the data warehouse forms a foundation for reusability and reconciliation of data.

This chapter describes some of the more important aspects of the data warehouse. A data warehouse is a subject-oriented, integrated, nonvolatile, and time-variant collection of data in support of management's decisions. The data warehouse contains granular corporate data. Data in the data warehouse is able to be used for many different purposes, including sitting and waiting for future requirements which are unknown today.

The subject orientation of the data warehouse is shown in Figure 2-1. Classical operations systems are organized around the functional applications of the company. For an insurance company, the applications may be for the processing of auto, life, health, and casualty. The major subject areas of the insurance corporation might be customer, policy, premium, and claim. For a manufacturer, the major subject areas might be product, order, vendor, bill of material, and raw goods. For a retailer, the major subject areas may be product, SKU, sale, vendor, and so forth. Each type of company has its own unique set of subjects.

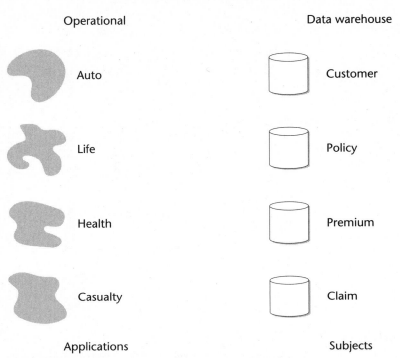

SUBJECT ORIENTATION

Operational   Data warehouse

Auto   Customer

Life   Policy

Health   Premium

Casualty   Claim

Applications   Subjects

Figure 2-1   An example of a subject orientation of data.

The second salient characteristic of the data warehouse is that it is integrated. Of all the aspects of a data warehouse, integration is the most important. Data is fed from multiple, disparate sources into the data warehouse. As the data is fed, it is converted, reformatted, resequenced, summarized, and so forth. The result is that data — once it resides in the data warehouse — has a single physical corporate image. Figure 2-2 illustrates the integration that occurs when data passes from the application-oriented operational environment to the data warehouse.

Design decisions made by applications designers over the years show up in different ways. In the past, when application designers built an application, they never considered that the data they were operating on would ever have to be integrated with other data. Such a consideration was only a wild theory. Consequently, across multiple applications there is no application consistency in encoding, naming conventions, physical attributes, measurement of attributes, and so forth. Each application designer has had free rein to make his or her own design decisions. The result is that any application is very different from any other application.

INTEGRATION

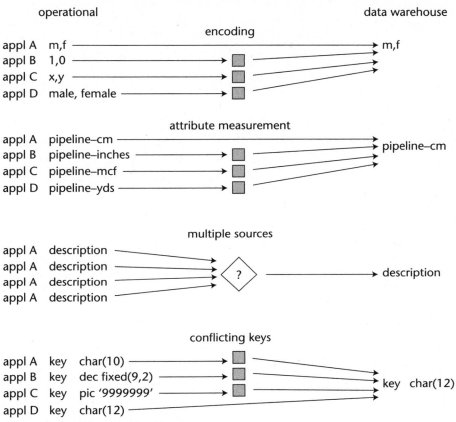

Figure 2-2 The issue of integration.

Data is entered into the data warehouse in such a way that the many inconsistencies at the application level are undone. For example, as previously shown in Figure 2-2, as far as encoding of gender is concerned, it matters little whether data in the warehouse is encoded as m/f or 1/0. What does matter is that regardless of method or source application, warehouse encoding is done consistently. If application data is encoded as X/Y for gender, it is converted as it is moved to the warehouse. The same consideration of consistency applies to all application design issues, such as naming conventions, key structure, measurement of attributes, and physical characteristics of data.

The third important characteristic of a data warehouse is that it is nonvolatile. Figure 2-3 illustrates nonvolatility of data and shows that operational data is regularly accessed and manipulated one record at a time. Data is updated in the operational environment as a regular matter of course, but data warehouse data exhibits a very different set of characteristics. Data warehouse data is loaded (usually, but not always, en masse) and accessed, but it is not updated (in the general sense). Instead, when data in the data warehouse is loaded, it is loaded in a snapshot, static format. When subsequent changes occur, a new snapshot record is written. In doing so, a historical record of data is kept in the data warehouse.

The last salient characteristic of the data warehouse is that it is time variant. Time variancy implies that every unit of data in the data warehouse is accurate as of some moment in time. In some cases, a record is time stamped. In other cases, a record has a date of transaction. But in every case, there is some form of time marking to show the moment in time during which the record is accurate. Figure 2-4 illustrates how time variancy of data warehouse data can show up in several ways.

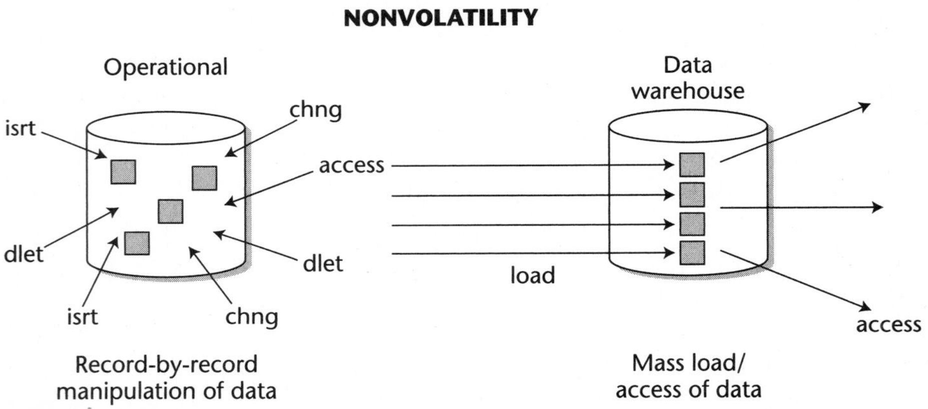

NONVOLATILITY

Operational

Data warehouse

isrt

chng

access

dlet

dlet

load

isrt

chng

access

Record-by-record
manipulation of data

Mass load/
access of data

Figure 2-3 The issue of nonvolatility.

TIME VARIANCY

Operational

Data warehouse

- Time horizon – current to 60–90 days
- Update of records
- Key structure may or may not contain an element of time

- Time horizon – 5–10 years
- Sophisticated snapshots of data
- Key structure contains an element of time

Figure 2-4 The issue of time variancy.

Different environments have different time horizons associated with them. A *time horizon* is the length of time data is represented in an environment. The collective time horizon for the data found inside a data warehouse is significantly longer than that of operational systems. A 60-to-90-day time horizon is normal for operational systems; a 5-to-10-year time horizon is normal for the data warehouse. As a result of this difference in time horizons, the data warehouse contains *much* more history than any other environment.

The data warehouse can be extended to include a "cache" or "overflow" area, often called *near-line storage*. The data in near-line storage is merely an extension of the data found in the data warehouse. Data in near-line storage is inexpensive to store. The time horizon for near-line storage can be almost limitless — 10, 15, 20 years, and even longer.

Operational databases contain *current-value data,* or data whose accuracy is valid as of the moment of access. For example, a bank knows how much money a customer has on deposit at any moment in time, an insurance company knows what policies are in force at any moment in time, or an airline knows who has reservations for a flight at a given moment in time. As such, current-value data can be updated as business conditions change. The bank balance is changed when the customer makes a deposit. The insurance coverage is changed when a customer lets a policy lapse. An airline takes a seat off the availability list when a reservation is made. Data warehouse data is very unlike current-value data, however. Data warehouse data can be thought of as nothing more than a sophisticated series of snapshots, each snapshot taken at one moment in time. The effect created by the series of snapshots is that the data warehouse has a historical sequence of activities and events, something not at all apparent in a current-value environment where only the most current value can be found.

The key structure of operational data may or may not contain some element of time, such as year, month, day, and so on. The key structure of the data warehouse always contains some element of time. The embedding of the element of time in the data warehouse record can take many forms, such as a time stamp on every record, a time stamp for a whole database, and so forth.

The Structure of the Data Warehouse

Figure 2-5 shows that there are different levels of detail in the data warehouse environment. There is an older level of detail (usually on alternate, bulk storage), a current level of detail, a level of lightly summarized data (the data mart level), and a level of highly summarized data. Data flows into the data warehouse from the operational environment. Usually significant transformation of data occurs at the passage from the operational level to the data warehouse level.

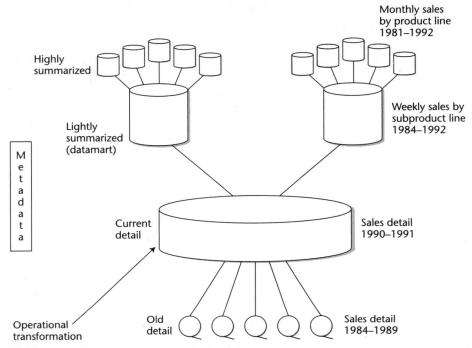

Figure 2-5 The structure of the data warehouse.

Once the data in the data warehouse ages, it passes from current detail to older detail. As the data is summarized, it passes from current detail to lightly summarized data, and then from lightly summarized data to highly summarized data.

Subject Orientation

The data warehouse is oriented to the major subject areas of the corporation that have been defined in the high-level corporate data model. Typical subject areas include the following:

- Customer
- Product
- Transaction or activity
- Policy
- Claim
- Account

Each major subject area is physically implemented as a series of related tables in the data warehouse. A subject area may consist of 10, 100, or even more physical tables that are all related. For example, the subject area implementation for a customer might look like Figure 2-6.

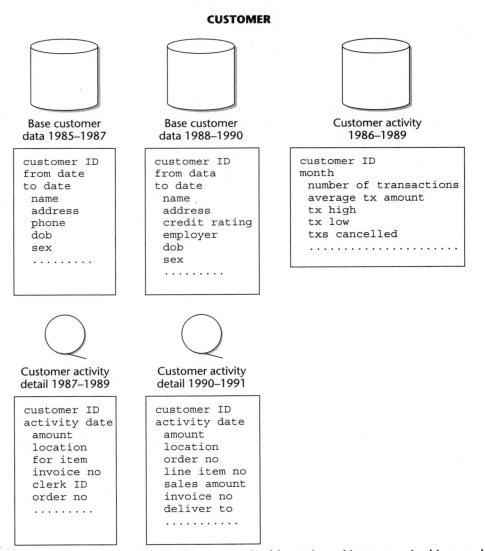

Figure 2-6 Data warehouse data is organized by major subject area — in this case, by customer.

There are five related physical tables in Figure 2-6, each of which has been designed to implement a part of a major subject area — customer. There is a base table for customer information as defined from 1985 to 1987. There is another for the definition of customer data between 1988 and 1990. There is a cumulative customer activity table for activities between 1986 and 1989. Each month, a summary record is written for each customer record based on customer activity for the month.

There are detailed activity files by customer for 1987 through 1989 and other files for 1990 through 1991. The definition of the data in the files is different, based on the year.

All of the physical tables for the customer subject area are related by a common key. Figure 2-7 shows that the key — customer ID — connects all of the data found in the customer subject area. Another interesting aspect of the customer subject area is that it may reside on different media, as shown in Figure 2-8. There is nothing to say that a physical table must reside on disk, even if it relates to other data that does reside on a disk.

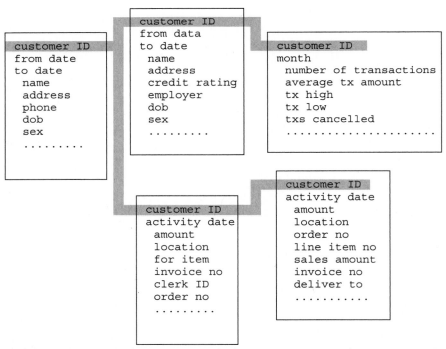

Figure 2-7   The collections of data that belong to the same subject area are tied together by a common key.

CUSTOMER

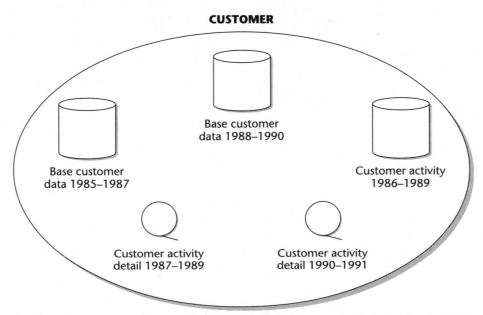

Figure 2-8 The subject area may contain data on different media in the data warehouse.

Figure 2-8 shows that some of the related subject area data resides on a *direct access storage device (DASD)*, and some resides on *magnetic tape*. One implication of data residing on different media is that there may be more than one DBMS managing the data in a warehouse, or that some data may not be managed by a DBMS at all. Just because data resides on magnetic tape or some storage media other than disk storage does not mean that the data is not a part of the data warehouse.

Data that has a high probability of access and a low volume of storage resides on a medium that is fast and relatively expensive. Data that has a low probability of access and is bulky resides on a medium that is cheaper and slower to access. Usually (but not always), data that is older has a lower probability of access. As a rule, the older data resides on a medium other than disk storage.

DASD and magnetic tape are the two most popular media on which to store data in a data warehouse. But they are not the only media. Two others that should not be overlooked are *fiche* and the *optical disk*. Fiche is good for storing detailed records that never have to be reproduced in an electronic medium again. Legal records are often stored on fiche for an indefinite period of time. Optical disk storage is especially good for data warehouse storage because it is cheap, relatively fast, and able to hold a mass of data. Another reason why optical disk storage is useful is that data warehouse data, once written, is seldom, if ever, updated. This last characteristic makes optical disk storage a very desirable choice for data warehouses.

Another interesting aspect of the files (previously shown in Figure 2-8) is that there is both a level of summary and a level of detail for the same data. Activity by month is summarized. The detail that supports activity by month is stored at the magnetic tape level of data. This is a form of a "shift in granularity," which will be discussed later in this chapter.

When data is organized around the subject (in this case, the customer), each key has an element of time, as shown in Figure 2-9.

Some tables are organized on a from-date-to-date basis. This is called a *continuous organization of data*. Other tables are organized on a cumulative monthly basis, and others on an individual date of record or activity basis. But all records have some form of date attached to the key, usually the lower part of the key.

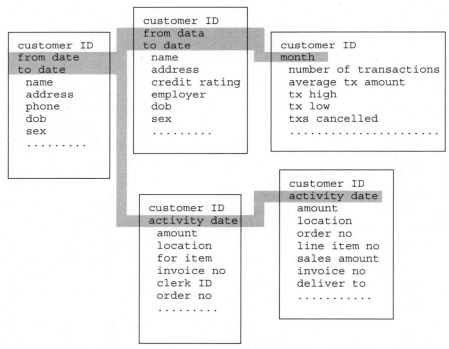

Figure 2-9   Each table in the data warehouse has an element of time as a part of the key structure, usually the lower part.

Day 1 to Day *n* Phenomenon

Data warehouses are not built all at once. Instead, they are designed and populated a step at a time, and as such are evolutionary, not revolutionary. The costs of building a data warehouse all at once, the resources required, and the disruption to the environment all dictate that the data warehouse be built in an orderly, iterative, step-at-a-time fashion. The "big bang" approach to data warehouse development is simply an invitation to disaster and is never an appropriate alternative.

Figure 2-10 shows the typical process of building a data warehouse. On day 1, there is a polyglot of legacy systems essentially doing operational, transactional processing. On day 2, the first few tables of the first subject area of the data warehouse are populated. At this point, a certain amount of curiosity is raised, and the users start to discover data warehouses and analytical processing.

On day 3, more of the data warehouse is populated, and with the population of more data comes more users. Once users find there is an integrated source of data that is easy to get to and has a historical basis designed for looking at data over time, there is more than curiosity. At about this time, the serious DSS analyst becomes attracted to the data warehouse.

On day 4, as more of the warehouse becomes populated, some of the data that had resided in the operational environment becomes properly placed in the data warehouse. And the data warehouse is now discovered as a source for doing analytical processing. All sorts of DSS applications spring up. Indeed, so many users and so many requests for processing (coupled with a rather large volume of data that now resides in the warehouse) appear that some users are put off by the effort required to get to the data warehouse. The competition to get at the warehouse becomes an obstacle to its usage.

On day 5, departmental databases (data mart or OLAP) start to blossom. Departments find that it is cheaper and easier to get their processing done by bringing data from the data warehouse into their own departmental processing environment. As data goes to the departmental level, a few DSS analysts are attracted.

On day 6, the land rush to departmental, multidimensional systems takes place. It is cheaper, faster, and easier to get departmental data than it is to get data from the data warehouse. Soon, end users are weaned from the detail of the data warehouse to departmental processing.

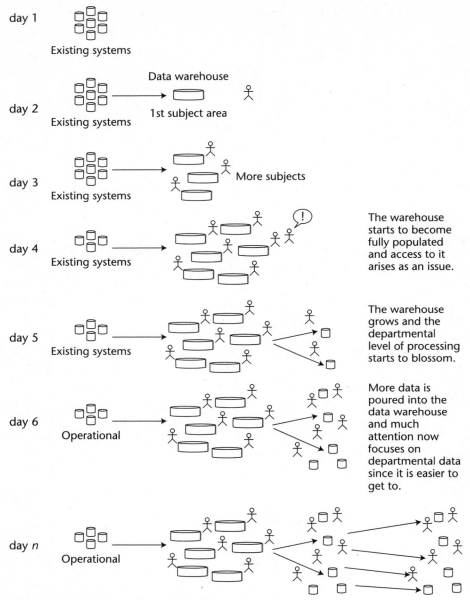

day 1

Existing systems

Data warehouse

day 2

Existing systems

1st subject area

day 3

Existing systems

More subjects

day 4

Existing systems

The warehouse starts to become fully populated and access to it arises as an issue.

day 5

Existing systems

The warehouse grows and the departmental level of processing starts to blossom.

day 6

Operational

More data is poured into the data warehouse and much attention now focuses on departmental data since it is easier to get to.

day n

Operational

Figure 2-10 Day 1 to day n phenomenon.

On day n, the architecture is fully developed. All that is left of the original set of production systems is operational processing. The warehouse is full of data. There are a few direct users of the data warehouse. There are a lot of departmental databases. Most of the DSS analytical processing occurs at the departmental level because it is easier and cheaper to get the data needed for processing there.

Of course, evolution from day 1 to day *n* takes a long time. The evolution does not happen in a matter of days. Several years is the norm. During the process of moving from day 1 to day *n*, the DSS environment is up and functional.

Note that the spider web seems to have reappeared in a larger, more grandiose form. Such is not the case at all, although the explanation is rather complex. Refer to "The Cabinet Effect," in the May 1991 edition of *Data Base Programming Design*, for an in-depth explanation of why the architected environment is not merely a re-creation of the spider web environment.

The day 1 to day *n* phenomenon described here is the ideal way to get to the data warehouse. There are many other paths. One such path is through the building of data marts first. This path is short-sighted and leads to a great deal of waste.

Granularity

The single most important aspect of the design of a data warehouse is the issue of granularity. Indeed, the issue of granularity permeates the entire architecture that surrounds the data warehouse environment. *Granularity* refers to the level of detail or summarization of the units of data in the data warehouse.

The more detail there is, the lower the level of granularity. The less detail there is, the higher the level of granularity. For example, a simple transaction would be at a low level of granularity. A summary of all transactions for the month would be at a high level of granularity.

Granularity of data has always been a major design issue. In early operational systems, granularity was taken for granted. When detailed data is being updated, it is almost a given that data be stored at the lowest level of granularity. In the data warehouse environment, though, granularity is not assumed. Figure 2-11 illustrates the issues of granularity.

Granularity is the single most critical design issue in the data warehouse environment because it profoundly affects the volume of data that resides in the data warehouse and the type of query that can be answered. The volume of data in a warehouse is traded off against the level of detail of a query. The lower the level of granularity, the more versatile the query that can be issued. The higher the level of granularity, the less versatile the query that can be issued.

In almost all cases, data comes into the data warehouse at too high a level of granularity. This means that the developer must spend a lot of design and development resources breaking the data apart before it can be stored in the data warehouse. Occasionally, though, data enters the warehouse at too low a level of granularity. An example of data at too low a level of granularity is the Web log data generated by the Web-based eBusiness environment (often called *clickstream data*). Web log clickstream data must be edited, filtered, and summarized before its granularity is fit for the data warehouse environment.

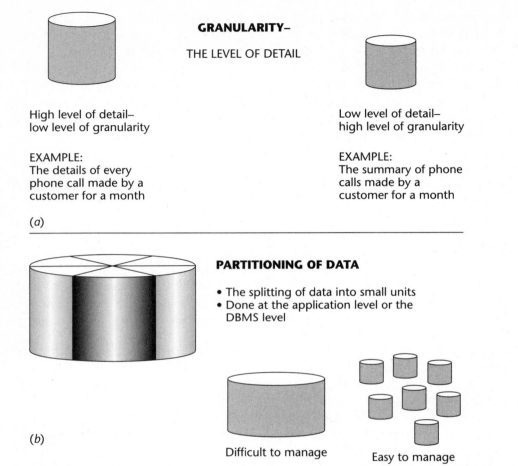

Figure 2-11 Major design issues of the data warehouse: granularity, partitioning, and proper design.

The Benefits of Granularity

Many organizations are surprised to find that data warehousing provides an invaluable foundation for many different types of DSS processing. Organizations may build a data warehouse for one purpose, and then discover that it can be used for many other kinds of DSS processing. Although infrastructure for the data warehouse is expensive and difficult to build, it has to be built only once. After the data warehouse has been properly constructed, it provides the organization with a foundation that is extremely flexible and reusable.

The granular data found in the data warehouse is the key to reusability, because it can be used by many people in different ways. For example, within a corporation, the same data might be used to satisfy the needs of marketing, sales, and accounting. All three departments look at the same basic data. Marketing may want to see sales on a monthly basis by geographic district, sales may want to see sales by salesperson by sales district on a weekly basis, and finance may want to see recognizable revenue on a quarterly basis by product line. All of these types of information are closely related, yet slightly different. With a data warehouse, the different organizations are able to look at the data as they wish to see it.

Looking at the data in different ways is only one advantage of having a solid foundation. A related benefit is the ability to reconcile data, if needed. Once there is a single foundation on which everyone relies, if there is a need to explain a discrepancy in analyses between two or more departments, then reconciliation is relatively simple.

Another related benefit of a low level of granularity is flexibility. Suppose that marketing wishes to alter how it looks at data. Having a granular foundation in place allows this to be accomplished easily.

Another benefit of granular data is that it contains a history of activities and events across the corporation. And the level of granularity is detailed enough that the data can be reshaped across the corporation for many different needs.

Perhaps the largest benefit of a data warehouse foundation is that future unknown requirements can be accommodated. Suppose there is a new requirement to look at data, or the state legislature passes a new law, or OPEC changes its rules for oil allocation, or the stock market crashes. There is a constant stream of new requirements for information because change is inevitable. With the data warehouse in place, the corporation can easily respond to change. When a new requirement arises and there is a need for information, the data warehouse is already available for analysis, and the organization is prepared to handle the new requirements.

An Example of Granularity

Figure 2-12 shows an example of the issues of granularity. The left side shows a low level of granularity. Each activity — in this case, a phone call — is recorded in detail. At the end of the month, each customer has, on average, 200 records (one for each recorded phone call throughout the month) that require about 40,000 bytes collectively.

The right side of the figure shows a higher level of granularity. A high level of detail refers to a low level of granularity. A low level of detail refers to a high level of granularity. The data shown in Figure 2-12 is at a high level of granularity. It represents the summary information set. Each record summarizes one month's activity for one customer, which requires about 200 bytes.

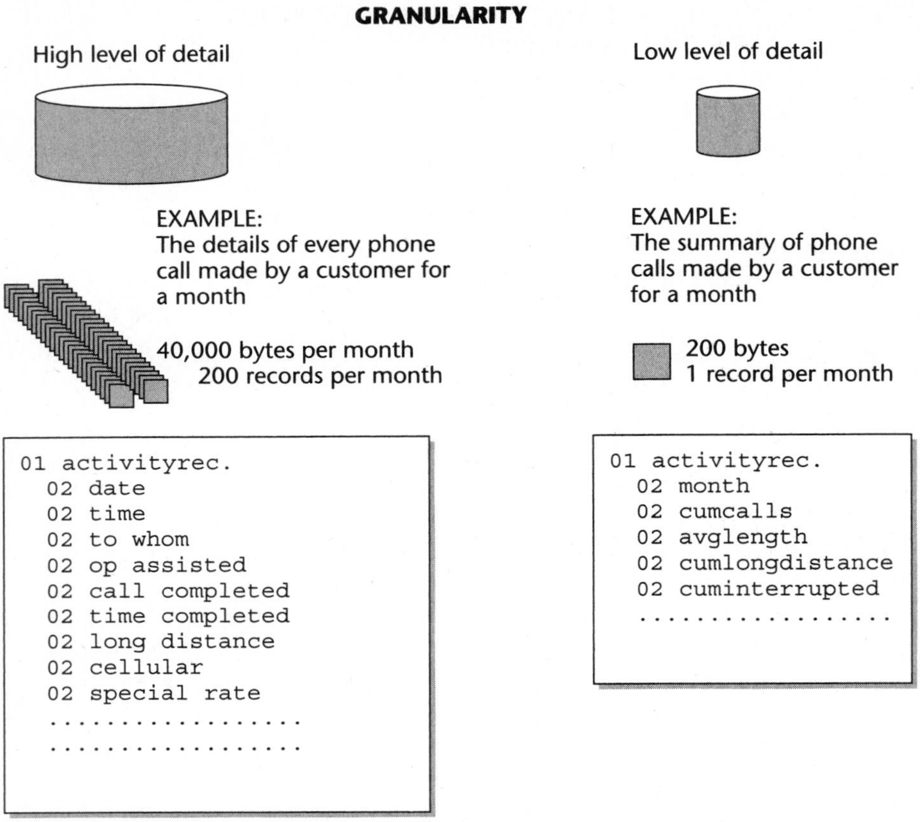

GRANULARITY

High level of detail   Low level of detail

EXAMPLE: EXAMPLE:
The details of every phone   The summary of phone
call made by a customer for   calls made by a customer
a month   for a month

40,000 bytes per month   200 bytes
    200 records per month   1 record per month

```
01 activityrec.
  02 date
  02 time
  02 to whom
  02 op assisted
  02 call completed
  02 time completed
  02 long distance
  02 cellular
  02 special rate
  .................
  .................
```

```
01 activityrec.
  02 month
  02 cumcalls
  02 avglength
  02 cumlongdistance
  02 cuminterrupted
  .................
```

Figure 2-12 Determining the level of granularity is the most important design issue in the data warehouse environment.

It is obvious that if space is a problem in a data warehouse (and volume of data is always the first and major issue in the data warehouse), a high level of granularity is a much more efficient way of representing data than a representation using a low level of granularity.

Not only are many fewer bytes of data required with a higher level of granularity, but fewer index entries are needed. However, the volume of data and the issue of raw space are not the only relevant issues. The amount of processing power that needs to be used in the face of a large volume of data to access the data is a factor as well.

There is, then, a very good case for the compaction of data in a data warehouse. When data is compacted, significant savings can be realized in the amount of DASD used, the number of index entries required, and the processor resources required to manipulate data.

Another aspect to the compaction of data occurs when the level of granularity is raised. Figure 2-13 demonstrates the trade-off. As the level of granularity of data rises, there is a corresponding loss in the ability to answer queries using the data. Put another way, with a very low level of granularity, you can answer practically any query. But a high level of granularity limits the number of questions that the data can handle.

Another consideration in designing granularity is determining which architectural entities will feed off the data warehouse. Each DSS architectural entity has its own unique considerations. The data warehouse must be designed to feed the lowest level of granularity needed by any architectural entity.

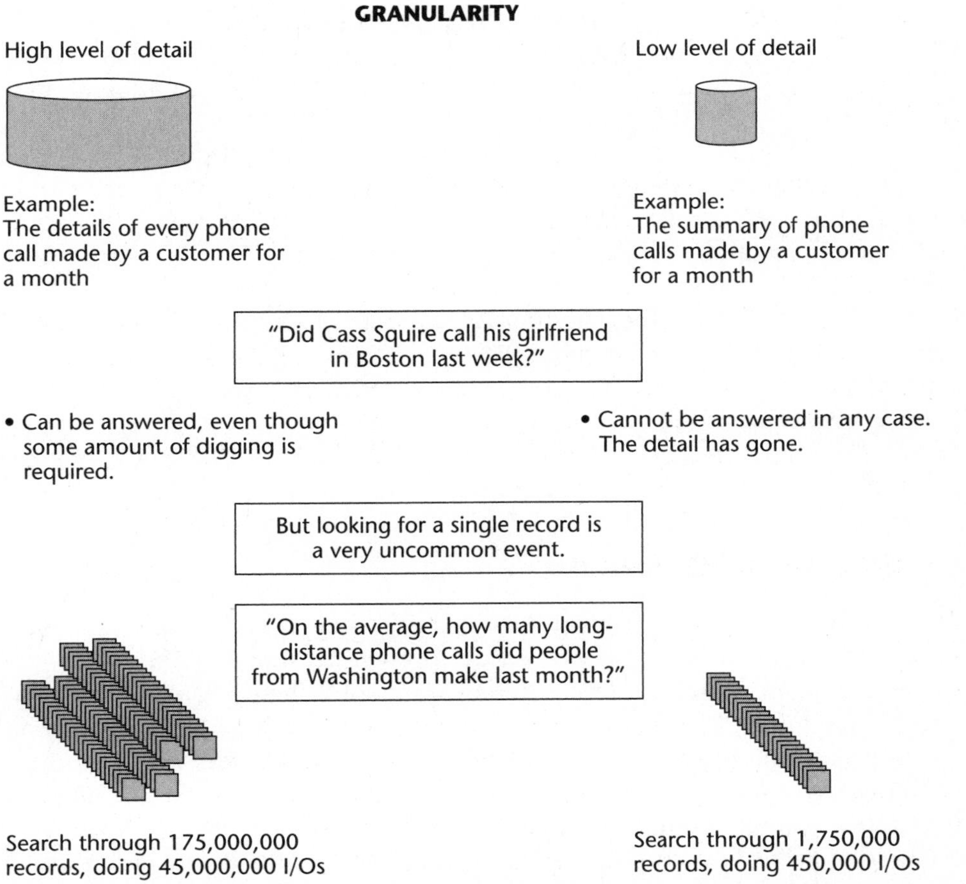

GRANULARITY

High level of detail

Low level of detail

Example:
The details of every phone call made by a customer for a month

Example:
The summary of phone calls made by a customer for a month

"Did Cass Squire call his girlfriend in Boston last week?"

• Can be answered, even though some amount of digging is required.

• Cannot be answered in any case. The detail has gone.

But looking for a single record is a very uncommon event.

"On the average, how many long-distance phone calls did people from Washington make last month?"

Search through 175,000,000 records, doing 45,000,000 I/Os

Search through 1,750,000 records, doing 450,000 I/Os

Figure 2-13 The level of granularity has a profound effect both on what questions can be answered and on what resources are required to answer a question.

To illustrate the effect of granularity on the ability to do queries, in Figure 2-13, the following query was made: "Did Cass Squire call his girlfriend in Boston last week?"

With a low level of granularity, the query can be answered. It may take a lot of resources to thumb through a lot of records, but at the end of the day, whether Cass called his girlfriend in Boston last week can be determined.

But with a high level of detail, there is no way to definitively answer the question. If all that is kept about Cass Squire in the data warehouse is the total number of calls that he made for a given week or month, whether one of those calls went to Boston cannot be determined.

When doing DSS processing in the data warehouse environment, examining only a single event is rare. A collective view of data is much more common. To achieve a collective view requires looking at a large number of records.

For example, suppose the following collective query is made: "On the average, how many long-distance phone calls did people from Washington make last month?"

This type of query is normal in a DSS environment. Of course, it can be answered by both the high level and the low level of granularity. In answering it, though, there is a tremendous difference in the resources used. A low level of granularity requires sorting through each record, because many resources are required when using very detailed data.

By using the high level of granularity, the data is much more compact and can provide an answer relatively quickly. If it contains sufficient detail, data with a high level of granularity is much more efficient to use.

Figure 2-14 shows the trade-off in determining the level of data granularity to use. This trade-off must be considered very carefully at the outset of designing and constructing the data warehouse.

Dual Levels of Granularity

Most of the time, there is a great need for efficiency in storing and accessing data, and for the ability to analyze data in great detail. (In other words, the organization wants to have its cake and eat it, too.) When an organization has lots of data in the warehouse, it makes eminent sense to consider two (or more) levels of granularity in the detailed portion of the data warehouse. In fact, there is such a need for more than one level of granularity that a dual level of granularity design should be the default for almost every shop. Figure 2-15 shows two levels of granularity at the detailed level of the data warehouse.

Called a *dual level of granularity*, the design shown in Figure 2-15 — a phone company — fits the needs of most shops. There is a tremendous amount of detail at the operational level. Most of this detail is needed for the billing systems. Up to 30 days of detail is stored in the operational level.

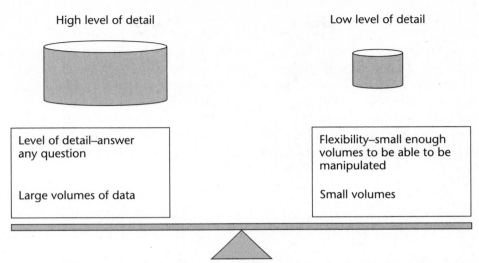

High level of detail   Low level of detail

Level of detail–answer any question	Flexibility–small enough volumes to be able to be manipulated
Large volumes of data	Small volumes

Figure 2-14 The trade-off with granularity is so stark that for most organizations the best solution is some form of multiple levels of granularity.

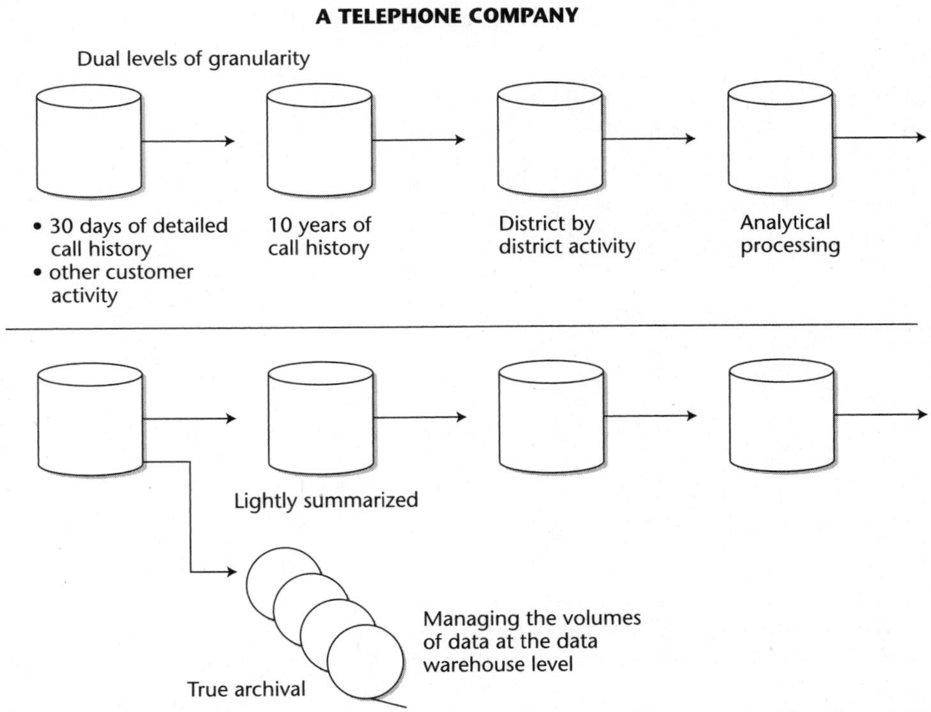

A TELEPHONE COMPANY

Dual levels of granularity

- 30 days of detailed call history
- other customer activity

10 years of call history

District by district activity

Analytical processing

Lightly summarized

True archival

Managing the volumes of data at the data warehouse level

Figure 2-15 The volume of data is such that most organizations need to have two levels of granularity in the data warehouse.

The data warehouse in this example contains two types of data — lightly summarized data and "true archival" detail data. The data in the data warehouse can go back 10 years. The data that emanates from the data warehouse is "district" data that flows to the different districts of the telephone company. Each district then analyzes its data independently from other districts. Much heuristic analytical processing occurs at the individual level.

Light summarization data is detailed data that has been summarized only to a very small extent. For example, phone call information may be summarized by the hour. Or, bank checking information may be summarized by the day. Figure 2-16 shows such a summarization.

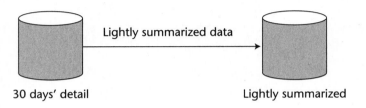

30 days' detail   Lightly summarized

```
J Jones
April 12 6:01 pm to 6:12 pm
415-566-9982 operator assisted
April 12 6:15 pm to 6:16 pm
415-334-8847 long distance
April 12 6:23 pm to 6:38 pm
408-223-7745
April 13 9:12 am to 9:23 am
408-223-7745
April 13 10:15 am to 10:21 am
408-223-7745 operator assisted
April 15 11:01 am to 11:21 am
415-964-4738
April 15 11:39 am to 12:01 pm
703-570-5770 incomplete
April 15 12:10 pm to 12:40 pm
703-841-5770 wrong number
April 16 12:34 pm to 12:56 pm
415-964-3130
.............................
.............................
```

```
April
J Jones
number of calls - 45
avg length of call - 14 minutes
number of long distance calls - 18
number of operator assisted calls - 2
number of incomplete calls - 1
```

Number of bytes required to house a record–225

For a single customer for a month, an average of 45,000 bytes are required to house 200 records.

Figure 2-16 With light summarization data, large quantities of data can be represented compactly.

As data is passed from the operational, 30-day store of data, it is summarized, by customer, into fields that are likely to be used for DSS analysis. The record for J Jones shows the number of calls made per month, the average length of each call, the number of long-distance calls made, the number of operator-assisted calls, and so forth.

There is a significantly less volume of data in the lightly summarized database than there is in the detailed database. Of course, there is a limit to the level of detail that can be accessed in the lightly summarized database.

The second tier of data in the data warehouse — the lowest level of granularity — is stored in the true archival level of data, as shown in Figure 2-17.

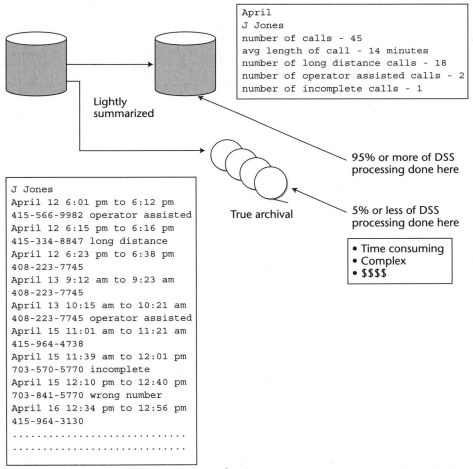

Figure 2-17 Dual levels of granularity allow you to process the majority of requests efficiently and answer any question that can be answered.

At the true archival level of data, all the detail coming from the operational environment is stored. There is truly a multitude of data at this level. For that reason, it makes sense to store the data on a medium such as magnetic tape or another bulk storage medium because the volume of data is so large.

By creating two levels of granularity in the data warehouse, the DSS architect has killed two birds with one stone — most DSS processing is performed against the lightly summarized data, where the data is compact and efficiently accessed. When some greater level of detail is required (5 percent of the time or less), there is the true archival level of data. It is expensive, cumbersome, and complex to access data at the true archival level of granularity, but if it is needed, it is there when necessary.

If a pattern of searching the true archival level of data develops over time, the designer may want to create some new fields of data at the lightly summarized level, so that most of the processing can occur there.

Because of the costs, efficiencies, ease of access, and ability to answer any query that can be answered, the dual level of data is the best architectural choice for the detailed level of the data warehouse for most shops. A single level of data should only be attempted when a shop has a relatively small amount of data in the data warehouse environment.

Exploration and Data Mining

The granular data found in the data warehouse supports more than data marts. It also supports the processes of exploration and data mining. Exploration and data mining take masses of detailed, historical data and examine it for previously unknown patterns of business activity.

The data warehouse contains a very useful source of data for the explorer and data miner. The data found in the data warehouse is cleansed, integrated, and organized. Plus, the data is historical. This foundation is precisely what the data miner and the explorer need in order to start the exploration and data mining activity. It is noteworthy that while the data warehouse provides an excellent source of data for the miner and the explorer, the data warehouse is often not the only source. External data and other data can be freely mixed with data warehouse data in the course of doing exploration and mining. Refer to the book *Exploration Warehousing: Turning Business Information into Business Opportunity* (Hoboken, N.J.: Wiley, 2000) for more information on this topic.

Living Sample Database

Occasionally, it is necessary to create a different kind of data warehouse. Sometimes there is simply too much data for normal access and analysis. When this happens, special design approaches may be used.

An interesting hybrid form of a data warehouse is the living sample database, which is useful when the volume of data in the warehouse has grown very large. The *living sample database* refers to a subset of either true archival data or lightly summarized data taken from a data warehouse. The term "living" stems from the fact that it is a subset — a sample — of a larger database, and the term "sample" stems from the fact that periodically the database needs to be refreshed. Figure 2-18 shows a living sample database.

In some circumstances (for example, statistical analysis of a population or profiling), a living sample database can be very useful and can save huge amounts of resources. But there are some severe restrictions, and the designer should not build such a database as part of the data warehouse infrastructure unless he or she is aware of the limitations.

A living sample database is not a general-purpose database. If you wanted to find out whether J Jones is a customer, you would not look into a living sample database for that information. It is absolutely possible for J Jones to be a customer but not be on record in the living sample. These databases are good for statistical analysis and looking at trends, and can offer some very promising results when data must be looked at collectively. They are not at all useful for dealing with individual records of data.

One of the important aspects of building a living sample database is how the data is loaded, which determines the amount of data in the database and how random the data will be. Consider how a living sample database is typically loaded. An extract, or selection, program rummages through a large database, choosing every one-hundredth or every one-thousandth record. The record is then shipped to the living sample database. The resulting living sample database, then, is one-hundredth or one-thousandth the size of the original database. The query that operates against this database then uses one-hundredth or one-thousandth the resources as a query that would operate directly against the full data warehouse.

The selection of records for inclusion into the living sample is usually random. On occasion, a *judgment sample* is taken, in which a record must meet certain criteria in order to be selected. The problem with judgment samples is that they almost always introduce bias into the living sample data. The problem with a random selection of data is that it may not produce statistical significance. But however it's done, a subset of the data warehouse is selected for the living sample. The fact that any given record is not found in the living sample database means nothing because the processing that operates against the living sample does not require every record in the data warehouse to be in the living sample.

The greatest asset of a living sample database is that it is very efficient to access. Because its size is a fraction of the larger database from which it was derived, it is correspondingly much more efficient to access and analyze.

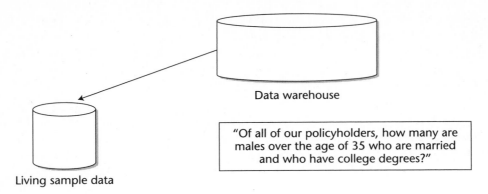

Living sample data

Data warehouse

"Of all of our policyholders, how many are males over the age of 35 who are married and who have college degrees?"

- A fraction of data in the warehouse
- Used for very efficient formulation of a query
- *Cannot be used for general purpose analysis— can only be used for statistical analysis*

Figure 2-18   Living simple data — another way of changing the granularity of data.

Put another way, suppose an analyst takes 24 hours to scan and analyze a large database. It may take as little as 10 minutes to scan and analyze a living sample database. In doing heuristic analysis, the turnaround time is crucial to the analysis that can be done. In *heuristic analysis*, the analyst runs a program, studies the results, reformulates the program, and runs it again. If it takes 24 hours to execute the program, the process of analysis and reformulation is greatly impaired (not to mention the resources required to do the reformulation).

With a living sample database small enough to be scanned in 10 minutes, the analyst can go through the iterative process very quickly. In short, the productivity of the DSS analyst depends on the speed of turning around the analysis being done.

One argument claims that doing statistical analysis yields incorrect answers. For example, an analyst may run against a large file of 25 million records to determine that 56.7 percent of the drivers on the road are men. Using a living sample database, the analyst uses 25,000 records to determine that 55.9 percent of the drivers on the road are men. One analysis has required vastly more resources than the other, yet the difference between the calculations is very small. Undoubtedly, the analysis against the large database was more accurate, but the cost of that accuracy is exorbitant, especially in the face of heuristic processing, where iterations of processing are the norm.

If very high degrees of accuracy are desired, a useful technique is to formulate the request and go through the iterative processing on the living sample database. In doing so, the DSS analyst quickly formulates the request. Then, after several iterations of analysis have been done, when the request is understood, it is run one final time against the large database.

Living sample data is just one more way of changing the level of granularity in the data warehouse to accommodate DSS processing.

Partitioning as a Design Approach

A second major design issue of data in the warehouse (after granularity) is partitioning (refer back to the b portion of Figure 2-11). Partitioning of data refers to the breakup of data into separate physical units that can be handled independently. In the data warehouse, the issues surrounding partitioning do not focus on whether partitioning should be done, but rather how it should be done.

It is often said that if both granularity and partitioning are done properly, then almost all other aspects of the data warehouse design and implementation come easily. If granularity is not handled properly, and if partitioning is not designed and implemented carefully, then no other aspects of design really matter.

Proper partitioning can benefit the data warehouse in several ways:

- Loading data
- Accessing data
- Archiving data
- Deleting data
- Monitoring data
- Storing data

Partitioning data properly allows data to grow and to be managed. Not partitioning data properly does not allow data to be managed or to grow gracefully.

There are other important design aspects of the data warehouse that will be discussed in later chapters.

Partitioning of Data

In the data warehouse environment, the question is not whether current detail data will be partitioned, but rather how current detail data will be partitioned. Figure 2-19 illustrates partitioning.

The purpose of partitioning current detail data is to break data up into small, manageable physical units. Why is this so important? The operations staff and the designer have more flexibility in managing small physical units of data than large ones.

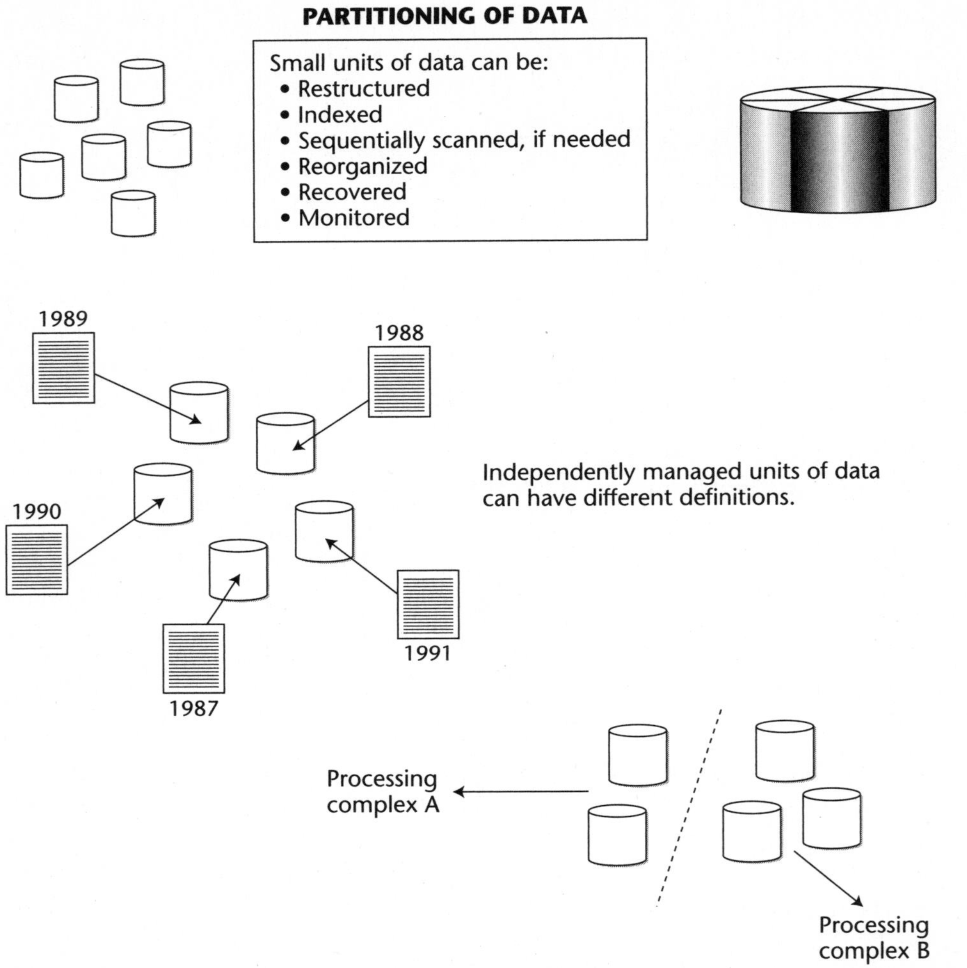

PARTITIONING OF DATA

Small units of data can be:
- Restructured
- Indexed
- Sequentially scanned, if needed
- Reorganized
- Recovered
- Monitored

1989

1988

1990

1987

1991

Independently managed units of data
can have different definitions.

Processing
complex A

Processing
complex B

Figure 2-19   Independently managed partitions of data can be sent to different processing complexes with no other system considerations.

Following are some of the tasks that cannot easily be performed when data resides in large physical units:

- Restructuring

- Indexing

- Sequential scanning, if needed

- Reorganization

- Recovery

- Monitoring

In short, one of the essences of the data warehouse is the flexible access of data. Large masses of data defeat much of the purpose of the data warehouse. Therefore, all current-detail data warehouse data will be partitioned.

Data is partitioned when data of a like structure is divided into more than one physical unit of data. In addition, any given unit of data belongs to one and only one partition.

Data can be divided by many criteria, such as:

- By date
- By line of business
- By geography
- By organizational unit
- By all of the above

The choices for partitioning data are strictly up to the developer. In the data warehouse environment, however, it is almost mandatory that one of the criteria for partitioning be by date.

As an example of how a life insurance company may choose to partition its data, consider the following physical units of data:

- 2000 health claims
- 2001 health claims
- 2002 health claims
- 1999 life claims
- 2000 life claims
- 2001 life claims
- 2002 life claims
- 2000 casualty claims
- 2001 casualty claims
- 2002 casualty claims

The insurance company has used the criteria of date — that is, year — and type of claim to partition the data.

Partitioning can be done in many ways. One of the major issues facing the data warehouse developer is whether to partition at the system level or at the application level. Partitioning at the system level is a function of the DBMS and the operating system to some extent. Partitioning at the application level is done by application code and is solely and strictly controlled by the developer and the programmer, so the DBMS and the system know of no relation between one partition and the other.

As a rule, it makes sense to partition data warehouse data at the application level. There are some important reasons for this. The most important is that at the application level there can be a different definition of data for each year. There can be 2000's definition of data and there can be 2001's definition of data, which may or may not be the same thing. The nature of data in a warehouse is the collection of data over a long period of time.

When the partitioning is done at the system level, the DBMS inevitably requires that there be a single definition of data. Given that the data warehouse holds data for a long period of time — up to 10 years — and given that the definition regularly changes, it does not make sense to allow the DBMS or the operating system to dictate that there should be a single definition of data.

By allowing the partitioning of data to be managed at the application level rather than the DBMS level, data can be moved from one processing complex to another with impunity. When the workload and volume of data become a real burden in the data warehouse environment, this feature may be a real advantage.

The acid test for the partitioning of data is to ask the question, "Can an index be added to a partition with no discernible interruption to other operations?" If an index can be added at will, then the partition is fine enough. If an index cannot be added easily, then the partition needs to be broken down more finely.

Structuring Data in the Data Warehouse

So far, we haven't delved into what the data structures found in the data warehouse really look like. Many kinds of structures are found and we will look at some of the more common ones now.

Perhaps the simplest and most common data structure found in the data warehouse is the simple cumulative structure, shown in Figure 2-20.

Figure 2-20 shows the daily transactions being transported from the operational environment. After that, they are summarized into data warehouse records, which may be by customer, by account, or by any subject area in the data warehouse. The transactions in Figure 2-20 are summarized by day. In other words, all daily activity for a customer for an account are totaled and passed into the data warehouse on a day-by-day basis.

Figure 2-21 shows a variation of the simple daily accumulation called the *storage of rolling summary data*.

SIMPLE CUMULATIVE DATA

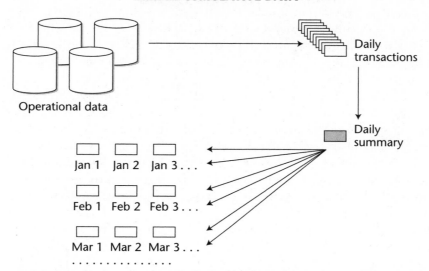

Figure 2-20   The simplest form of data in the data warehouse is the data that has been accumulated on a record-by-record basis, called simple cumulative data.

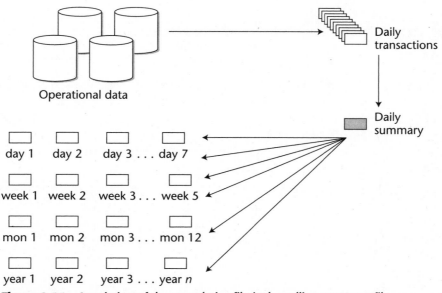

Figure 2-21   A variation of the cumulative file is the rolling summary file.

The data passes from the operational environment to the data warehouse environment as it did previously. In rolling summary data, however, the data is entered into a very different structure. For the first seven days of the week, activity is summarized into seven daily slots. On the eighth day, the seven daily slots are added together and placed into the first weekly slot. Then the daily totals are added into the first daily slot.

At the end of the month, the weekly slots are added together and placed in the first monthly slot. Then the weekly slots are reset to zero. At the end of the year, the monthly slots are added together, and the first yearly slot is loaded. Then the monthly slots are reset to zero.

A rolling summary data structure handles many fewer units of data than does a simple cumulative structuring of data. A comparison of the advantages and the disadvantages of rolling summary versus simple cumulative structuring of data is shown in Figure 2-22.

Another possibility for the structuring of data warehouse data is the *simple direct file*, shown in Figure 2-23.

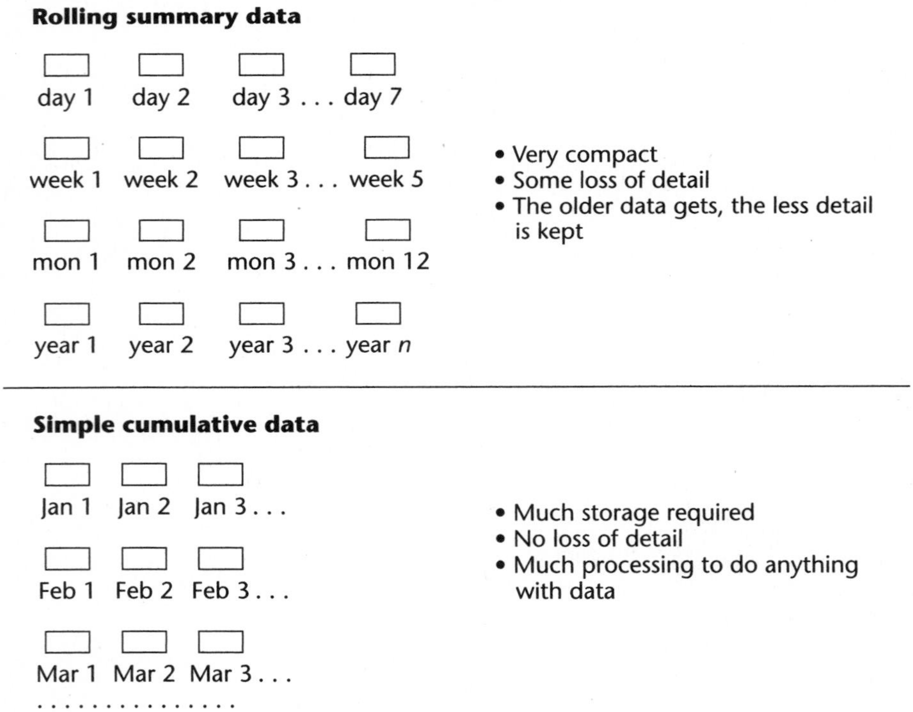

Rolling summary data

| day 1 | day 2 | day 3 . . . day 7 |

| week 1 | week 2 | week 3 . . . week 5 |

- Very compact
- Some loss of detail
- The older data gets, the less detail is kept

| mon 1 | mon 2 | mon 3 . . . mon 12 |

| year 1 | year 2 | year 3 . . . year *n* |

Simple cumulative data

| Jan 1 | Jan 2 | Jan 3 . . . |

- Much storage required
- No loss of detail
- Much processing to do anything with data

| Feb 1 | Feb 2 | Feb 3 . . . |

| Mar 1 | Mar 2 | Mar 3 . . . |

. . . .

Figure 2-22   Comparing simple cumulative data with rolling summary data.

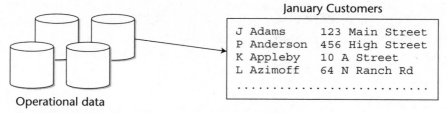

January Customers

```
J Adams       123 Main Street
P Anderson    456 High Street
K Appleby     10 A Street
L Azimoff     64 N Ranch Rd
. . . . . . . . . . . . . . . . . . . . . . . . . . .
```

Operational data

Figure 2-23   Creating a continuous file from direct files.

Figure 2-23 shows that data is merely pulled from the operational environment to the data warehouse environment; there is no accumulation. In addition, the simple direct file is not created on a daily basis. Instead, it is created over a longer period of time, such as a week or a month. As such, the simple direct file represents a snapshot of operational data taken as of one instant in time.

A *continuous file* can be created from two or more simple direct files, as shown in Figure 2-24. Two snapshots — one from January and one from February — are merged to create a continuous file of data. The data in the continuous file represents the data continuously from the first month to the last.

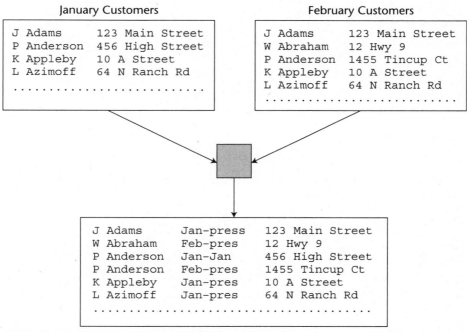

January Customers

```
J Adams      123 Main Street
P Anderson   456 High Street
K Appleby    10 A Street
L Azimoff    64 N Ranch Rd
. . . . . . . . . . . . . . . . . . . . . . . . . .
```

February Customers

```
J Adams      123 Main Street
W Abraham    12 Hwy 9
P Anderson   1455 Tincup Ct
K Appleby    10 A Street
L Azimoff    64 N Ranch Rd
. . . . . . . . . . . . . . . . . . . . . . . . . .
```

```
J Adams      Jan-press   123 Main Street
W Abraham    Feb-pres    12 Hwy 9
P Anderson   Jan-Jan     456 High Street
P Anderson   Feb-pres    1455 Tincup Ct
K Appleby    Jan-pres    10 A Street
L Azimoff    Jan-pres    64 N Ranch Rd
. . . . . . . . . . . . . . . . . . . . . . . . . . . . . . . . . . .
```

Figure 2-24   Creating a continuous file from direct files.

Of course, a continuous file can be created by appending a snapshot of data onto a previous version of the continuous file, as shown in Figure 2-25.

There are many more ways to structure data within the data warehouse. The most common are these:

- Simple cumulative
- Rolling summary
- Simple direct
- Continuous

At the key level, data warehouse keys are inevitably compounded keys. There are two compelling reasons for this:

- Date — year, year/month, year/month/day, and so on — is almost always a part of the key.
- Because data warehouse data is partitioned, the different components of the partitioning show up as part of the key.

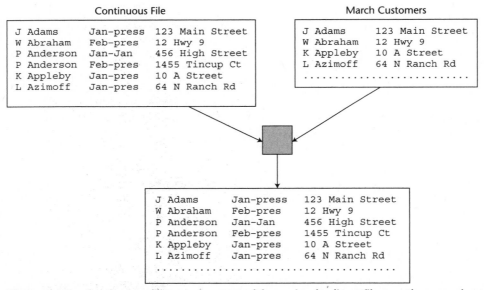

Figure 2-25 Continuous files can be created from simple direct files, or they may have simple direct files appended to them.

Auditing and the Data Warehouse

An interesting issue that arises with data warehouses is whether auditing can be or should be done from the data warehouse itself. Auditing can be done from the data warehouse. In the past, there have been a few examples of detailed audits being performed there. But there are many reasons why auditing — even if it can be done from the data warehouse — should not be done from there. The primary reasons for not doing so are the following:

- Data that otherwise would not find its way into the warehouse suddenly has to be there.
- The timing of data entry into the warehouse changes dramatically when an auditing capability is required.
- The backup and recovery restrictions for the data warehouse change drastically when an auditing capability is required.
- Auditing data at the warehouse forces the granularity of data in the warehouse to be at the very lowest level.

In short, it is possible to audit from the data warehouse environment, but because of the complications involved, it makes much more sense to audit elsewhere.

Data Homogeneity and Heterogeneity

At first glance, it may appear that the data found in the data warehouse is homogeneous in the sense that all of the types of records are the same. In truth, data in the data warehouse is heterogeneous. The data found in the data warehouse is divided into major subdivisions called *subject areas*. Figure 2-26 shows that a data warehouse has subject areas of Product, Customer, Vendor, and Transaction.

The first division of data inside a data warehouse is along the lines of the major subjects of the corporation. But with each subject area there are further subdivisions. Data within a subject area is divided into tables. Figure 2-27 shows this division of data into tables for the subject area product.

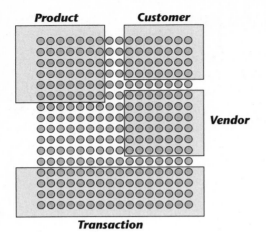

Figure 2-26   The data in the different parts of the data warehouse are grouped by subject area.

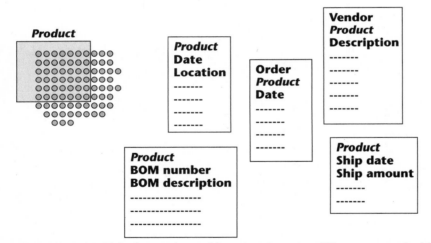

Figure 2-27   Within the product subject area there are different types of tables, but each table has a common product identifier as part of the key.

Figure 2-27 shows that there are five tables that make up the subject area inside the data warehouse. Each of the tables has its own data, and there is a common thread for each of the tables in the subject area. That common thread is the key, or foreign key, data element — Product.

Within the physical tables that make up a subject area, there are further subdivisions. These subdivisions are created by different occurrences of data values. For example, inside the product shipping table, there are January shipments, February shipments, March shipments, and so forth.

The data in the data warehouse then is subdivided by the following criteria:

- Subject area
- Table
- Occurrences of data within table

This organization of data within a data warehouse makes the data easily accessible and understandable for all the different components of the architecture that must build on the data found there. The result is that the data warehouse, with its granular data, serves as a basis for many different components, as shown in Figure 2-28.

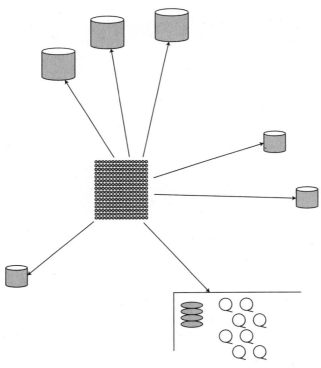

Figure 2-28   The data warehouse sits at the center of a large framework.

The simple yet elegant organization of data within the data warehouse environment shown in Figure 2-28 makes data accessible in many different ways for many different purposes.

Purging Warehouse Data

Data does not just eternally pour into a data warehouse. It has its own life cycle within the warehouse as well. At some point in time, data is purged from the warehouse. The issue of purging data is one of the fundamental design issues that must not escape the data warehouse designer.

In some cases, data is not purged from the warehouse at all. It is simply rolled up to higher levels of summary. There are several ways in which data is purged or the detail of data is transformed, including the following:

- Data is added to a rolling summary file where detail is lost.
- Data is transferred to a bulk storage medium from a high-performance medium such as DASD.
- Data is actually purged from the system.
- Data is transferred from one level of the architecture to another, such as from the operational level to the data warehouse level.

There are, then, a variety of ways in which data is purged or otherwise transformed inside the data warehouse environment. The life cycle of data — including its purge or final archival dissemination — should be an active part of the design process for the data warehouse.

Reporting and the Architected Environment

It is a temptation to say that once the data warehouse has been constructed, all reporting and informational processing will be done from there. That is simply not the case. There is a legitimate class of report processing that rightfully belongs in the domain of operational systems. Figure 2-29 shows where the different styles of processing should be located.

Figure 2-29 shows that operational reporting is for the clerical level and focuses primarily on the line item. Data warehouse or informational processing focuses on management and contains summary or otherwise calculated information. In the data warehouse style of reporting, little use is made of line-item, detailed information once the basic calculation of data is made.

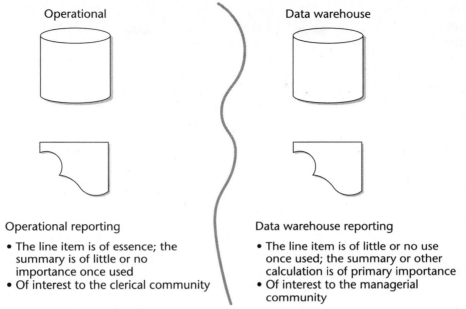

Operational

Data warehouse

Operational reporting

- The line item is of essence; the summary is of little or no importance once used
- Of interest to the clerical community

Data warehouse reporting

- The line item is of little or no use once used; the summary or other calculation is of primary importance
- Of interest to the managerial community

Figure 2-29   The differences between the two types of reporting.

As an example of the differences between operational reporting and DSS reporting, consider a bank. Every day before going home, a teller must balance the cash in his or her window. This means that the teller takes the starting amount of cash, tallies all the day's transactions, and determines what the day's ending cash balance should be. In order to do this, the teller needs a report of all the day's transactions. This is a form of operational reporting.

Now consider the bank vice president who is trying to determine how many new ATMs to place in a newly developed shopping center. The banking vice president looks at a whole host of information, some of which comes from within the bank and some of which comes from outside the bank. The bank vice president is making a long-term, strategic decision and uses classical DSS information for his or her decision.

There is then a real difference between operational reporting and DSS reporting. Operational reporting should always be done within the confines of the operational environment.

The Operational Window of Opportunity

In its broadest sense, archival represents anything older than right now. Thus, the information about the loaf of bread that you bought 30 seconds ago is archival information. The only thing that is not archival is information that is current.

The foundation of DSS processing — the data warehouse — contains nothing but archival information, most of it at least 24 hours old. But archival data is found elsewhere throughout the architected environment. In particular, some limited amounts of archival data are also found in the operational environment.

In the data warehouse, it is normal to have a vast amount of archival data — from 5 to 10 years of data is common. Because of the wide time horizon of archival data, the data warehouse contains a massive amount of data. The time horizon of archival data found in the operational environment — the *operational window* of data — is not nearly as long. It can be anywhere from 1 week to 2 years.

The time horizon of archival data in the operational environment is not the only difference between archival data in the data warehouse and in the operational environment. Unlike the data warehouse, the operational environment's archival data is nonvoluminous and has a high probability of access.

In order to understand the role of fresh, nonvoluminous, high-probability-of-access archival data in the operational environment, consider the way a bank works. In a bank environment, the customer can reasonably expect to find information about this month's transactions. Did this month's rent check clear? When was a paycheck deposited? What was the low balance for the month? Did the bank take out money for the electricity bill last week?

The operational environment of a bank, then, contains very detailed, very current transactions (which are still archival). Is it reasonable to expect the bank to tell the customer whether a check was made out to the grocery store 5 years ago or whether a check to a political campaign was cashed 10 years ago? These transactions would hardly be in the domain of the operational systems of the bank. These transactions are very old, and so the data has a very low probability of access.

The operational window of time varies from industry to industry and even in type of data and activity within an industry.

For example, an insurance company would have a very lengthy operational window — from 2 to 3 years. The rate of transactions in an insurance company is very low, at least compared to other types of industries. There are relatively few direct interactions between the customer and the insurance company. The operational window for the activities of a bank, on the other hand, is very short — from 0 to 60 days. A bank has many direct interactions with its customers.

The operational window of a company depends on what industry the company is in. In the case of a large company, there may be more than one operational window, depending on the particulars of the business being conducted. For example, in a telephone company, customer usage data may have an operational window of 30 to 60 days, while vendor or supplier activity may have a window of 2 to 3 years.

The following are some suggestions as to how the operational window of archival data may look in different industries:

- Insurance — 2 to 3 years
- Bank trust processing — 2 to 5 years
- Telephone customer usage — 30 to 60 days
- Supplier/vendor activity — 2 to 3 years
- Retail banking customer account activity — 30 days
- Vendor activity — 1 year
- Loans — 2 to 5 years
- Retailing SKU activity — 1 to 14 days
- Vendor activity — 1 week to 1 month
- Airlines flight seat activity — 30 to 90 days
- Vendor/supplier activity — 1 to 2 years
- Public utility customer utilization — 60 to 90 days
- Supplier activity — 1 to 5 years

The length of the operational window is very important to the DSS analyst because it determines where the analyst goes to do different kinds of analysis and what kinds of analysis can be done. For example, the DSS analyst can do individual-item analysis on data found within the operational window, but cannot do massive trend analysis over a lengthy period of time. Data within the operational window is geared to efficient individual access. Only when the data passes out of the operational window is it geared to mass data storage and access.

On the other hand, the DSS analyst can do sweeping trend analysis on data found outside the operational window. Data out there can be accessed and processed en masse, whereas access to any one individual unit of data is not optimal.

Incorrect Data in the Data Warehouse

The architect needs to know what to do about incorrect data in the data warehouse. The first assumption is that incorrect data arrives in the data warehouse on an exception basis. If data is being incorrectly entered in the data warehouse on a wholesale basis, then it is incumbent on the architect to find the offending ETL program and source and make adjustments. Occasionally, even with the best of ETL processing, a few pieces of incorrect data enter the data warehouse environment. How should the architect handle incorrect data in the data warehouse?

There are at least three options. Each approach has its own strengths and weaknesses, and none are absolutely right or wrong. Instead, under some circumstances one choice is better than another.

For example, suppose that on July 1 an entry for $5,000 is made into an operational system for account ABC. On July 2 a snapshot for $5,000 is created in the data warehouse for account ABC. Then on August 15 an error is discovered. Instead of an entry for $5,000, the entry should have been for $750. How can the data in the data warehouse be corrected?

- **Choice 1: Go back into the data warehouse for July 2 and find the offending entry. Then, using update capabilities, replace the value $5,000 with the value $750.** — This is a clean and neat solution when it works, but it introduces new issues:

  - The integrity of the data has been destroyed. Any report running between July 2 and Aug 16 will not be able to be reconciled.

  - The update must be done in the data warehouse environment.

  - In many cases, there is not a single entry that must be corrected, but many, many entries that must be corrected.

- **Choice 2: Enter offsetting entries.** — Two entries are made on August 16, one for –$5,000 and another for +$750. This is the best reflection of the most up-to-date information in the data warehouse between July 2 and August 16. There are some drawbacks to this approach:

  - Many entries may have to be corrected, not just one. Making a simple adjustment may not be an easy thing to do at all.

  - Sometimes the formula for correction is so complex that making an adjustment cannot be done.

- **Choice 3: Reset the account to the proper value on August 16.** — An entry on August 16 reflects the balance of the account at that moment regardless of any past activity. An entry would be made for $750 on August 16. But this approach has its own drawbacks:

  - The ability to simply reset an account as of one moment in time requires application and procedural conventions.

  - Such a resetting of values does not accurately account for the error that has been made.

Choice 3 is what likely happens when you cannot balance your checking account at the end of the month. Instead of trying to find out what the bank has done, you simply take the bank's word for it and reset the account balance.

There are then at least three ways to handle incorrect data as it enters the data warehouse. Depending on the circumstances, one of the approaches will yield better results than another approach.

Summary

The two most important design decisions that can be made concern the granularity of data and the partitioning of data. For most organizations, a dual level of granularity makes the most sense. Partitioning of data breaks it down into small physical units. As a rule, partitioning is done at the application level rather than at the system level.

Data warehouse development is best done iteratively. First, one part of the data warehouse is constructed, and then another part of the warehouse is constructed. It is *never* appropriate to develop the data warehouse under the "big bang" approach. One reason is that the end user of the warehouse operates in a discovery mode, so only *after* the warehouse's first iteration is built can the developer tell what is really needed in the warehouse.

The granularity of the data residing inside the data warehouse is of the utmost importance. A very low level of granularity creates too much data, and the system is overwhelmed by the volumes of data. A very high level of granularity is efficient to process, but precludes many kinds of analyses that need detail. In addition, the granularity of the data warehouse needs to be chosen in an awareness of the different architectural components that will feed off the data warehouse.

Surprisingly, many design alternatives can be used to handle the issue of granularity. One approach is to build a multitiered data warehouse with dual levels of granularity that serve different types of queries and analysis. Another approach is to create a living sample database where statistical processing can be done very efficiently from a living sample database.

Partitioning a data warehouse is very important for a variety of reasons. When data is partitioned it can be managed in separate, small, discrete units. This means that loading the data into the data warehouse will be simplified, building indexes will be streamlined, archiving data will be easy, and so forth. There are at least two ways to partition data — at the DBMS or operating system level and at the application level. Each approach to partitioning has its own set of advantages and disadvantages.

Each unit of data in the data warehouse environment has a moment associated with it. In some cases, the moment in time appears as a snapshot on every record. In other cases, the moment in time is applied to an entire table. Data is often summarized by day, month, or quarter. In addition, data is created in a continuous manner. The internal time structuring of data is accomplished in many ways.

Auditing can be done from a data warehouse, but auditing should not be done from a data warehouse. Instead, auditing is best done in the detailed operational transaction-oriented environment. When auditing is done in the data warehouse, data that would not otherwise be included is found there, the timing of the update into the data warehouse becomes an issue, and the level of granularity in the data warehouse is mandated by the need for auditing, which may not be the level of granularity needed for other processing.

A normal part of the data warehouse life cycle is that of purging data. Often, developers neglect to include purging as a part of the specification of design. The result is a warehouse that grows eternally, which, of course, is an impossibility.

CHAPTER 3

The Data Warehouse and Design

There are two major components to building a data warehouse: the design of the interface from operational systems and the design of the data warehouse itself. Yet, the term "design" is not entirely accurate because it suggests that elements can be planned out in advance. The requirements for the data warehouse cannot be known until it is partially populated and in use, and design approaches that have worked in the past will not necessarily suffice in subsequent data warehouses. Data warehouses are constructed in a heuristic manner, where one phase of development depends entirely on the results attained in the previous phase. First, one portion of data is populated. It is then used and scrutinized by the DSS analyst. Next, based on feedback from the end user, the data is modified and/or other data is added. Then another portion of the data warehouse is built, and so forth. This feedback loop continues throughout the entire life of the data warehouse.

Therefore, data warehouses cannot be designed the same way as the classical requirements-driven system. On the other hand, anticipating requirements is still important. Reality lies somewhere in between.

Beginning with Operational Data

Design begins with the considerations of placing data in the data warehouse. There are many considerations to be made concerning the placement of data into the data warehouse from the operational environment.

At the outset, operational transaction-oriented data is locked up in existing legacy systems. Though it is tempting to think that creating the data warehouse involves only extracting operational data and entering it into the warehouse, nothing could be further from the truth. Merely pulling data out of the legacy environment and placing it in the data warehouse achieves very little of the potential of data warehousing.

Figure 3-1 shows a simplification of how data is transferred from the existing legacy systems environment to the data warehouse. We see here that multiple applications contribute their data to the data warehouse.

Figure 3-1 is overly simplistic for many reasons. Most importantly, it does not take into account that the data in the operational environment is unintegrated. Figure 3-2 shows the lack of integration in a typical existing systems environment. Pulling the data into the data warehouse without integrating it is a grave mistake.

When the existing applications were constructed, no thought was given to possible future integration. Each application had its own set of unique and private requirements. It is no surprise, then, that some of the same data exists in various places with different names, some data is labeled the same way in different places, some data is all in the same place with the same name but reflects a different measurement, and so on. Extracting data from many places and integrating it into a unified picture is a complex problem.

This lack of integration is the extract programmer's nightmare. As illustrated in Figure 3-3, countless details must be programmed and reconciled just to bring the data properly from the operational environment.

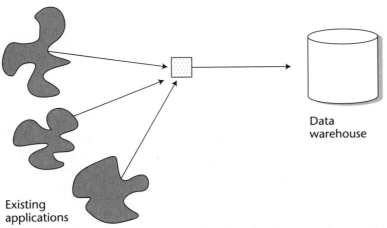

Figure 3-1 Moving from the operational to the data warehouse environment is not as simple as mere extraction.

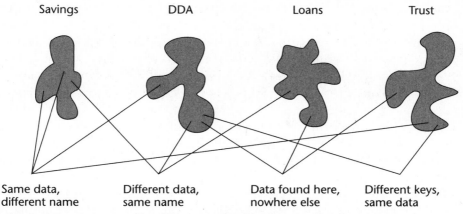

Savings   DDA   Loans   Trust

Same data,   Different data,   Data found here,   Different keys,
different name   same name   nowhere else   same data

Figure 3-2   Data across the different applications is severely unintegrated.

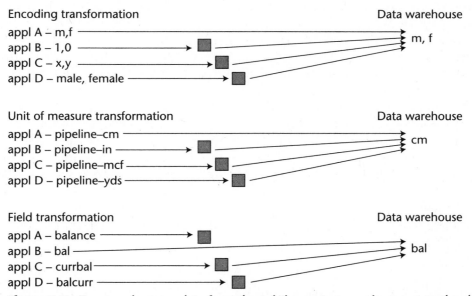

Encoding transformation   Data warehouse

appl A – m,f   m, f
appl B – 1,0
appl C – x,y
appl D – male, female

Unit of measure transformation   Data warehouse

appl A – pipeline–cm   cm
appl B – pipeline–in
appl C – pipeline–mcf
appl D – pipeline–yds

Field transformation   Data warehouse

appl A – balance   bal
appl B – bal
appl C – currbal
appl D – balcurr

Figure 3-3   To properly move data from the existing systems environment to the data warehouse environment, it must be integrated.

One simple example of lack of integration is data that is not encoded consistently, as shown by the encoding of gender. In one application, gender is encoded as m/f. In another, it is encoded as 0/1. In yet another, it is encoded as x/y. Of course, in the data warehouse, it doesn't matter how gender is encoded as long as it is done consistently. As data passes to the data warehouse, the applications' different values must be correctly deciphered and recoded with the proper value.

As another example, consider four applications that have the same field-pipeline. The pipeline field is measured differently in each application. In one application, pipeline is measured in inches, in another in centimeters, and so forth. It does not matter how pipeline is measured in the data warehouse, as long as it is measured consistently. As each application passes its data to the warehouse, the measurement of pipeline is converted into a single consistent corporate measurement.

Semantic field transformation is another integration issue. Say that the same field exists in four applications under four different names. To transform the data to the data warehouse properly, a mapping from the different source fields to the data warehouse fields must occur.

Yet another issue is that legacy data exists in many different formats under many different DBMSs. Some legacy data is under IMS, some legacy data is under DB2, and still other legacy data is under VSAM. In order to populate the data warehouse, all of these technologies must have the data they protect brought forward into a single technology. Such a translation of technology is not always straightforward.

These simple examples hardly scratch the surface of integration, and they are not complex in themselves. But when they are multiplied by the thousands of existing systems and files, compounded by the fact that documentation is usually out-of-date or nonexistent, the issue of integration becomes burdensome.

But integration of existing legacy systems is not the only difficulty in the transformation of data from the operational, existing systems environment to the data warehouse environment. Another major problem is the efficiency of accessing existing systems data. How does the program that scans existing systems know whether a file has been scanned previously? The existing systems environment holds tons of data, and attempting to scan all of it every time a data warehouse load needs to be done is wasteful and unrealistic.

Three types of loads are made into the data warehouse from the operational environment:

- Archival data
- Data currently contained in the operational environment
- Ongoing changes to the data warehouse environment from the changes (updates) that have occurred in the operational environment since the last refresh

As a rule, loading archival data from the legacy environment as the data warehouse is first loaded presents a minimal challenge for two reasons. First, it often is not done at all. Organizations find the use of old data not cost-effective in many environments. Second, even when archival data is loaded, it is a one-time-only event.

Loading current, nonarchival data from the existing operational environment likewise presents a minimal challenge because it must be done only once. Usually, the existing systems environment can be downloaded to a sequential file, and the sequential file can be downloaded into the warehouse with no disruption to the online environment. Although system resources are required, because the process is done only once, the event is minimally disruptive.

Loading data on an ongoing basis — as changes are made to the operational environment — presents the largest challenge to the data architect. Efficiently trapping those ongoing daily changes and manipulating them is not easy. Scanning existing files, then, is a major issue facing the data warehouse architect.

Five common techniques are used to limit the amount of operational data scanned at the point of refreshing the data warehouse, as shown in Figure 3-4. The first technique is to scan data that has been time stamped in the operational environment. When an application stamps the time of the last change or update on a record, the data warehouse scan can run quite efficiently because data with a date other than that applicable does not have to be touched. It usually is only by happenstance, though, that existing data has been time stamped.

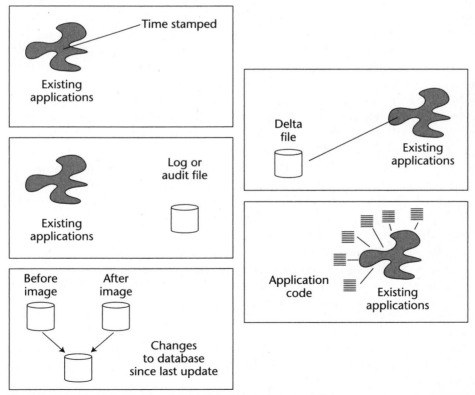

Figure 3-4 How do you know what source data to scan? Do you scan every record every day? Every week?

The second technique to limiting the data to be scanned is to scan a delta file. A *delta file* contains only the changes made to an application as a result of the transactions that have run through the operational environment. With a delta file, the scan process is very efficient because data that is not a candidate for scanning is never touched. Not many applications, however, build delta files.

The third technique is to scan a log file or an audit file created as a by-product of transaction processing. A log file contains essentially the same data as a delta file. However, there are some major differences. Many times, computer operations protects the log files because they are needed in the recovery process. Computer operations is not particularly thrilled to have its log file used for something other than its primary purpose. Another difficulty with a log tape is that the internal format is built for systems purposes, not applications purposes. A technological guru may be needed to interface the contents of data on the log tape. Another shortcoming is that the log file usually contains much more information than that desired by the data warehouse developer. Audit files have many of the same shortcomings as log files. An example of the use of log files to update a data warehouse is the Web logs created by the Web-based eBusiness environment.

The fourth technique for managing the amount of data scanned is to modify application code. This is never a popular option, because much application code is old and fragile.

The last option (in most respects, a hideous one from a resource-utilization perspective, mentioned primarily to convince people that there must be a better way) is rubbing a "before" and an "after" image of the operational file together. In this option, a snapshot of a database is taken at the moment of extraction. When another extraction is performed, another snapshot is taken. The two snapshots are serially compared to each other to determine the activity that has transpired. This approach is cumbersome and complex, and it requires an inordinate amount of resources. It is simply a last resort to be done when nothing else works.

Integration and performance are not the only major discrepancies that prevent a simple extract process from being used to construct the data warehouse. A third difficulty is that operational data must undergo a time-basis shift as it passes into the data warehouse, as shown in Figure 3-5.

Existing operational data is almost always current-value data. Such data's accuracy is valid as of the moment of access, and it can be updated. But data that goes into the data warehouse cannot be updated. Instead, an element of time must be attached to it. A major shift in the modes of processing surrounding the data is necessary as it passes into the data warehouse from the operational environment.

Yet another major consideration when passing data is the need to manage the volume of data that resides in and passes into the warehouse. Data must be condensed both at the moment of extraction and as it arrives at the warehouse. If condensation is not done, the volume of data in the data warehouse will grow rapidly out of control. Figure 3-6 shows a simple form of data condensation.

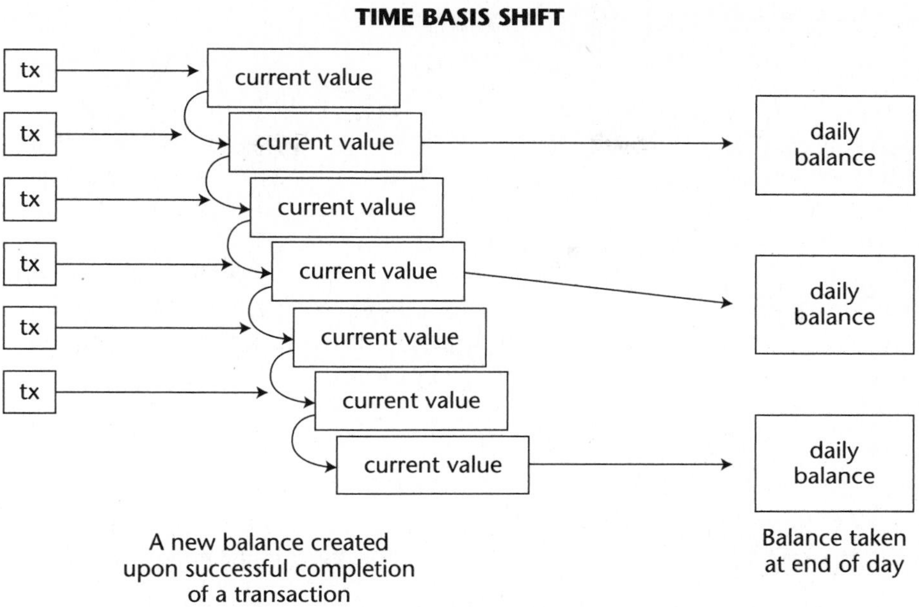

TIME BASIS SHIFT

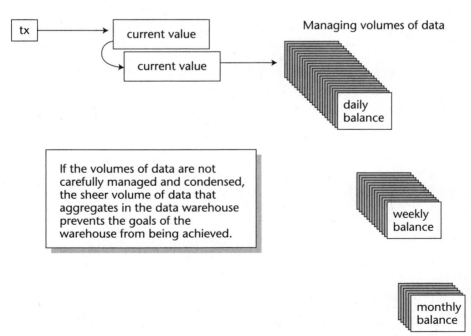

A new balance created
upon successful completion
of a transaction

Balance taken
at end of day

Figure 3-5   A shift in the time-basis is required as data is moved over from the operational to the data warehouse environment.

Managing volumes of data

If the volumes of data are not carefully managed and condensed, the sheer volume of data that aggregates in the data warehouse prevents the goals of the warehouse from being achieved.

daily balance

weekly balance

monthly balance

Figure 3-6   Condensation of data is a vital factor in the managing of warehouse data.

Process and Data Models and the Architected Environment

Before attempting to apply conventional database design techniques, the designer must understand the applicability and the limitations of those techniques. Figure 3-7 shows the relationship among the levels of the architecture and the two types of models for the information systems environment — process models and data models. The *process model* applies only to the operational environment. The *data model* applies to both the operational environment and the data warehouse environment. Trying to use a process or data model in the wrong place produces nothing but frustration.

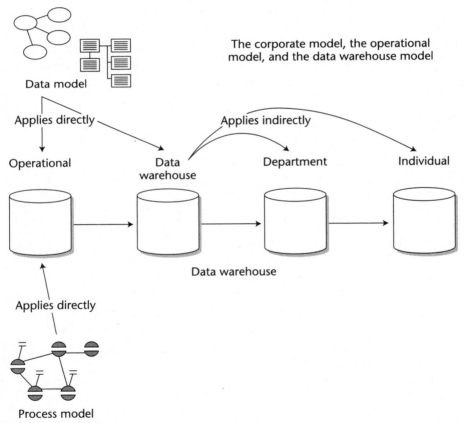

Figure 3-7   How the different types of models apply to the architected environment.

Data models are discussed in depth in the following section. For now, we will address process models. A process model typically consists of the following (in whole or in part):

- Functional decomposition
- Context-level zero diagram
- Data flow diagram
- Structure chart
- State transition diagram
- HIPO chart
- Pseudocode

There are many contexts and environments in which a process model is invaluable — for example, when building the data mart. However, because the process model is requirements-based, it is not suitable for the data warehouse. The process model assumes that a set of known processing requirements exists *a priori*, that is, before the details of the design are established. With processes, such an assumption can be made. But those assumptions do not hold for the data warehouse.

The Data Warehouse and Data Models

As shown in Figure 3-8, the data model is applicable to both the existing systems environment and the data warehouse environment. Here, an overall corporate data model has been constructed with no regard for a distinction between existing operational systems and the data warehouse. The corporate data model focuses on and represents only primitive data. To construct a separate existing data model, the beginning point is the corporate model, as shown. Performance factors are added into the corporate data model as the model is transported to the existing systems environment. All in all, very few changes are made to the corporate data model as it is used operationally.

However, a fair number of changes are made to the corporate data model as it is applied to the data warehouse. First, data that is used purely in the operational environment is removed. Next, the key structures of the corporate data model are enhanced with an element of time if they don't already have an element of time. Derived data is added to the corporate data model where the derived data is publicly used and calculated once, not repeatedly. Finally, data relationships in the operational environment are turned into "artifacts" of the relationship in the data warehouse.

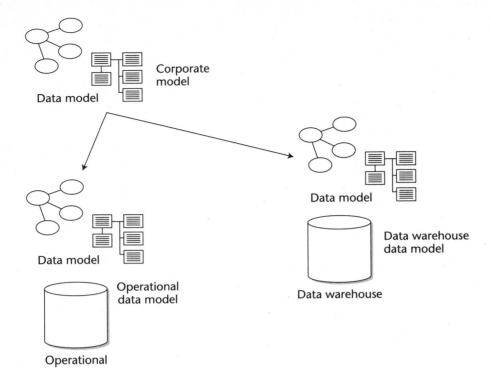

- Operational data model equals corporate data model

- Performance factors are added prior to database design

- Remove pure operational data

- Add element of time to key

- Add derived data where appropriate

- Create artifacts of relationships

Figure 3-8   How the different levels of modeling relate.

A final design activity in transforming the corporate data model to the data warehouse data model is to perform stability analysis. *Stability analysis* involves grouping attributes of data together based on their propensity for change. Figure 3-9 illustrates stability analysis for the manufacturing environment. Three tables are created from one large general-purpose table based on the stability requirements of the data contained in the tables.

In Figure 3-9, data that seldom changes is grouped, data that sometimes changes is grouped, and data that frequently changes is grouped. The net result of stability analysis (which usually is the last step of data modeling before physical database design) is to create groups of data with similar characteristics.

There is, then, a common genesis of data models. As an analogy, say the corporate data model is Adam, the operational data model is Cain, and the data warehouse data model is Abel. They are all from the same lineage, but at the same time, they are all different.

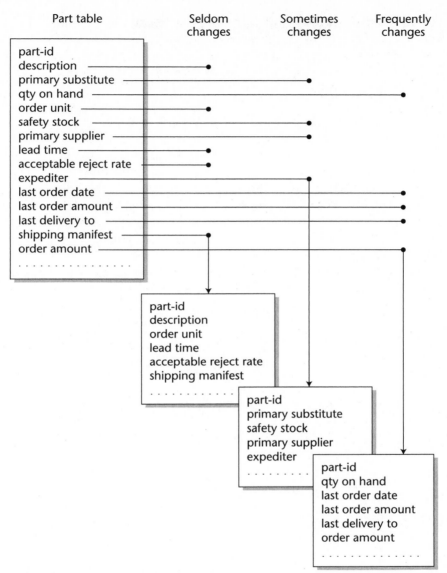

Figure 3-9 An example of stability analysis.

The Data Warehouse Data Model

There are three levels of data modeling: high-level modeling (called the *entity relationship diagram, or ERD*), midlevel modeling (called the *data item set, or DIS*), and low-level modeling (called the *physical model*).

> **NOTE** Other books have been written on data modeling, detailing several different approaches. Any number can be used successfully in building a data warehouse. The approach summarized here can be further explored in my previous book, *Information Systems Architecture: Development in the 90s* (Hoboken, N.J.: Wiley, 1993).

The high level of modeling features entities and relationships, as shown in Figure 3-10. The name of the entity is surrounded by an oval. Relationships among entities are depicted with arrows. The direction and number of the arrowheads indicate the cardinality of the relationship, and only direct relationships are indicated. In doing so, transitive dependencies are minimized.

The entities that are shown in the ERD level are at the highest level of abstraction. What entities belong in the scope of the model and what entities do not are determined by what is termed the *scope of integration*, as shown in Figure 3-11. The scope of integration defines the boundaries of the data model and must be defined before the modeling process commences. The scope is agreed on by the modeler, the management, and the ultimate user of the system. If the scope is not predetermined, there is the great chance that the modeling process will continue forever. The definition of the scope of integration should be written in no more than five pages and in language understandable to the businessperson.

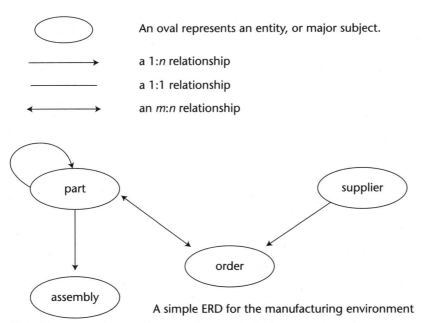

An oval represents an entity, or major subject.

a 1:*n* relationship

a 1:1 relationship

an *m*:*n* relationship

A simple ERD for the manufacturing environment

Figure 3-10   Representing entities and relationships.

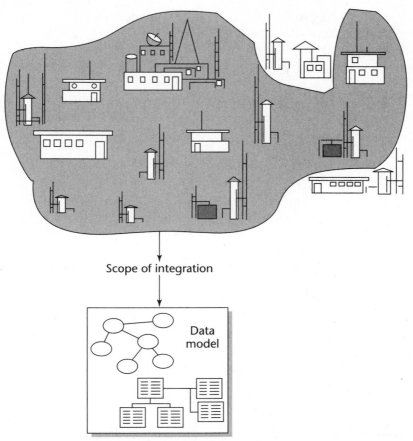

Figure 3-11   The scope of integration determines what portion of the enterprise will be reflected in the data model.

As shown in Figure 3-12, the corporate ERD is a composite of many individual ERDs that reflect the different views of people across the corporation. Separate high-level data models have been created for different communities within the corporation. Collectively, they make up the corporate ERD.

The ERDs representing the known requirements of the DSS community are created by means of user view sessions or *Joint Application Design (JAD) sessions*, which are interview sessions with the appropriate personnel in the various departments.

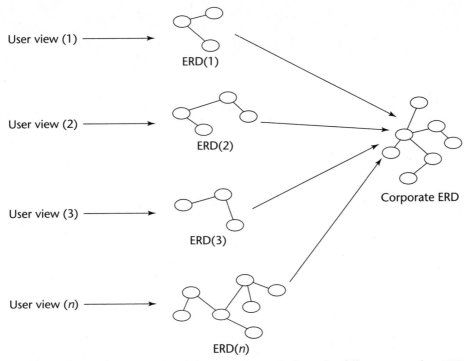

Figure 3-12   The construction of the corporate ERD from the different user view ERDs.

The Midlevel Data Model

After the high-level data model is created, the next level is established — the midlevel model, or the DIS. For each major subject area, or entity, identified in the high-level data model, a midlevel model is created, as seen in Figure 3-13. The high-level data model has identified four entities, or major subject areas. Each area is subsequently developed into its own midlevel model.

Interestingly, only very rarely are all of the midlevel models developed at once. The midlevel data model for one major subject area is expanded, and then a portion of the model is fleshed out while other parts remain static, and so forth.

As shown in Figure 3-14, four basic constructs are found at the midlevel model:

- **A primary grouping of data** — The *primary grouping* exists once, and only once, for each major subject area. It holds attributes that exist only once for each major subject area. As with all groupings of data, the primary grouping contains attributes and keys for each major subject area.

THE RELATIONSHIP BETWEEN THE ERD AND THE DIS

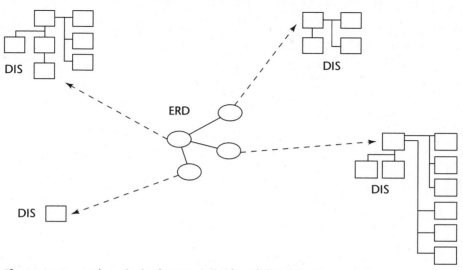

Figure 3-13 Each entity in the ERD is further defined by its own DIS.

- **A secondary grouping of data** — The *secondary grouping* holds data attributes that can exist multiple times for each major subject area. This grouping is indicated by a line emanating downward from the primary grouping of data. There may be as many secondary groupings as there are distinct groups of data that can occur multiple times.

- **A connector** — This signifies the relationships of data between major subject areas. The *connector* relates data from one grouping to another. A relationship identified at the ERD level results in an acknowledgment at the DIS level. The convention used to indicate a connector is an underlining of a foreign key.

- **"Type of" data** — This data is indicated by a line leading to the right of a grouping of data. The grouping of data to the left is the *supertype*. The grouping of data to the right is the *subtype* of data.

These four data modeling constructs are used to identify the attributes of data in a data model and the relationship among those attributes. When a relationship is identified at the ERD level, it is manifested by a pair of connector relationships at the DIS level. Figure 3-15 shows one of those pairs.

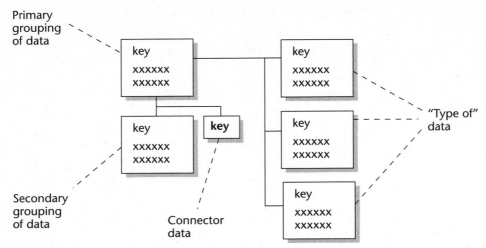

Figure 3-14   The four constructs that make up the midlevel data model.

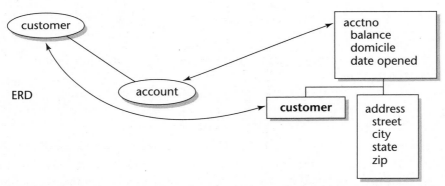

Figure 3-15   The relationships identified in the ERD are reflected by connectors in the DIS. Note that only one connector — from acctno to customer — is shown in this diagram. In reality, another connector from customer to acctno would be shown elsewhere in the DIS for customer.

At the ERD, a relationship between `customer` and `account` has been identified. At the DIS level for `account`, there exists a connector beneath `account`. This indicates that an account may have multiple customers attached to it. Not shown is the corresponding relationship beneath the customer in the `customer` DIS. Here will be a connector to `account`, indicating that a customer can have an account or accounts.

Figure 3-16 shows what a full-blown DIS might look like, where a DIS exists for an account for a financial institution. In this example, all of the different constructs are shown in the DIS.

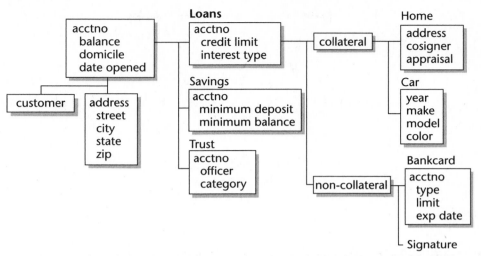

Figure 3-16 An expanded DIS showing the different types of loans that a bank may support.

Of particular interest is the case where a grouping of data has two "type of" lines emanating from it, as shown in Figure 3-17. The two lines leading to the right indicate that there are two "type of" criteria. One type of criteria is by activity type — either a deposit or a withdrawal. The other line indicates another activity type — either an ATM activity or a teller activity. Collectively, the two types of activity encompass the following transactions:

- ATM deposit
- ATM withdrawal
- Teller deposit
- Teller withdrawal

Another feature of the diagram is that all common data is to the left and all unique data is to the right. For example, the attributes date and time are common to all transactions, but cashbox balance relates only to teller activity.

The relationship between the data model and the physical tables that result from the data model is shown in Figure 3-18. In general, each grouping of data results in a table being defined in the database design process. Assuming that to be the case, two transactions result in several table entries, as shown in Figure 3-18. The physical table entries that resulted came from the following two transactions:

- An ATM withdrawal that occurred at 1:31 p.m. on January 2
- A teller deposit that occurred at 3:15 p.m. on January 5

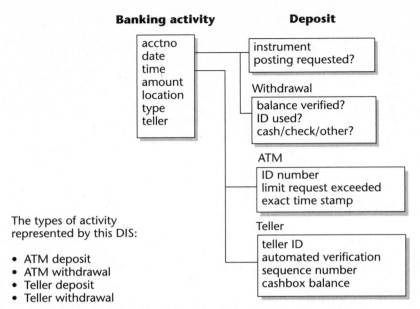

Figure 3-17 A DIS showing different subcategorization criteria.

The two transactions caused six entries in five separate tables to be generated.

Like the corporate ERD that is created from different ERDs reflecting the community of users, the corporate DIS is created from multiple DISs, as illustrated in Figure 3-19. When the interviews or JAD sessions are done for a particular user, a DIS as well as an ERD are created. The parochial DIS is then merged with all other DISs to form the corporate view of a DIS.

The Physical Data Model

The physical data model is created from the midlevel data model merely by extending the midlevel data model to include keys and physical characteristics of the model. At this point, the physical data model looks like a series of tables, sometimes called *relational tables*.

Although it is tempting to say that the physical data base tables are ready to be cast into the concrete of physical database design, one last design step remains — factoring in the optimization of performance characteristics. With the data warehouse, the first step in design is deciding on the granularity and partitioning of the data. This step is crucial. (Of course, the key structure is changed to add the element of time, to which each unit of data is relevant.)

THE DIFFERENT TYPES OF DATA THAT WOULD EXIST IN SEPERATE TABLES AS A RESULT OF THE DIS

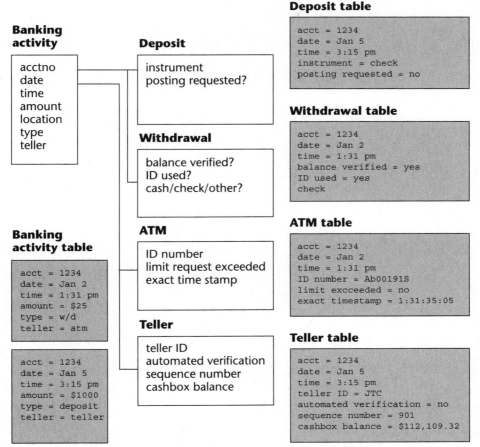

Figure 3-18   The table entries represented by the two transactions.

After granularity and partitioning are factored in, a variety of other physical design activities are embedded into the design, as outlined in Figure 3-20. At the heart of the physical design considerations is the usage of physical I/O (input/output). Physical I/O is the activity that brings data into the computer from storage or sends data to storage from the computer. Figure 3-21 shows a simple case of I/O.

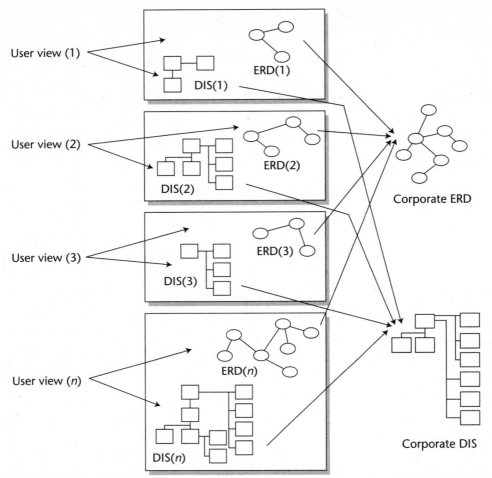

Figure 3-19   The corporate DIS is made up of the DIS created as a result of each user view session.

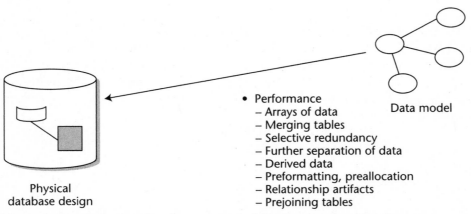

Figure 3-20   Getting good performance out of the data warehouse environment.

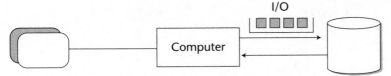

Figure 3-21   Getting the most out of the physical I/Os that have to be done.

Data is transferred to and from the computer to storage in blocks. The I/O event is vital to performance because the transfer of data to and from storage to the computer occurs roughly two to three orders of magnitude slower than the speeds at which the computer runs. The computer runs internally in terms of nanosecond speed. Transfer of data to and from storage occurs in terms of milliseconds. Thus, physical I/O is normally the main impediment to performance.

The job of the data warehouse designer is to organize data physically for the return of the maximum number of records from the execution of a physical I/O.

NOTE This is not an issue of blindly transferring a large number of records from DASD to main storage. Instead, it is a more sophisticated issue of transferring a bulk of records that have a high probability of being accessed.

For example, suppose a programmer must fetch five records. If those records are organized into different blocks of data on storage, then five I/Os will be required. But if the designer can anticipate that the records will be needed as a group and can physically juxtapose those records into the same block, then only one I/O will be required, thus making the program run much more efficiently.

There is another mitigating factor regarding physical placement of data in the data warehouse: Data in the warehouse normally is not updated. At least data is updated in the data warehouse on an exception basis. The freedom from having to do updates frees the designer to use physical design techniques that otherwise would not be acceptable if the data warehouse were regularly updated.

The Data Model and Iterative Development

In all cases, the data warehouse is best built iteratively. This means that first one part of the data warehouse is built, and then another part of the data warehouse is built, and so forth. The following are some of the many reasons why *iterative development* is important:

- The industry track record of success strongly suggests it.
- The end user is unable to articulate many requirements until the first iteration is done.

- Management will not make a full commitment until at least a few actual results are tangible and obvious.

- Visible results must be seen quickly.

What may not be obvious is the role of the data model in iterative development. To understand the role of the data model during this type of development, consider the typical iterative development suggested by Figure 3-22. First, one development effort is undertaken, then another, and so forth. The data warehouse serves as a roadmap for each of the development efforts, as seen in Figure 3-23. Not only does the data model tell what needs to be done, the data model suggests how any one development effort will be integrated with any other development effort.

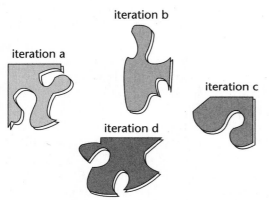

Figure 3-22   The different iterations of data warehouse development.

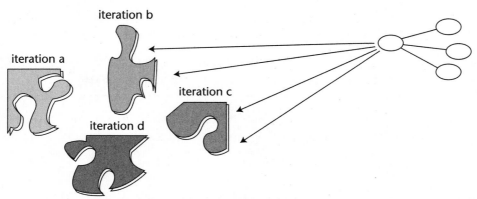

Figure 3-23   The data model allows the different iterations of development to be built in a cohesive manner.

When the second development effort (that is, the second iteration) ensues, the developer is confident that he or she will intersect his or her effort with the first development effort because all development efforts are being driven from the data model. Each succeeding development effort builds on the preceding one. The result is that the different development efforts are done under a unifying data model. And because they are built under a single data model, the individual iterative efforts produce a cohesive and tightly orchestrated whole, as shown in Figure 3-24.

When the different iterations of development are done with no unifying data model, there is much overlap of effort and much separate, disjoint development. Figure 3-25 illustrates this cacophonous result.

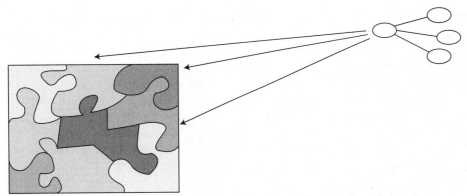

Figure 3-24   At the end of the development effort, all the iterations fit together.

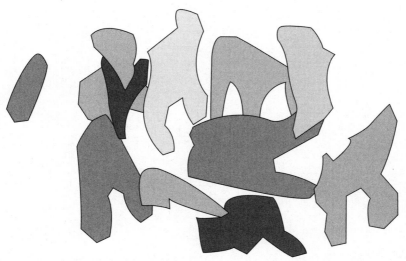

Figure 3-25   When there is no data model, the iterations do not form a cohesive pattern. There is much overlap and lack of uniformity.

There is, then, an indirect, yet important, correlation between the data model and the ability to achieve long-term integration and a harmonious effort in the incremental and iterative development of a data warehouse.

Normalization and Denormalization

The output of the data model process is a series of tables, each of which contains keys and attributes. The normal output produces numerous tables, each with only a modicum of data. While there is nothing wrong (per se) with lots of little tables, there is a problem from a performance perspective. Consider the work the program must do to interconnect the tables dynamically, as shown in Figure 3-26.

In Figure 3-26, a program goes into execution. First, one table is accessed, then another. To execute successfully, the program must jump around many tables. Each time the program jumps from one table to the next, I/O is consumed, in terms of both accessing the data and accessing the index to find the data. If only one or two programs had to pay the price of I/O, there would be no problem. But when all programs must pay a stiff price for I/O, performance in general suffers, and that is precisely what happens when many small tables, each containing a limited amount of data, are created as a physical design.

A more rational approach is to physically merge some of the tables so that minimal I/O is consumed, as shown in Figure 3-27. Now the same program operates as before, only it needs much less I/O to accomplish the same task.

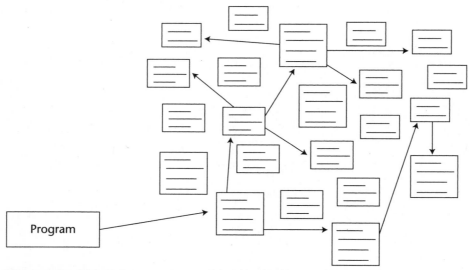

Figure 3-26 When there are many tables, much I/O is required for dynamic interconnectability.

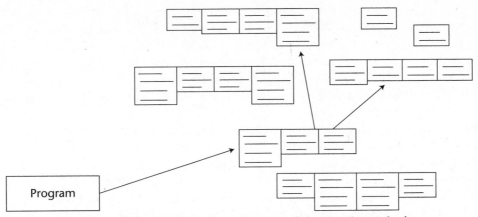

Figure 3-27   When tables are physically merged, much less I/O is required.

The question, then, becomes what is a sane strategy to merge the tables so that the maximum benefit is derived? It is in answering this question that the physical database designer earns his or her reward.

Merging tables is only one design technique that can save I/O. Another very useful technique is creating an array of data. In Figure 3-28, data is normalized so that each occurrence of a sequence of data resides in a different physical location. Retrieving each occurrence, $n, n + 1, n + 2, \ldots$, requires a physical I/O to get the data. If the data were placed in a single row in an array, then a single I/O would suffice to retrieve it, as shown at the bottom of Figure 3-28.

CREATING ARRAYS OF DATA FOR PERFORMANCE

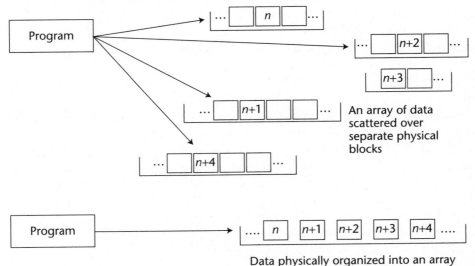

Figure 3-28   Under the right circumstances, creating arrays of data can save considerable resources.

Of course, it does not make sense to create an array of data in every case. Only when there are a stable number of occurrences, where the data is accessed in sequence, where it is created and/or updated in a statistically well-behaved sequence, and so forth, does creating an array pay off.

Interestingly, in the data warehouse these circumstances occur regularly because of the time-based orientation of the data. Data warehouse data is always relevant to some moment in time, and units of time occur with great regularity. In the data warehouse, creating an array by month, for example, is a very easy, natural thing to do.

Another important physical design technique that is especially relevant to the data warehouse environment is the deliberate introduction of redundant data. Figure 3-29 shows an example where the deliberate introduction of redundant data pays a big dividend. In the top of Figure 3-29, the field — description (desc) — is normalized and exists nonredundantly. In doing so, all processes that must see the description of a part must access the base parts table. The access of the data is very expensive, although the insertion of the data is optimal.

In the bottom of Figure 3-29, the data element "description" (desc) has been deliberately placed in the many tables where it is likely to be used. In doing so, the access of data is more efficient, and the update of data is not optimal. For data that is widely used (such as description), and for data that is stable (such as description), however, there is little reason to worry about update. In particular, in the data warehouse environment there is no concern whatsoever for update.

Another useful technique is the further separation of data when there is a wide disparity in the probability of access. Figure 3-30 shows such a case.

In Figure 3-30, concerning a bank account, the domicile of the account and the data opened for the account are normalized together with the balance of the account. Yet the balance of the account has a very different probability of access than the other two data elements. The balance of an account is very popular, while the other data is hardly ever accessed. To make I/O more efficient and to store the data more compactly, it makes sense to further reduce the normalized table into two separate tables, as shown.

Occasionally, the introduction of *derived* (that is, *calculated*) *data* into the physical database design can reduce the amount of I/O needed. Figure 3-31 shows such a case. A program accesses payroll data regularly in order to calculate the annual pay and taxes that have been paid. If the program is run regularly and at the year's end, it makes sense to create fields of data to store the calculated data. The data has to be calculated only once. Then all future requirements can access the calculated field. This approach has another advantage in that once the field is calculated, it will not have to be calculated again, eliminating the risk of faulty algorithms from incorrect evaluations.

SELECTIVE USE OF REDUNDANCY

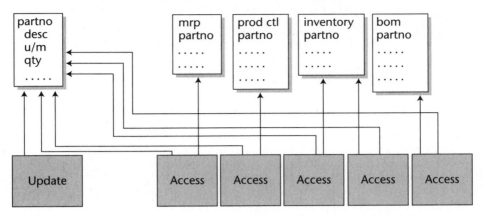

Description is nonredundant and is used frequently, but is seldom updated.

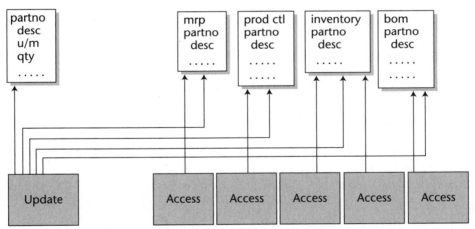

Figure 3-29   Description is redundantly spread over the many places it is used. It must be updated in many places when it changes, but it seldom, if ever, does.

One of the most innovative techniques in building a data warehouse is what can be termed a *creative index*, or a *creative profile*. Figure 3-32 shows an example of a creative index. This type of creative index is created as data is passed from the operational environment to the data warehouse environment. Because each unit of data must be handled in any case, it requires very little overhead to calculate or create an index at this point.

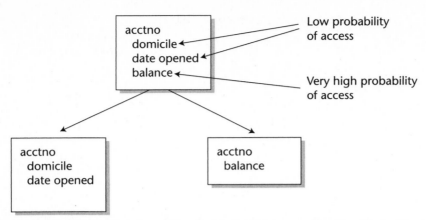

Figure 3-30 Further separation of data based on a wide disparity in the probability of access.

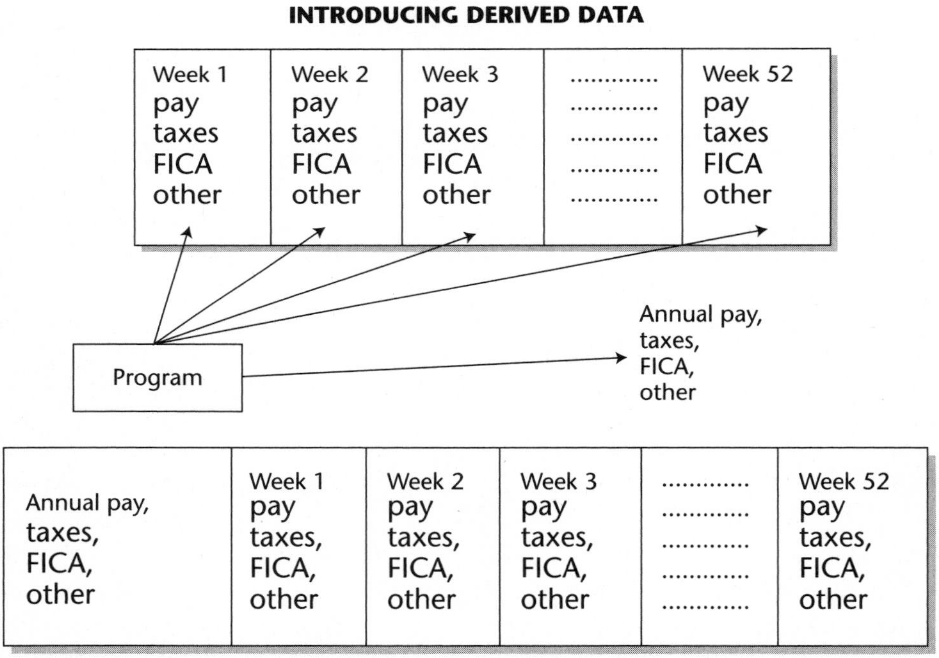

INTRODUCING DERIVED DATA

Figure 3-31 Derived data, calculated once, then forever available.

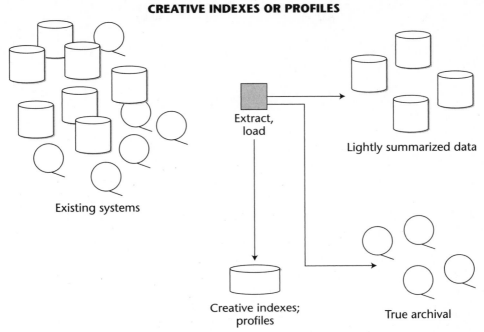

Figure 3-32 Examples of creative indexes.

The creative index does a profile on items of interest to the end user, such as the largest purchases, the most inactive accounts, the latest shipments, and so on. If the requirements that might be of interest to management can be anticipated (admittedly, they cannot in every case), at the time of passing data to the data warehouse, it makes sense to build a creative index.

A final technique that the data warehouse designer should keep in mind is the management of *referential integrity*. Figure 3-33 shows that referential integrity appears as "artifacts" of relationships in the data warehouse environment.

In the operational environment, referential integrity appears as a dynamic link among tables of data. But because of the volume of data in a data warehouse, because the data warehouse is not updated, and because the warehouse represents data over time and relationships do not remain static, a different approach should be taken toward referential integrity. In other words, relationships of data are represented by an artifact in the data warehouse environment. Therefore, some data will be duplicated, and some data will be deleted when other data is still in the warehouse. In any case, trying to replicate referential integrity in the data warehouse environment is a patently incorrect approach.

DATA WAREHOUSE AND REFERENTIAL INTEGRITY

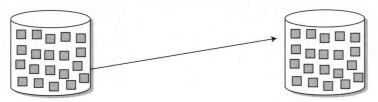

In operational systems, the relationships between databases are
handled by referetial integrity.

But, in the data warehouse environment:

- There is much more data than in the operational environment.
- Once in the warehouse, the data doesn't change.
- There is a need to represent more than one business rule over time.
- Data purges in the warehouse are not tightly coordinated.

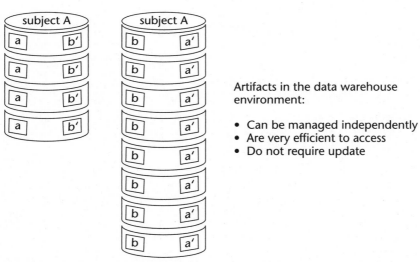

Artifacts in the data warehouse
environment:

- Can be managed independently
- Are very efficient to access
- Do not require update

Figure 3-33   Referential integrity in the data warehouse environment.

Snapshots in the Data Warehouse

Data warehouses are built for a wide variety of applications and users, such as
customer systems, marketing systems, sales systems, and quality control systems. Despite the very diverse applications and types of data warehouses, a common thread runs through all of them. Internally, each of the data warehouses

centers around a structure of data called a *snapshot*. Figure 3-34 shows the basic components of a data warehouse snapshot.

Snapshots are created as a result of some event occurring. Several kinds of events can trigger a snapshot. One event is the recording of information about a discrete activity, such as writing a check, placing a phone call, the receipt of a shipment, the completion of an order, or the purchase of a policy. In the case of a discrete activity, some business occurrence has occurred, and the business must make note of it. In general, discrete activities occur randomly.

The other type of snapshot trigger is time, which is a predictable trigger, such as the end of the day, the end of the week, or the end of the month.

The snapshot triggered by an event has four basic components:

- A key
- A unit of time
- Primary data that relates only to the key
- Secondary data captured as part of the snapshot process that has no direct relationship to the primary data or key

NOTE Of these components, only secondary data is optional.

The key can be unique or nonunique and it can be a single element of data. In a typical data warehouse, however, the key is a composite made up of many elements of data that serve to identify the primary data. The key identifies the record and the primary data.

The unit of time, such as year, month, day, hour, and quarter, usually (but not always) refers to the moment when the event being described by the snapshot has occurred. Occasionally, the unit of time refers to the moment when the capture of data takes place. (In some cases, a distinction is made between when an event occurs and when the information about the event is captured. In other cases, no distinction is made.) In the case of events triggered by the passage of time, the time element may be implied rather than directly attached to the snapshot.

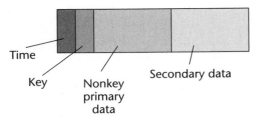

Figure 3-34   A data warehouse record of data is a snapshot taken at one moment in time and includes a variety of types of data.

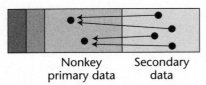

Nonkey   Secondary
primary data   data

Figure 3-35   The artifacts of a relationship are captured as a result of the implied relationship of secondary data residing in the same snapshot as primary data.

The primary data is the nonkey data that relates directly to the key of the record. As an example, suppose the key identifies the sale of a product. The element of time describes when the sale was finalized. The primary data describes what product was sold at what price, conditions of the sale, location of the sale, and who the representative parties were.

The secondary data (if it exists) identifies other extraneous information captured at the moment when the snapshot record was created. An example of secondary data that relates to a sale is incidental information about the product being sold (such as how much is in stock at the moment of sale). Other secondary information might be the prevailing interest rate for a bank's preferred customers at the moment of sale. Any incidental information can be added to a data warehouse record, if it appears at a later time that the information can be used for DSS processing. Note that the incidental information added to the snapshot may or may not be a foreign key. A foreign key is an attribute found in table that is a reference to the key value of another table where there is a business relationship between the data found in the two tables.

Once the secondary information is added to the snapshot, a relationship between the primary and secondary information can be inferred, as shown in Figure 3-35. The snapshot implies that there is a relationship between secondary and primary data. Nothing other than the existence of the relationship is implied, and the relationship is implied only as of the instant of the snapshot. Nevertheless, by the juxtaposition of secondary and primary data in a snapshot record, at the instant the snapshot was taken, there is an inferred relationship of data. Sometimes this inferred relationship is called an *artifact*. The snapshot record that has been described is the most general and most widely found case of a record in a data warehouse.

Metadata

An important component of the data warehouse environment is *metadata* (or data about data), which has been a part of the information processing milieu for as long as there have been programs and data. But in the world of data warehouses, metadata takes on a new level of importance, for it affords the most effective use of the data warehouse. Metadata allows the end user or DSS analyst to navigate through the possibilities. Put differently, when a user approaches a data warehouse where there is no metadata, the user does not know where to begin the analysis. The user must poke and probe the data warehouse to find out what data is there and what data is not there and considerable time is wasted. Even after the user pokes around, there is no guarantee that he or she will find the right data or correctly interpret the data encountered. With the help of metadata, however, the end user can quickly go to the necessary data or determine that it isn't there.

Metadata then acts like an index to the contents of the data warehouse. It sits above the warehouse and keeps track of what is where in the warehouse. Typically, items the metadata store tracks are as follows:

- Structure of data as known to the programmer
- Structure of data as known to the DSS analyst
- Source data feeding the data warehouse
- Transformation of data as it passes into the data warehouse
- Data model
- Relationship between the data model and the data warehouse
- History of extracts

Managing Reference Tables in a Data Warehouse

When most people think of data warehousing, their thoughts turn to the normal, large databases constantly being used by organizations to run day-to-day business such as customer files, sales files, and so forth. Indeed, these common files form the backbone of the data warehousing effort. Yet another type of data belongs in the data warehouse and is often ignored: *reference data*.

Reference tables are often taken for granted, and that creates a special problem. For example, suppose in 1995 a company has some reference tables and starts to create its data warehouse. Time passes, and much data is loaded into the data warehouse. In the meantime, the reference table is used operationally and occasionally changes. In 1999, the company needs to consult the reference table. A reference is made from 1995 data to the reference table. But the reference table has not been kept historically accurate, and the reference from 1995 data warehouse data to reference entries accurate as of 1999 produces very inaccurate results. For this reason, reference data should be made time-variant, just like all other parts of the data warehouse.

Reference data is particularly applicable to the data warehouse environment because it helps reduce the volume of data significantly. There are many design techniques for the management of reference data. Two techniques — at the opposite ends of the spectrum — are discussed here. In addition, there are many variations on these options.

Figure 3-36 shows the first design option, where a snapshot of an entire reference table is taken every six months. This approach is quite simple and at first glance appears to make sense. But the approach is logically incomplete. For example, suppose some activity had occurred to the reference table on March 15. Say a new entry, ddw, was added, and then on May 10 the entry for ddw was deleted. Taking a snapshot every six months would not capture the activity that transpired from March 15 to May 10.

A second approach is shown in Figure 3-37. At some starting point, a snapshot is made of a reference table. Throughout the year, all the activities against the reference table are collected. To determine the status of a given entry to the reference table at a moment in time, the activity is reconstituted against the reference table. In such a manner, logical completeness of the table can be reconstructed for any moment in time. Such a reconstruction, however, is a not a trivial matter; it may represent a very large and complex task.

```
Jan 1                    July 1                   Jan 1
  AAA - Amber Auto          AAA - Amber Auto         AAA - Alaska Alt
  AAT - Allison's           AAR - Ark Electric       AAG - German Air
  AAZ - AutoZone            BAE - Brit Eng           AAR - Ark Electric
  BAE - Brit Eng            BAG - Bill's Garage      BAE - Brit Eng

  ...............          ...............          ...............
```

Figure 3-36 A snapshot is taken of a reference table in its entirety every six months — one approach to the management of reference tables in the data warehouse.

```
Jan 1                        Jan 1  - add TWQ -      Taiwan Dairy
  AAA - Amber Auto           Jan 16 - delete ATT
  AAT - Allison's            Feb 3  - add AAG -      German Power
  AAZ - AutoZone             Feb 27 - change GYY - German Govt
  BAE - Brit Eng
                             ...................................
  ...............
                             ...................................
  ...............
```

A complete snapshot is taken on the first of the year.

Changes to the reference table are collected throughout the year and can be used to reconstruct the table at any moment in time.

Figure 3-37 Another approach to the management of reference data.

The two approaches outlined here are opposite in intent. The first approach is simple, but logically incomplete. The second approach is very complex, but logically complete. Many design alternatives lie between these two extremes. However they are designed and implemented, reference tables must be managed as a regular part of the data warehouse environment.

Cyclicity of Data — The Wrinkle of Time

One of the intriguing issues of data warehouse design is the *cyclicity of data*, or the length of time a change of data in the operational environment takes to be reflected in the data warehouse. Consider the data in Figure 3-38.

The current information is shown for Judy Jones. The data warehouse contains the historical information about Judy. Now suppose Judy changes addresses. Figure 3-39 shows that as soon as that change is discovered, it is reflected in the operational environment as quickly as possible.

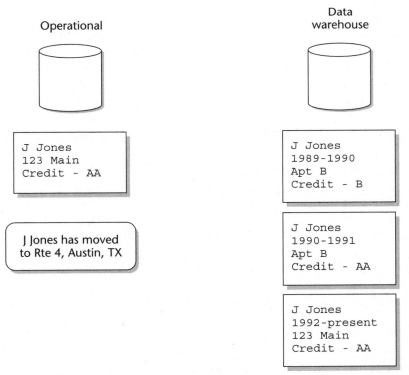

Figure 3-38   What happens when the corporation finds out that J Jones has moved?

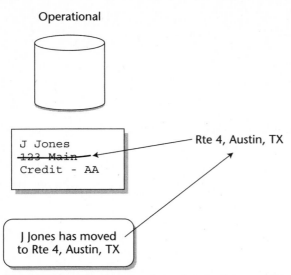

Operational

J Jones
~~123 Main~~ ◄────── Rte 4, Austin, TX
Credit - AA

J Jones has moved
to Rte 4, Austin, TX

Figure 3-39   The first step is to change the operational address of J Jones.

Once the data is reflected in the operational environment, the changes need to be moved to the data warehouse. Figure 3-40 shows that the data warehouse has a correction to the ending date of the most current record and a new record has been inserted reflecting the change.

The issue is, how soon should this adjustment to the data warehouse data be made? As a rule, at least 24 hours should pass from the time the change is known to the operational environment until the change is reflected into the data warehouse (see Figure 3-41). There should be no rush to try to move the change into the data warehouse as quickly as possible. This "wrinkle of time" should be implemented for several reasons.

The first reason is that the more tightly the operational environment is coupled to the data warehouse, the more expensive and complex the technology is. A 24-hour wrinkle of time can easily be accomplished with conventional technology. A 12-hour wrinkle of time can be accomplished, but at a greater cost of technology. A 6-hour wrinkle of time can be accomplished, but at an even greater cost in technology.

A more powerful reason for the wrinkle of time is that it imposes a certain discipline on the environments. With a 24-hour wrinkle, there is no temptation to do operational processing in the data warehouse and data warehouse processing in the operational environment. But if the wrinkle of time is reduced (say, to 4 hours) there is the temptation to do such processing, and that is patently a mistake.

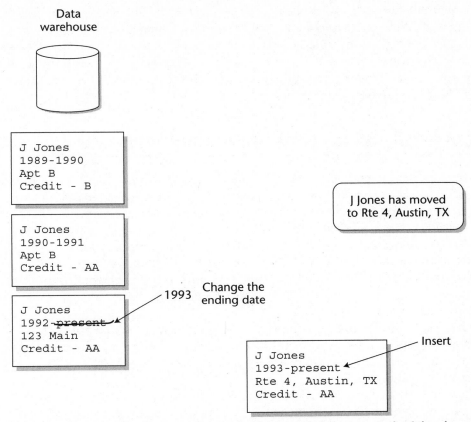

Figure 3-40   The activities that occur in the data warehouse as a result of the change of address.

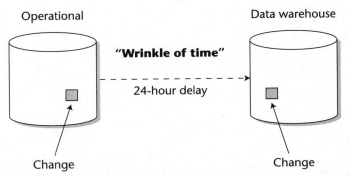

Figure 3-41   There needs to be at least a 24-hour lag — a "wrinkle of time" — between the time a change is known to the operational environment and the time when the change is reflected into the data warehouse.

Another benefit of the wrinkle of time is opportunity for data to settle before it is moved to the data warehouse. Adjustments can be made in the operational environment before the data is sent to the data warehouse. If data is quickly sent to the warehouse and then it is discovered that adjustments must be made, those adjustments must be made in both the operational environment and the data warehouse environment.

Complexity of Transformation and Integration

At first glance, when data is moved from the legacy environment to the data warehouse environment, it appears that nothing more is going on than simple extraction of data from one place to the next. Because of the deceptive simplicity, many organizations start to build their data warehouses manually. The programmer looks at the movement of data from the old operational environment to the new data warehouse environment and declares, "I can do that!" With pencil and coding pad in hand, the programmer anxiously jumps into the creation of code within the first three minutes of the design and development of the data warehouse.

First impressions, though, can be very deceiving. What at first appears to be nothing more than the movement of data from one place to another quickly turns into a large and complex task — far larger and more complex than the programmer thought.

Precisely what kind of functionality is required as data passes from the operational, legacy environment to the data warehouse environment? The following lists some of the necessary functionality:

- The extraction of data from the operational environment to the data warehouse environment requires a change in technology. This normally includes reading the operational DBMS technology (such as IMS) and writing the data out in newer, data warehouse DBMS technology (such as DB2/UDB). There is a need for a technology shift as the data is being moved. And the technology shift is not just one of changing the DBMS. The operating system changes, the hardware changes, and even the hardware-based structure of the data changes.

- The selection of data from the operational environment may be very complex. To qualify a record for extraction processing, several coordinated lookups to other records in a variety of other files may be necessary, requiring keyed reads, connecting logic, and so on. In some cases, the extraneous data cannot be read in anything but the online environment. When this is the case, extraction of data for the data warehouse must occur in the online operating window, a circumstance to be avoided if at all possible.

■ Operational input keys usually must be restructured and converted before they are written out to the data warehouse. Very seldom does an input key remain unaltered as it is read in the operational environment and written out to the data warehouse environment. In simple cases, an element of time is added to the output key structure. In complex cases, the entire input key must be rehashed or otherwise restructured.

■ Nonkey data is reformatted as it passes from the operational environment to the data warehouse environment. As a simple example, input data about a date is read as YYYY/MM/DD and is written to the output file as DD/MM/YYYY. (Reformatting of operational data before it is ready to go into a data warehouse often becomes much more complex than this simple example.)

■ Data is cleansed as it passes from the operational environment to the data warehouse environment. In some cases, a simple algorithm is applied to input data in order to make it correct. In complex cases, artificial intelligence subroutines are invoked to scrub input data into an acceptable output form. There are many forms of data cleansing, including domain checking, cross-record verification, and simple formatting verification.

■ Multiple input sources of data exist and must be merged as they pass into the data warehouse. Under one set of conditions, the source of a data warehouse data element is one file, and under another set of conditions the source of data for the data warehouse is another file. Logic must be spelled out to have the appropriate source of data contribute its data under the right set of conditions.

■ When there are multiple input files, key resolution must be done before the files can be merged. This means that if different key structures are used in the different input files, the merging program must have the logic embedded that allows resolution.

■ With multiple input files, the sequence of the files may not be the same or even compatible. In this case, the input files need to be resequenced. This is not a problem unless many records must be resequenced, which unfortunately is almost always the case.

■ Multiple outputs may result. Data may be produced at different levels of summarization by the same data warehouse creation program.

■ Default values must be supplied. Under some conditions an output value in the data warehouse will have no source of data. In this case, the default value to be used must be specified.

■ The efficiency of selection of input data for extraction often becomes a real issue. Consider the case where at the moment of refreshment there is no way to distinguish operational data that needs to be extracted from operational data that does not need to be extracted. When this occurs, the entire operational file must be read. Reading the entire file is especially inefficient because only a fraction of the records is actually needed. This type of processing causes the online environment to be active, which further squeezes other processing in the online environment.

■ Summarization of data is often required. Multiple operational input records are combined into a single "profile" data warehouse record. To do summarization, the detailed input records to be summarized must be properly sequenced. In the case where different record types contribute to the single summarized data warehouse record, the arrival of the different input record types must be coordinated so that a single record is produced.

■ Renaming of data elements as they are moved from the operational environment to the data warehouse must be tracked. As a data element moves from the operational environment to the data warehouse environment, it usually changes its name. Documentation of that change must be made.

■ The input records that must be read have exotic or nonstandard formats. There are a whole host of input types that must be read, and then converted on entry into the data warehouse:

   ■ Fixed-length records

   ■ Variable-length records

   ■ Occurs depending on

   ■ Occurs clause

Conversion must be made. But the logic of conversion must be specified, and the mechanics of conversion (what the "before" and "after" look like) can be quite complex. In some cases, conversion logic becomes very twisted.

■ Perhaps worst of all, data relationships at the semantic level that have been built into old legacy program logic must be understood and unraveled before those files can be used as input. These semantic relationships are often Byzantine, arcane, and undocumented. But they must patiently be unwound and deciphered as the data moves into the data warehouse. This is especially difficult when there is no documentation or when the documentation that exists is out-of-date. And, unfortunately, on many operational legacy systems, there is no documentation. There is an old saying, "Real programmers don't do documentation."

- Data format conversion must be done. EBCDIC to ASCII (or vice versa) must be spelled out.

- Massive volumes of input must be accounted for. Where there is only a small amount of data being entered as input, many design options can be accommodated. But where many records are being input, special design options (such as parallel loads and parallel reads) may have to be used.

- The design of the data warehouse must conform to a corporate data model. As such, there is order and discipline to the design and structuring of the data warehouse. The input to the data warehouse conforms to design specifications of an application that were written a long time ago. The business conditions behind the application have probably changed ten times since the application was originally written. Much undocumented maintenance was done to the application code. In addition, the application probably had no integration requirements to fit with other applications. All of these mismatches must be accounted for in the design and building of the data warehouse.

- The data warehouse reflects the historical need for information, while the operational environment focuses on the immediate, current need for information. This means that an element of time may need to be added as the data moves from the operational environment to the data warehouse environment.

- The data warehouse addresses the informational needs of the corporation, while the operational environment addresses the up-to-the-second clerical needs of the corporation.

- Transmission of the newly created output file that will go into the data warehouse must be accounted for. In some cases, this is very easy to do; in other cases, it is not simple at all, especially when operating systems are crossed. Another issue is the location where the transformation will take place. Will the transformation take place on the machine hosting the operational environment? Or, will raw data be transmitted and the transformation take place on the machine hosting the data warehouse?

And there is more. This list is merely a sampling of the complexities facing the programmer when setting off to load the data warehouse.

In the early days of data warehouse, there was no choice but to build the programs that did the integration by hand. Programmers using COBOL, C, and other languages wrote these. But soon people noticed that these programs were tedious and repetitive. Furthermore, these programs required ongoing maintenance. Soon technology appeared that automated the process of integrating data from the operational environment, called *extract/transform/load (ETL) software*. The first ETL software was crude, but it quickly matured to the point where almost any transformation could be handled.

ETL software comes in two varieties — software that produces code and software that produces a run-time module that is parameterized. The code-producing software is much more powerful than the run-time software. The code-producing software can access legacy data in its own format. The run-time software usually requires that legacy data be flattened. Once flattened, the run-time module can read the legacy data. Unfortunately, much intelligence is lost in the flattening of the legacy data.

In any case, ETL software automates the process of converting, reformatting, and integrating data from multiple legacy operational sources. Only under very unusual circumstances does attempting to build and maintain the operational or data warehouse interface manually make sense.

An alternative to ETL software is *extract/load/transform (ELT) software*. The advantage of ELT software is that transformation can be done where reference to large amounts of data are possible at the moment of doing transformation. The disadvantage of ELT software is that it is a temptation to extract and load data, and skip the transformation process. When the transformation process is skipped, the value of the data warehouse is greatly diminished.

Triggering the Data Warehouse Record

The basic business interaction that causes the data warehouse to become populated with data is one that can be called an *event-snapshot interaction*. In this type of interaction, some event (usually in the operational environment) triggers a snapshot of data, which in turn is moved to the data warehouse environment. Figure 3-42 symbolically depicts an event-snapshot interaction.

Events

As mentioned earlier in the chapter, the business event that triggers a snapshot might be the occurrence of some notable activity, such as the making of a sale, the stocking of an item, the placing of a phone call, or the delivery of a shipment. This type of business event is called an *activity-generated event*. The other type of business event that may trigger a snapshot is the marking of the regular passage of time, such as the ending of the day, the ending of the week, or the ending of the month. This type of business event is called a *time-generated event*.

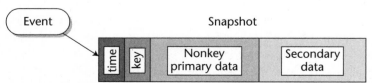

Figure 3-42   Every snapshot in the data warehouse is triggered by some event.

Whereas events caused by business activities are random, events triggered by the passage of time are not. The time-related snapshots are created quite regularly and predictably.

Components of the Snapshot

As mentioned earlier in this chapter, the snapshot placed in the data warehouse normally contains several components. One component is the *unit of time* that marks the occurrence of the event. Usually (not necessarily always) the unit of time marks the moment of the taking of the snapshot. The next component of the snapshot is the key that identifies the snapshot. The third normal component of a data warehouse snapshot is the *primary (nonkey) data* that relates to the key. Finally, an optional component of a snapshot is *secondary data* that has been incidentally captured as of the moment of the taking of the snapshot and placed in the snapshot. As mentioned, sometimes this secondary data is called an *artifact of the relationship*.

In the simplest case in a data warehouse, each operational activity important to the corporation will trigger a snapshot. In this case, there is a one-to-one correspondence between the business activities that have occurred and the number of snapshots that are placed in the data warehouse. When there is a one-to-one correspondence between the activities in the operational environment and the snapshots in the data warehouse, the data warehouse tracks the history of all the activity relating to a subject area.

Some Examples

An example of a simple snapshot being taken every time there is an operational, business activity might be found in a customer file. Every time a customer moves, changes phone numbers, or changes jobs, the data warehouse is alerted, and a continuous record of the history of the customer is made. One record tracks the customer from 1989 to 1991. The next record tracks the customer from 1991 to 1993. The next record tracks the customer from 1993 to the present. Each activity of the customer results in a new snapshot being placed in the data warehouse.

As another example, consider the premium payments on an insurance policy. Suppose premiums are paid semiannually. Every six months, a snapshot record is created in the data warehouse describing the payment of the premium — when it was paid, how much, and so on.

Where there is little volume of data, where the data is stable (that is, the data changes infrequently), and where there is a need for meticulous historical detail, the data warehouse can be used to track each occurrence of a business event by storing the details of every activity. But where data changes frequently, each change in business status cannot be tracked in the data warehouse.

Profile Records

There are many cases in which data in the data warehouse does not meet the criteria of stability and infrequency of change. In some cases, there will be massive volumes of data. In other cases, the content of data changes frequently. And in still other cases, there is no business need for meticulous historical detail of data. When one or more of these conditions prevail, a different kind of data warehouse record, called a *profile* or an *aggregate record*, can be created. A profile record groups many different, detailed occurrences of operational data into a single record. The single profile record represents the many operational records in aggregation.

Profile records represent snapshots of data, just like individual activity records. The difference between the two is that individual activity records in the data warehouse represent a single event, while profile records in the data warehouse represent multiple events.

Like individual activity records, profile records are triggered by some event — either a business activity or the marking of the regular passage of time. Figure 3-43 shows how an event causes the creation of a profile record.

A profile record is created from the grouping of many detailed records. As an example, a phone company may at the end of the month take all of a customer's phone activities for the month and wrap those activities into a single customer record in the data warehouse. In doing so, a single representative record can be created for the customer that reflects all of his or her monthly activity. Or, a bank may take all the monthly activities of a customer and create an aggregate data warehouse record that represents all of his or her banking activities for the month.

The aggregation of operational data into a single data warehouse record may take many forms, including the following:

- Values taken from operational data can be summarized.

- Units of operational data can be tallied, where the total number of units is captured.

- Units of data can be processed to find the highest, lowest, average, and so forth.

- First and last occurrences of data can be trapped.

- Data of certain types, falling within the boundaries of several parameters, can be measured.

- Data that is effective as of some moment in time can be trapped.

- The oldest and the youngest data can be trapped.

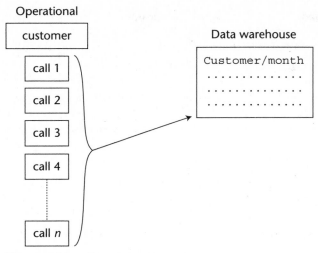

Operational

The monthly call records are aggregated in order to provide a single composite record.

Figure 3-43   The creation of a profile record from a series of detailed records.

The ways to perform representative aggregation of operational data into a profile record are limitless.

Another very appealing benefit to the creation of profile records is organizing the data in a compact and convenient form for the end user to access and analyze. Done properly, the end user is quite comfortable with the distillation of many records into a single record because he or she has to look only in a single place to find what is needed. By prepackaging the data into an aggregate record in the data warehouse, the data architect saves the end user from tedious processing.

Managing Volume

In many cases, the volume of data to be managed in the data warehouse is a significant issue. Creating profile records is an effective technique for managing the volume of data. The reduction of the volume of data possible in moving detailed records in the operational environment into a profile record is remarkable. It is possible (indeed, normal) to achieve a 2-to-3 order-of-magnitude reduction of data by the creation of profile records in a data warehouse. Because of this benefit, the ability to create profile records is a powerful one that should be in the portfolio of every data architect.

There is, however, a downside to profiling records in the data warehouse. Whenever the use of the profile technique is contemplated, note that a certain capability or functionality of the data warehouse is lost. Of necessity, detail is lost whenever aggregation is done. Keep in mind, however, that losing detail is not necessarily a bad thing. The designer of the profile record must ensure that the lost detail is not important to the DSS analyst who will ultimately be using the data warehouse. The data architect's first line of defense (and easily the most effective one) is to ensure that such detail is not terribly important and to build the profile records iteratively. By doing so, the data architect has the maneuverability to make changes gracefully.

The first iteration of the design of the contents of the profile record suggests the second iteration of design, and so forth. As long as the iterations of data warehouse development are small and fast, and as long as the architect listens carefully to the end user throughout the building of the iterations, there is little danger the end user will find many important requirements left out of the profile record. The danger comes when profile records are created and the first iteration of development is large. In this case, the data architect probably will paint himself or herself into a nasty corner because important detail will have been omitted.

A second approach (which can be used in conjunction with the iterative approach) to ensure that important detail is not permanently lost is to create an alternative level of historical detail along with the profile record, as shown in Figure 3-44. The alternative detail is not designed to be used frequently. It is stored on slow, inexpensive, sequential storage and is difficult to get to and awkward to work with. But the detail is there should it be needed. When management states that they must have a certain detail, however arcane, it can always be retrieved, albeit at a cost of time and money.

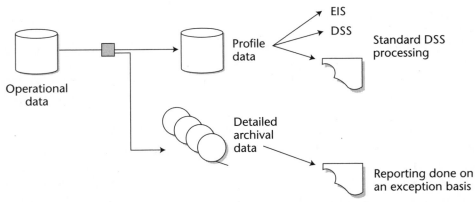

Figure 3-44 An alternative to the classical data warehouse architecture — all the detail that is needed is available while good performance for most DSS processing is the norm.

Creating Multiple Profile Records

Multiple profile records can be created from the same detail. In the case of a phone company, individual call records can be used to create a customer profile record, a district traffic profile record, a line analysis profile record, and so forth.

The profile records can be used to go into the data warehouse, ODS, or a data mart that is fed by the data warehouse. When the profile records go into a data warehouse, they are for general-purpose use. When the profile records go into the data mart, they are customized for the department that uses the data mart. When the profile records go into an ODS (Operational Data Store), they can be accessed in an OLTP manner.

The aggregation of the operational records into a profile record is frequently done on the operational server because this server is large enough to manage volumes of data and because that is where the data resides in any case. Usually creating the profile record involves sorting and merging data. Once the process of creating the snapshot becomes complicated and drawn out, whether the snapshot should be taken at all becomes questionable.

The metadata records written for profile records are very similar to the metadata records written for single activity snapshots, with the exception that the process of aggregating the records becomes an important piece of metadata in itself. (Technically speaking, the record of the process of aggregation is "meta process" information, not "metadata" information.)

Going from the Data Warehouse to the Operational Environment

The operational environment and the data warehouse environment are about as different as any two environments can be in terms of content, technology, usage, communities served, and a hundred other ways. The interface between the two environments is well-documented. Data undergoes a fundamental transformation as it passes from the operational environment to the data warehouse environment. For a variety of reasons — the sequence in which business is conducted, the high-performance needs of operational processing, the aging of data, the strong application orientation of operational processing, and so forth — the flow of data from the operational environment to the data warehouse environment is natural and normal. This normal flow of data is shown in Figure 3-45.

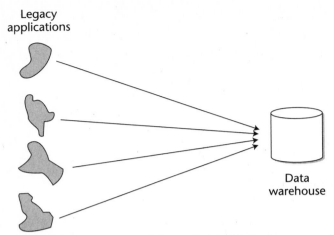

Legacy
applications

Data
warehouse

Figure 3-45 The normal flow of data in the legacy application and data warehouse architected environment.

The question occasionally arises, is it possible for data to pass from the data warehouse environment to the operational environment? In other words, can data pass in a reverse direction from that normally experienced? From the standpoint of technology, the answer certainly is "yes, such a passage of data is technologically possible." Although it is not normal, there are a few isolated circumstances in which data does indeed flow "backward."

Direct Operational Access of Data Warehouse Data

Figure 3-46 illustrates the dynamics of the simplest of circumstances — the direct access of data from the data warehouse by the operational environment. A request has been made within the operational environment for data that resides in the data warehouse. The request is transferred to the data warehouse environment, and the data is located and transferred to the operational environment. Apparently, from the standpoint of dynamics, the transfer could not be easier.

There are a number of serious and uncompromising limitations to the scenario of the direct access of data in the data warehouse from the operational environment. Some of these are as follows:

- The request must be a casual one in terms of response time. It may take as long as 24 hours for it to be satisfied. This means that the operational processing that requires the data warehouse data is decidedly not of an online nature.

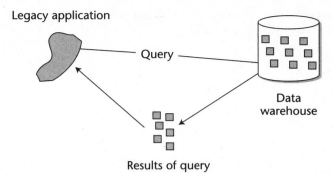

Figure 3-46 A direct query against the data warehouse from the legacy applications environment.

- The request for data must be for a minimal amount of data. The data being transferred is measured in terms of bytes, not megabytes or gigabytes.
- The technology managing the data warehouse must be compatible with the technology managing the operational environment in terms of capacity, protocol, and so on.
- The formatting of data after it is retrieved from the data warehouse in preparation for transport to the operational environment must be nonexistent (or minimal).

These conditions preclude most data ever being directly transferred from the data warehouse to the operational environment. It is easy to see why there is a minimal amount of backward flow of data in the case of direct access.

Indirect Access of Data Warehouse Data

Because of the severe and uncompromising conditions of transfer, direct access of data warehouse data by the operational environment is a rare occurrence. Indirect access of data warehouse data is another matter entirely. Indeed, one of the most effective uses of the data warehouse is the indirect access of data warehouse data by the operational environment. Some examples of indirect access of data warehouse data follow.

An Airline Commission Calculation System

One effective indirect use of data warehouse data occurs in the airline environment. Consider, for example, an airline ticketing transaction. A travel agent has contacted the airline reservation clerk on behalf of a customer. The customer has requested a ticket for a flight and the travel agent wants to know the following:

- Is there a seat available?
- What is the cost of the seat?
- What is the commission paid to the travel agent?

If the airline pays too much of a commission, it will get the agent's business, but it will lose money. If the airline pays too little commission, the travel agent will "shop" the ticket and the airline will lose it to another airline that pays a larger commission. It is in the airline's best interest to calculate the commission it pays very carefully because the calculation has a direct effect on its bottom line.

The interchange between the travel agent and the airline clerk must occur in a fairly short amount of time — within two to three minutes. In this two-to-three-minute window, the airline clerk must enter and complete several transactions:

- Are there any seats available?
- Is seating preference available?
- What connecting flights are involved?
- Can the connections be made?
- What is the cost of the ticket?
- What is the commission?

If the response time of the airline clerk (who is running several transactions while carrying on a conversation with the travel agent) starts to be excessive, the airline will find that it is losing business merely because of the poor response time. It is in the best interest of the airline to ensure brisk response time throughout the dialogue with the travel agent.

The calculation of the optimal commission becomes a critical component of the interchange. The optimal commission is best calculated by looking at a combination of two factors — current bookings and the load history of the flight. The current bookings tell how heavily the flight is booked, and the load history yields a perspective of how the flight has been booked in the past. Between current bookings and historical bookings, an optimal commission can be calculated.

Though tempting to perform the bookings and flight history calculations online, the amount of data that must be manipulated is such that response time suffers if they are calculated in this manner. Instead, the calculation of commission and analysis of flight history are done offline, where there are ample machine resources. Figure 3-47 shows the dynamics of offline commission calculation.

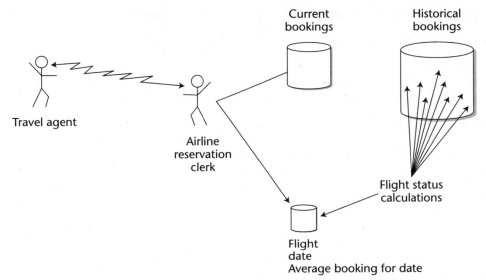

Figure 3-47 The flight status file is created periodically by reading the historical data. It is then a very quick matter for the airline agent to get current bookings and to compare those bookings against the historical average.

The offline calculation and analysis are done periodically, and a small, easy-to-access flight status table is created. When the airline clerk has to interact with the travel agent, it is an easy matter to look at current bookings and the flight status table. The result is a very fast and smooth interaction with the travel agent and the ability to use the data stored in the data warehouse.

A Retail Personalization System

Another example of the indirect use of data warehouse data in the operational environment occurs in the retail personalization system. In this system, a customer reads a catalog or other flyer issued by the retailer. The customer is inspired to make a purchase or to at least inquire about the catalog. A phone call to the retailer ensues.

The interchange is about 5 to 8 minutes long. During this time, the retail sales representative has a fair amount of processing to do — identify the customer, take down the specifics of the order, and so forth. The response time is critical; otherwise, the customer will lose interest.

While the customer is placing the order or making an inquiry, the retail sales representative finds out some other information relevant to the interchange, such as the following:

- The last time the customer made a purchase
- The last type of purchase made
- The market segment or segments in which the customer belongs

While engaging the customer in conversation, the sales representative says such things as these:

- "I see it's been since February that we last heard from you."
- "How was that blue sweater you purchased?"
- "Did the problems you had with the pants get resolved?"

In short, the retail sales representative is able to personalize the conversation. The personalization makes the customer more amenable to purchases.

In addition, the retail sales clerk has market segment information available, such as the following:

- Male/female
- Professional/other
- City/country
- Children
- Ages
- Sex
- Sports
- Fishing
- Hunting
- Beach

Because the phone call can be personalized and the direct marketing segment for a customer is available when the customer calls in, the retail sales representative is able to ask pointed questions, such as these:

- "Did you know we have an unannounced sale on swimsuits?"
- "We just got in some Italian sunglasses that I think you might like."
- "The forecasters predict a cold winter for duck hunters. We have a special on waders right now."

The customer has already taken the time to make a phone call. The personalization of the phone call and the knowledge of what products the customer is interested in give the retailer a very good chance at raising revenue with no further outlay of cash or advertising. The personalization of the phone call is achieved by the indirect use of the data warehouse. Figure 3-48 shows the dynamics of how personalization is achieved.

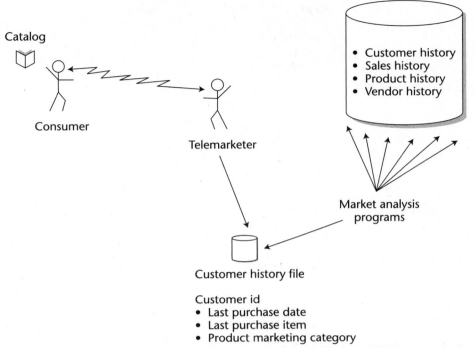

Figure 3-48 The customer history is at the disposal of the telemarketer at a moment's notice.

In the background (that is, in the data warehouse environment), an analysis program is constantly reading and analyzing customer records. This program scans and analyzes historical customer data in a very sophisticated manner. Periodically, the analysis program spins off a file to the operational environment that contains such information as the following:

- Last purchase date
- Last purchase type
- Market analysis/segmenting

When the customer rings in, the online prepared file is waiting for use by the retail sales representative.

Credit Scoring

Another example of the indirect use of a data warehouse in the operational environment is credit scoring in the banking or finance environment. Credit scoring refers to qualifying (or not qualifying) a person for a loan. Say, for example, a customer walks up to the teller's window and asks for a loan. The teller takes in some basic information about the customer and decides whether the loan should be approved. The interchange occurs in a very short amount of time — 5 to 10 minutes.

To determine whether the loan should be approved, a certain amount of processing must be performed. The loan request is first put through a simple screening process. If the loan is for a small enough amount and if the person has a stable financial background, then it may be approved with no further processing. If the loan is for a fair amount and/or the customer does not have a stable, predictable background, then a further check is required.

The background check relies on the data warehouse. In truth, the check is an eclectic one, in which many aspects of the customer are investigated, such as the following:

- Past payback history
- Home/property ownership
- Financial management
- Net worth
- Gross income
- Gross expenses
- Other intangibles

This extensive background check requires quite a bit of diverse historical data. Completing this part of the loan qualification process requires more than a few minutes.

To satisfy the most customers in the shortest amount of time, an analysis program is written. Figure 3-49 shows how the analysis program fits in with the other components of credit scoring. The analysis program is run periodically and produces a prequalified file for use in the operational environment. In addition to other data, the prequalified file includes the following:

- Customer identification
- Approved credit limit
- Special approval limit

Now when the customer wishes to apply for and get a loan, in a high-performance, online mode the teller qualifies (or does not qualify) the loan request from the customer. Only if the customer asks for a loan for an amount greater than the preapproved limit does there need to be an interaction by a loan officer.

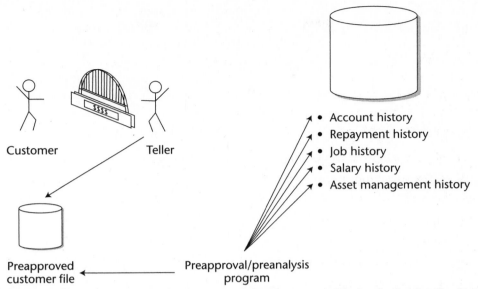

Figure 3-49   The preapproved customer credit file is accessible by the bank teller in an instant.

Indirect Use of Data Warehouse Data

There is, then, an emerging pattern to the indirect use of data warehouse data, as shown in Figure 3-50.

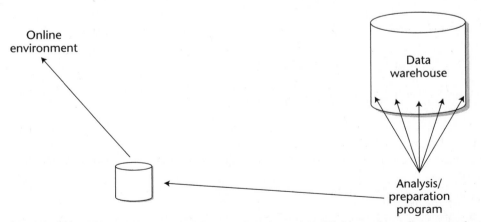

Figure 3-50   The way that data warehouse data is made available to the online operational environment — indirectly.

The data warehouse is analyzed periodically by a program that examines relevant characteristics and criteria. The analysis then creates a small file in the online environment that contains succinct information about the business of the enterprise. The small online file is used quickly and efficiently, fitting in with the style of the other processing that occurs in the operational environment.

Following are a few considerations of the elements of the indirect use of data warehouse data:

- The analysis program:
  - Has many characteristics of artificial intelligence
  - Has free rein to run on any data warehouse data that is available
  - Is run in the background, where processing time is not an issue (or at least not a large issue)
  - Is run in harmony with the rate at which data warehouse changes
- The periodic refreshment:
  - Occurs infrequently
  - Operates in a replacement mode
  - Moves the data from the technology supporting the data warehouse to the technology supporting the operational environment
- The online preanalyzed data file:
  - Contains only a small amount of data per unit of data
  - May contain collectively a large amount of data (because there may be many units of data)
  - Contains precisely what the online clerk needs
  - Is not updated, but is periodically refreshed on a wholesale basis
  - Is part of the online high-performance environment
  - Is efficient to access
  - Is geared for access of individual units of data, not massive sweeps of data

Star Joins

Data warehouse design is decidedly a world in which a normalized or relational approach is the proper one. There are several very good reasons why normalization and a relational approach produces the optimal design for a data warehouse:

- It produces flexibility.
- It fits well with very granular data.
- It is not optimized for any given set of processing requirements.
- It fits very nicely with the data model.

Of course, some small accommodations can be made away from the normalized model when the entire organization views the data in the same way. For example, suppose that monthly data is kept and when the organization looks at the monthly data, it looks at all monthly data. In this case, storing data for all months together makes sense.

A different approach to database design sometimes mentioned in the context of data warehousing is the multidimensional approach. This approach entails star joins, fact tables, and dimensions. The multidimensional approach applies exclusively to data marts, not data warehouses.

Unlike data warehouses, data marts are very much shaped by processing requirements. To build a data mart, you have to know a lot about the processing requirements that surround the data mart. Once those requirements are known, the data mart can be shaped into an optimal star join structure.

But data warehouses are essentially different because they serve a very large and diverse community, and as such, they are not optimized for the convenience or performance of any one set of requirements. Data warehouses are shaped around the corporate requirements for information, not the departmental requirements for information. Therefore, creating a star join for the data warehouse is a mistake because the end result will be a data warehouse optimized for one community at the expense of all other communities.

The appeal of the multidimensional approach to database design for data marts begins with the data model. For all of the practical uses of a data model as one of the foundations of design, there are some shortcomings. Consider the simple data model in Figure 3-51.

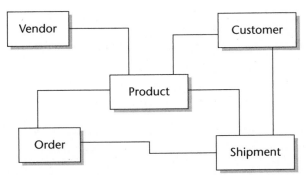

Figure 3-51 A simple two-dimensional data model gives the impression that all entities are equal.

The data model in the figure shows four simple entities with relationships. If all that is considered is the data model for database design, the inference can be drawn that all entities are equal. In other words, from a design standpoint the data model appears to make all entities peers with each other. Approaching database design for the data warehouse solely from the perspective of the data model produces a "flat" effect. In actuality, for a variety of reasons, entities in the world of data marts are anything but peers. Some entities demand their own special treatment.

To see why the data model perspective of the data and the relationships in an organization are distorted, consider the three-dimensional perspective shown in Figure 3-52. Here entities representing vendor, customer, product, and shipment will be sparsely populated, while entities for orders will be heavily populated. There will be many more occurrences of data residing in the table or tables representing the order entity than there will be for any other entity.

Because of the massive volume of data populating the entity, a different design treatment (order) is required.

The design structure that is required to manage large amounts of data residing in an entity in a data mart is called a *star join*. As a simple example of a star join, consider the data structure shown in Figure 3-53. Order is at the center of the star join and is the entity that will be heavily populated. Surrounding ORDER are the entities Part, Date, Supplier, and Shipment. Each of the surrounding entities will have only a modest number of occurrences of data. The center of the star join (Order) is called the *fact table*. The surrounding entities — Part, Date, Supplier, and Shipment — are called "dimension tables." The fact table contains unique identifying data for Order, as well as data unique to the order itself. The fact table also contains prejoined foreign key references to tables outlying itself — the dimension tables. The foreign key relationships may be accompanied by nonforeign key information inside the star join if, in fact, the nonforeign key information is used frequently with the fact table. As an example, the description of a Part may be stored inside the fact table along with the Part number if, in fact, the description is used frequently as part of Order processing.

There can be any number of foreign key relationships to the dimension tables. A foreign key relationship is created when there is a need to examine the foreign key data along with data in the fact table. It is typical for a star join to have as many as 20 to 30 dimensions.

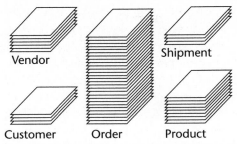

Figure 3-52   A three-dimensional perspective of the entities shows that the entities are anything but equals. Some contain far more occurrences of the data than others.

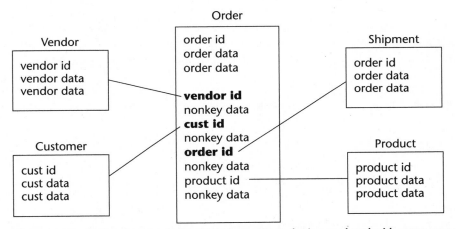

Figure 3-53   A simple star join in which the entity Order is populated with many occurrences and other entities are prejoined with the data.

One of the interesting aspects of the star join is that, in many cases, textual data is divided from numeric data. Consider the diagram in Figure 3-54. Textual data often ends up in the dimension tables, and numeric data ends up in the fact table. Such a division occurs in almost every case.

The benefit of creating star joins is to streamline data for DSS processing. By prejoining data and by creating selective redundancy, the designer greatly simplifies and streamlines data for access and analysis, which is exactly what is needed for the data mart. Note that if star joins were used outside of the DSS data mart environment, there would be many drawbacks. Outside the DSS data mart environment, where updates occur and where data relationships are managed up to the second, a star join most likely would be a very cumbersome structure to build and maintain. But because the data mart is a load-and-access environment, because the data mart contains historical data, and because massive amounts of data need to be managed, the star join data structure is ideal for the processing that occurs inside the star join.

The star join then has its rightful place as a foundation for data mart design. Figure 3-55 shows how the star join and the data model fit as foundations for data mart DSS design. The star join applies as a design foundation to the very large entities that will exist in the data mart. The data model applies as a design foundation to the nonvoluminous entities found in the data mart.

One of the issues of data warehouses and data marts is how data gets from the data warehouse to the data mart. Data in the data warehouse is very granular. Data in the data mart is very compact and summarized. Periodically data must be moved from the data warehouse to the data mart. This movement of data from the data warehouse to the data mart is analogous to the movement of data into the data warehouse from the operational legacy environment.

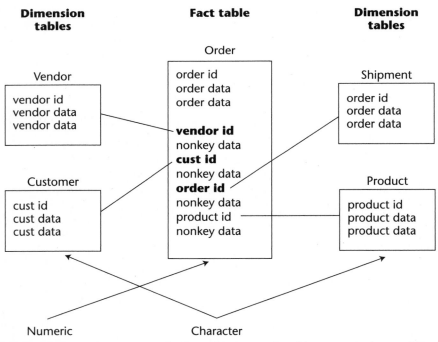

Figure 3-54   In many cases, the fact table is populated by numeric data and foreign keys, while the dimension table is populated by character data.

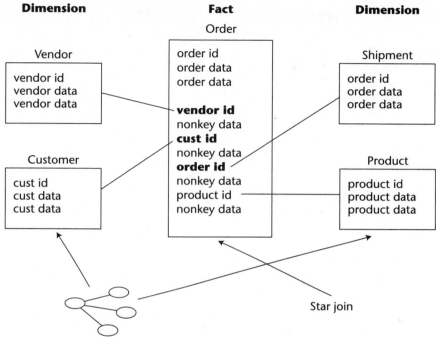

Figure 3-55 Classical data modeling applies to the dimension tables (that is, the nonpopulous entities), and star join design applies to the fact tables (that is, the populous entities).

DATA MARTS: A SUBSTITUTE FOR A DATA WAREHOUSE?

There is an argument in the IT community that says that a data warehouse is expensive and troublesome to build. Indeed, a data warehouse requires resources in the best of cases. But building a data warehouse is absolutely worth the effort. The argument for not building a data warehouse usually leads to building something short of a data warehouse, usually a data mart. The premise is that you can get a lot out of a data mart without the high cost and investment for a data warehouse.

From a short-term perspective, there is some merit to this argument. But from a long-term perspective, a data mart is never a substitute for a data warehouse. The following figure shows why.

(continued)

DATA MARTS: A SUBSTITUTE FOR A DATA WAREHOUSE? *(continued)*

The relationship between the data warehouse and the data mart.

The structure of the data found in the data mart is shaped by the particular requirements of the department. The finance department will have one structure for its data mart, the sales department will have another structure for its data mart, and the marketing department will have another data structure for its data mart. All of their structures will be fed from the granular data found in the data warehouse.

The data structure found in any given data mart is different from the data structure for any other data mart. For example, the sales data mart data structure will be different from the marketing data mart data. The data mart structures are typically known as star joins and contain fact tables and dimensions. The data mart structures are typically known as multidimensional structures and are served by OLAP technology.

Because there is a different data structure for each data mart, making any data mart into a data warehouse doesn't make sense. When a data mart star join is made into a data warehouse, the data warehouse is optimal for one data mart and its users and is not optimal (or really usable) for anyone else. Data marts produce structures that are not reusable except by someone operating in the department that is optimized.

Data mart data structures — in general, across the enterprise — are not reusable, are not flexible, are not useful as a foundation for reconciliation, and are not standing ready for a new set of unknown requirements. But the normalized granular data found in a data warehouse is indeed all of those things.

Data warehouse data must be selected, accessed, and then reshaped to meet the needs of the data mart. Often the data mart data resides in cubes. The cubes need to be formed, and many different calculations need to be performed on the detailed data that resides in the data warehouse. In short, a nontrivial process occurs as data is passed from a normalized world into a multidimensional world.

One of the important issues here is how much data must be accessed and how often is the refreshment process to be performed.

Supporting the ODS

In general, there are four classes of ODS:

- **Class I** — In a class I ODS, updates of data from the operational environment to the ODS are synchronous.

- **Class II** — In a class II ODS, the updates between the operational environment and the ODS occur within a two-to-three-hour time frame.

- **Class III** — In a class III ODS, the synchronization of updates between the operational environment and the ODS occurs overnight.

- **Class IV** — In a class IV ODS, updates into the ODS from the data warehouse are unscheduled. Figure 3-56 shows this support.

The data in the data warehouse is analyzed, and periodically the data is placed in the ODS. The data that is shipped to the ODS is shipped in the form of profile data, which is data that represents many different physical occurrences of data. As a simple example of profile data, suppose the details of a customer's transactions are analyzed. The customer has been active for several years. The analysis of the transactions in the data warehouse is used to produce the following profile information about a single customer:

- Customer name and ID
- Customer volume — high/low
- Customer profitability — high/low
- Customer frequency of activity — very frequent/very infrequent
- Customer likes/dislikes (fast cars, single malt scotch)

Each of the categories of information found in the profile record is created from the examination and analysis of the many detailed records found in the data warehouse. There is then a very fundamental difference between the data found in the data warehouse and the profile data found in the class IV ODS.

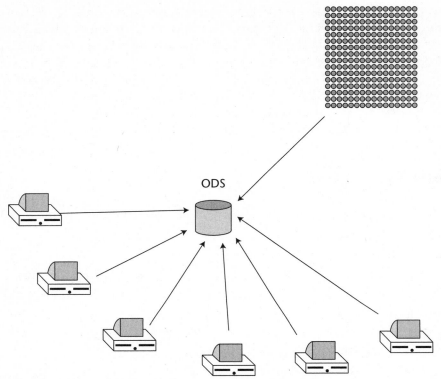

Figure 3-56 The data warehouse supports a class IV ODS.

Requirements and the Zachman Framework

Data warehouses are not built from processing requirements, but data warehouses are designed from enterprise requirements. Enterprise requirements focus on the entire enterprise, not just the immediate application. Enterprise requirements look at the full set of requirements for processing, data, and infrastructure.

One of the best ways to gather and organize enterprise requirements is through an approach that is called the *Zachman framework* approach. The Zachman framework approach is named after its inventor, John Zachman, one of the pioneers in enterprise architecture. The Zachman framework is depicted in Figure 3-57.

The Zachman framework is a convenient device for ensuring that all the aspects of the enterprise have been considered in the development of a system. The matrix approach demands that all perspectives be considered, not just a few perspectives. The building of a Zachman framework requires discipline and requires looking at organizational needs for information in different ways. In many ways, the output from having built a Zachman framework for an organization is perspective and context. Many times, designers design a system without first having to examine all the many ways information is needed and used. Building the Zachman framework forces an organization into a way of thinking that is healthy for the organization and its long-term information needs. After having built a Zachman framework, the organization has built a blueprint that can be used for articulating enterprise requirements.

Those enterprise information requirements can then be extracted from the Zachman framework, once built. From the requirements that have been extracted, an enterprise data model can be built. And then from the enterprise data model, the data warehouse is built in an iterative manner, as has been discussed.

Figure 3-58 shows the progression from the Zachman framework to the development of the data warehouse.

There is then a symbiotic relationship between the data warehouse design and development and the enterprise perspective that results from the building of a Zachman framework.

	Data	Function	Network	People	Time	Motivation
Scope						
Enterprise model						
System model						
Technical model						
Components						
Functional system						

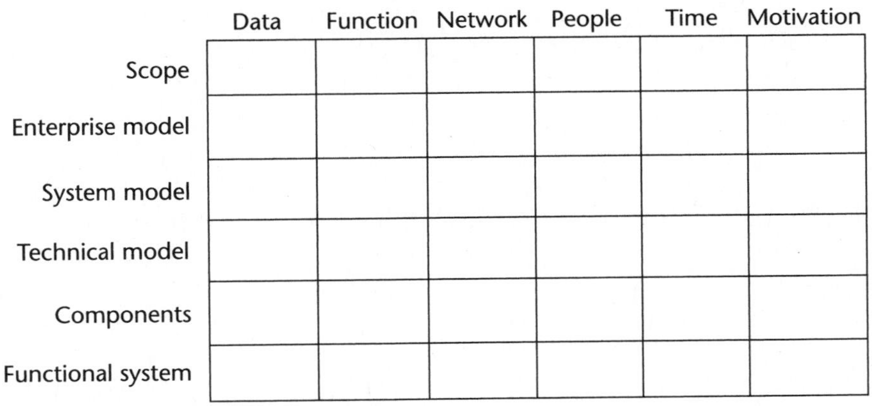

Figure 3-57 The Zachman framework.

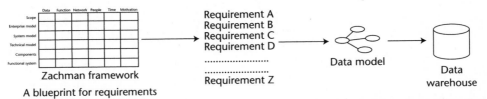

Zachman framework
A blueprint for requirements

Requirement A
Requirement B
Requirement C
Requirement D
....
....
Requirement Z

Data model

Data warehouse

Figure 3-58 Progression from the Zachman framework to the development of the data warehouse.

Summary

The design of the data warehouse begins with the data model. The corporate data model is used for the design of the operational environment, and a variation of the corporate data model is used for the data warehouse. The data warehouse is constructed in an iterative fashion. Requirements for the data warehouse cannot be known *a priori*. The construction of the data warehouse is under a development life cycle completely different from that of classical operational systems.

The primary concern of the data warehouse developer is managing volume. To that end, granularity and partitioning of data are the two most important issues of database design. There are, however, many other physical design issues, most of which center around the efficiency of access to data.

The data warehouse is fed data as it passes from the legacy operational environment. Data goes through a complex process of conversion, reformatting, and integration as it passes from the legacy operational environment into the data warehouse environment. Often, as data passes into the data warehouse environment, there is a shift of time. In some cases, the operational data has no time stamping, and in other cases, the level of granularity of the operational data needs to be adjusted.

The data model exists at three levels — high level, midlevel, and low level. The data model is the key to being able to build the data warehouse in iterations. The entities found in the high-level model relate to the major subject areas of the corporation. The low-level model relates to the physical database design of the data warehouse.

At the lowest level of database design, slight denormalization can occur when the entire organization looks at the data in the same way. Some techniques for slight denormalization of data include creating arrays of data, creating redundant data judiciously, and making creative indexes.

The basic structure of the data warehouse record is one that contains a time stamp, a key, direct data, and secondary data. All data warehouse database designs (in one form or the other) follow this simple pattern.

Reference tables must be placed in the data warehouse and managed on a time-variant basis just like any other data. There are many approaches to the inclusion and design of reference data in the data warehouse.

Data is loaded into the data warehouse under what can be termed a "wrinkle of time." This means that as soon as an activity occurs in the operational environment, that data is not immediately rushed to the data warehouse. Instead, data that has been newly updated in the operational environment is allowed to stand in the operational environment for up to 24 hours before being moved to the data warehouse.

The transformation that occurs as data moves from the operational environment to the data warehouse environment is complex. There is a change in DBMS, a change in operating systems, a change in hardware architecture, a change in semantics, a change in coding, and so forth. Many, many considerations are involved in the movement of data from the operational environment to the data warehouse environment.

The creation of a data warehouse record is triggered by an activity or an event that has occurred in the operational environment. In some cases, an event (such as a sale) has occurred. In other cases, the regular passage of time has occurred, such as the end of the month or the end of the week.

A profile record is a composite record made up of many different historical activities. The profile record is a composite representation of data.

The star join is a database design technique that is sometimes mistakenly applied to the data warehouse environment. The star join multidimensional approach is an approach where database design is based on the occurrences of data within a subject area and how that data will be accessed. Star join design applies to the world of data marts, not the world of data warehouses. It is a mistake to build a data warehouse with a star join because the data warehouse will end up being optimal for one set of users at the expense of everyone else.

Granularity in the Data Warehouse

The single most important design issue facing the data warehouse developer is determining the proper level of granularity of the data that will reside in the data warehouse. When the level of granularity is properly set, the remaining aspects of design and implementation flow smoothly; when it is not properly set, every other aspect is awkward.

Granularity is also important to the warehouse architect because it affects all the environments that depend on the warehouse for data. Granularity affects how efficiently data can be shipped to the different environments and determines the types of analysis that can be done.

The primary issue of granularity is that of getting it at the right level. The level of granularity needs to be neither too high nor too low.

The trade-off in choosing the right levels of granularity (as discussed in Chapter 2) centers around managing the volume of data and storing data at too high a level of granularity, to the point that detailed data is so voluminous that it is unusable. In addition, if there is to be a truly large amount of data, consideration must be given to putting the inactive portion of the data into overflow storage.

Raw Estimates

The starting point for determining the appropriate level of granularity is to do a raw estimate of the number of rows of data and the DASD (direct access storage device) that will be in the data warehouse. Admittedly, in the best of circumstances, only an estimate can be made. But all that is required at the inception of building the warehouse is an order-of-magnitude estimate.

The raw estimate of the number of rows of data that will reside in the data warehouse tells the architect a great deal. If there are only 10,000 rows, almost any level of granularity will do. If there are 10 million rows, a low level of granularity is possible. If there are 10 billion rows, not only is a higher level of granularity needed, but a major portion of the data will probably go into overflow storage.

Figure 4-1 shows an algorithmic path to calculate the space occupied by a data warehouse. The first step is to identify all the tables to be built. As a rule of thumb, there will be one or two really large tables and many smaller supporting tables. Next, estimate the size of the row in each table. It is likely that the exact size will not be known. A lower-bound estimate and an upper-bound estimate are sufficient.

Estimating rows/space for the warehouse environment

1. For each known table:
     How big is a row (in bytes)?
       – Biggest estimate
       – Smallest estimate
     For the 1-year horizon
       What is the maximum number of rows possible?
       What is the minimum number of rows possible?
     For the 5-year horizon·
       What is the maximum number of rows possible?
       What is the minimum number of rows possible?
     For each key of the table
       What is the size of the key (in bytes)?
     Total maximum 1-year space = biggest row x 1-year max rows
     Total minimum 1-year space = smallest row x 1-year min rows
       plus index space

2. Repeat (1) for all known tables.

Figure 4-1   Space/row calculations.

Next, on the one-year horizon, estimate the maximum and minimum number of rows in the table. This estimate is the one that is the most problematic for the designer. If the table is for customers, use today's estimate, factoring in business conditions and the corporate business plan. If there is no existing business today, estimate the total market multiplied by the expected market share. If the market share is unpredictable, use an estimate of what a competitor has achieved. In short, start with a reasonable estimate of customers gathered from one or more sources.

If the warehouse is to contain information about activity, go from the estimated number of customers to the estimated activity per unit of time. Again, the same logic is used — looking at current business profiles, a competitor's profile, economic projections, average customer activity for the time period selected, and so forth.

Once the estimate of number of units of data in the data warehouse is made (using a high and a low projection), repeat the process, but this time for the five-year horizon.

After the raw data projections are made, the index data space projections are calculated. For each table — for each key in the table or element of data that will be searched directly — identify the length of the key or element of data and determine whether the key will exist for each entry in the primary table.

Now the high and low numbers for the occurrences of rows in the tables are multiplied, respectively, by the maximum and minimum lengths of data. In addition, the number of index entries is multiplied by the length of the key and added to the total amount of data to determine the volume of data that will be required.

After the index calculations are made, consider what space will be needed for back up and recovery. In some cases, disk storage will be used for backup and recovery. In other cases, off-line storage will be used. In some cases, only portions of tables will be backed up. In other cases, entire tables are locked together and must be backed up together.

A word of caution: Estimates projecting the size of the data warehouse almost always are low. Furthermore, the growth rate of the warehouse is usually faster than the projection.

Input to the Planning Process

The estimate of rows and DASD then serves as input to the planning process, as shown in Figure 4-2. When the estimates are made, accuracy is actually important (or even desirable) only to the order of magnitude. A fine degree of accuracy here is a waste of time.

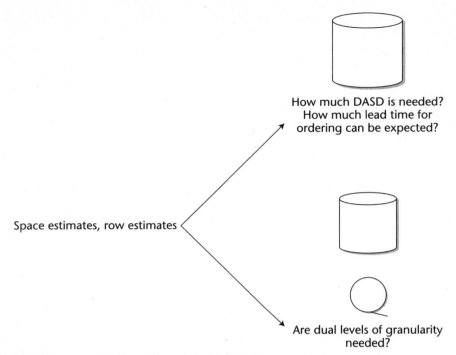

Figure 4-2   Using the output of the space estimates.

Data in Overflow

Once the raw estimate as to the size of the data warehouse is made, the next step is to compare the total number of rows in the warehouse environment to the charts shown in Figure 4-3. Depending on how many total rows will be in the warehouse environment, different approaches to design, development, and storage are necessary. For the one-year horizon, if the number of rows totals fewer than 1 million, practically any design and implementation will work, and no data will have to go to overflow. If there will be 10 million total rows or fewer, design must be done with a reasonable amount of care, and it is unlikely that any data will have to go into overflow. If the total number of rows will exceed 100 million, design must be done carefully, and it is likely that at least some data will go to overflow. And if the total number of rows in the data warehouse environment is to exceed 1,000 million rows, surely some amount of data will go to overflow storage, and a very careful design and implementation of the data warehouse is required.

1-YEAR HORIZON		5-YEAR HORIZON	
100,000,000	Data in overflow and on disk; majority in overflow; very careful consideration of granularity	1,000,000,000	Data in overflow and on disk; majority in overflow; very careful consideration of granularity
10,000,000	Possibly some data in overflow; most data on disk; some consideration of granularity	100,000,000	Possibly some data in overflow; most data on disk; some consideration of granularity
1,000,000	Data on disk; almost any database design	10,000,000	Data on disk; almost any database design
100,000	Any database design; all data on disk	1,000,000	Any database design; all data on disk

Figure 4-3 Compare the total number of rows in the warehouse environment to the charts.

On the five-year horizon, the totals shift by about an order of magnitude or perhaps even more. The theory is that after five years, these factors will be in place:

- There will be more expertise available in managing the data warehouse volumes of data.
- Hardware costs will have dropped to some extent.
- More powerful software tools will be available.
- The end user will be more sophisticated.

All of these factors point to a different volume of data that can be managed over a long period of time. Unfortunately, it is almost impossible to accurately forecast the volume of data into a five-year horizon. Therefore, this estimate is used as merely a raw guess.

An interesting point is that the total number of bytes used in the warehouse has relatively little to do with the design and granularity of the data warehouse. In other words, it does not particularly matter whether the record being considered is 25 bytes long or 250 bytes long. As long as the length of the record is of reasonable size, then the chart previously shown in Figure 4-3 still applies. Of course, if the record being considered is 250,000 bytes long, then the length of the record makes a difference. Not many records of that size are found in the data warehouse environment, however. The reason for the indifference to record size has as much to do with the indexing of data as anything else. The same number of index entries is required regardless of the size of the record being indexed. Only under exceptional circumstances does the actual size of the record being indexed play a role in determining whether the data warehouse should go into overflow.

Overflow Storage

Data in the data warehouse environment grows at a rate never before seen by IT professionals. The combination of historical data and detailed data produces a growth rate that is phenomenal. The terms "terabyte" and "petabyte" were used only in theory prior to data warehousing.

As data grows large, a natural subdivision of data occurs between actively used data and inactively used data. Inactive data is sometimes called *dormant data* or *infrequently used data*. At some point in the life of the data warehouse, the vast majority of the data in the warehouse becomes stale and unused. At this point, it makes sense to start separating the data onto different storage media.

Most professionals have never built a system on anything but disk storage. But as the data warehouse grows large, it simply makes economic and technological sense to place the data on multiple storage media. The actively used portion of the data warehouse remains on high-performance disk storage, while the inactive portion of the data in the data warehouse is placed on alternative storage or near-line storage.

Data that is placed on alternative or near-line storage is stored much less expensively than data that resides on disk storage. And just because data is placed on alternative or near-line storage does not mean that the data is inaccessible. Data placed on alternate or near-line storage is just as accessible as data placed on disk storage. By placing inactive data or dormant data on alternate or near-line storage, the architect removes impediments to performance from the high-performance active data. In fact, moving data to near-line storage greatly accelerates the performance of the entire environment.

In fact, there are several alternatives to high-performance disk storage. There is low-performance disk storage (sometimes called "fat" storage). There is near-line storage, which is robotically controlled cartridge-based sequential tape. Then there is sequential tape, which is considerably less sophisticated than near-line storage. In fact, there are all sorts of physical storage media other than high-performance disk storage.

To make data accessible throughout the system and to place the proper data in the proper part of storage, software support of the alternate storage or near-line environment is needed. Figure 4-4 shows some of the more important components of the support infrastructure needed for the alternate storage or near-line storage environment.

Figure 4-4 shows that a data monitor is needed to determine the usage of data. The data monitor tells where to place data by determining what data is and is not being used in the data warehouse. The movement between disk storage and near-line storage is controlled by means of software called a *cross-media storage manager* (CMSM). The data in alternate storage or near-line storage can be accessed directly by means of software that has the intelligence to know where data is located in near-line storage. These three software components are the minimum required for alternate storage or near-line storage to be used effectively.

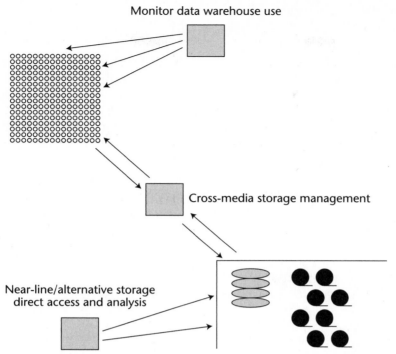

Figure 4-4 The support software needed to make storage overflow possible.

In many regards, alternate storage or near-line storage acts as overflow storage for the data warehouse. Logically, the data warehouse extends over both disk storage and alternate storage or near-line storage in order to form a single image of data. Of course, physically the data may be placed on any number of volumes of data.

An important component of the data warehouse is *overflow storage*, where infrequently used data is held. Overflow storage has an important effect on granularity. Without this type of storage, the designer is forced to adjust the level of granularity to the capacity and budget for disk technology. With overflow storage, the designer is free to create as low a level of granularity as desired.

Overflow storage can be on any number of storage media. Some of the popular media are photo optical storage, magnetic tape (sometimes called "near-line storage"), and cheap disk. The magnetic tape storage medium is not the same as the old-style mag tapes with vacuum units tended by an operator. Instead, the modern rendition is a robotically controlled silo of storage where the human hand never touches the storage unit, where masses of data can be stored, where cartridges can be retrieved quickly, and so forth.

The alternate forms of storage are cheap, reliable, and capable of storing huge amounts of data, much more so than is feasible for storage on high-performance disk devices. In doing so, the alternate forms of storage act as overflow for the data warehouse. In some cases, a query facility that can operate independently of the storage device is desirable. In this case, when a user makes a query, there is no prior knowledge of where the data resides. The query is issued, and the system then finds the data regardless of where it is.

While it is convenient for the end user to merely "go get the data" without knowing where the data is, there is a serious performance implication. If the end user frequently accesses data that is in alternate storage, the query will not run quickly, and many machine resources will be consumed in the servicing of the request. Therefore, the data architect is best advised to make sure that the data that resides in alternate storage is accessed infrequently.

There are several ways to ensure infrequently accessed data resides in alternate storage. A simple (but crude) way is to place data in alternate storage when it reaches a certain age — say, 24 months. Another way is to place certain types of data in alternate storage and other types in disk storage. A monthly summary of customer records may be placed in disk storage, while details that support the monthly summary are placed in alternate storage.

In other cases of query processing, separating the disk-based queries from the alternate-storage-based queries is desirable. Here, one type of query goes against disk-based storage and another type goes against alternate storage. In this case, there is no need to worry about the performance implications of a query having to fetch alternate-storage-based data.

This sort of query separation can be advantageous — particularly with regard to protecting systems resources. Usually, the types of queries that operate against alternate storage end up accessing huge amounts of data. Because these long-running activities are performed in a completely separate environment, the data administrator never has to worry about query performance in the disk-based environment.

For the overflow storage environment to operate properly, several types of software become mandatory. Figure 4-5 shows these types and where they are positioned.

Figure 4-5 shows that two pieces of software are needed for the overflow environment to operate properly — a CMSM and an activity monitor. The CMSM manages the traffic of data going to and from the disk storage environment to the alternate storage environment. Data moves from the disk to alternate storage when it ages or when its probability of access drops. Data from the alternate storage environment can be moved to disk storage when there is a request for the data or when it is detected that there will be multiple future requests for the data. By moving the data to and from disk storage to alternate storage, the data administrator is able to get maximum performance from the system.

The second piece that is required, the activity monitor, determines what data is and is not being accessed. The activity monitor supplies the intelligence to determine where data is to be placed — on disk storage or on alternate storage.

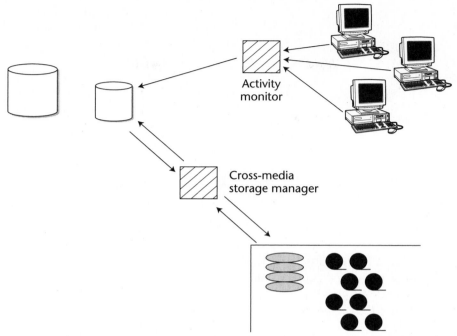

Figure 4-5 For overflow storage to function properly, at least two types of software are needed — a cross-media storage manager and an activity monitor.

What the Levels of Granularity Will Be

Once the simple analysis of how much data there will be in the data warehouse is done (and, in truth, many companies discover that they need to put at least some data into overflow storage), the next step is to determine the level of granularity for data residing on disk storage. This step requires common sense and a certain amount of intuition. Creating a disk-based data warehouse at a very low level of detail doesn't make sense because too many resources are required to process the data. On the other hand, creating a disk-based data warehouse with a level of granularity that is too high means that much analysis must be done against data that resides in overflow storage. So, the first cut at determining the proper level of granularity is to make an educated guess.

Such a guess is only the starting point, however. To refine the guess, a certain amount of iterative analysis is needed, as shown in Figure 4-6. The only real way to determine the proper level of granularity for the lightly summarized data is to put the data in front of the end user. Only after the end user has actually seen the data can a definitive answer be given. Figure 4-6 shows the iterative loop that must transpire.

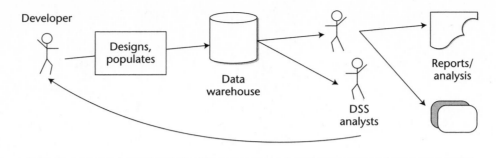

Developer

Designs, populates

Data warehouse

DSS analysts

Reports/ analysis

Rule of Thumb:
If 50% of the first iteration of design is correct, the design effort has been a success.

• Building very small subsets quickly and carefully listening to feedback
• Prototyping
• Looking at what other people have done
• Working with an experienced user
• Looking at what the organization has now
• JAD sessions with simulated output

Figure 4-6   The attitude of the end user: "Now that I see what can be done, I can tell you what would really be useful."

The second consideration in determining the granularity level is to antici-pate the needs of the different architectural entities that will be fed from the data warehouse. In some cases, this determination can be done scientifically. But, in truth, this anticipation is really an educated guess. As a rule, if the level of granularity in the data warehouse is small enough, the design of the data warehouse will suit all architectural entities. Data that is too fine can always be summarized, whereas data that is not fine enough cannot be easily broken down. Therefore, the data in the data warehouse needs to be at the lowest com-mon denominator.

Some Feedback Loop Techniques

Following are techniques to make the feedback loop harmonious:

■ Build the first parts of the data warehouse in very small, very fast steps, and carefully listen to the end users' comments at the end of each step of development. Be prepared to make adjustments quickly.

■ If available, use prototyping and allow the feedback loop to function using observations gleaned from the prototype.

- Look at how other people have built their levels of granularity and learn from their experience.

- Go through the feedback process with an experienced user who is aware of the process occurring. Under no circumstances should you keep your users in the dark as to the dynamics of the feedback loop.

- Look at whatever the organization has now that appears to be working, and use those functional requirements as a guideline.

- Execute *joint application design (JAD)* sessions and simulate the output to achieve the desired feedback.

Granularity of data can be raised in many ways, such as the following:

- Summarize data from the source as it goes into the target.

- Average or otherwise calculate data as it goes into the target.

- Push highest and/or lowest set values into the target.

- Push only data that is obviously needed into the target.

- Use conditional logic to select only a subset of records to go into the target.

The ways that data may be summarized or aggregated are limitless.

When building a data warehouse, keep one important point in mind: In classical requirements systems development, it is unwise to proceed until the vast majority of the requirements are identified. But in building the data warehouse, it is unwise not to proceed if at least half of the requirements for the data warehouse are identified. In other words, if in building the data warehouse, the developer waits until many requirements are identified, the warehouse will never be built. It is vital that the feedback loop with the DSS analyst be initiated as soon as possible.

As a rule, when transactions are created in business, they are created from lots of different types of data. An order contains part information, shipping information, pricing, product specification information, and the like. A banking transaction contains customer information, transaction amounts, account information, banking domicile information, and so forth. When normal business transactions are being prepared for placement in the data warehouse, their level of granularity is too high, and they must be broken down into a lower level. The normal circumstance then is for data to be broken down. There are at least two other circumstances in which data is collected at too low a level of granularity for the data warehouse, however:

- **Manufacturing process control** — Analog data is created as a by-product of the manufacturing process. The analog data is at such a deep level of granularity that it is not useful in the data warehouse. It must be edited and aggregated so that its level of granularity is raised.

- **Clickstream data generated in the Web environment** — Web logs collect clickstream data at a level of granularity that it is much too fine to be placed in the data warehouse. Clickstream data must be edited, cleansed, resequenced, summarized, and so forth before it can be placed in the warehouse.

These are a few notable exceptions to the rule that business-generated data is at too high of a level of granularity.

Levels of Granularity — Banking Environment

Consider the simple data structures shown in Figure 4-7 for a banking or financial environment.

To the left — at the operational level — is operational data, where the details of banking transactions are found. Sixty days' worth of activity are stored in the operational online environment.

In the lightly summarized level of processing — shown to the right of the operational data — are up to 10 years' history of activities. The activities for an account for a given month are stored in the lightly summarized portion of the data warehouse. While there are many records here, they are much more compact than the source records. Much less DASD and many fewer rows are found in the lightly summarized level of data.

Of course, there is the archival level of data (that is, the overflow level of data), in which every detailed record is stored. The archival level of data is stored on a medium suited to bulk management of data. Note that not all fields of data are transported to the archival level. Only those fields needed for legal reasons, informational reasons, and so forth are stored. The data that has no further use, even in an archival mode, is purged from the system as data is passed to the archival level.

The overflow environment can be held in a single medium, such as magnetic tape, which is cheap for storage and expensive for access. It is entirely possible to store a small part of the archival level of data online, when there is a probability that the data might be needed. For example, a bank might store the most recent 30 days of activities online. The last 30 days is archival data, but it is still online. At the end of the 30-day period, the data is sent to magnetic tape, and space is made available for the next 30 days' worth of archival data.

Now consider another example of data in an architected environment in the banking or financial environment. Figure 4-8 shows customer records spread across the environment. In the operational environment is shown current-value data whose content is accurate as of the moment of usage. The data that exists at the light level of summarization is the same data (in terms of definition of data) but is taken as a snapshot once a month.

DUAL LEVELS OF GRANULARITY IN THE BANKING ENVIRONMENT

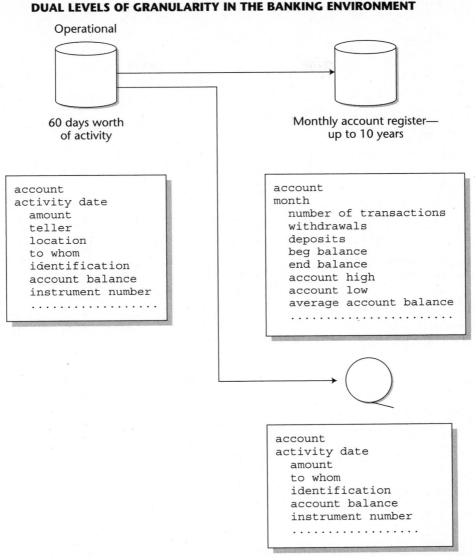

Figure 4-7 A simple example of dual levels of granularity in the banking environment.

Where the customer data is kept over a long span of time — for the past 10 years — a continuous file is created from the monthly files. In such a fashion, the history of a customer can be tracked over a lengthy period of time.

Now let's move to another industry — manufacturing. In the architected environment shown in Figure 4-9, at the operational level is the record of manufacture upon the completion of an assembly for a given lot of parts. Throughout the day, many records aggregate as the assembly process runs.

DUAL LEVELS OF GRANULARITY IN THE BANKING ENVIRONMENT

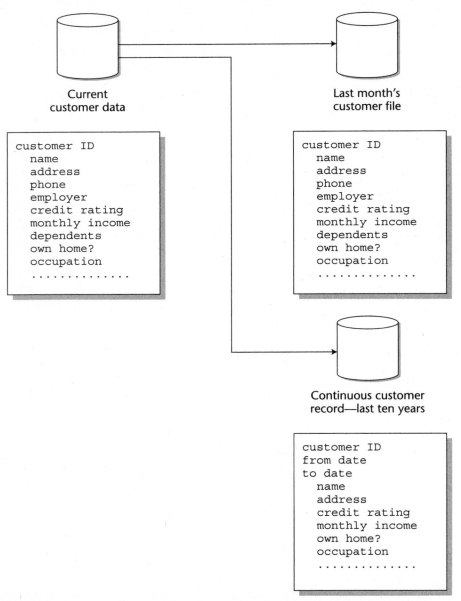

Figure 4-8 Another form of dual levels of granularity in the banking environment.

DUAL LEVELS OF GRANULARITY IN THE MANUFACTURING ENVIRONMENT

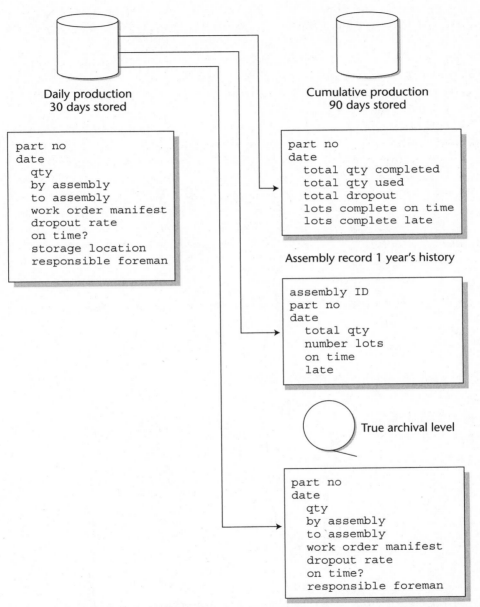

Daily production
30 days stored

```
part no
date
  qty
  by assembly
  to assembly
  work order manifest
  dropout rate
  on time?
  storage location
  responsible foreman
```

Cumulative production
90 days stored

```
part no
date
  total qty completed
  total qty used
  total dropout
  lots complete on time
  lots complete late
```

Assembly record 1 year's history

```
assembly ID
part no
date
  total qty
  number lots
  on time
  late
```

True archival level

```
part no
date
  qty
  by assembly
  to assembly
  work order manifest
  dropout rate
  on time?
  responsible foreman
```

Figure 4-9   Some of the different levels of granularity in a manufacturing environment.

The light level of summarization contains two tables — one for all the activities for a part summarized by day, another by assembly activity by part. The parts' cumulative production table contains data for up to 90 days. The assembly record contains a limited amount of data on the production activity summarized by date.

The archival or overflow environment contains a detailed record of each manufacture activity. As in the case of a bank, only those fields that will be needed later are stored. (Actually, those fields that have a reasonable probability of being needed later are stored.)

Another example of data warehouse granularity in the manufacturing environment is shown in Figure 4-10, where an active-order file is in the operational environment. All orders that require activity are stored there. In the data warehouse is stored up to 10 years' worth of order history. The order history is keyed on the primary key and several secondary keys. Only the data that will be needed for future analysis is stored in the warehouse. The volume of orders was so small that going to an overflow level was not necessary. Of course, should orders suddenly increase, it may be necessary to go to a lower level of granularity and into overflow.

DUAL LEVELS OF GRANULARITY IN THE MANUFACTURING ENVIRONMENT

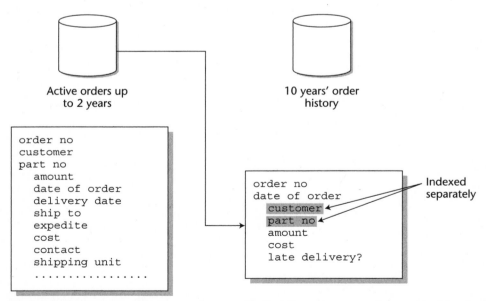

Figure 4-10   There are so few order records that there is no need for a dual level of granularity.

Another adaptation of a shift in granularity is seen in the data in the architected environment of an insurance company, shown in Figure 4-11. Premium payment information is collected in an active file. Then, after a period of time, the information is passed to the data warehouse. Because only a relatively small amount of data exists, overflow data is not needed. However, because of the regularity of premium payments, the payments are stored as part of an array in the warehouse.

As another example of architecture in the insurance environment, consider the insurance claims information shown in Figure 4-12. In the current claims system (the operational part of the environment), much detailed information is stored about claims. When a claim is settled (or when it is determined that a claim is not going to be settled), or when enough time passes that the claim is still pending, the claim information passes over to the data warehouse. As it does so, the claim information is summarized in several ways — by agent by month, by type of claim by month, and so on. At a lower level of detail, the claim is held in overflow storage for an unlimited amount of time. As in the other cases in which data passes to overflow, only data that might be needed in the future is kept (which is most of the information found in the operational environment).

DUAL LEVELS OF GRANULARITY IN THE INSURANCE ENVIRONMENT

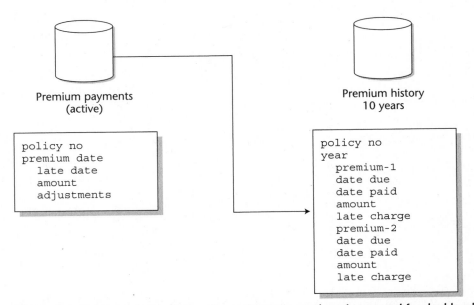

Figure 4-11   Because of the low volume of premiums, there is no need for dual levels of granularity, and because of the regularity of premium billing, there is the opportunity to create an array of data.

DUAL LEVELS OF GRANULARITY IN THE INSURANCE ENVIRONMENT

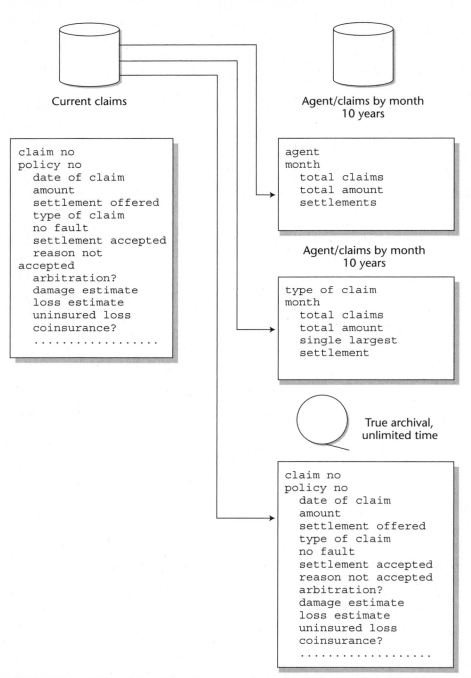

Figure 4-12 Claims information is summarized on other than the primary key in the lightly summarized part of the warehouse. Claims information must be kept indefinitely in the true archival portion of the architecture.

Feeding the Data Marts

Another important consideration in the choosing of the granularity of data that resides in the data warehouse is that of understanding what level of granularity the data marts will need. It is the job of the data warehouse to feed data marts. Different data marts need to look at data differently. One of the ways that data marts look at data is in terms of granularity.

The data that resides in the data warehouse must be at the lowest level of granularity needed by *any* of the data marts. In other words, to feed all the data marts properly, the data in the data warehouse must be at the level of granularity needed at the lowest level by any data mart. Data in the data warehouse then becomes the lowest common denominator for the DSS analytical environment.

Summary

Choosing the proper levels of granularity for the architected environment is vital to success. The normal way the levels of granularity are chosen is to use common sense, create a small part of the warehouse, and let the user access the data. Then listen very carefully to the user, take the feedback he or she gives, and adjust the levels of granularity appropriately.

The worst stance that can be taken is to design all the levels of granularity *a priori*, and then build the data warehouse. Even in the best of circumstances, if 50 percent of the design is done correctly, the design is a good one. The nature of the data warehouse environment is such that the DSS analyst cannot envision what is really needed until he or she actually sees the reports.

The process of granularity design begins with a raw estimate of how large the warehouse will be on the one-year and the five-year horizon. Once the raw estimate is made, then the estimate tells the designer just how fine the granularity should be. In addition, the estimate tells whether overflow storage should be considered.

There is an important feedback loop for the data warehouse environment. Upon building the data warehouse's first iteration, the data architect listens very carefully to the feedback from the end user. Adjustments are made based on the user's input.

Another important consideration is the levels of granularity needed by the different architectural components that will be fed from the data warehouse. When data goes into overflow — away from disk storage to a form of alternate storage — the granularity can be as low as desired. When overflow storage is not used, the designer will be constrained in the selection of the level of granularity when there is a significant amount of data.

For overflow storage to operate properly, two pieces of software are necessary — a cross-media storage manager (CMSM) that manages the traffic to and from the disk environment to the alternate storage environment and an activity monitor. The activity monitor is needed to determine what data should be in overflow and what data should be on disk.

CHAPTER 5

The Data Warehouse and Technology

In many ways, the data warehouse requires a simpler set of technological features than its operational predecessors. Online updating with the data warehouse is not needed, locking and integrity needs are minimal, only a very basic teleprocessing interface is required, and so forth. Nevertheless, there are a fair number of technological requirements for the data warehouse. This chapter outlines some of these.

Managing Large Amounts of Data

Prior to data warehousing, the terms *terabytes* and *petabytes* were unknown; data capacity was measured in megabytes and gigabytes. After data warehousing, the whole perception changed. Suddenly, what was large one day was trifling the next. The explosion of data volume came about because the data warehouse required that both detail and history be mixed in the same environment. The issue of storing and managing large volumes of data is so important that it pervades all other aspects of data warehousing. With this in mind, the first and most important technological requirement for the data warehouse is the ability to manage large amounts of data, as shown in Figure 5-1. There are many approaches, and in a large warehouse environment, more than one approach will be used.

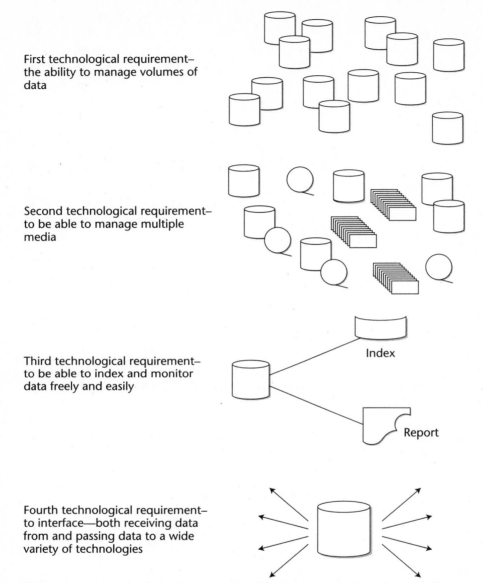

First technological requirement–
the ability to manage volumes of
data

Second technological requirement–
to be able to manage multiple
media

Third technological requirement–
to be able to index and monitor
data freely and easily

Index

Report

Fourth technological requirement–
to interface—both receiving data
from and passing data to a wide
variety of technologies

Figure 5-1   Some basic requirements for technology supporting a data warehouse.

Large amounts of data need to be managed in many ways — through flexibility of addressability of data stored inside the processor and stored inside disk storage, through indexing, through extensions of data, through the efficient management of overflow, and so forth. No matter how the data is managed, however, two fundamental requirements are evident — the ability to manage large amounts of data at all and the ability to manage it well. Some approaches can be used to manage large amounts of data but do so in a clumsy manner. Other approaches can manage large amounts and do so in an efficient, elegant manner. To be effective, the technology used must satisfy the requirements for both volume and efficiency.

In the ideal case, the data warehouse developer builds a data warehouse under the assumption that the technology that houses the data warehouse can handle the volumes required. When the designer has to go to extraordinary lengths in design and implementation to map the technology to the data warehouse, then there is a problem with the underlying technology. When technology is an issue, it is normal to engage more than one technology. The ability to participate in moving dormant data to overflow storage is perhaps the most strategic capability that a technology can have.

Of course, beyond the basic issue of technology and its efficiency is the cost of storage and processing.

Managing Multiple Media

In conjunction with managing large amounts of data efficiently and cost-effectively, the technology underlying the data warehouse must handle multiple storage media. It is insufficient to manage a mature data warehouse on DASD alone. Following is a hierarchy of storage of data in terms of speed of access and cost of storage:

Main memory	Very fast	Very expensive
Expanded memory	Very fast	Expensive
Cache	Very fast	Expensive
DASD	Fast	Moderate
Magnetic tape	Not fast	Not expensive
Near line	Not fast*	Not expensive
Optical disk	Not slow	Not expensive
Fiche	Slow	Cheap

The volume of data in the data warehouse and the differences in the probability of access dictates that a fully populated data warehouse reside on more than one level of storage.

*Not fast to find first record sought; very fast to find all other records in the block.

Indexing and Monitoring Data

The very essence of the data warehouse is the flexible and unpredictable access of data. This boils down to the ability to access the data quickly and easily. If data in the warehouse cannot be easily and efficiently indexed, the data warehouse will not be a success. Of course, the designer uses many practices to make data as flexible as possible, such as spreading data across different storage media and partitioning data. But the technology that houses the data must be able to support easy indexing as well. Some of the indexing techniques that often make sense are the support of secondary indexes, the support of sparse indexes, the support of dynamic, temporary indexes, and so forth. Furthermore, the cost of creating the index and using the index cannot be significant.

In the same vein, the data must be monitored at will. The overhead of monitoring data cannot be so high and the complexity of monitoring data so great as to inhibit a monitoring program from being run whenever necessary. Unlike the monitoring of transaction processing, where the transactions themselves are monitored, data warehouse activity monitoring determines what data has and has not been used.

Monitoring data warehouse data determines such factors as the following:

- If a reorganization needs to be done
- If an index is poorly structured
- If too much or not enough data is in overflow
- The statistical composition of the access of the data
- Available remaining space

If the technology that houses the data warehouse does not support easy and efficient monitoring of data in the warehouse, it is not appropriate.

Interfaces to Many Technologies

Another extremely important component of the data warehouse is the ability both to receive data from and to pass data to a wide variety of technologies. Data passes into the data warehouse from the operational environment and the ODS, and from the data warehouse into data marts, DSS applications, exploration and data mining warehouses, and alternate storage. This passage must be smooth and easy. The technology supporting the data warehouse is practically worthless if there are major constraints for data passing to and from the data warehouse.

In addition to being efficient and easy to use, the interface to and from the data warehouse must be able to operate in a batch mode. Operating in an online mode is interesting, but not terribly useful. Usually, a period of dormancy exists from the moment that the data arrives in the operational environment until the data is ready to be passed to the data warehouse. Because of this latency, online passage of data into the data warehouse is almost nonexistent (as opposed to online movement of data into a class I ODS).

The interface to different technologies requires several considerations:

- Does the data pass from one DBMS to another easily?
- Does it pass from one operating system to another easily?
- Does it change its basic format in passage (EBCDIC, ASCII, and so forth)?
- Can passage into multidimensional processing be done easily?
- Can selected increments of data, such as changed data capture (CDC) be passed rather than entire tables?
- Is the context of data lost in translation as data is moved to other environments?

Programmer or Designer Control of Data Placement

Because of efficiency of access and update, the programmer or designer must have specific control over the placement of data at the physical block or page level, as shown in Figure 5-2.

The technology that houses the data in the data warehouse can place the data where it thinks is appropriate, as long as the technology can be explicitly overridden when needed. Technology that insists on the physical placement of data with no overrides from the programmer is a serious mistake.

The programmer or designer often can arrange for the physical placement of data to coincide with its usage. In doing so, many economies of resource utilization can be gained in the access of data.

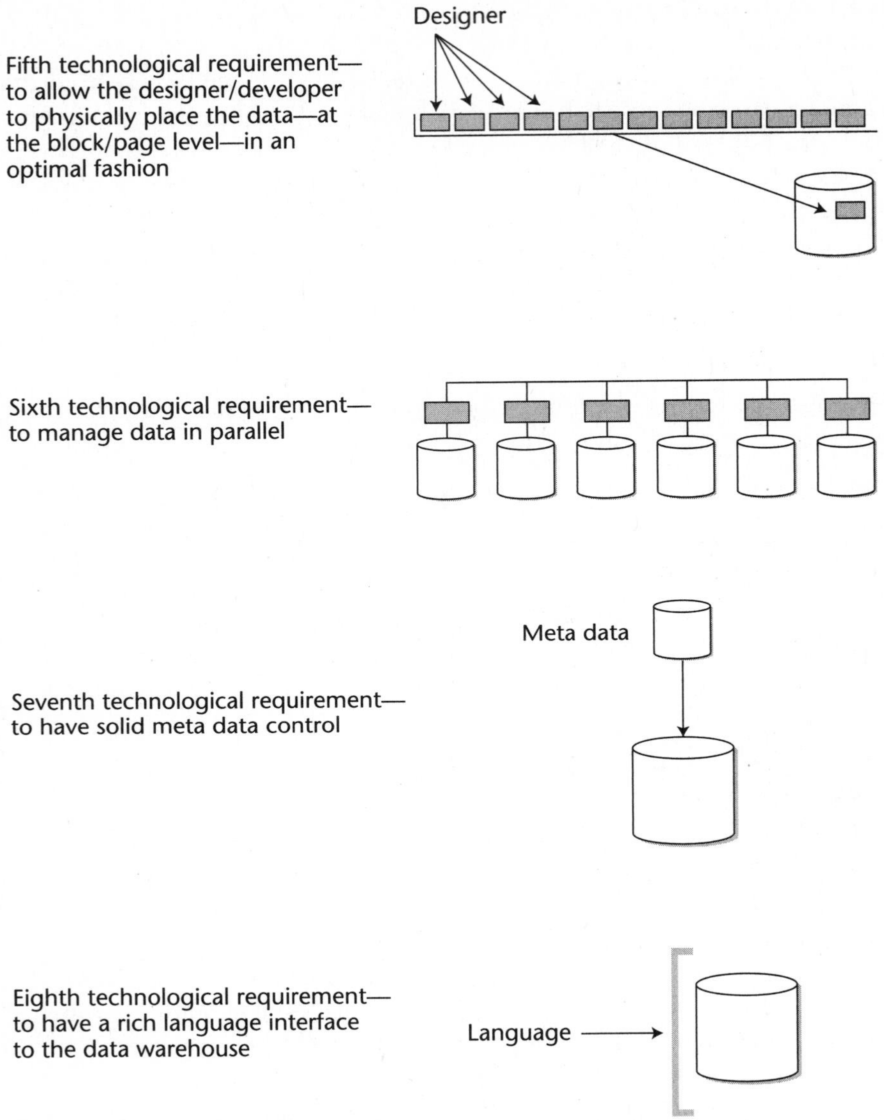

Fifth technological requirement—
to allow the designer/developer
to physically place the data—at
the block/page level—in an
optimal fashion

Designer

Sixth technological requirement—
to manage data in parallel

Meta data

Seventh technological requirement—
to have solid meta data control

Eighth technological requirement—
to have a rich language interface
to the data warehouse

Language

Figure 5-2   More technological requirements for the data warehouse.

Parallel Storage and Management of Data

One of the most powerful features of data warehouse data management is parallel storage and management. When data is stored and managed in a parallel fashion, the gains in performance can be dramatic. Furthermore, with a parallel approach, the volumes of data that can be managed grow significantly. As a rule, the performance boost is inversely proportional to the number of physical devices over which the data is physically distributed, assuming there is an even probability of access for the data.

The entire issue of parallel storage and management of data is a complex one. In general, when data management can be parallelized, there is no limit to the volume of data that can be managed. Instead, the limit of data that can be managed is an economic limit, not a technical limit.

Metadata Management

As mentioned in Chapter 3, for a variety of reasons, metadata becomes even more important in the data warehouse than in the classical operational environment. Metadata is vital because of the fundamental difference in the development life cycle that is associated with the data warehouse. The data warehouse operates under a heuristic, iterative development life cycle. To be effective, the user of the data warehouse must have access to metadata that is accurate and up-to-date. Without a good source of metadata to operate from, the job of the DSS analyst is much more difficult. Typically, the technical metadata that describes the data warehouse contains the following:

- Data warehouse table structures
- Data warehouse table attribution
- Data warehouse source data (the system of record)
- Mapping from the system of record to the data warehouse
- Data model specification
- Extract logging
- Common routines for access of data
- Definitions and/or descriptions of data
- Relationships of one unit of data to another

It is noteworthy that metadata comes in different varieties. One set of flavors that metadata comes in is that of business metadata versus technical metadata. *Business metadata* is that metadata that is of use and value to the business person. *Technical metadata* is that metadata that is of use and value to the technician.

Another consideration of metadata is that every technology in the business intelligence environment has its own metadata. Report writers, business intelligence tools, ODS environments, and ETL all have their own metadata.

Language Interface

The data warehouse must have a rich language specification. The languages used by the programmer and the DSS end user to access data inside the data warehouse should be easy to use and robust. Without a robust language interface, entering and accessing data in the warehouse become difficult. In addition, the language used to access data inside the data warehouse needs to operate efficiently.

Typically, the language interface to the data warehouse should do the following:

- Be able to access data a set at a time
- Be able to access data a record at a time
- Specifically ensure that one or more indexes will be used in the satisfaction of a query
- Have an SQL interface
- Be able to insert, delete, or update data

There are, in fact, many different kinds of languages depending on the processing being performed. These include languages for statistical analysis of data, where data mining and exploration are done; languages for the simple access of data; languages that handle prefabricated queries; and languages that optimize on the graphic nature of the interface. Each of these languages has its own strengths and weaknesses.

Because of the complexity of SQL, it is highly desirable to have a language interface that creates and manages the query in SQL so that the end user doesn't have to actually know or use SQL. In other words, a language interface that does not appear to be SQL based is highly preferable for organizations with "normal" end users.

In most organizations, only very technical people write direct SQL queries. All other people, including end users, need to have a language interface that is much simpler than SQL.

Efficient Loading of Data

An important technological capability of the data warehouse is the ability to load the data warehouse efficiently, as shown in Figure 5-3. The need for an efficient load capability is important everywhere, but even more so in a large warehouse.

Ninth technological requirement—
to be able to load the warehouse
efficiently

Tenth technological requirement—
to use indexes efficiently

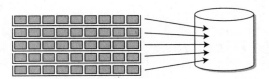

Eleventh technological requirement—
to be able to store data in a
compact way

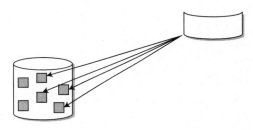

Twelfth technological requirement—
to support compound keys

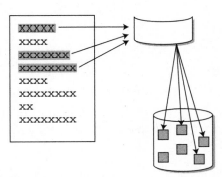

Figure 5-3   Further technological requirements.

Data is loaded into a data warehouse in two fundamental ways: a record at a time through a language interface or en masse with a utility. As a rule, loading data by means of a utility is much faster. In addition, indexes must be efficiently loaded at the same time the data is loaded. In some cases, the loading of the indexes may be deferred in order to spread the workload evenly.

As the burden of the volume of loading becomes an issue, the load is often parallelized. When this happens, the data being loaded is divided into one of several job streams. Once the input data is divided, each job stream is executed independently of the other job streams. In doing so, the elapsed time needed for loading is reduced by the number of job streams (roughly speaking).

Another related approach to the efficient loading of very large amounts of data is staging the data prior to loading. As a rule, large amounts of data are gathered into a buffer area before being processed by extract/transfer/load (ETL) software. The staged data is merged (perhaps edited, summarized, and so forth) before it passes into the ETL layer. Staging of data is needed where the amount of data is large and the complexity of processing is high. The other case for a staging area is that of needing to coordinate the merging of data. Suppose data from source ABC is ready for entry into the data warehouse at 9:00 am. But data from source BCD must be merged with ABC. However, data from source BCD is not ready until 6:00 p.m. Data from ABC then waits in the staging area until data from BCD is ready for processing.

Efficient Index Utilization

Not only must the technology underlying the data warehouse be able to easily support the creation and loading of new indexes, but those indexes must be able to be accessed efficiently. Technology can support efficient index access in several ways:

- Using bit maps
- Having multileveled indexes
- Storing all or parts of an index in main memory
- Compacting the index entries when the order of the data being indexed allows such compaction
- Creating selective indexes and range indexes

In addition to the efficient storage and scanning of the index, the subsequent access of data at the primary storage level is important. Unfortunately, there are not nearly as many options for optimizing the access of primary data as there are for the access of index data.

Compaction of Data

The very essence of success in the data warehouse environment is the ability to manage large amounts of data. Central to this goal is the ability to compact data. Of course, when data is compacted, it can be stored in a minimal amount of space. In addition, when data can be stored in a small space, the access of the data is very efficient. Compaction of data is especially relevant to the data warehouse environment because data in the warehouse environment is seldom updated once inserted in the warehouse. The stability of warehouse data minimizes the problems of space management that arise when tightly compacted data is being updated.

Another advantage is that the programmer gets the most out of a given I/O when data is stored compactly. Of course, there is always the corresponding issue of decompaction of data on access. While it is true that the process of decompaction requires overhead, the overhead is measured in CPU resources, not I/O resources. As a rule, in the data warehouse environment, I/O resources are much scarcer than CPU resources, so decompaction of data is not a major issue.

Compound Keys

A simple (but important) technological requirement of the data warehouse environment is the ability to support compound keys. Compound keys occur everywhere in the data warehouse environment, primarily because of the time variancy of data warehouse data and because key-foreign key relationships are quite common in the atomic data that makes up the data warehouse.

Variable-Length Data

Another simple but vital technological requirement of the data warehouse environment is the ability to manage variable-length data efficiently, as seen in Figure 5-4. Variable-length data can cause tremendous performance problems when it is constantly being updated and changed. Where variable-length data is stable, as in the case of a data warehouse, there is no inherent performance problem.

In addition, because of the variety of data found in the data warehouse, variable-length structuring of data must be supported.

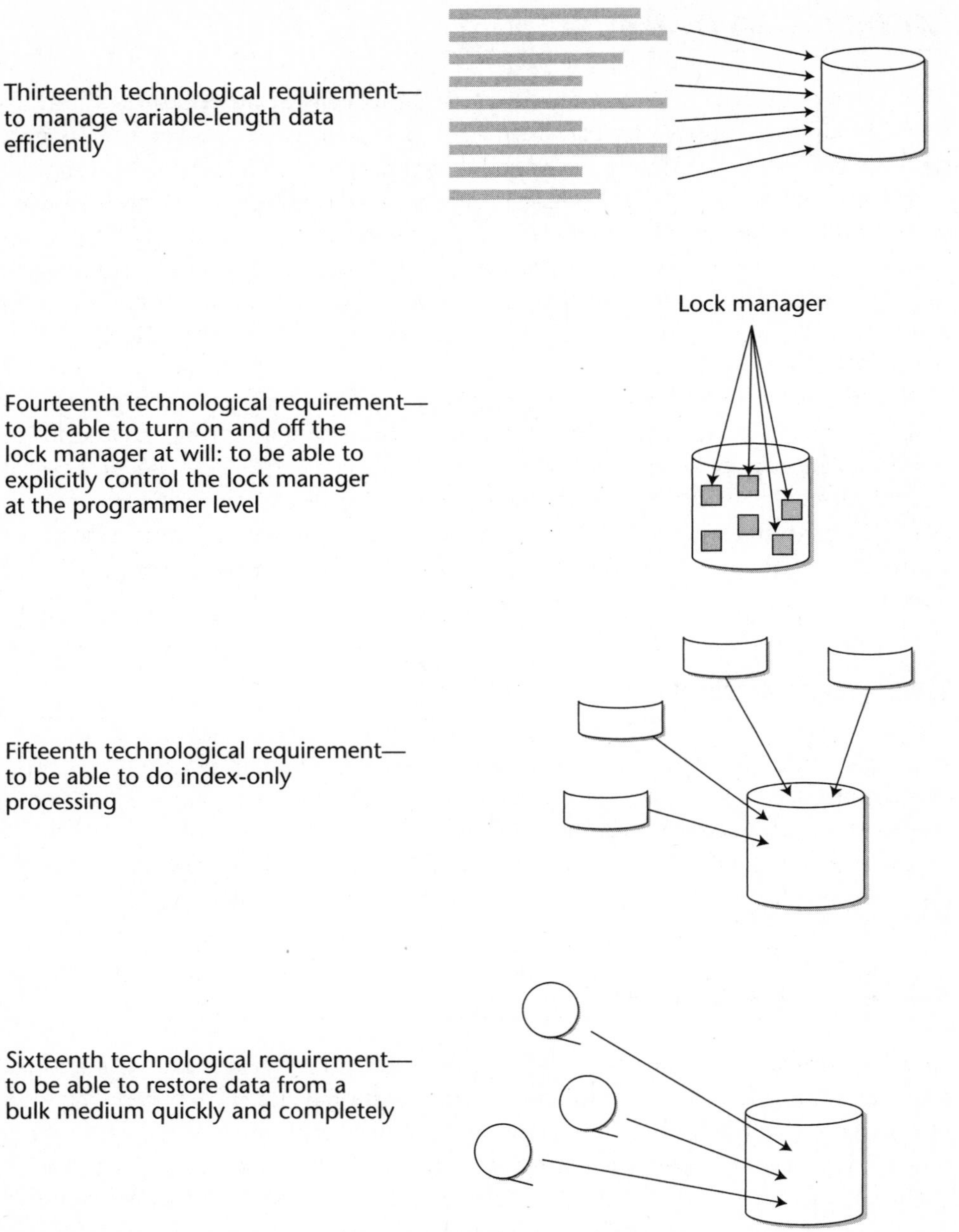

Thirteenth technological requirement—
to manage variable-length data
efficiently

Lock manager

Fourteenth technological requirement—
to be able to turn on and off the
lock manager at will: to be able to
explicitly control the lock manager
at the programmer level

Fifteenth technological requirement—
to be able to do index-only
processing

Sixteenth technological requirement—
to be able to restore data from a
bulk medium quickly and completely

Figure 5-4   Still more technological requirements for the data warehouse.

Lock Management

A standard part of database technology is the *lock manager*, which ensures that two or more people are not updating the same record at the same time. But an update is not done in the data warehouse; instead, data is stored in a series of snapshot records. When a change occurs, a new snapshot record is added, rather than an update being done.

One of the effects of the lock manager is that it consumes a fair amount of resources, even when data is not being updated. Merely turning the lock manager on requires overhead. Therefore, to streamline the data warehouse environment, being able to selectively turn the lock manager off and on is necessary.

Index-Only Processing

A fairly standard database management system feature is the ability to do index-only processing. On many occasions, it is possible to service a request by simply looking in an index (or indexes) — without going to the primary source of data. This is, of course, much more efficient. Not all DBMSs, though, are intelligent enough to know that a request can be satisfied in the index.

Technology that is optimal for the data warehouse environment looks for data in the indexes exclusively if such a request can be formulated and/or allow the query user to specify that such an index query has been specified. The DBMS technology must offer the DSS end user the option of specifying that if an index query can be executed, the query be satisfied in that manner.

Fast Restore

A simple (but important) technological feature of the data warehouse environment is the capability to quickly restore a data warehouse table from non-DASD storage. When a restore can be done from secondary storage, enormous savings may be possible. Without the ability to restore data quickly from secondary storage, the standard practice is to double the amount of DASD and use one-half of the DASD as a recovery and restore repository.

The quick-restore capability must be able to restore both full databases and partial databases. The size of the data found in the data warehouse mandates that only partial databases be able to be recovered.

In addition, the DBMS needs to sense that an error has occurred in as automated a manner as possible. Leaving the detection of data corruption to the end user is a very crude way to process. Another useful technology is the ability to create diagnostic tools to determine exactly what data has been corrupted. The diagnostic tool must operate within huge amounts of data.

Other Technological Features

The features discussed here are only the most important. Many others support data warehousing, but they are too numerous to mention here.

It is noteworthy that many other features of DBMS technology found in the classical transaction processing DBMS play only a small role (if they play a role at all) in the support of the data warehouse environment. Some of those features include the following:

- Transaction integrity
- High-speed buffering
- Row- or page-level locking
- Referential integrity
- VIEWs of data
- Partial block loading

Indeed, whenever a transaction-based DBMS is used in the data warehouse environment, it is desirable to turn off such features, because they interfere with the efficient processing of data inside the data warehouse.

DBMS Types and the Data Warehouse

With the advent of data warehousing and the recognition of DSS as an integral part of the modern information systems infrastructure, a new class of DBMS has arisen. This class can be called a *data warehouse-specific DBMS*. The data warehouse-specific DBMS is optimized for data warehousing and DSS processing.

Prior to data warehousing was transaction processing, and DBMSs supported the needs of this processing type. Processing in the data warehouse, though, is quite different. Data warehouse processing can be characterized as *load-and-access processing*. Data is integrated, transformed, and loaded into the data warehouse from the operational legacy environment and the ODS. Once in the data warehouse, the integrated data is accessed and analyzed there. An update is not normally done in the data warehouse once the data is loaded. If corrections or adjustments need to be made to the data warehouse, they are made at off hours, when no analysis is occurring against the data warehouse data. In addition, such changes are often made by including a more current snapshot of data.

Another important difference between classical transaction processing database environments and the data warehouse environment is that the data warehouse environment tends to hold much more data, measured in terabytes and petabytes, than classical transaction processing databases under a general-purpose DBMSs. Data warehouses manage massive amounts of data because they contain the following:

- Granular, atomic detail
- Historical information
- Summary as well as detailed data

In terms of basic data management capability, data warehouses are optimized around a very different set of parameters than standard operational DBMSs.

The first and most important difference between a classical, general-purpose DBMS and a data warehouse-specific DBMS is how updates are performed. A classical, general-purpose DBMS must be able to accommodate record-level, transaction-based updates as a normal part of operations. Because record-level, transaction-based updates are a regular feature of the general-purpose DBMS, the general-purpose DBMS must offer facilities for such items as the following:

- Locking
- COMMITs
- Checkpoints
- Log tape processing
- Deadlock
- Backout

Not only do these features become a normal part of the DBMS, they consume a tremendous amount of overhead. Interestingly, the overhead is consumed even when it isn't being used. In other words, at least some update and locking overhead — depending on the DBMS — is required by a general-purpose DBMS even when read-only processing is being executed. Depending on the general-purpose DBMS, the overhead required by update can be minimized, but it cannot be completely eliminated. For a data warehouse-specific DBMS, there is no need for any of the overhead of update.

A second major difference between a general-purpose DBMS and a data warehouse-specific DBMS regards basic data management. For a general-purpose DBMS, data management at the block level includes space that is reserved for future block expansion at the moment of update or insertion. Typically, this space is referred to as *freespace*. For a general-purpose DBMS, freespace may be as high as 50 percent. For a data warehouse-specific DBMS, freespace always equals 0 percent because there is no need for expansion in the physical block, once loaded; after all, update is not done in the data warehouse environment. Indeed, given the amount of data to be managed in a data warehouse, it makes no sense to reserve vast amounts of space that may never be used.

Another relevant difference between the data warehouse and the general-purpose environment that is reflected in the different types of DBMS is indexing. A general-purpose DBMS environment is restricted to a finite number of indexes. This restriction exists because as updates and insertions occur, the indexes themselves require their own space and their own data management. In a data warehouse environment where there is no update and there is a need to optimize access of data, there is a need (and an opportunity) for many indexes. Indeed, a much more robust and sophisticated indexing structure can be employed for data warehousing than for operational, update-oriented databases.

Beyond indexing, update, and basic data management at the physical block level, there are some other very basic differences between the data management capabilities and philosophies of general-purpose transaction processing DBMSs and data warehouse-specific DBMSs. Perhaps the most basic difference is the ability to physically organize data in an optimal fashion for different kinds of access. A general-purpose DBMS typically physically organizes data for optimal transaction access and manipulation. Organizing in this fashion allows many different types of data to be gathered according to a common key and efficiently accessed in one or two I/Os. Data that is optimal for informational access usually has a very different physical profile. Data that is optimal for informational access is organized so that many different occurrences of the same type of data can be accessed efficiently in one or two physical I/Os.

Data can be physically optimized for transaction access or DSS access, but not both at the same time. A general-purpose, transaction-based DBMS allows data to be optimized for transaction access, and a data warehouse-specific DBMS allows data to be physically optimized for DSS access and analysis.

Changing DBMS Technology

An interesting consideration of the information warehouse is changing the DBMS technology after the warehouse has already been populated. Such a change may be in order for several reasons:

- DBMS technologies may be available today that simply were not an option when the data warehouse was first populated.

- The size of the warehouse has grown to the point that a new technological approach is mandated.

- Use of the warehouse has escalated and changed to the point that the current warehouse DBMS technology is not adequate.
- The basic DBMS decision must be revisited from time to time.

Should the decision be made to go to a new DBMS technology, what are the considerations? A few of the more important ones follow:

- Will the new DBMS technology meet the foreseeable requirements?
- How will the conversion from the older DBMS technology to the newer DBMS technology be done?
- How will the transformation programs be converted?

Of all of these considerations, the last is the most vexing. Trying to change the transformation programs is a complex task in the best of circumstances.

The fact remains that once a DBMS has been implemented for a data warehouse, change at a later point in time is a possibility. Such was never the case in the world of transaction processing; once a DBMS had been implemented, that DBMS stayed as long as the transactions were being run.

Multidimensional DBMS and the Data Warehouse

One of the technologies often discussed in the context of the data warehouse is *multidimensional DBMS processing* (sometimes called *OLAP processing*). Multidimensional database management systems, or data marts, provide an information system with the structure that allows an organization to have very flexible access to data, to slice and dice data any number of ways, and to dynamically explore the relationship between summary and detail data. Multidimensional DBMSs offer both flexibility and control to the end user, and as such they fit well in a DSS environment. A very interesting and complementary relationship exists between multidimensional DBMSs and the data warehouse, as shown in Figure 5-5.

The detailed data housed in a data warehouse provides a very robust and convenient source of data for the multidimensional DBMS. Data flows from the data warehouse into the multidimensional DBMS on a regular basis as the multidimensional DBMS needs to be periodically refreshed. Because legacy application data is integrated as it enters the data warehouse, the multidimensional DBMS does not need to extract and integrate the data it operates on from the operational environment. In addition, the data warehouse houses data at its lowest level, providing "bedrock" data for the lowest level of analysis that anyone using the multidimensional DBMS would ever want.

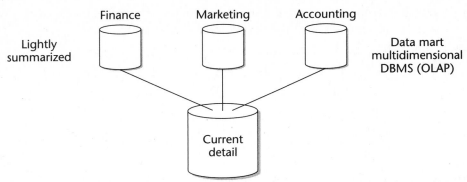

Figure 5-5   The classical structure of the data warehouse and how current detail data and departmental data (or multidimensional DBMS, data mart) data fit together.

Though tempting to think that multidimensional DBMS technology should be the database technology for the data warehouse, in all but the most unusual cases, this is a mistake. The properties that make multidimensional DBMS technology optimal for what it does are not the properties of primary importance for the data warehouse, and the properties that are the most important in the data warehouse are not those found in multidimensional DBMS technology.

Consider the differences between the multidimensional DBMS and the data warehouse:

- The data warehouse holds massive amounts of data; the multidimensional DBMS holds at least an order of magnitude less data.

- The data warehouse is geared for a limited amount of flexible access; the multidimensional DBMS is geared for very heavy and unpredictable access and analysis of data.

- The data warehouse contains data with a very lengthy time horizon (from 5 to 10 years); the multidimensional DBMS holds a much shorter time horizon of data.

- The data warehouse allows analysts to access its data in a constrained fashion; the multidimensional DBMS allows unfettered access.

- Instead of the data warehouse being housed in a multidimensional DBMS, the multidimensional DBMS and the data warehouse enjoy a complementary relationship.

One of the interesting features of the relationship between the data warehouse and the multidimensional DBMS is that the data warehouse can provide a basis for very detailed data that is normally not found in the multidimensional DBMS. The data warehouse can contain a very fine degree of detail, which is lightly summarized as it is passed up to the multidimensional DBMS.

Once in the multidimensional DBMS, the data can be further summarized. In such a fashion, the multidimensional DBMS can house all but the most detailed level of data. The analyst using the multidimensional DBMS can drill down in a flexible and efficient manner over all the different levels of data found in it. Then, if needed, the analyst can actually drill down to the data warehouse. By marrying the data warehouse and the multidimensional DBMS in such a manner, the DSS analyst gets the best of both worlds. The DSS analyst enjoys the efficiency of operating most of the time in the world of the multidimensional DBMS, while at the same time being able to drill down to the lowest level of detail.

Another advantage is that summary information may be calculated and collected in the multidimensional DBMS and then stored in the data warehouse. When this is done, the summary data can be stored in the data warehouse for a much longer time than if it were stored in the multidimensional DBMS.

There is still another way that the multidimensional DBMS and data warehouse worlds are complementary. The multidimensional DBMS houses data over a modest length of time — say 12 to 15 months, depending on the application. The data warehouse houses data over a much longer time — 5 to 10 years. In such a manner, the data warehouse becomes a source of research for multidimensional DBMS analysts. Multidimensional DBMS analysts have the luxury of knowing that huge amounts of data are available if needed, but they do not have to pay the price of storing all that data in their environment.

Multidimensional DBMSs come in several flavors. Some multidimensional DBMSs operate on a foundation of relational technology, and some operate on a technological foundation optimal for "slicing and dicing" the data, where data can be thought of as existing in multidimensional cubes. The latter technological foundation is sometimes called a *cube* or *OLAP foundation*.

Both foundations can support multidimensional DBMS data marts. But there are some differences between the two types of technological foundations.

Following is the relational foundation for multidimensional DBMS data marts:

- Strengths:
    - Can support a lot of data.
    - Can support dynamic joining of data.
    - Has proven technology.
    - Is capable of supporting general-purpose update processing.
    - If there is no known pattern of usage of data, then the relational structure is as good as any other.
- Weaknesses:
    - Has performance that is less than optimal.
    - Cannot be purely optimized for access processing.

Following is the cube foundation for multidimensional DBMS data marts:

- Strengths:
    - Performance that is optimal for DSS processing.
    - Can be optimized for very fast access of data.
    - If pattern of access of data is known, then the structure of data can be optimized.
    - Can easily be sliced and diced.
    - Can be examined in many ways.
- Weaknesses:
    - Cannot handle nearly as much data as a standard relational format.
    - Does not support general-purpose update processing.
    - May take a long time to load.
    - If access is desired on a path not supported by the design of the data, the structure is not flexible.
    - Questionable support for dynamic joins of data.

Multidimensional DBMS (OLAP) is a technology, while the data warehouse is an architectural infrastructure, and a symbiotic relationship exists between the two. In the normal case, the data warehouse serves as a foundation for the data that will flow into the multidimensional DBMS — feeding selected subsets of the detailed data into the multidimensional DBMS where it is summarized and otherwise aggregated. But in some circles, there is the notion that multidimensional DBMSs do not need a data warehouse for their foundation of data.

Without a data warehouse serving as the foundation for the multidimensional DBMS, the data flowing into the multidimensional DBMS comes directly from the older, legacy applications environment. Figure 5-6 shows the flow of data from the legacy environment directly to the multidimensional DBMS. The design is appealing because it is straightforward and easily achieved. A programmer can immediately start to work on building it.

Legacy application

Finance

Multidimensional
DBMS data mart

Figure 5-6 Building the multidimensional DBMS data mart from an application with no current detail.

Unfortunately, some major pitfalls in the architecture, as suggested by Figure 5-6, are not immediately apparent. For a variety of reasons, it makes sense to feed the multidimensional DBMS environment from the current level of detail of the data warehouse, rather than feeding it directly from the legacy applications operational environment.

Figure 5-7 illustrates the feeding of the multidimensional DBMS environment from the current level of detail of the data warehouse environment. Old, legacy operational data is integrated and transformed as it flows into the data warehouse.

Once in the data warehouse, the integrated data is stored in the current level of detailed data. From this level, the multidimensional DBMS is fed.

At first glance, there may not appear to be substantive differences between the architectures shown in Figure 5-6 and Figure 5-7. In fact, putting data first into a data warehouse may even appear to be a wasted effort. However, there is a very good reason why integrating data into the data warehouse is the first step in creating the multidimensional DBMS.

Consider that, under normal conditions, a corporation will want to build multiple multidimensional DBMSs. Finance will want its multidimensional DBMS, as will accounting. Marketing, sales, and other departments will want their own multidimensional DBMSs. Because multiple multidimensional DBMSs will be in the corporation, the scenario previously shown in Figure 5-6 becomes much more complex. In Figure 5-8, this scenario has been expanded into a realistic scenario where there are multiple multidimensional DBMSs being directly and individually fed from the legacy systems environment.

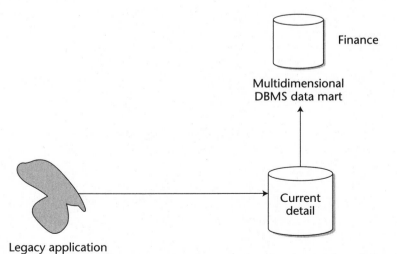

Finance

Multidimensional
DBMS data mart

Current
detail

Legacy application

Figure 5-7   The flow of data from the application environment to the current level of detail to the multidimensional DBMS data mart.

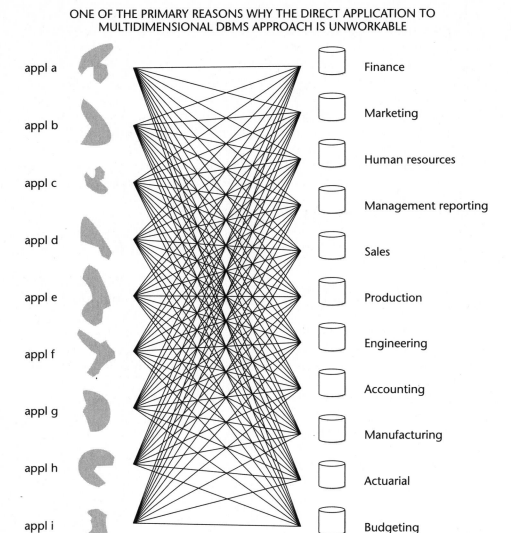

ONE OF THE PRIMARY REASONS WHY THE DIRECT APPLICATION TO
MULTIDIMENSIONAL DBMS APPROACH IS UNWORKABLE

appl a

appl b

appl c

appl d

appl e

appl f

appl g

appl h

appl i

Finance

Marketing

Human resources

Management reporting

Sales

Production

Engineering

Accounting

Manufacturing

Actuarial

Budgeting

Figure 5-8   There are many applications, and there are many data marts. An interface application is needed between each occurrence. The result of bypassing the current level of detail is an unmanageable "spider web."

Figure 5-8 shows that multiple multidimensional DBMSs are being fed directly from the same legacy applications. So, what is so wrong with this architecture? The problems are as follows:

- The amount of development required in extraction is enormous. Each different departmental multidimensional DBMS must have its own set of extraction programs developed for it on a customized basis. There is a tremendous overlap of extract processing. The amount of wasted development work is enormous. When the multidimensional DBMSs are fed from the data warehouse, only one set of integration and transformation programs is needed.

- There is no integrated foundation when the multidimensional DBMSs are fed directly from the legacy systems environment. Each departmental, multidimensional DBMS has its own interpretation as to how different applications should be integrated. Unfortunately, the way one department integrates data is most likely not the way another department integrates the same data. The result is that there is no single integrated, definitive source of data. Conversely, when the data warehouse is built, there is a single, definitive, integrated source of data that can be built upon.

- The amount of development work required for maintenance is enormous. A single change in an old legacy application ripples through many extraction programs. The change must be accommodated wherever there is an extraction program, and there are many. With a data warehouse, the effect of change is minimized because a minimal number of programs must be written to manage the interface between the legacy environment and the data warehouse.

- The amount of hardware resources consumed is great. The same legacy data is sequentially and repeatedly passed for each extraction process for each department. In the case of the data warehouse, the legacy data is passed only once to refresh the data in the data warehouse.

- The complexity of moving data directly from the legacy environment to the multidimensional DBMS environment precludes effective metadata management and control. With the data warehouse, capturing and managing metadata are both straightforward.

- The lack of reconcilability of data is an issue. When a difference in opinion exists among various departments, each having its own multidimensional DBMS, there is no easy resolution. With a data warehouse, resolution of conflicts is natural and easy.

- Each time a new multidimensional DBMS environment must be built, it must be built from the legacy environment, and the amount of work required is considerable. When a foundation of data is in a data warehouse, however, building a new multidimensional DBMS environment is quick and easy.

When an organization takes a short-term approach, justifying the data warehouse is hard to do. The long-term cost of building many multidimensional database environments is very high. When an organization takes a long-term view and builds a data warehouse, the long-term total cost of data warehousing and data marts drops significantly.

Data Warehousing across Multiple Storage Media

One interesting aspect of a data warehouse is the dual environments often created when a large amount of data is spread across more than one storage medium. One processing environment is the DASD environment where online, interactive processing is done. The other processing environment is often a tape or mass store environment, which has essentially different features. Logically, the two environments combine to form a single data warehouse. Physically, however, the two environments are very different. In many cases, the underlying technology that supports the DASD environment is not the same technology that supports the mass store environment. Mixing technologies in the data warehouse environment is normal and natural when done this way.

However, there is another way that technology can be split that is not normal or natural. It is conceivable that the data warehouse environment — the DASD portion — is split over more than one technology. In other words, part of the DASD-based data warehouse resides on one vendor's technology and another part of the data warehouse resides on another vendor's database technology. If the split is deliberate and part of a larger distributed data warehouse, such a split is just fine. But if the split occurs for political or historical reasons, splitting part of a data warehouse onto different vendor platforms is not advisable.

The Role of Metadata in the Data Warehouse Environment

The role of metadata in the data warehouse environment is very different from the role of metadata in the operational environment. In the operational environment, metadata is treated almost as an afterthought and is relegated to the same level of importance as documentation. Metadata in the data warehouse environment takes on an enhanced role.

The importance of its role in the data warehouse environment is illustrated in Figure 5-9. Two different communities are served by operational metadata and data warehouse metadata. Operational metadata is used by the IT professional. For years, the IT professional has used metadata casually. The IT professional is computer-literate and is able to find his or her way around systems. The data warehouse, though, serves the DSS analyst community, and the DSS analyst is usually a professional, first and foremost. There usually is not a high degree of computer literacy in the DSS analyst community. The DSS analyst needs as much help as possible to use the data warehouse environment effectively, and metadata serves this end quite well. In addition, metadata is the first thing the DSS analyst looks at in planning how to perform informational, analytical processing. Because of the difference in the communities served and because of the role that metadata plays in the day-to-day job function, metadata is much more important in the data warehouse environment than it ever was in the operational environment.

There are other reasons why data warehouse metadata is important. One such reason concerns managing the mapping between the operational environment and the data warehouse environment. Figure 5-10 illustrates this point.

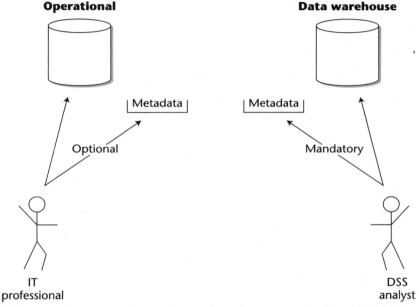

Figure 5-9 The IT professional uses metadata on a casual basis; the DSS analyst uses metadata regularly and as the first step of an analysis.

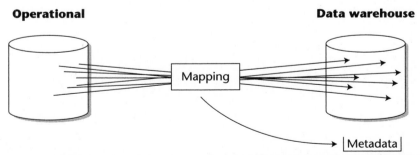

Figure 5-10 The mapping between the operational environment and the data warehouse environment is another major reason for the need for metadata; without the mapping, controlling the interface is extremely difficult.

Data undergoes a significant transformation as it passes from the operational environment to the data warehouse environment. Conversion, filtering, summarization, and structural changes all occur. There is a need to keep careful track of the transformation, and the metadata in the data warehouse is the ideal place to do so. The importance of keeping a careful record of the transformation is highlighted by the events that occur when a manager needs to trace data from the data warehouse back to its operational source (the ultimate in the drill-down process). In this case, the record of the transformation describes exactly how to get from the data warehouse to the operational source of data.

Yet another important reason for the careful management of metadata in the data warehouse environment is shown in Figure 5-11. As mentioned, data in a data warehouse exists for a lengthy time span — from 5 to 10 years. Over a 5-to-10-year time span, it is absolutely normal for a data warehouse to change its structure. Keeping track of the changing structure of data over time is a natural task for the metadata in the data warehouse.

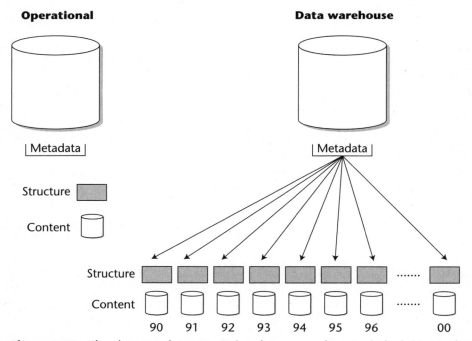

Figure 5-11 The data warehouse contains data over a long period of time and must manage multiple structures or definitions of data. The operational environment assumes that there is only a single correct definition of data at any one time.

Contrast the notion that there will be many structures of data over time in the data warehouse environment with the metadata found in the operational environment. In the operational environment, it is assumed that at any one moment, there is one and only one correct definition of the structure of data.

Context and Content

In the past, classical operational information systems have focused their attention on the very current data of a corporation. In the operational world, the emphasis is on how much an account balance is right now, how much is in inventory right now, or what the status of a shipment is right now. Of course, every organization needs to know about current information. But there is real value in looking at information over time, as is possible with data warehousing. For example, trends become apparent that simply are not observable when looking at current information. One of the most important defining characteristics of the data warehouse is this ability to store, manage, and access data over time.

With the lengthy spectrum of time that is part of a data warehouse comes a new dimension of *data-context*. To explain the importance of contextual information, an example is in order.

Suppose a manager asks for a report from the data warehouse for 1995. The report is generated, and the manager is pleased. In fact, the manager is so pleased that a similar report for 1990 is requested. Because the data warehouse carries historical information, such a request is not hard to accommodate. The report for 1990 is generated. Now the manager holds the two reports — one for 1995 and one for 1990 — in his hands and declares that the reports are a disaster.

The data warehouse architect examines the reports and sees that the financial statement for 1995 shows $50 million in revenue, while the report for 1990 shows a value of $10,000 for the same category. The manager declares that there is no way that any account or category could have increased in value that much in five years' time.

Before giving up, the data warehouse architect points out to the manager that there are other relevant factors that do not show up in the report. In 1990, there was a different source of data than in 1995. In 1990, the definition of a product was not the same as in 1995. In 1990, there were different marketing territories than in 1995. In 1990, there were different calculations, such as for depreciation, than in 1995. In addition, there were many different external considerations, such as a difference in inflation, taxation, economic forecasts, and so forth. Once the context of the reports is explained to the manager, the contents now appear to be quite acceptable.

In this simple but common example where the contents of data stand naked over time, the contents by themselves are quite inexplicable and unbelievable. When context is added to the contents of data over time, the contents and the context become quite enlightening.

To interpret and understand information over time, a whole new dimension of context is required. While content of information remains important, the comparison and understanding of information over time mandates that context be an equal partner to content. And in years past, context has been an undiscovered, unexplored dimension of information.

Three Types of Contextual Information

Three levels of contextual information must be managed:

- Simple contextual information
- Complex contextual information
- External contextual information

Simple contextual information relates to the basic structure of data itself, and includes such things as these:

- The structure of data
- The encoding of data
- The naming conventions used for data
- The metrics describing the data, such as:
  - How much data there is
  - How fast the data is growing
  - What sectors of the data are growing
  - How the data is being used

Simple contextual information has been managed in the past by dictionaries, directories, system monitors, and so forth. Complex contextual information describes the same data as simple contextual information, but from a different perspective. This type of information addresses such aspects of data as these:

- Product definitions
- Marketing territories
- Pricing
- Packaging
- Organization structure
- Distribution

Complex contextual information is some of the most useful and, at the same time, some of the most elusive information there is to capture. It is elusive because it is taken for granted and is in the background. It is so basic that no one thinks to define what it is or how it changes over time. And yet, in the long run, complex contextual information plays an extremely important role in understanding and interpreting information over time.

External contextual information is information outside the corporation that nevertheless plays an important role in understanding information over time. Some examples of external contextual information include the following:

- Economic forecasts:
  - Inflation
  - Financial trends
  - Taxation
  - Economic growth
- Political information
- Competitive information
- Technological advancements
- Consumer demographic movements

External contextual information says nothing directly about a company, but says everything about the universe in which the company must work and compete. External contextual information is interesting both in terms of its immediate manifestation and its changes over time. As with complex contextual information, there are very few organized attempts to capture and measure this information. It is so large and so obvious that it is taken for granted, and it is quickly forgotten and difficult to reconstruct when needed.

Capturing and Managing Contextual Information

Complex and external contextual types of information are hard to capture and quantify because they are so unstructured. Compared to simple contextual information, external and complex contextual types of information are amorphous. Another mitigating factor is that contextual information changes quickly. What is relevant one minute is passé the next. It is this constant flux and the amorphous state of external and complex contextual information that makes these types of information so hard to systematize.

Looking at the Past

You could argue that the information systems profession has had contextual information in the past. Dictionaries, repositories, directories, and libraries are all attempts at the management of simple contextual information. For all the good intentions, there have been some notable limitations in these attempts that have greatly short-circuited their effectiveness. Some of these shortcomings are as follows:

- The information management attempts were aimed at the information systems developer, not the end user. As such, there was very little visibility to the end user. Consequently, the end user had little enthusiasm or support for something that was not apparent.

- Attempts at contextual management were passive. A developer could opt to use or not use the contextual information management facilities. Many chose to work around those facilities.

- Attempts at contextual information management were in many cases removed from the development effort. In case after case, application development was done in 1965, and the data dictionary was done in 1985. By 1985, there were no more development dollars. Furthermore, the people who could have helped the most in organizing and defining simple contextual information were long gone to other jobs or companies.

- Attempts to manage contextual information were limited to only simple contextual information. No attempt was made to capture or manage external or complex contextual information.

Refreshing the Data Warehouse

Once the data warehouse is built, attention shifts from the building of the data warehouse to its day-to-day operations. Inevitably, the discovery is made that the cost of operating and maintaining a data warehouse is high, and the volume of data in the warehouse is growing faster than anyone had predicted. The widespread and unpredictable usage of the data warehouse by the end-user DSS analyst causes contention on the server managing the warehouse. Yet the largest unexpected expense associated with the operation of the data warehouse is the periodic refreshment of legacy data. What starts out as an almost incidental expense quickly turns very significant.

The first step most organizations take in the refreshment of data warehouse data is to read the old legacy databases. For some kinds of processing and under certain circumstances, directly reading the older legacy files is the only way refreshment can be achieved, for example, when data must be read from different legacy sources to form a single unit that is to go into the data warehouse. In addition, when a transaction has caused the simultaneous update of multiple legacy files, a direct read of the legacy data may be the only way to refresh the warehouse.

As a general-purpose strategy, however, repeated and direct reads of the legacy data are very costly. The expense of direct legacy database reads mounts in two ways. First, the legacy DBMS must be online and active during the read process. The window of opportunity for lengthy sequential processing for the legacy environment is always limited. Stretching the window to refresh the data warehouse is never welcome. Second, the same legacy data is needlessly passed many times. The refreshment scan must process 100 percent of a legacy file when only 1 or 2 percent of the legacy file is actually needed. This gross waste of resources occurs each time the refreshment process is done. Because of these inefficiencies, repeatedly and directly reading the legacy data for refreshment is a strategy that has limited usefulness and applicability.

A much more appealing approach is to trap the data in the legacy environment as it is being updated. By trapping the data, full table scans of the legacy environment are unnecessary when the data warehouse must be refreshed. In addition, because the data can be trapped as it is being updated, there is no need to have the legacy DBMS online for a long sequential scan. Instead, the trapped data can be processed offline.

Two basic techniques are used to trap data as an update is occurring in the legacy operational environment. One technique is called *data replication*; the other is called *change data capture*, where the changes that have occurred are pulled out of log or journal tapes created during online update. Each approach has its pros and cons.

Replication requires that the data to be trapped be identified prior to the update. Then, as update occurs, the data is trapped. A trigger is set that causes the update activity to be captured. One of the advantages of replication is that the process of trapping can be selectively controlled. Only the data that needs to be captured is, in fact, captured. Another advantage of replication is that the format of the data is "clean" and well-defined. The content and structure of the data that has been trapped are well-documented and readily understandable to the programmer. The disadvantages of replication are that extra I/O is incurred as a result of trapping the data and, because of the unstable, ever-changing nature of the data warehouse, the system requires constant attention to the definition of the parameters and triggers that control trapping. The amount of I/O required is usually nontrivial. Furthermore, the I/O that is consumed is taken out of the middle of the high-performance day, at the time when the system can least afford it.

The second approach to efficient refreshment is changed data capture (CDC). One approach to CDC is to use the log tape to capture and identify the changes that have occurred throughout the online day. In this approach, the log or journal tape is read. Reading a log tape is no small matter, however. Many obstacles are in the way, including the following:

- The log tape contains much extraneous data.
- The log tape format is often arcane.
- The log tape contains spanned records.
- The log tape often contains addresses instead of data values.
- The log tape reflects the idiosyncrasies of the DBMS and varies widely from one DBMS to another.

The main obstacle in CDC, then, is that of reading and making sense out of the log tape. But once that obstacle is passed, there are some very attractive benefits to using the log for data warehouse refreshment. The first advantage is efficiency. Unlike replication processing, log tape processing requires no extra I/O. The log tape will be written regardless of whether it will be used for data warehouse refreshment. Therefore, no incremental I/O is necessary. The second advantage is that the log tape captures all update processing. There is no need to go back and redefine parameters when a change is made to the data warehouse or the legacy systems environment. The log tape is as basic and stable as you can get.

There is a second approach to CDC: lift the changed data out of the DBMS buffers as change occurs. In this approach, the change is reflected immediately. So, reading a log tape becomes unnecessary, and there is a time-savings from the moment a change occurs to when it is reflected in the warehouse. However, because more online resources are required (including system software sensitive to changes), there is a performance impact. Still, this direct buffer approach can handle large amounts of processing at a very high speed.

The progression described here mimics the mindset of organizations as they mature in their understanding and operation of the data warehouse. First, the organization reads legacy databases directly to refresh its data warehouse. Then it tries replication. Finally, the economics and the efficiencies of operation lead it to CDC as the primary means to refresh the data warehouse. Along the way, it is discovered that a few files require a direct read. Other files work best with replication. But for industrial-strength, full-bore, general-purpose data warehouse refreshment, CDC looms as the long-term final approach to data warehouse refreshment.

Testing

In the classical operational environment, two parallel environments are set up — one for production and one for testing. The *production environment* is where live processing occurs. The *testing environment* is where programmers test out new programs and changes to existing programs. The idea is that it is safer when programmers have a chance to see if the code they have created will work before it is allowed into the live online environment.

It is very unusual to find a similar test environment in the world of the data warehouse, for the following reasons:

- Data warehouses are so large that a corporation has a hard time justifying one of them, much less two of them.

- The nature of the development life cycle for the data warehouse is iterative. For the most part, programs are run in a heuristic manner, not in a repetitive manner. If a programmer gets something wrong in the data warehouse environment (and programmers do all the time), the environment is set up so that the programmer simply redoes it.

The data warehouse environment, then, is fundamentally different from the classical production environment because, under most circumstances, a test environment is simply not needed.

Summary

Some technological features are required for satisfactory data warehouse processing. These include a robust language interface, the support of compound keys and variable-length data, and the abilities to do the following:

- Manage large amounts of data
- Manage data on a diverse media
- Easily index and monitor data
- Interface with a wide number of technologies
- Allow the programmer to place the data directly on the physical device
- Store and access data in parallel
- Have metadata control of the warehouse
- Efficiently load the warehouse
- Efficiently use indexes
- Store data in a compact way
- Support compound keys
- Selectively turn off the lock manager
- Do index-only processing
- Quickly restore from bulk storage

Additionally, the data architect must recognize the differences between a transaction-based DBMS and a data warehouse-based DBMS. A transaction-based DBMS focuses on the efficient execution of transactions and update. A data warehouse-based DBMS focuses on efficient query processing and the handling of a load and access workload.

Multidimensional OLAP technology is suited for data mart processing and not data warehouse processing. When the data mart approach is used as a basis for data warehousing, many problems become evident:

- The number of extract programs grows large.

- Each new multidimensional database must return to the legacy operational environment for its own data.

- There is no basis for reconciliation of differences in analysis.

- A tremendous amount of redundant data among different multidimensional DBMS environments exists.

Finally, metadata in the data warehouse environment plays a very different role than metadata in the operational legacy environment.

CHAPTER 6

The Distributed Data Warehouse

Most organizations build and maintain a single centralized data warehouse environment. This setup makes sense for many reasons:

- The data in the warehouse is integrated across the corporation, and an integrated view is used only at headquarters.

- The corporation operates on a centralized business model.

- The volume of data in the data warehouse is such that a single centralized repository of data makes sense.

- Even if data could be integrated, if it were dispersed across multiple local sites, it would be cumbersome to access.

In short, the politics, the economics, and the technology greatly favor a single centralized data warehouse. Still, in a few cases, a distributed data warehouse makes sense, as you'll see in this chapter.

Types of Distributed Data Warehouses

The three types of distributed data warehouses are as follows:

- Business is distributed geographically or over multiple, differing product lines. In this case, there is what can be called a *local data warehouse* and a *global data warehouse*. The local data warehouse represents data and processing at a remote site, and the global data warehouse represents that part of the business that is integrated across the business.

■ The data warehouse environment will hold a lot of data, and the volume of data will be distributed over multiple processors. Logically there is a single data warehouse, but physically there are many data warehouses that are all tightly related but reside on separate processors. This configuration can be called the *technologically distributed data warehouse*.

■ The data warehouse environment grows up in an uncoordinated manner — first one data warehouse appears, then another. The lack of coordination of the growth of the different data warehouses is usually a result of political and organizational differences. This case can be called the *independently evolving distributed data warehouse*.

Each of these types of distributed data warehouse has its own concerns and considerations, which we will examine in the following sections.

Local and Global Data Warehouses

When a corporation is spread around the world, information is needed both locally and globally. The global needs for corporate information are met by a central data warehouse where information is gathered. But there is also a need for a separate data warehouse at each local organization — that is, in each country. In this case, a distributed data warehouse is needed. Data will exist both centrally and in a distributed manner.

A second case for a local and global distributed data warehouse occurs when a large corporation has many lines of business. Although there may be little or no business integration among the different vertical lines of business, at the corporate level — at least as far as finance is concerned — there is. The different lines of business may not meet anywhere else but at the balance sheet, or there may be considerable business integration, including such things as customers, products, vendors, and the like. In this scenario, a corporate centralized data warehouse is supported by many different data warehouses for each line of business.

In some cases, part of the data warehouse exists centrally (that is, globally), and other parts of the data warehouse exist in a distributed manner (that is, locally).

To understand when a geographically or distributed business distributed data warehouse makes sense, consider some basic topologies of processing. Figure 6-1 shows a very common processing topology.

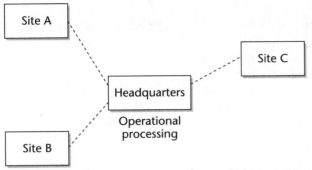

Figure 6-1   A topology of processing representative of many enterprises.

In Figure 6-1, all processing is done at the organization's headquarters. If any processing is done at the local geographically dispersed level, it is very basic, involving, perhaps, a series of dumb terminals. In this type of topology it is very unlikely that a distributed data warehouse will be necessary.

One step up the ladder in terms of sophistication of local processing is the case where basic data and transaction capture activity occurs at the local level, as shown in Figure 6-2. In this scenario, some small amount of very basic processing occurs at the local level. Once the transactions that have occurred locally are captured, they are shipped to a central location for further processing.

Under this simple topology, it is very unlikely that a distributed data warehouse is needed. From a business standpoint, no great amount of business occurs locally, and decisions made locally do not warrant a data warehouse.

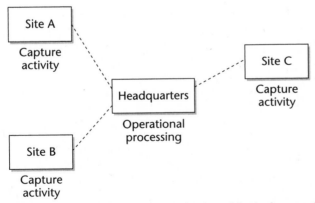

Figure 6-2   In some cases, very basic activity is done at the site level.

Now, contrast the processing topology shown in Figure 6-3 with the previous two. In Figure 6-3, a fair amount of processing occurs at the local level. Sales are made. Money is collected. Bills are paid locally. As far as operational processing is concerned, the local sites are autonomous. Only on occasion and for certain types of processing will data and activities be sent to the central organization. A central corporate balance sheet is kept. It is for this type of organization that some form of distributed data warehouse makes sense.

There is the even larger case where much processing occurs at the local level. Products are made. Sales forces are hired. Marketing is done. An entire mini-corporation is set up locally. Of course, the local corporations report to the same balance sheet as all other branches of the corporation. But, at the end of the day, the local organizations are effectively their own company, and there is little business integration of data across the corporation. In this case, a full-scale data warehouse at the local level is needed.

Just as there are many different kinds of distributed business models, there is more than one type of local and global distributed data warehouse, as will be discussed. It is a mistake to think that the model for the local and global distributed data warehouse is a binary proposition. Instead, there are degrees of distributed data warehouse.

Most organizations that do not have a great deal of local autonomy and processing have a central data warehouse, as shown in Figure 6-4.

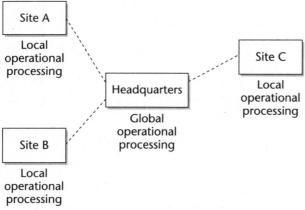

Figure 6-3   At the other end of the spectrum of the distributed data warehouse, much of the operational processing is done locally.

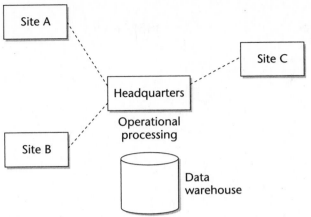

Figure 6-4 Most organizations have a centrally controlled, centrally housed data warehouse.

The Local Data Warehouse

A form of data warehouse, known as a local data warehouse, contains data that is of interest only to the local level. There might be a local data warehouse for Brazil, one for France, and one for Hong Kong. Or there might be a local data warehouse for car parts, motorcycles, and heavy trucks. Each local data warehouse has its own technology, its own data, its own processor, and so forth. Figure 6-5 shows a simple example of a series of local data warehouses.

In Figure 6-5, a local data warehouse exists for different geographical regions or for different technical communities. The local data warehouse serves the same function that any other data warehouse serves, except that the scope of the data warehouse is local. For example, the data warehouse for Brazil does not have any information about business activities in France, or the data warehouse for car parts does not have any data about motorcycles. In other words, the local data warehouse contains data that is historical in nature and is integrated within the local site. There is no coordination of data or structure of data from one local data warehouse to another.

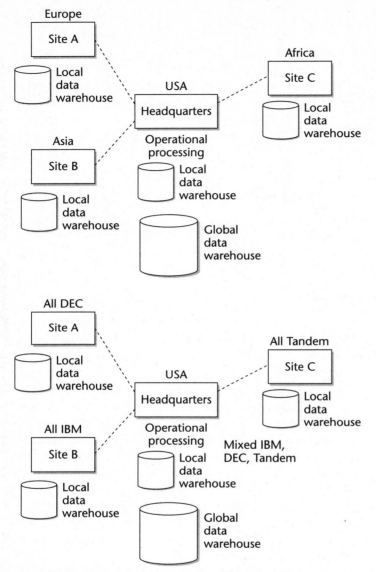

Figure 6-5 Some circumstances in which you might want to create a two-tiered level of data warehouse.

The Global Data Warehouse

Of course, there can also be a global data warehouse, as shown in Figure 6-6. The global data warehouse has as its scope the corporation or the enterprise, while each of the local data warehouses within the corporation has as its scope the local site that it serves. For example, the data warehouse in Brazil does not coordinate or share data with the data warehouse in France, but the local data warehouse in Brazil does share data with the corporate headquarters data warehouse in Chicago; or the local data warehouse for car parts does not share data with the local data warehouse for motorcycles, but it does share data with the corporate data warehouse in Detroit. The scope of the global data warehouse is the business that is integrated across the corporation. In some cases, there is considerable corporate integrated data; in other cases, there is very little. The global data warehouse contains historical data, as do the local data warehouses. The source of the data for the local data warehouses is shown in Figure 6-7, where we see that each local data warehouse is fed by its own operational systems. The source of data for the corporate global data warehouse is the local data warehouses, or in some cases, a direct update can go into the global data warehouse.

The global data warehouse contains information that must be integrated at the corporate level. In many cases, this consists only of financial information. In other cases, this may mean integration of customer information, product information, and so on. While a considerable amount of information will be peculiar to and useful to only the local level, other corporate common information will need to be shared and managed corporately. The global data warehouse contains the data that needs to be managed globally.

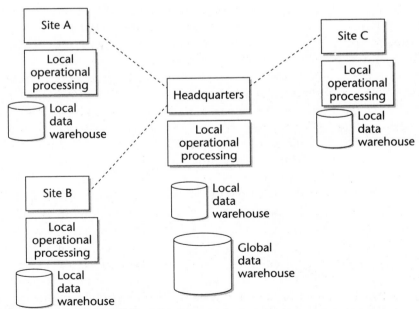

Figure 6-6 What a typical distributed data warehouse might look like.

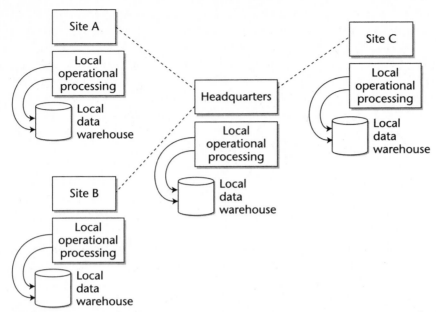

Figure 6-7 The flow of data from the local operational environment to the local data warehouse.

An interesting issue is commonality of data among the different local data warehouses. Figure 6-8 shows that each local warehouse has its own unique structure and content of data. In Brazil, there may be much information about the transport of goods up and down the Amazon. This information is of no use in Hong Kong and France. Conversely, information might be stored in the French data warehouse about the trade unions in France and about trade under the euro that is of little interest or relevance in Hong Kong or Brazil.

In the case of the car parts data warehouse, an interest might be shared in spark plugs among the car parts, motorcycle, and heavy trucks data warehouses, but the tires used by the motorcycle division are not of interest to the heavy trucks or the car parts division. There is, then, both commonality and uniqueness among local data warehouses.

Any intersection or commonality of data from one local data warehouse to another is purely coincidental. There is no coordination whatsoever of data, processing structure, or definition between the local data warehouses previously shown in Figure 6-8.

However, it is reasonable to assume that a corporation will have at least some natural intersections of data from one local site to another. If such an intersection exists, it is best contained in a global data warehouse. Figure 6-9 shows that the global data warehouse is fed from existing local operational systems. The common data may be financial information, customer information, parts vendors, and so forth.

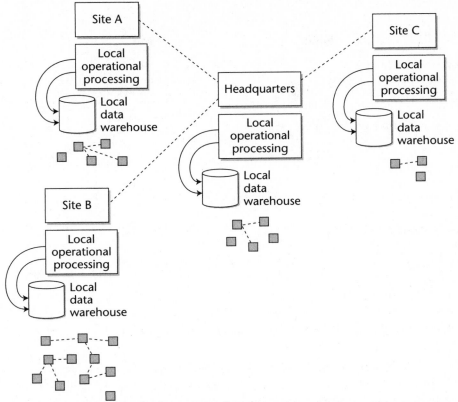

Figure 6-8   The structure and content of the local data warehouses are very different.

Intersection of Global and Local Data

Figure 6-9 showed that data is being fed from the local data warehouse environment to the global data warehouse environment. The data may be carried in both warehouses, and a simple transformation of data may occur as the data is placed in the global data warehouse. For example, one local data warehouse may carry its information in the Hong Kong dollar, but convert to the U.S. dollar on entering the global data warehouse; or the French data warehouse may carry parts specifications in metric in the French data warehouse, but convert metric to English measurements on entering the global data warehouse.

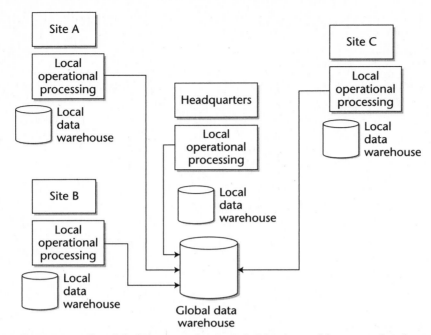

Figure 6-9 The global data warehouse is fed by the outlying operational systems.

The global data warehouse contains data that is common across the corporation and data that is integrated. Central to the success and usability of the distributed data warehouse environment is the mapping of data from the local operational systems to the data structure of the global data warehouse, as seen in Figure 6-10. This mapping determines which data goes into the global data warehouse, the structure of the data, and any conversions that must be done. The mapping is the most important part of the design of the global data warehouse, and it will be different for each local data warehouse. For instance, the way that the Hong Kong data maps into the global data warehouse is different from how the Brazil data maps into the global data warehouse, which is yet different from how the French map their data into the global data warehouse. It is in the mapping to the global data warehouse that the differences in local business practices are accounted for.

The mapping of local data into global data is easily the most difficult aspect of building the global data warehouse.

Figure 6-10 showed that for some types of data, there is a common structure of data for the global data warehouse. The common data structure encompasses and defines all common data across the corporation, but there is a different mapping of data from each local site into the global data warehouse. In other words, the global data warehouse is designed and defined centrally based on the definition and identification of common corporate data, but the mapping of the data from existing local operational systems is a choice made by the local designer and developer.

It is entirely likely that the mapping from local operational systems into global data warehouse systems will not be done as precisely as possible the first time. Over time, as feedback from the user is accumulated, the mapping at the local level improves. If ever there were a case for iterative development of a data warehouse, it is in the creation and solidification of global data based on the local mapping.

MAPPING INTO THE GLOBAL DATA STRUCTURE

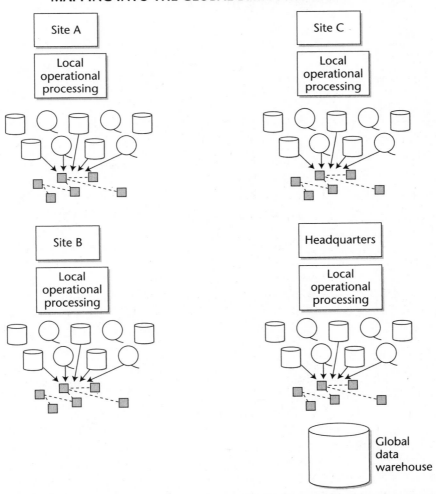

Figure 6-10 There is a common structure for the global data warehouse. Each local site maps into the common structure differently.

A variation of the local and global data warehouse structure that has been discussed is to allow a global data warehouse "staging" area to be kept at the local level. Figure 6-11 shows that each local area stages global warehouse data before passing the data to the central location. For example, say that in France are two data warehouses — one a local data warehouse used for French decisions. In this data warehouse, all transactions are stored in the French franc. In addition, there is a "staging area" in France, where transactions are stored in U.S. dollars. The French are free to use either their own local data warehouse or the staging area for decisions. In many circumstances, this approach may be technologically mandatory. An important issue is associated with this approach. Should the locally staged global data warehouse be emptied after the data that is staged inside of it is transferred to the global level? If the data is not deleted locally, redundant data will exist.

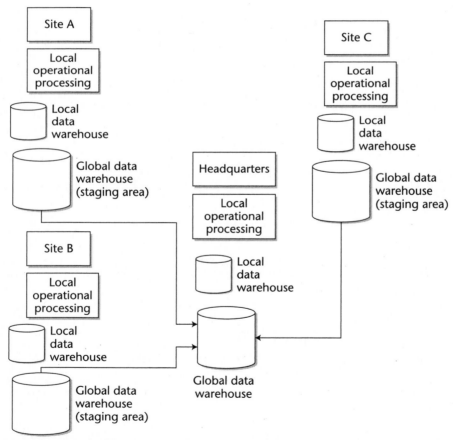

Figure 6-11 The global data warehouse may be staged at the local level, and then passed to the global data warehouse at the headquarters level.

Under certain conditions, some amount of redundancy may be called for. This issue must be decided and policies and procedures put into place. For example, the Brazilian data warehouse may create a staging area for its data based on American dollars and the product descriptions that are used globally. In the background, the Brazilians may have their own data warehouse in Brazilian currency and the product descriptions as they are known in Brazil. The Brazilians may use both their own data warehouse and the staged data warehouse for reporting and analysis.

Though any of several subject areas may be candidates for the first global data warehouse development effort, many corporations begin with corporate finance. Finance is a good starting point for the following reasons:

- It is relatively stable.
- It enjoys high visibility.
- It is only a fraction of the business of the organization (except, of course, for organizations whose business is finance).
- It is always at the nerve center of the organization.
- It entails only a modicum of data.

In the case of the global warehouse being discussed, the Brazilian, the French, and the Hong Kong data warehouses would all participate in the building of a corporate-wide financial data warehouse. There would be lots of other data in the operations of the Brazilian, French, and Hong Kong business units, but only the financial information would flow into the global data warehouse.

Because the global data warehouse does not fit the classical structure of a data warehouse as far as the levels of data are concerned, when building the global data warehouse, one must recognize that there will be some anomalies. One such anomaly is that the detailed data (or, at least, the source of the detailed data) resides at the local level, while the lightly summarized data resides at the centralized global level. For example, suppose that the headquarters of a company is in New York and it has outlying offices in Texas, California, and Illinois. The details of sales and finance are managed independently and at a detailed level in Texas, California, and Illinois. The data model is passed to the outlying regions, and the needed corporate data is translated into the form that is necessary to achieve integration across the corporation. Upon having made the translation at the local level, the data is transmitted to New York. The raw, untranslated detail still resides at the local level. Only the transformed, lightly summarized data is passed to headquarters. This is a variation on the theme of the classical data warehouse structure.

Redundancy

One of the issues of a global data warehouse and its supporting local data warehouses is redundancy or overlap of data. Figure 6-12 shows that, as a policy, only minimal redundant data exists between the local levels and the global levels of data (and in this regard, it matters not whether global data is stored locally in a staging area or locally). On occasion, some detailed data will pass through to the global data warehouse untouched by any transformation or conversion. In this case, a small overlap of data from the global data warehouse to the local data warehouse will occur. For example, suppose a transaction occurs in France for US$10,000. That transaction may pass through to the global data warehouse untouched.

On the other hand, most data passes through some form of conversion, transformation, reclassification, or summarization as it passes from the local data warehouse to the data warehouse. In this case, there is (strictly speaking) no redundancy of data between the two environments. For example, suppose that a HK$175,000 transaction is recorded in Hong Kong. The transaction may be broken apart into several smaller transactions, the dollar amount may be converted, the transaction may be combined with other transactions, and so forth. In this case, there is certainly a relationship between the detailed data found in the local data warehouse and the data found in the global data warehouse. But there is no redundancy of data between the two environments.

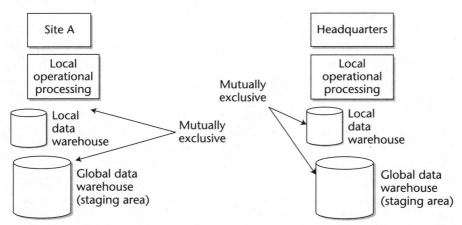

Figure 6-12 Data can exist in either the local data warehouse or the global data warehouse, but not both.

A massive amount of redundancy of data between the local and the global data warehouse environments indicates that the scopes of the different warehouses probably have not been defined properly. When massive redundancy of data exists between the local and the global data warehouse environments, it is only a matter of time before spider web systems start to appear. With the appearance of such systems come many problems — reconciliation of inconsistent results, inability to create new systems easily, costs of operation, and so forth. For this reason, it should be a matter of policy that global data and local data be mutually exclusive with the exception of very small amounts of data that incidentally overlap between the two environments.

Access of Local and Global Data

In line with policies required to manage and structure the local and the global data warehouses is the issue of access of data. At first, this issue seems to be almost trivial. The obvious policy is that anyone should be able to get at any data. Some important ramifications and nuances come into play, however.

Figure 6-13 shows that some local sites are accessing global data. Depending on what is being asked for, this may or may not be an appropriate use of data warehouse data. For example, an analyst in Brazil may be analyzing how Brazilian revenues compare to total corporate revenues. Or a person in France may be looking at total corporate profitability. If the intent of the local analysis is to improve local business, the access of global data at the local level is probably a good policy. If the global data is being used informationally, on a one-time-only basis, and to improve local business practices, the access of global data at the local level is probably acceptable.

As a principle, local data should be used locally and global data should be used globally. The question must be raised, then: Why is global analysis being done locally? For example, suppose a person in Hong Kong is comparing total corporate profitability with that of another corporation. There is nothing wrong per se with this analysis, except that this sort of global analysis is best performed at the headquarters level. The question must be asked: What if the person in Hong Kong finds that globally the corporation is not competing well with other corporations? What is the person in Hong Kong going to do with that information? The person may have input into global decisions, but he or she is not in a position to effect such a decision. Therefore, it is questionable whether a local business analyst should be looking at global data for any other purpose than that of improving local business practices. As a rule, the local business analyst should be satisfied using local data.

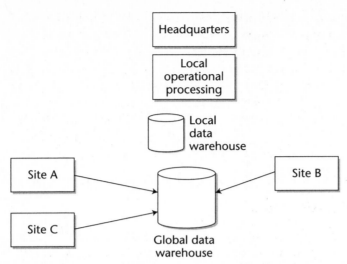

Figure 6-13   An important issue to be resolved is whether local sites should be accessing the global data warehouse.

Another issue is the routing of requests for information into the architected information environment. When only a single central data warehouse existed, the source of a request for information was not much of an issue. But when data is distributed over a complex landscape (such as a distributed data warehouse landscape, as shown in Figure 6-14), there is the consideration of ensuring the request originated from the appropriate place.

For example, asking a local site to determine total corporate salaries is inappropriate, as is asking the central data warehouse group what a contractor was paid last month at a particular site for a particular service. With local and global data, there is the issue of origin of request, something not encountered in the simple centralized data warehouse environment.

Another important issue of local and global distributed data warehousing is the transfer of data from the local data warehouse to the global data warehouse. There are many facets to this issue:

- How frequently will the transfer of data from the local environment to the global environment be made? Daily? Weekly? Monthly? The rate of transfer depends on a combination of factors. How quickly is the data needed in the global data warehouse? How much activity has occurred at the local level? What volume of data is being transported?

- Is the transportation of the data from the local environment to the global data warehouse across national lines legal? Some countries have Draconian laws that prevent the movement of certain kinds of data across their national boundaries.

- What network will be used to transport the data from the local environment to the global environment? Is the Internet safe enough? Is it reliable enough? Can the Internet safely transport enough data? What is the backup strategy? What safeguards are in place to determine if all of the data has been passed?

- What safeguards are in place to determine whether data is being hacked during transport from the local environment to the global environment?

- What window of processing is open for transport of data from the local environment to the global environment? Will transportation have to be done during the hours when processing against the data warehouse will be heavy?

- What technology is the local data in, and what technology is the global data in? What measures must be taken to convert the local technology to the global technology? Will data be lost in the translation?

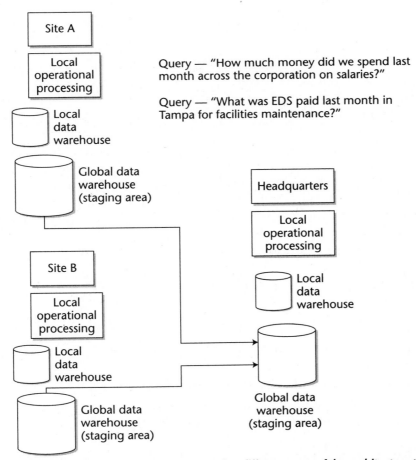

Site A

Local operational processing

Local data warehouse

Global data warehouse (staging area)

Query — "How much money did we spend last month across the corporation on salaries?"

Query — "What was EDS paid last month in Tampa for facilities maintenance?"

Headquarters

Local operational processing

Local data warehouse

Site B

Local operational processing

Local data warehouse

Global data warehouse (staging area)

Global data warehouse (staging area)

Figure 6-14   Queries need to be routed to different parts of the architecture to be answered properly.

Many issues relate to the physical movement of the data into the global data warehouse environment. In some cases, these issues are mundane; in others, they are anything but.

A related yet separate issue is global operational data. Thus far, this chapter has assumed that every local site has its own unique operational data and processing. However, it is entirely possible that there is a degree of commonality between the operational systems found at each local site. In this case, some degree of corporate operational data and processing might be desirable. For example, some customers may need to be handled globally, such as large multinational corporations like Coca-Cola, McDonalds, IBM, and AT&T. Pricing considerations, size-of-order considerations, and delivery considerations may be treated differently globally than similar decisions are treated locally. In the case of global operational processing, that global operational data merely becomes another source of data into the global data warehouse. But there is still the distinction between operational data and DSS informational data.

Underlying the whole issue of the distributed data warehouse is complexity. In a simple central data warehouse environment, roles and responsibilities are fairly straightforward. In a distributed data warehouse environment, however, the issues of scope, coordination, metadata, responsibilities, transfer of data, local mapping, and more make the environment complex indeed.

One of the major considerations for a global data warehouse is whether the data warehouse should be built centrally or globally. While it is tempting to say that a global data warehouse should be designed and built centrally, doing so is patently a mistake. With a centralized construction of a global data warehouse, there is (at best) only a marginal local buy-in to the global data warehouse. This means that the definition of the mapping between the local systems and the needs for global data is done centrally, not locally. To succeed, there must be local management and control of the mapping process. Stated differently, the single most difficult part of the building and population of the global data warehouse is the mapping of the local data to the global data. And this mapping cannot be done centrally; it must be done locally.

For example, suppose the headquarters organization tries to map Brazilian data into the global data warehouse. This poses the following problems:

- Portuguese is not the native tongue of the headquarters organization.

- Headquarters personnel do not understand local business practices and customs.

- Headquarters personnel do not understand local legacy applications.

- Headquarters personnel do not understand the local data warehouse.

- Headquarters personnel are not on hand to keep abreast of day-to-day changes in local systems.

There are then a plethora of reasons why the mapping of local data into the global data warehouse environment cannot be done by centralized personnel. Therefore, the local organization must be a part of the building of the global data warehouse.

A final observation is that the local data needs to be in as flexible a form as possible. This usually means that the local data must be organized relationally and at a low level of granularity. If the local data is organized in a star join multidimensional format, it will be difficult to break apart and restructure for the global data warehouse.

The Technologically Distributed Data Warehouse

The spread of a company over multiple geographical locations or over many different product lines is not the only reason why a distributed data warehouse is appealing. There are other rationales as well. One case for a different type of a distributed warehouse is that of placing a data warehouse on the distributed technology of a vendor. Client/server technology fits this requirement nicely.

The first question is: Can a data warehouse be placed on distributed technology? The answer is "yes." The next question is: What are the advantages and disadvantages of using distributed technology for a data warehouse? The first advantage of a technologically distributed data warehouse is that the entry cost is cheap. In other words, the cost of hardware and software for a data warehouse when initially loaded onto distributed technology is much less than if the data warehouse were initially loaded onto classical, large, centralized hardware. The second advantage is that there is no theoretical limit to how much data can be placed in the data warehouse. If the volume of data inside the warehouse begins to exceed the limit of a single distributed processor, then another processor can be added to the network, and the progression of adding data continues in an unimpeded fashion. Whenever the data grows too large, another processor is added.

Figure 6-15 depicts a world in which there may be an infinite amount of data in the data warehouse. This is appealing because a data warehouse will contain much data (but not an infinite amount).

There are, however, some considerations. As the data warehouse starts to expand beyond a few processors (that is, servers), an excessive amount of traffic starts to appear on the network. The increased traffic appears when a request for data overlaps from one processor to another. For example, suppose one processor holds data for the year 1998, another processor for 1999, another for 2000, and yet another for 2001. When a request is made for data from 1998 to 2001, the result set for that query must pass over the boundaries of the processor that originally held the data. In this case, data from four processors must be gathered. In the process, data passes across the network and increases the traffic.

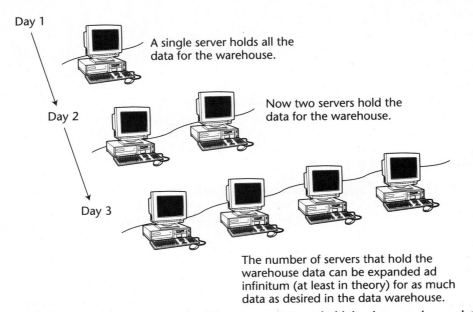

Figure 6-15 The progression of adding more servers to hold the data warehouse data.

The issue arises not only of a query accessing data housed by multiple processors, but of a large amount of data needing to be transported from a single processor. For example, suppose a query wishes to access all 1999 data and all 2000 data. Such a query will pull data from one or the other processor. Figure 6-16 depicts a query that wishes to access a large amount of data from multiple servers.

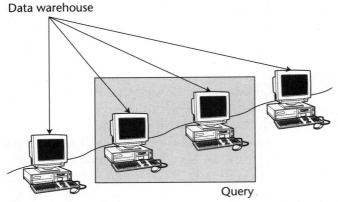

Figure 6-16 A query that accesses a large amount of data from multiple data warehouse servers.

Techniques and approaches do, of course, exist to deal with a data warehouse that is technically distributed over multiple servers. Ironically, the problems grow with time, as the warehouse becomes fully populated and as the number of servers grows. In the early days of a distributed data warehouse, when there is very little data and only a few servers, the problems discussed here are hardly obvious. In the more mature days of a data warehouse, however, the data and the processing environment become more difficult to manage.

The Independently Evolving Distributed Data Warehouse

Yet a third flavor of distributed data warehouse is one in which independent data warehouses are developed concurrently and in an uncontrolled manner.

The first step many corporations take in data warehousing is to put up a data warehouse for a financial or marketing organization. Once success follows the initial warehouse effort, other parts of the corporation naturally want to build on the successful first effort. In short order, the data warehouse architect has to manage and coordinate multiple data warehouse efforts within the organization.

The Nature of the Development Efforts

The first issue facing the data architect who must manage multiple data warehouse development efforts is the nature of the development efforts. Unless the data architect knows what kinds of efforts are occurring and how they relate to the overall architecture, he or she will have a very difficult time managing and coordinating them. Because the issues of development vary considerably depending on the approach, different types of data warehouse development efforts require very different approaches to management.

Multiple data warehouse development efforts occur in four typical cases, as outlined in Figure 6-17.

In the first, rare case shown in Figure 6-17, a corporation has totally separate and unintegrated lines of business for which data warehouses are being independently built by different development groups. The diverse lines of business report to the corporation, but other than sharing a company name, there is no business integration or sharing of data within the company. Such a corporate structure is not unknown, but it is not common. In this case, there is very little danger that one data warehouse development effort will conflict with another. Accordingly, there is little or no need for cross-management and coordination of data warehouse development efforts.

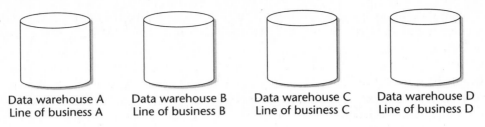

Data warehouse A
Line of business A

Data warehouse B
Line of business B

Data warehouse C
Line of business C

Data warehouse D
Line of business D

Completely unintegrated lines of business each with their own data warehouses

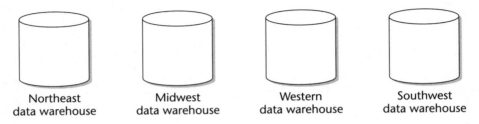

Northeast
data warehouse

Midwest
data warehouse

Western
data warehouse

Southwest
data warehouse

The same data warehouse but with distributed parts

Lightly
summarized

Detailed
data

OLAP

Different levels of data within the same data warehouse

Different non-distributed parts of the detailed level of the data warehouse

Figure 6-17 Four possible meanings to "multiple groups building the data warehouse"; each interpretation is very different from the others.

The second case of multiple data warehouse efforts occurring simultaneously happens when a corporate distributed data warehouse is being built and various development groups are creating different parts of the same data warehouse. In this case, the same detailed data is being built by different groups of developers, but the data is distributed across different locations. For example, suppose a car manufacturer is building a manufacturing data warehouse in Detroit and another manufacturing data warehouse in Canada. The same detailed data finds its way into the data warehouse in both places. Unless extraordinary measures are taken, likely many conflicting analyses will occur. This case for multiple development efforts is as common as the previous case is rare. Yet, because this case is so common, it requires a great deal of attention. It requires discipline and close coordination among the groups to achieve a collectively satisfying result. The danger of not coordinating this effort is that much waste may occur through redundant storage and manipulation of massive amounts of data. If data is created redundantly, the resulting data warehouse may well be ineffective because there will be a classic spider web in the DSS environment.

The third case of multiple data warehouse development occurring simultaneously happens when different groups are building different levels of data (that is, summarized data and detailed data) in the data warehouse environment. Like the preceding case, this scenario is also very common. However, for a variety of reasons, it is much easier to manage than either of the two previous cases. Because of the differences in the levels of data, there are different uses and expectations. And coordination between the two groups is likely to be a straightforward exercise. For example, one group of people might be building a data warehouse to capture and analyze each bank transaction at the lowest level of detail. Another group of analysts might be creating customer records summarized up to the monthly level. The interface between the two groups is simple. The detailed transactions are summarized on a monthly basis to create the aggregate or summary record for the customer.

The fourth case occurs when multiple groups are trying to build different parts of the current level of detail of the data warehouse environment in a nondistributed manner. This is a somewhat rare phenomenon, but when it occurs, it mandates special attention. There is much at stake in this last case, and the data architect must be aware of what the issues are and how they relate to success.

Each of these cases is discussed in the following sections, along with their issues, advantages, and disadvantages.

Completely Unrelated Warehouses

The building and operation of completely unrelated warehouses is shown in Figure 6-18. A corporation has four lines of business — a fast-food franchise, a steel mill, retail banking, and golf course management. There is no integration of the businesses whatsoever. A customer of one business may be a customer of another business, and there is no desire to link the two relationships. The ongoing data warehouse efforts have no reason to be coordinated. All the way from modeling to selection of base technology (that is, platform, DBMS, access tools, development tools, and so forth), each of the different businesses could operate as if it were completely autonomous.

For all the autonomy of the lines of business, they are necessarily integrated at one level: the financial balance sheet. If the different lines of business report to a single financial entity, there must be integration at the balance-sheet level. In this situation, a corporate data warehouse might need to be built that reflects the corporate finances. Figure 6-19 shows a corporate financial data warehouse sitting above the different businesses.

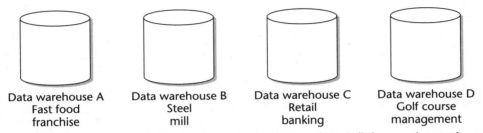

Data warehouse A	Data warehouse B	Data warehouse C	Data warehouse D
Fast food	Steel	Retail	Golf course
franchise	mill	banking	management

Figure 6-18 Four totally independent enterprises where there is little or no integration of data at the business level.

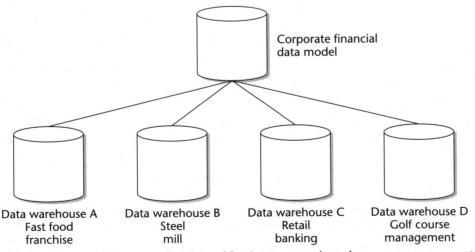

Corporate financial data model

Data warehouse A	Data warehouse B	Data warehouse C	Data warehouse D
Fast food	Steel	Retail	Golf course
franchise	mill	banking	management

Figure 6-19 Even the most disparate of business enterprises share common corporate financial data.

The financial corporate data warehouse contains simple (and abstract) entities such as expenses, revenues, capital expenditures, depreciation, and the like. There is very little, if any, business data beyond that found on every balance sheet. (In other words, no attempt is made for a common corporate description of customer, product, sale, and so on in the financial data warehouse.) Of course, the data feeding the corporate financial data warehouse that was depicted in Figure 6-19 may come either from the "local" data warehouse or from the operational systems found at the individual operating company level.

Metadata is vital at the local level. With a corporate financial data warehouse, it is also needed at the corporate financial level. However, in this case, because no real business integration exists, there is no need to tie any of the metadata together.

Distributed Data Warehouse Development

Unlike the case of the unrelated warehouses, most businesses have some degree of integration among their disparate parts. Very few businesses are as autonomous as those previously depicted in Figure 6-19. A much more common scenario for the development of multiple data warehouse efforts is shown in Figure 6-20.

In Figure 6-20 a corporation has different sites in different parts of the world — one in the United States and Canada, one in South America, one in the Far East, and one in Africa. Each site has its own unique data, with no overlap of data — particularly of detailed transaction data — from one site to the next. The company wants to create a data warehouse for each of the disparate entities as a first effort in achieving an architected environment. There is some degree of business integration among the different organizations. At the same time, it is assumed that distinct business practices are carried on in each locale. Such an organization of corporate entities is common to many companies.

Africa
data
warehouse

U.S.
data
warehouse

Canada
data
warehouse

Far East
data
warehouse

South America
data
warehouse

Figure 6-20   Logically the same data warehouse.

The first step many organizations make toward data warehousing is to create a local data warehouse at each geographical entity. Figure 6-21 shows the creation of a local data warehouse.

Each locale builds its own unique autonomous data warehouse according to its needs. Note that there is no redundant detailed data among the different locales, at least as far as transaction data is concerned. In other words, a unit of data reflecting transactions that belongs in Africa would never be found in the local data warehouse for Europe.

There are several pros and cons to this approach to building the distributed corporate data warehouse. One advantage is that it is quick to accomplish. Each local group has control over its design and resources. A sense of autonomy and control may make each local organization happy. As such, the benefits of the data warehouse can be proven throughout the corporation on a real-time basis. Within six months, the local data warehouses can be up and running, and the organization at the local level can be deriving the benefits. The disadvantage is that if there is any commonality in the structure (not the content) of data across the organization, this approach does nothing to recognize or rationalize that commonality.

Coordinating Development across Distributed Locations

An alternative approach is to try to coordinate the local data warehouse development efforts across the different local organizations. This sounds good in theory, but in execution it has not proved to be effective. The local development groups never collectively move at the same pace, and the local groups look on the central development group trying to coordinate the many local development efforts as a hindrance to progress. A separate data model is built to provide the foundation of the data warehouse design for each of the separate locales.

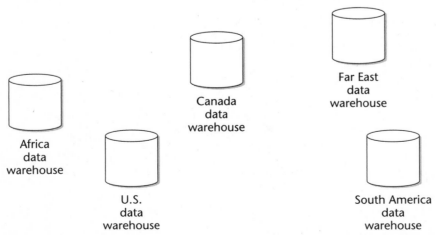

Figure 6-21 Local data warehouses are built at each of the autonomous operating divisions.

Following along with this scenario, let's say that one day, after the worth of data warehousing has been proven at the local level, the corporation decides to build a corporate data warehouse (see Figure 6-22).

The corporate data warehouse will reflect the business integration across the different divisions and locales. The corporate data warehouse will be related to, but still distinct from, the local data warehouses. The first step in building the corporate data warehouse is to create a corporate data model for that portion of the business that will be reflected in the corporate data warehouse. As a general rule, the corporate data model that is built for the first iteration of the corporate data warehouse will be small and simple, and it will be limited to a subset of the business. Figure 6-23 illustrates the building of the corporate data model after which the corporate data warehouse will be shaped.

The Corporate Data Model — Distributed

The corporate data model reflects the integration of business at the corporate level. As such, the corporate data model may overlap considerably with portions of the local data models. Such an overlap is healthy and normal. In other cases, the corporate data model will be different from the local data models. In any case, it is up to the local organization to determine how the fit is to be made between the corporate need for data and the local ability to provide it. The local organization knows its own data better than anyone, and it is best equipped to show how local data needs to be shaped and reshaped to meet the specifications of the corporate design of data for the data warehouse.

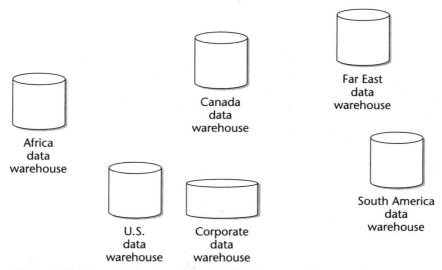

Figure 6-22 The decision is made to build a corporate data warehouse.

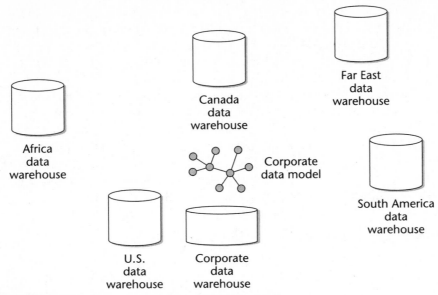

Figure 6-23 The corporate data model is created.

While there may very well be overlap in the structural design of data from one local level to the next, there is no overlap to any great extent in the content of data. Figure 6-24 shows the building and population of the corporate data warehouse from the local levels.

The source of the data going to the corporate data warehouse can come from the local data warehouse or from the local operational systems. The determination of the system of record should be a decision that is made entirely at the local level. Most certainly, several iterations of definition of the system of record will be needed.

In addition, an important design issue is how to create and transport the local system of record data from the technology found at the local level into the technology of the corporate data warehouse. In some cases, the official "staged" data is kept at the local level. In other cases, the staged data is passed on to the corporate environment with no access at the local level.

As a rule, the data in the corporate data warehouse is simple in structure and concept. Figure 6-25 shows that data in the corporate data warehouse appears to be detailed data to the DSS analyst at the corporate level, and at the same time it appears to be summary data to the DSS analyst at the local level. This apparent contradiction is reconciled by the fact that the appearance of summarization or detail is strictly in the eye of the beholder.

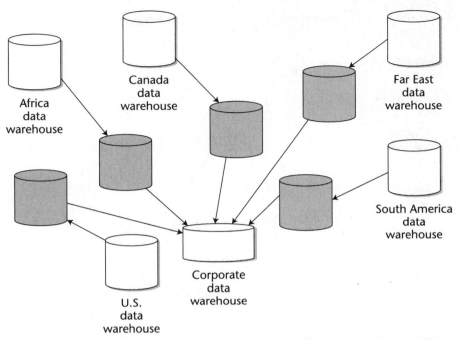

Figure 6-24   The corporate data warehouse is loaded from the different autonomous operating companies.

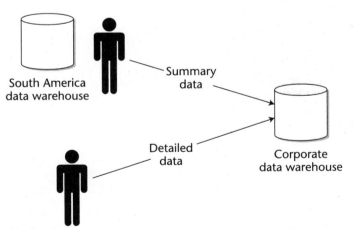

Figure 6-25   What is summary at one level is detailed at another.

The corporate data warehouse of the distributed database can be contrasted with the corporate financial data warehouse of the completely unrelated companies. Figure 6-26 makes this comparison.

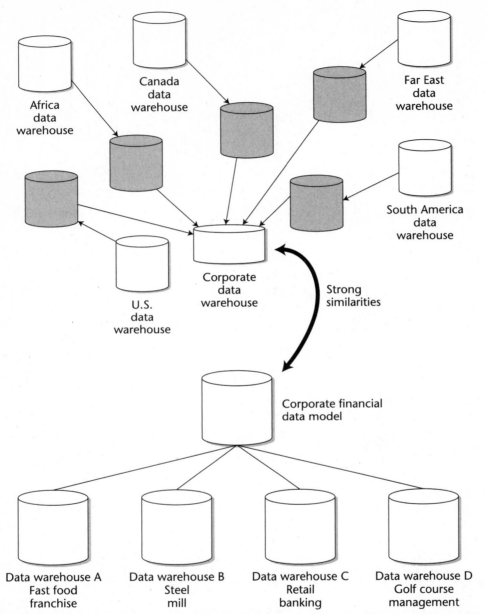

Figure 6-26 The data warehouse of a distributed corporation can be very similar to that of unrelated companies.

In many ways, the data warehouse of the distributed corporation is very similar to the data warehouse of the unrelated companies. However, although there are similarities in design and operation, there is one major difference.

The corporate distributed data warehouse extends into the business itself, reflecting the integration of customer, vendor, product, and so forth. As such, the corporate distributed data warehouse represents the very fabric of the business itself. The corporate data warehouse for unrelated companies, though, is for finance alone. The instant that there is a desire to use the corporate financial data warehouse for anything other than the financial relationship of the different parts of the corporation, there will be disappointment with the corporate financial data warehouse. The difference between the two data warehouses, then, is one of depth.

Metadata in the Distributed Warehouse

Metadata plays a very important role across the distributed corporate data warehouse. It is through metadata that the coordination of the structure of data is achieved across the many different locations where the data warehouse is found. Not surprisingly, metadata provides the vehicle for the achievement of uniformity and consistency.

Building the Warehouse on Multiple Levels

The third scenario of a company's simultaneous data warehouse development occurs when different development groups are building different levels of the data warehouse, as seen in Figure 6-27. This case is very different from the case of the distributed data warehouse development. In this case, Group A is building the high level of summarization of data, Group B is building the middle level of summarization, and Group C is building the current level of detail.

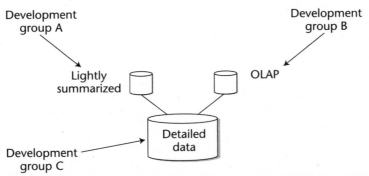

Figure 6-27 Different development groups are developing different parts of the data warehouse environment at different levels of the architecture.

The scenario of multiple levels of data warehouse development is very common. Fortunately, it is the easiest scenario to manage, with the fewest risks.

The primary concern of the data architect is to coordinate the efforts of the different development teams, both in terms of the specification of content and structure and in terms of the timing of development. For example, if Group A is significantly ahead of Group B or C, there will be a problem. When Group A is ready to populate its databases at the summary level, there may be no detailed data to work with.

One of the interesting aspects of different groups building different levels of summarization of the same data warehouse is that it is the group that is building the current level of detail that uses the data warehouse data model. Figure 6-28 illustrates this relationship.

The data model for the data warehouse directly reflects the design and development effort by the group doing current-level detailed analysis and design. Of course, indirectly the data warehouse data model reflects the needs of all groups. But because other groups are summarizing from the data found at the current level of detail, they have their own interpretation of what is needed. In most cases, the groups working on the higher levels of summarization have their own data models that reflect their own specialized needs.

One of the issues of managing multiple groups building different levels of summarization is the technological platforms on which the data warehouse levels are built. Normally, different groups choose different technological platforms. In fact, for the different development groups to choose the same platform would be very unusual. There are several reasons for this, though the primary one is cost. The detailed level of data requires an industrial-strength platform because of the large volume of data that will have to be handled. The different levels of summarization will require much less data, especially at the higher levels of summarization. It is overkill (and expensive) to place the higher levels of summarized data on the same platform as the detailed data (although it can be done).

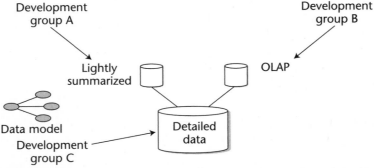

Figure 6-28 The development organization that is developing the lowest level of detail is the organization that uses the data model.

Another reason is that the alternative platforms offer a wide variety of specialized software, much of which is not to be found on the monolithic platforms that house detailed data. In any case, whether the different levels of data are on a single platform or on multiple platforms, metadata must be carefully stored and managed, so that continuity from one level of detail to the next can be maintained.

Because different platforms are commonly used for the different levels of data that are being developed by different groups, the issue of interconnectivity arises. Figure 6-29 shows the need for interconnectivity from one level to the next.

Several aspects of interconnectivity need to be addressed. One issue is the compatibility of access at the call level. In other words, is there compatible syntax between the two technologies that make up the detailed and the summary data between any two levels of the warehouse? If there is not at least some degree of compatibility, the interface will not be usable. Another aspect of the interconnectivity issue is the effective bandwidth of the interface. If very heavy traffic is being created by processing that occurs on either level of the data warehouse, the interface between the two environments can become a bottleneck.

However the groups that work on the data warehouse are coordinated, one requirement remains clear: The group that manages the lower-level detail must form a proper foundation of data for those groups that will be summarizing the data and creating a new level. This need is depicted in Figure 6-30.

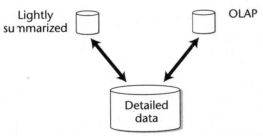

Figure 6-29 Interconnectivity between the different levels of the data warehouse is an important issue.

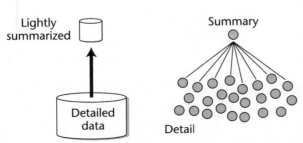

Figure 6-30 The detailed level forms the foundation for the summary level of data.

The coordination among the groups can be as simple as an agreement on a data model that satisfies the needs of all parties, or the agreement can be much more elaborate if circumstances warrant. The coordination of the development efforts is another matter. There must be a time-sequenced arrangement among the different development groups so that no one group arrives at a point of needing data that has not yet been gathered at a lower level.

Multiple Groups Building the Current Level of Detail

An infrequent set of circumstances occurs when multiple development groups attempt to build the current level of detail in a data warehouse in a non-distributed manner. Figure 6-31 illustrates this phenomenon.

As long as the groups that are developing the current level of detail are developing mutually exclusive sets of data, there is little difficulty. In this case, if the development groups are working from a common data model and the different groups' platforms are compatible, no problems should ensue. Unfortunately, mutually exclusive data sets are the exception rather than the rule. It is much more common for the multiple development groups to be designing and populating some or all of the same data.

A series of problems arises when the groups overlap. The first problem is cost — in particular, the cost of storage and processing. The volumes of data that are found at the current detailed level are such that any amount of redundancy must be questioned, much less wholesale redundancy. The cost of processing the detail is likewise a major issue.

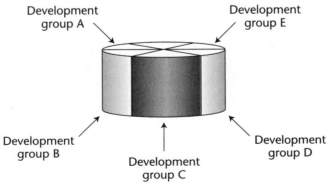

Figure 6-31 Different development groups that are developing the current level of detail for the data warehouse.

The second, more insidious issue is the introduction of the spider web into the DSS environment. With massive amounts of redundant detailed data, it is almost axiomatic that misinterpretation of data caused by redundancy will occur, where there is no effective reconcilability. Creating large amounts of redundant detailed data is a very undesirable condition for the detailed level of data in the data warehouse and defeats its purpose. If multiple development groups will be doing concurrent design and population in the current level of detail, great care must be taken to ensure that no redundant detailed data is created.

To ensure that no redundant data is developed, it is necessary to create a data model that reflects the common detailed data. Figure 6-32 shows that multiple development groups have combined their interests to create a common data model.

In addition to the currently active development groups, other groups that will have future requirements, but who are not currently in a development mode may also contribute their requirements. (Of course, if a group knows it will have future requirements but is unable to articulate them, then those requirements cannot be factored into the common detailed data model.) The common detailed data model reflects the collective need among the different groups for detailed data in the data warehouse.

The data model forms the basis of the design for the data warehouse. Figure 6-33 shows that the data model will be broken up into many tables as design progresses, each of which physically becomes part of the warehouse.

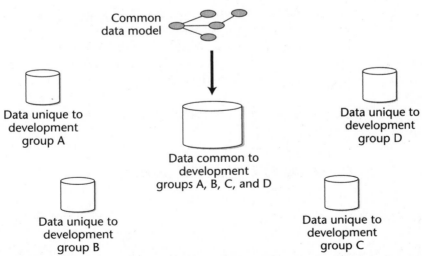

Figure 6-32 A data model identifies data that is common to all the development groups.

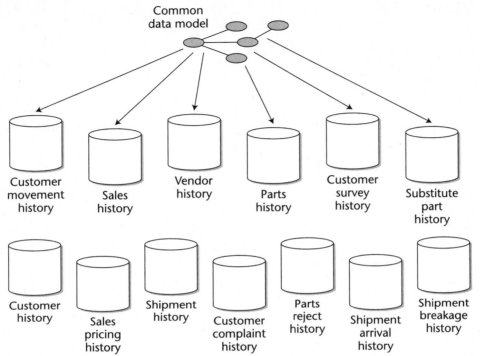

Figure 6-33 The data warehouse is physically manifested over multiple physical tables and databases.

Because the data model is broken into multiple physical tables at the moment of implementation, the development process for the data warehouse can proceed in an iterative manner. There is no need to build all of the tables at once. In fact, a good reason to build only a few tables at a time is so that the end-user feedback can be factored into the modification of the table, if necessary, with a minimum of fuss. In addition, because the common data model is broken into multiple tables, adding new tables at a later time to reflect requirements that are now unknown is not a problem.

Different Requirements at Different Levels

Normally, different groups have unique requirements (see Figure 6-34). These requirements result in what can be termed "local" current-level detail. The local data is certainly part of the data warehouse. It is, however, distinctively different from the "common" part. The local data has its own data model, usually much smaller and simpler than the common detailed data model.

There is, of necessity, nonredundancy of data across all of the detailed data. Figure 6-35 makes this point clear.

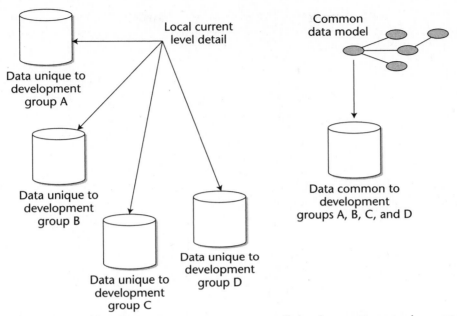

Figure 6-34   Just because data is not common to all development groups does not mean that it does not belong in the current-level detail of the data warehouse.

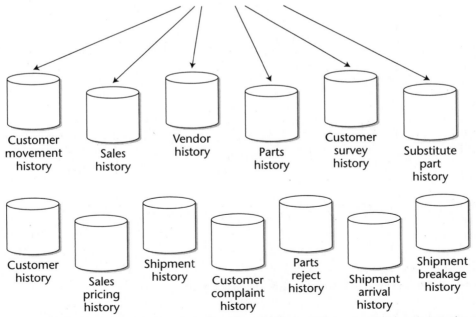

Figure 6-35   Nonredundancy of nonkey data throughout the many tables that make up the detailed level of the data warehouse.

Of course, the nonredundancy of the data is restricted to nonkey data. Redundancy exists at the key level because a form of foreign key relationships is used to relate the different types of data. Figure 6-36 shows the use of foreign keys.

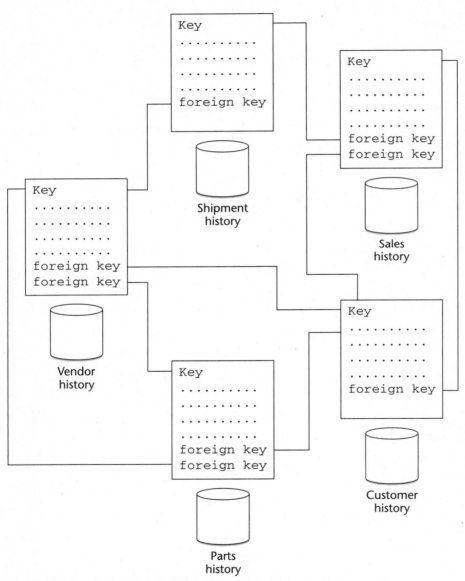

Figure 6-36 Foreign keys in the data warehouse environment.

The foreign keys found in the tables shown in Figure 6-36 are quite different from the classical foreign key relationships that are governed by referential integrity. Because the data in the data warehouse is gathered by and stored in terms of snapshots of data, the foreign key relationships that are found are organized in terms of "artifacts" of relationships. For an in-depth explanation of artifacts of relationships, refer to the www.inmoncif.com Tech Topic white paper on the subject, found in the "References" section at the end of this book.

An issue that arises is whether to place all of the detailed tables — common and local — under the same technology, as shown in Figure 6-37. There are many good arguments for doing so. One argument is that the cost of a single platform versus multiple platforms is much less. Another is that the cost of support and training will be less. In fact, about the only argument for multiple platforms for detailed data is that with multiple platforms, there may not be the need for a single massively large platform, and as a consequence, the cost of the multiple smaller platforms may be less than a single larger platform. In any case, many organizations adopt the strategy of a single platform for all their detailed data warehouse data, and the strategy works well.

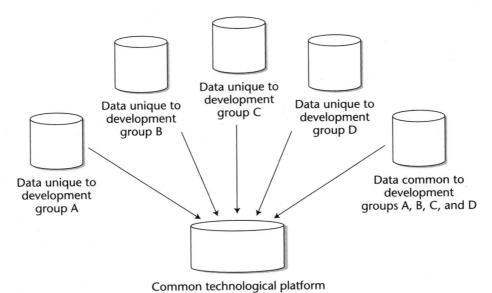

Figure 6-37   The different types of data in the detailed level of the data warehouse all on a common platform.

Other Types of Detailed Data

Another strategy is to use different platforms for the different types of data found at the detailed level. Figure 6-38 shows one example of this option. Some of the local data is on one platform, the common data is on another platform, and other local data is on yet another. This option is certainly one that is valid, and it often satisfies the different political needs of the organization. With this option, each group doing development can feel that it has some degree of control of at least its own peculiar needs. Unfortunately, this option has several major drawbacks. First, multiple technologies must be purchased and supported. Second, the end user needs to be trained in different technologies. And finally, the boundaries between the technologies may not be as easy to cross. Figure 6-39 illustrates this dilemma.

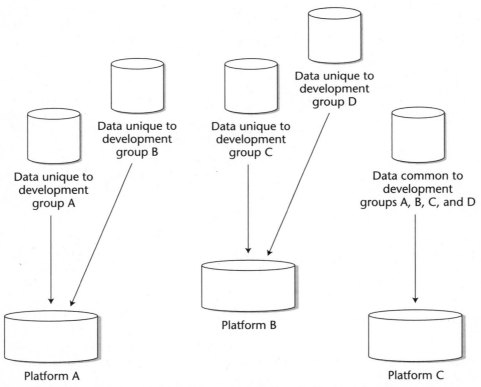

Figure 6-38 In this case, the different parts of the detailed level of the data warehouse are scattered across different technological platforms.

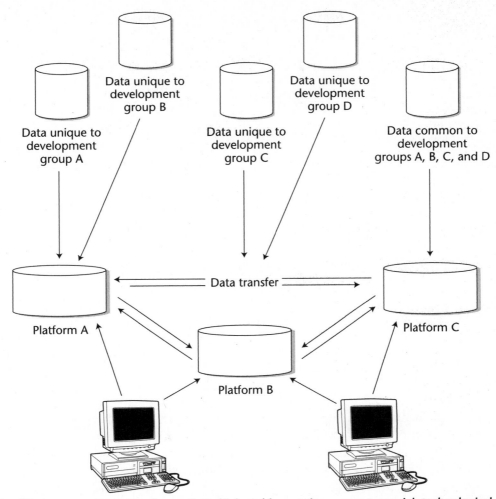

Figure 6-39 Data transfer and multiple table queries present special technological problems.

If there are to be multiple technologies supporting the different levels of detail in the data warehouse, it will be necessary to cross the boundaries between the technologies frequently. Software that is designed to access data across different technological platforms is available. Some of the problems that remain are shown in Figure 6-40.

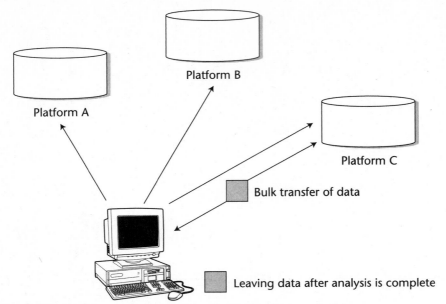

Figure 6-40 Some problems with interfacing different platforms.

One problem is in the passage of data. If multi-interfaced technology is used for the passage of small amounts of data, then there is no problem with performance. But if multi-interfaced technology is used to pass large amounts of data, then the software can become a performance bottleneck. Unfortunately, in a DSS environment it is almost impossible to know how much data will be accessed by any one request. Some requests access very little data; other requests access large amounts of data. This problem of resource utilization and management manifests itself when detailed data resides on multiple platforms.

Another related problem is "leaving" detailed data on one side of the data warehouse after it has been transported from the other side. This casual redeployment of detailed data has the effect of creating redundancy of data at the detailed level, something that is not acceptable.

Metadata

In any case, whether detailed data is managed on a single technology or on multiple technologies, the role of metadata is not diminished. Figure 6-41 shows that metadata is needed to sit on top of the detailed data warehouse data.

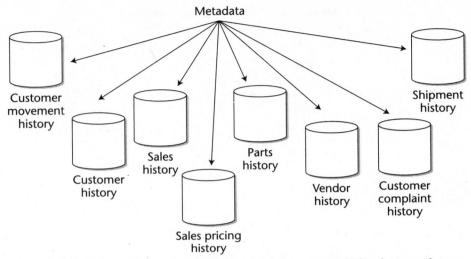

Figure 6-41   Metadata sits on top of the actual data contents of the data warehouse.

Multiple Platforms for Common Detail Data

One other possibility worth mentioning is using multiple platforms for common detail of data. Figure 6-42 outlines this scenario.

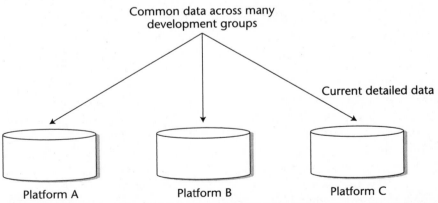

Figure 6-42   Common detailed data across multiple platforms — a real red flag in all cases.

While such a possibility is certainly an option, it is almost never a good choice. Managing common current detailed data is difficult enough. The volumes of data found at that level present their own unique problems for management. Adding the complication of having to cross multiple technological platforms merely makes life more difficult. Unless there are very unusual mitigating circumstances, this option is not recommended.

The only advantage of multiple platforms for the management of common detail is that this option satisfies immediate political and organizational differences of opinion.

Summary

Most environments operate from a single centralized data warehouse. But in some circumstances, there can be a distributed data warehouse. The three types of distributed data warehouses are as follows:

- Data warehouses serving global businesses where there are local operations and a central operation
- Technologically distributed data warehouses where the volume of data is such that the data is spread over multiple physical volumes
- Disparate data warehouses that have grown separately through lack of organizational or political alignment

Each type of distributed data warehouses has its own considerations.

The most difficult aspect of a global data warehouse is the mapping done at the local level. The mapping must account for conversion, integration, and different business practices. The mapping is done iteratively. In many cases, the global data warehouse will be quite simple because only the corporate data that participates in business integration will be found in the global data warehouse. Much of the local data will never be passed to or participate in the loading of the global data warehouse. Access of global data is done according to the business needs of the analyst. As long as the analyst is focusing on a local business practice, access to global data is an acceptable practice.

The local data warehouses often are housed on different technologies. In addition, the global data warehouse may be on a different technology than any of the local data warehouses. The corporate data model acts as the glue that holds the different local data warehouses together, as far as their intersection at the global data warehouse is concerned. There may be local data warehouses that house data unique to and of interest to the local operating site. There may also be a globally distributed data warehouse. The structure and content of the distributed global data warehouse are determined centrally, whereas the mapping of data into the global data warehouse is determined locally.

The coordination and administration of the distributed data warehouse environment is much more complex than that of the single-site data warehouse. Many issues relate to the transport of the data from the local environment to the global environment, including the following questions:

- What network technology will be used?
- Is the transport of data legal?
- Is there a processing window large enough at the global site?
- What technological conversion must be done?

Executive Information Systems and the Data Warehouse

Prior to data warehousing, there were Executive Information Systems (EIS). EIS was a notion that computation should be available to everyone in the corporation, not just the clerical community doing day-to-day transactions. EIS presented the executive with a set of appealing screens. The idea was that the elegance of the screen presentation would beguile the executive. While there certainly is merit to the idea that the world of computation should be open to the executive, the founders of EIS had no concept of the infrastructure needed to get those numbers to the executive. The entire idea behind EIS was presentation of information with no real understanding of the infrastructure needed to create that information in the first place.

When the data warehouse first appeared, the EIS community roundly derided it as a complex discipline that required getting the hands dirty. EIS was a high-minded, elegant discipline that was above the hard work and management of complexity involved in a data warehouse. The EIS community decided that executives had better things to do than worry about such issues as sources of data, quality of data, currency of data, and so forth. And so EIS eventually died for lack of an infrastructure. (It can be argued that when the data warehouse appeared, EIS morphed into business intelligence.) It hardly mattered that the presentation to the executive was elegant if the numbers being presented were unbelievable, inaccurate, or just plain unavailable.

This chapter first appeared as a white paper just as EIS was on its way out (or as EIS was being morphed). As originally written, this chapter was an attempt to appeal to the EIS community, based on the rationality of the necessity of an infrastructure. But the wisdom of the EIS community and its venture capital backers was such that there was to be no relationship between data warehousing and EIS. When it came to the infrastructure needed to support the grandiose plans of the EIS community, the EIS community and their venture capital community just didn't get it.

EIS as it was known in its earliest manifestation has all but disappeared, but the promises made by EIS are still valuable and real. Consequently, EIS has reappeared in many forms today — such as OLAP processing and DSS applications like customer relationship management (CRM). Those more modern forms of EIS are very much related to data warehousing, unlike the earliest forms of EIS.

EIS — The Promise

EIS is one of the most potent forms of computing. Through EIS, the executive analyst can pinpoint problems and detect trends that are of vital importance to management. In a sense, EIS represents one of the most sophisticated applications of computer technology.

EIS processing is designed to help the executive make decisions. In many regards, EIS becomes the executive's window into the corporation. EIS processing looks across broad vistas and picks out the aspects that are relevant to the running of the business. Some of the typical uses of EIS are these:

- Trend analysis and detection
- Key ratio indicator measurement and tracking
- Drill-down analysis
- Problem monitoring
- Competitive analysis
- Key performance indicator monitoring

A Simple Example

As an example of how EIS analysis might appear to an executive, consider Figure 7-1, which shows information on policies offered by an insurance company. Quarter by quarter, the new life, health, and casualty policy sales are tracked. The simple graph shown in Figure 7-1 is a good starting point for an executive's probing into the state of the business. Once the executive has seen the overall information, he or she can probe more deeply, as shown by the trend analysis in Figure 7-2.

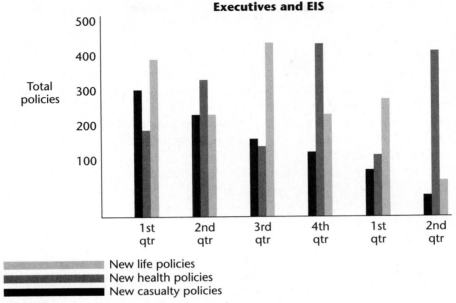

Figure 7-1   A chart typical of EIS processing.

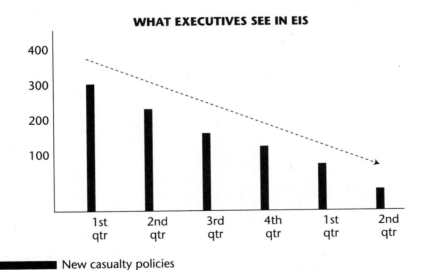

Figure 7-2   Trends — new casualty policy sales are dropping off.

In Figure 7-2, the executive has isolated new casualty sales from new life sales and new health sales. Looking just at new casualty sales, the executive identifies a trend: New casualty sales are dropping off each quarter. Having identified the trend, the executive can investigate why sales are dropping.

The EIS analysis alerts the executive as to what the trends are. It is then up to him or her to discover the underlying reasons for the trends.

The executive is interested in both negative and positive trends. If business is getting worse, why, and at what rate? What can be done to remedy the situation? Or, if business is picking up, who and what are responsible for the upturn? What can be done to accelerate and accentuate the success factors? Can the success factors be applied to other parts of the business?

Trends are not the only type of analysis accommodated by EIS. Another type of useful analysis is comparisons. Figure 7-3 shows a comparison that might be found in an EIS analysis.

Looking at fourth-quarter data, first-quarter data, and second-quarter data in Figure 7-3, the question can be asked, "Why is there such a difference in sales of new health policies for the past three quarters?" The EIS processing alerts the manager to these differences. It is then the job of the EIS analyst to determine the underlying reasons.

For the manager of a large, diverse enterprise, EIS allows a look at the activities of the enterprise in many ways. Trying to keep track of a large number of activities is much more difficult than trying to keep track of just a few activities. In that sense, EIS can be used to expand the scope of control of a manager.

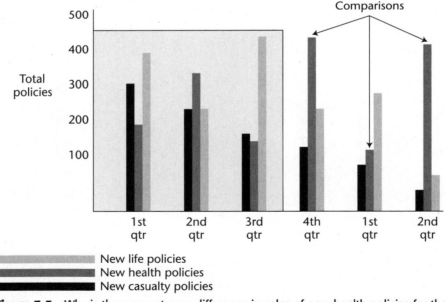

Figure 7-3   Why is there an extreme difference in sales of new health policies for the past three quarters?

But trend analysis and comparisons are not the only ways that the manager can use EIS effectively. Another approach is to "slice-and-dice." Here the analyst takes basic information, groups it one way, and analyzes it, and then groups it another way and reanalyzes it. Slicing and dicing allows the manager to have many different perspectives of the activities that are occurring.

Drill-Down Analysis

To do slicing and dicing, it is necessary to be able to *drill down* on data. Drilling down refers to the ability to start at a summary number and to break that summary into a successively finer set of summarizations. By being able to get at the detail beneath a summary number, the manager can get a feel for what is happening, especially where the summary number is surprising. Figure 7-4 shows a simple example of drill-down analysis.

In Figure 7-4, the manager has seen second-quarter summary results and wants to explore them further. The manager then looks at the regions that have contributed to the summary analysis. The figures analyzed are those of the Western region, the Southeast region, the Northeast region, and the Central region. In looking at the numbers of each region, the manager decides to look more closely at the Northeast region's numbers.

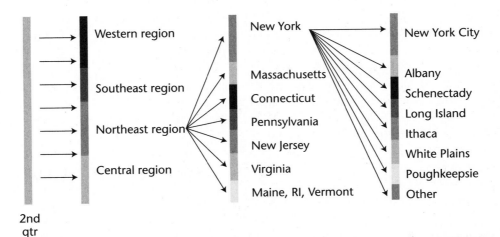

Figure 7-4   To make sense of the numbers shown by EIS, the numbers need to support a drill-down process.

The Northeast's numbers are made up of totals from New York, Massachusetts, Connecticut, Pennsylvania, New Jersey, Virginia, Maine, Rhode Island, and Vermont. Of these states, the manager then decides to look more closely at the numbers for New York. The different cities in New York that have outlets are then queried.

In each case, the manager has selected a path of going from summary to detail, and then to a successively lower level. In such a fashion, he or she can determine where the troublesome results are. Once the anomalies have been identified, the manager then knows where to look more closely.

Yet another important aspect of EIS is the ability to track key performance indicators. Although each corporation has its own set, typical key performance indicators might be the following:

- Cash on hand
- Customer pipeline
- Length of sales cycle
- Collection time
- New product channel
- Competitive products

Each corporation has several key performance indicators that — in a single measurement — tell an important story about some aspect of the life of the corporation. On their own, the key performance indicators say a lot about what is going on in the corporation. Taken over time, the key performance indicators say even more because they indicate trends.

It is one thing to say that the cash on hand is $X. It is even more powerful to say that two months ago the cash on hand was $Z, one month ago the cash on hand was $Y, and this month the cash on hand is $X. Looking at key performance indicators over time is one of the most important things an executive can do, and EIS is ideal for this purpose.

There is plenty of very sophisticated software that can be used in EIS to present the results to a manager. The difficult part of EIS is not in the graphical presentation, but in discovering and preparing the numbers – accurately, completely, and integrated — that go into the graphics, as shown in Figure 7-5.

EIS is perfectly capable of supporting the drill-down process from the graphical perspective as long as the underlying data exists in the first place. However, if the data to analyze does not exist, the drill-down process becomes very tedious and awkward, and is certainly not something the executive wants to do.

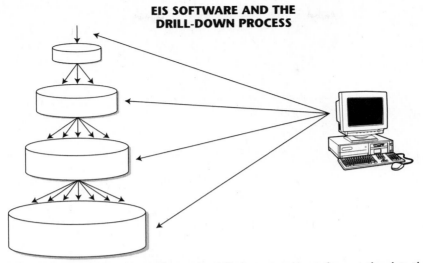

**EIS SOFTWARE AND THE
DRILL-DOWN PROCESS**

Figure 7-5   EIS software supports the drill-down process as long as the data that is needed is available and is structured properly.

Supporting the Drill-Down Process

Creating the basis of data on which to perform drill-down analysis, then, is the major obstacle to successfully implementing the drill-down process, as shown in Figure 7-6. Indeed, some studies indicate that $9 is spent on drill-down data preparation for every $1 spent on EIS software and hardware.

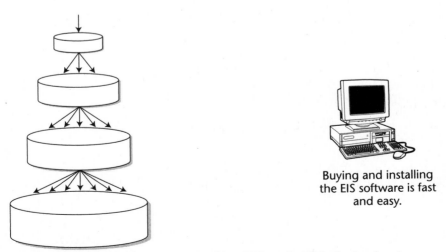

Buying and installing
the EIS software is fast
and easy.

Figure 7-6   Creating the base of data on which to do EIS is the hard part.

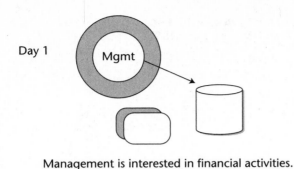

Management is interested in financial activities.

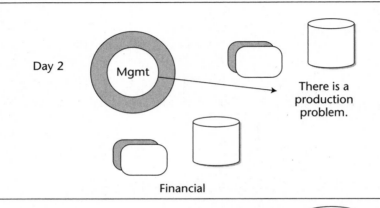

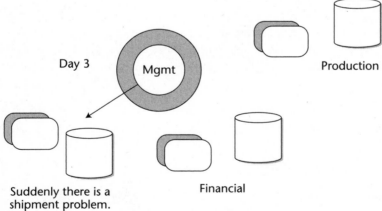

Figure 7-7 The constantly changing interests of executives.

Exacerbating the problem is the fact that the executive is constantly changing his or her mind about what is of interest, as shown in Figure 7-7. On day 1, the executive is interested in the corporation's financial activities. The EIS analyst makes a big effort to develop the underlying data to support EIS interest. Then on day 2, there is an unexpected production problem, and management's attention turns there. The EIS analyst scurries around and tries to gather the data needed by the executive. On day 3, the EIS analyst is directed to the problems that have developed in shipping. Each day there is a new focus for the executive. The EIS analyst simply cannot keep up with the rate at which the executive changes his or her mind.

Don't blame management for changing its mind. Management needs to change its mind every time business changes, and if there is one fact of life it is that business conditions change every day all day.

Management's focus in the running of the business shifts with every new problem or opportunity that arises. There simply is no predictable pattern for what management will be interested in tomorrow. In turn, the EIS analyst is at the end of a whip — the wrong end. The EIS analyst is forever in a reactive state. Furthermore, given the work that is required of the EIS analyst to build the base of data needed for EIS analysis, the EIS analyst is constantly swamped.

The problem is that there is no basis of data from which the EIS analyst can easily work. Each new focus of management requires an entirely different set of data for the EIS analyst. There is no infrastructure to support the EIS environment.

The Data Warehouse as a Basis for EIS

It is in the EIS environment that the data warehouse operates in its most effective state. The data warehouse is tailor-made for the needs of the EIS analyst. Once the data warehouse has been built, the job of the EIS is infinitely easier than when there is no foundation of data on which the EIS analyst can operate. Figure 7-8 shows how the data warehouse supports the need for EIS data.

With a data warehouse, the EIS analyst does not have to worry about the following:

- Searching for the definitive source of data
- Creating special extract programs from existing systems
- Dealing with unintegrated data
- Compiling and linking detailed and summary data and the linkage between the two
- Finding an appropriate time basis of data (finding historical data)
- Management constantly changing its mind about what needs to be looked at next

In addition, the EIS analyst has a rich supply of summary data available.

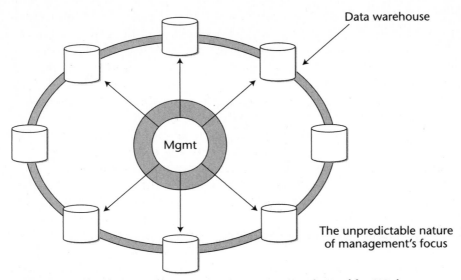

Data warehouse

Mgmt

The unpredictable nature of management's focus

Figure 7-8 The data warehouse supports management's need for EIS data.

In short, the data warehouse provides the basis of data (the infrastructure) that the EIS analyst needs to support EIS processing effectively. With a fully populated data warehouse in place, the EIS analyst can be in a proactive stance — not an eternally reactive stance — with regard to answering management's needs. The EIS analyst's job changes from that of playing data engineer to that of doing true analysis, thanks to the data warehouse.

Yet another very important reason why the data warehouse serves the needs of the world of EIS is this: The data warehouse operates at a low level of granularity. The data warehouse contains — for lack of a better word — *atomic data*. The atomic data can be shaped one way, and then another. When management has a new set of needs for information that has never before been encountered in the corporation, the very detailed data found in the data warehouse sits, waiting to be shaped in a manner suited to management's needs. Because of the granular atomic data that resides in the data warehouse, analysis is flexible and responsive. The detailed data in the data warehouse sits and waits for future unknown needs for information. This is why the data warehouse turns an organization from a reactive stance to a proactive stance.

Where to Turn

The EIS analyst can turn to various places in the architecture to get data. As shown in Figure 7-9, the EIS analyst can go to the individual level of processing, the departmental (data mart) level of processing, the lightly summarized level of processing, or the archival/dormant level of data. In addition, there is a normal sequence or hierarchy in which the EIS analyst goes after data to serve management's needs.

There is a very good reason for the order shown, as indicated in Figure 7-10. By going from the individual level of processing to the archival or dormant level, the analyst does de facto drill-down analysis. The most summarized data found in the architected environment is at the individual level. The supporting level of summary for the individual level is the departmental (data mart) level. Supporting the summaries at the departmental (data mart) level is data at the data warehouse lightly summarized level. Finally, the light summarization at the data warehouse level is supported by archival, dormant data. The sequence of summaries just described is precisely what is required to support drill-down EIS analysis.

Almost by default, the data warehouse lays a path for drill-down analysis. At the different levels of the data warehouse, and throughout the summarization process, data is related by means of a key structure. The key structure itself, or the derivations of the key structure, allow the data to be related so that drill-down analysis is easy and natural.

The ways that EIS is supported by the data warehouse are illustrated in Figure 7-11.

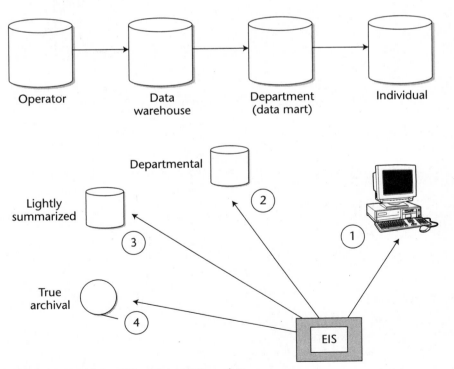

Figure 7-9   Where EIS goes to retrieve data.

REPETITIVE SUMMARY DATA

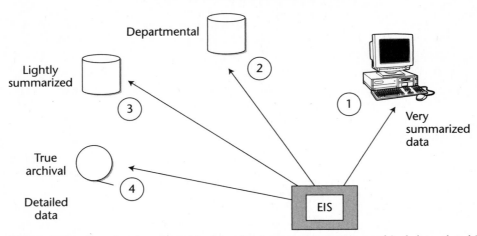

Figure 7-10   In going from individual levels of processing to true archival data, the drill-down process is accommodated.

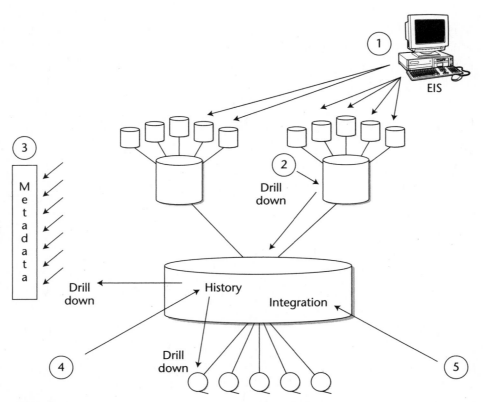

Figure 7-11   How EIS is supported by the data warehouse.

The EIS function uses the following:

- The data warehouse for a readily available supply of summary data
- The structure of the data warehouse to support the drill-down process
- Data warehouse metadata for the DSS analyst to plan how the EIS system is built
- The historical content of the data warehouse to support the trend analysis that management wishes to see
- The integrated data found throughout the data warehouse to look at data across the corporation

Event Mapping

A useful technique in using the data warehouse for EIS processing is event mapping. The simplest way to depict event mapping is to start with a simple trend line.

Figure 7-12 shows that corporate revenues have varied by month, as expected. The trend has been calculated from data found in the data warehouse. The trend of revenues in and of itself is interesting, but gives only a superficial view of what is going on with the corporation. To enhance the view, events are mapped onto the trend line.

In Figure 7-13, three notable events have been mapped to the corporate revenue trend line — the introduction of a "spring colors" line of products, the advent of a sales incentive program, and the introduction of competition. Now the relationship between corporate revenue and significant events begins to take on a different perspective. Looking at the diagram in Figure 7-13, you might draw the conclusion that the introduction of a new line of products and a new incentive plan have boosted revenue and that competition is starting to have an effect in the latter part of the year.

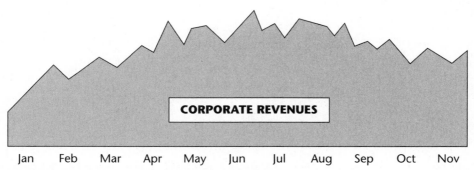

Figure 7-12 Corporate revenue varies by month.

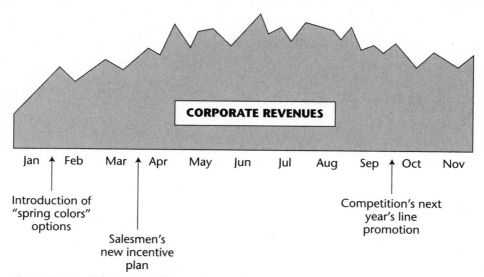

Figure 7-13   Mapping events against a trend line.

For some sorts of events, event mapping is the only way to measure the results. Some events and activities cannot be measured directly and have to be measured in a correlative fashion. Cost justification and actual cost benefit cannot be measured any other way for some types of events.

Misleading conclusions can be drawn, though, by looking at correlative information. It often helps to look at more than one set of trends that relate to the events at hand. As an example, Figure 7-14 shows that corporate revenues are matched against the consumer confidence index to produce a diagram packed with even more perspective. Looking at the figure shown, the executive can make up his or her own mind whether events that have been mapped have shaped sales.

The data warehouse can store both the internally generated revenue numbers and the externally generated consumer confidence numbers.

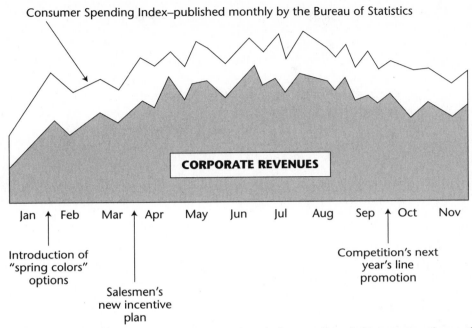

Consumer Spending Index–published monthly by the Bureau of Statistics

CORPORATE REVENUES

Jan   Feb   Mar   Apr   May   Jun   Jul   Aug   Sep   Oct   Nov

Introduction of "spring colors" options

Salesmen's new incentive plan

Competition's next year's line promotion

Figure 7-14   Superimposing another trend analysis over the existing one to gain another perspective.

Detailed Data and EIS

Just how much detailed data do you need to run your EIS/DSS environment? One school of thought says that you need as much detail as possible. By storing as much data as possible, you can do any kind of analysis that might happen along. Because the nature of DSS is delving into the unknown, who knows what detail you will need? To be on the safe side, you'd better keep all the detailed data you can get your hands on. Furthermore, the more historical detailed data you can get, the better, because you never can tell how far back you need to go to do a given DSS analysis.

The logic at the heart of the argument for the storage of massive amounts of detail for DSS processing is hard to argue with. Intellectually, it must be correct to say that you need as much detail as possible for DSS and EIS processing. But, in some important ways, the argument suggests Zeno's paradox. In *Zeno's paradox*, logic inescapably "proves" that a rabbit can never outrun a turtle as long as the turtle has a head start on the rabbit. Of course, reality and our own observations tell us something quite different, warning us that any conclusion based purely on logic is circumspect.

What, then, is so wrong with keeping all the detail in the world around when you are building an EIS/DSS environment? There are several things wrong. First, the amount of money required for both storage and processing costs can go sky-high. The sheer cost of storing and processing huge amounts of detailed data prohibits the establishment of an effective EIS/DSS environment. Second, massive amounts of data form an obstacle to the effective use of analysis techniques. Given very large amounts of data to be processed, important trends and patterns can hide behind the mask of endless records of detailed data. Third, with the detail, reuse of previous analysis is not fostered. As long as there is a massive amount of detail around, DSS analysts are encouraged to create new analyses from scratch. Such a practice is wasteful and potentially harmful. When new analysis is not done in quite the same way as older analysis, very similar analyses are done and ironically conflicting results are obtained.

There is, then, a very real case for storing summary data as well as detailed data. DSS and EIS processing ought to make as much use of summary data as they do of detailed data. Summary data is much less voluminous and much easier to manage than detailed data. From an access and presentation perspective, summary data is ideal for management. Summary data represents a foundation on which future analysis can build and for which existing analysis does not have to be repeated. For these reasons alone, summary data is an integral part of the EIS/DDS environment.

Keeping Only Summary Data in the EIS

Some very real problems become evident with keeping just summary data. First, summary data implies a process — the summary is always created as a result of the process of calculation. The calculation may be very simple or complex. In any case, there is no such thing as summary data that stands alone — summary data of necessity stands with its process. To effectively use summary data, the DSS analyst must have access to and an understanding of the process that has been used to shape it. As long as EIS and DSS understand this relationship between process and summary data, and as long as EIS and DSS can profitably use the summary data that has resulted from the process of calculation, then summary data constitutes an ideal foundation for EIS and DSS. However, if the analysts that are doing EIS/DSS analysis do not understand that process is intimately related to summary data, the results of the analysis can be very misleading.

The second problem with summary data is that it may or may not be at the appropriate level of granularity for the analytical purpose at hand. A balance needs to be struck between the level of detail and the level of summarization for EIS and DSS processing.

Summary

There is a very strong affinity between the needs of the EIS analyst and the data warehouse. The data warehouse explicitly supports all of the EIS analyst's needs. With a data warehouse in place, the EIS analyst can be in a proactive rather than a reactive position.

The data warehouse enables the EIS analyst to deal with the following management needs:

- Accessing information quickly
- Changing their minds (that is, flexibility)
- Looking at integrated data
- Analyzing data over a spectrum of time
- Drilling down

The data warehouse provides an infrastructure on which the EIS analyst can build.

CHAPTER 8

External Data and the Data Warehouse

Most organizations build their first data warehouse efforts on data whose source is existing systems (that is, on data internal to the corporation). In almost every case, this data can be termed internal, structured data. The data comes internally from the corporation and has been already shaped into a regularly occurring format.

A whole host of other data is of legitimate use to a corporation that is not generated from the corporation's own systems. This class of data is called *external data* and usually enters the corporation in an unpredictable format. Figure 8-1 shows external data entering the data warehouse.

The data warehouse is the ideal place to store external data. If external data is not stored in a centrally located place, several problems are sure to arise. Figure 8-2 shows that when this type of data enters the corporation in an undisciplined fashion, the identity of the source of the data is lost, and there is no coordination whatsoever in the orderly use of the data.

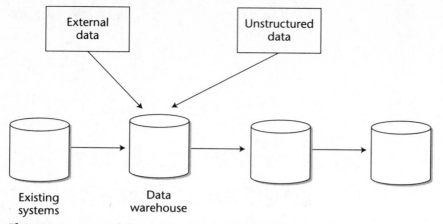

Figure 8-1   External data belongs in the data warehouse.

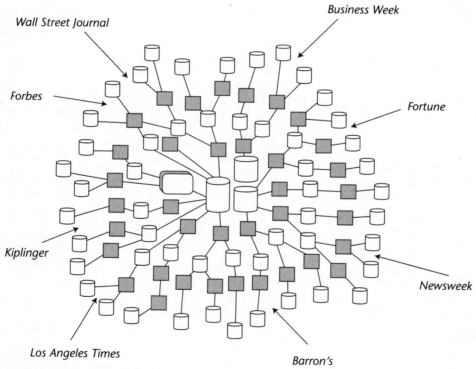

Figure 8-2   Problems with external data.

Typically, when external data is not entered into the data warehouse, it comes into the corporation by means of the personal computer (the PC). There is nothing wrong per se with entering data at the PC level. But almost always, the data is entered manually through a spreadsheet or some other informal system, and absolutely no attempt is made to capture information about its source or the integrity of the data. For example, in Figure 8-2, an analyst sees a report in the *Wall Street Journal*. The next day, the analyst uses the data from the *Wall Street Journal* as part of a report, but the original source of the data is lost as it is entered into the corporate mainstream of data.

Another difficulty with the laissez-faire approach to external data is that, at a later time, it is hard to recall the data. It is entered into the corporation's systems, used once, and then it disappears. Even a few weeks later, it is hard to find and then reprocess the external data for further use. This is unfortunate because much of the data coming from external sources is quite useful over the spectrum of time.

There are two basic types of external data:

- Records of external data collected by some source (such as a drug store, a supermarket, and so forth)
- External data from random reports, articles, and other sources

Some of the sources for external data records might be Dun and Bradstreet, Acxiom, IMS, and others.

The types of data from non-record-oriented external sources are many and diverse. Some typical sources of interesting and useful external data include the following:

- *Wall Street Journal*
- *Business Week*
- *Forbes*
- *Fortune*
- Industry newsletters
- Technology reports
- Reports generated by consultants specifically for the corporation
- Equifax reports
- Competitive analysis reports
- Marketing comparison and analysis reports
- Sales analysis and comparison reports
- New product announcements

In addition, reports internal to the corporation are of interest as well:

- Auditor's quarterly report
- Annual report
- Consultant reports

In a sense, the data generated by the Web-based eBusiness environment is external data, as well. But data coming from the Web environment is at such a low level of detail that the data must be reconstituted before it is useful. This clickstream data, then, is merely a sophisticated form of external data.

External Data in the Data Warehouse

Several issues relate to the use and storage of external data in the data warehouse. One problem of external data is the *frequency of availability*. Unlike internally appearing data, there is no real fixed pattern of appearance for external data. This irregularity is a problem because constant monitoring must be set up to ensure that the right external data is captured. For some environments (such as the Internet), monitoring programs can be created and used to build automated alerts and automated loads.

The second problem with external data is that it is *totally undisciplined*. To be useful, and for placement in the warehouse, a certain amount of reformatting and structuring of external data is needed to transform it into an internally acceptable and usable form in the data warehouse. A common practice is to convert the external data as it enters the data warehouse environment. External key data is converted to internal key data. Or, external data is passed through simple edits, such as a domain check. In addition, the data is often restructured so that it is compatible with internal data.

In some cases, the level of granularity of the external data will not match that of the internal systems of the corporation. For example, suppose a corporation has individual household information. Now, suppose the corporation purchases a list of income by ZIP code. The external list says that the average household income in the ZIP code is $X. The matching of the internal household information is done in such a way that each household in a ZIP code is assigned the income specified by the external file. (This means that some households will be assigned an income level below their means and that other households will be assigned an income level above their means — but, on average, the household income will be about right.) Once this arbitrary assignment of income is done, the data can be sliced and diced into many other patterns.

The third factor that makes external data hard to capture and use is its *unpredictability*. External data may come from practically any source at almost any time.

There are many methods to capture and store external information. One of the best places to locate external data if it is voluminous is on a bulk storage medium such as near-line storage. With near-line storage, the external data is still accessible, but it doesn't cost huge amounts of money to store. Of course, extensive indexing of the external data can be done, and those indexes can be stored in both disk storage and near-line storage. In such a manner, many requests about the external data can be managed without actually having to go to the external data. In addition, some requests can be handled entirely inside the index of the external data itself. Also, if an extensive index of external data is created, the external data can be tied to structured data and the data warehouse. The index can then be used to determine what external data to bring to disk storage. In this case, only external data that is prequalified and preselected would be brought to disk storage.

Another technique for handling external data that is sometimes effective is to create two stores of external data. One store contains all of the external data, and another, much smaller store contains only a subset. The subset of external data can be accessed and analyzed before the large, complete external store is analyzed. When this is done, the potential to save on processing is huge.

The external data becomes an adjunct to the data warehouse. The external data is connected to the data warehouse by means of an index, and the external data is brought into the data warehouse only when there is a specific, prequalified request for it.

Metadata and External Data

As previously discussed, metadata is an important component of the data warehouse in any scenario, but it takes on an entirely different dimension in the face of storing and managing external data. Figure 8-3 shows the role of metadata.

Metadata is vital when it comes to the issue of external data because it is through metadata that external data is registered, accessed, and controlled in the data warehouse environment. The importance of metadata is best understood by noting what it typically encompasses:

- Document ID
- Date of entry into the warehouse
- Description of the document
- Source of the document
- Date of source of the document

- Classification of the document
- Index words
- Purge date
- Physical location reference
- Length of the document
- Related references

It is through the metadata that a manager determines much information about the external data. In many instances, the manager will look at the metadata without ever looking at the source document. Scanning metadata eliminates much work because it filters out documents that are not relevant or are out-of-date. Therefore, properly built and maintained metadata is absolutely essential to the operation of the data warehouse — particularly with regard to external data.

Associated with metadata is another type of data — *notification data*. Shown in Figure 8-4, notification data is merely a file created for users of the system that indicates classifications of data interesting to the users. When data is entered into the data warehouse and into the metadata, a check is made to see who is interested in it. The person is then notified that the external data has been captured.

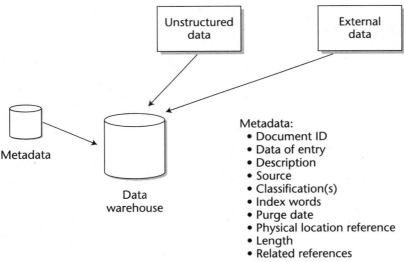

Figure 8-3   Metadata takes on a new role in the face of external data.

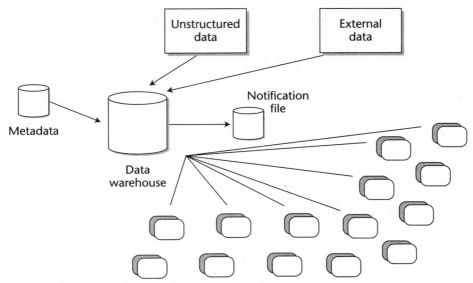

Figure 8-4 Another nice feature of external data and metadata is the ability to create a tailored notification file.

Storing External Data

External data can actually be stored in the data warehouse if it is convenient and cost-effective to do so. But in many cases, it will not be possible or economical to store all external data in the data warehouse. Instead, an entry is made in the metadata of the warehouse describing where the actual body of external data can be found. The external data is then stored elsewhere, where it is convenient, as shown in Figure 8-5. External data may be stored in a filing cabinet, on fiche, on magnetic tape, and so on.

However it is done, storing external data requires considerable resources. By associating external data with a data warehouse, the external data becomes available for all parts of the organization (such as finance, marketing, accounting, sales, engineering, and so forth). The implication is that once the data is captured and managed centrally, the organization has to undergo the expense of dealing with such data only once. But when external data is not associated with a data warehouse, then there is the very real chance that different parts of the organization will capture and store the same data. This duplication of effort and resources is very wasteful and carries with it a very high price tag.

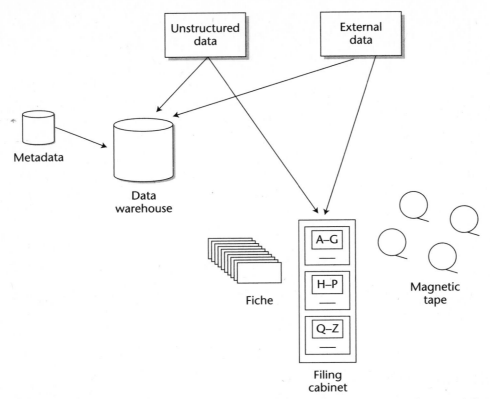

Figure 8-5   In every case, external data is registered with metadata, but the actual data may or may not be stored in the data warehouse based on the size of the data and the probability of access.

Different Components of External Data

One of the important design considerations of external data is that it often contains many different components, some of which are of more use than others. As an example, suppose the complete manufacturing history of a product is purchased. Certain aspects of production are very important, such as the length of time from first to final assembly. Another important production measurement is total cost of unassembled raw goods. But many other unimportant pieces of information accompany the manufacturing information, such as actual date of production, shipment specification, and temperature at production.

To manage the data, an experienced DSS analyst or industrial engineer must determine the most important units of data. Then those units are stored in an online, easy-to-get-to location. There is efficiency of storage and efficiency of access. The remaining, less important detail is not discarded, but is placed in a bulk storage location. In such a manner, large amounts of external data can be efficiently stored and managed.

Modeling and External Data

What is the relationship between the data model and external data? Figure 8-6 reflects the dilemma. The normal role of the data model is the shaping of the environment, usually in terms of design. But external data is not malleable to any extent at all. Therefore, it appears that there is very little relationship between the data model and external data. About the best that can be done is to note the differences between the data model and external data as far as the interpretation of key phrases and words are concerned. Attempting to use the data model for any serious reshaping of the external data is a mistake. The most that can be done is to create subsets of the data that are compatible with the existing internal data.

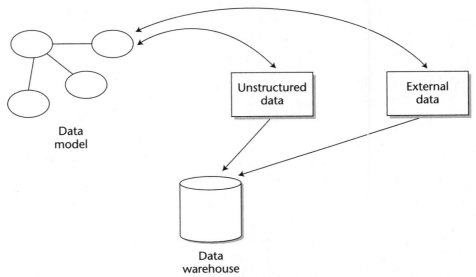

Figure 8-6   There is only a faint resemblance of external data to a data model. Furthermore, nothing can be done about reshaping external data.

Secondary Reports

Not only can primary data be put in the data warehouse, but when data is repetitive in nature, secondary reports can be created from the detailed data over time. For example, take the month-end Dow Jones Industrial Average report shown in Figure 8-7.

In the figure, Dow Jones information comes into the data warehouse environment daily. The daily information is useful, but of even more interest are the long-term trends that are formed. At the end of the month, the Dow Jones average is shuffled off into a secondary report. The secondary report then becomes part of the store of external data contained in the data warehouse.

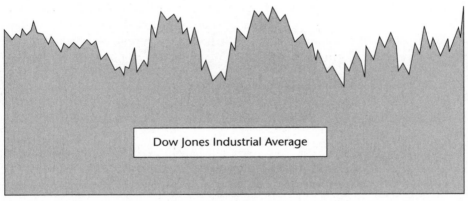

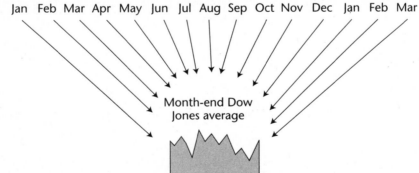

Figure 8-7   Creating a summary report from daily or monthly recurring information.

Archiving External Data

Every piece of information — external or otherwise — has a useful lifetime. Once that lifetime is past, it is not economical to keep the information. An essential part of managing external data is deciding what the useful lifetime of the data is. Even after this is determined, there remains the issue of whether the data should be discarded or put into archives. As a rule, external data may be removed from the data warehouse and placed on less-expensive storage. The metadata reference to the external data is updated to reflect the new storage place and is left in the metadata store. The cost of an entry into the metadata store is so low that once put there, it is best left there.

Comparing Internal Data to External Data

One of the most useful things to do with external data is to compare it to internal data over a period of time. The comparison allows management a unique perspective. For example, being able to contrast immediate and personal activities and trends against global activities and trends allows an executive to have insights that simply are not possible elsewhere. Figure 8-8 shows such a comparison.

When the comparison between external and internal data is made, the assumption is that the comparison is made on a common key. If any other assumption is made, the comparison between external and internal data loses much of its usefulness. Unfortunately, actually achieving a common-key basis between external and internal data is not easy.

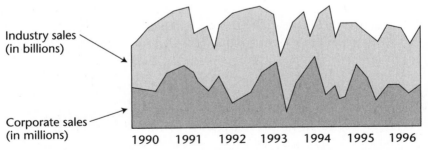

Figure 8-8 Comparing external data to internal data can be very elucidating.

To understand the difficulty, consider two cases. In one case, the commodity being sold is a large, expensive item, such as a car or a television set. For a meaningful comparison, sales-by-actual outlet data needs to be measured. The actual sales-by-dealer data is the basis for comparison. Unfortunately, the key structure used for dealers by the external source of data is not the same key structure used by internal systems. Either the external source must be converted to the key structure of the internal source, or vice versa. Such a conversion is a nontrivial task.

Now consider the measurement of sales of a high-volume, low-cost item such as colas (or sodas). The internal sales figures of the company reflect the sale of colas. But the external sales data has mixed the sales of colas with the sales of other beverages such as beer. Making a comparison between the two types of sales data will lead to some very misleading conclusions. For a meaningful comparison, there needs to be a "cleansing" of the external sales data to include only colas. In fact, if at all possible, colas only of the variety produced and sold by the bottler should be included. Not only should beer be removed from the external sales data, but noncompeting cola types should be removed as well.

Summary

The data warehouse is capable of holding much more than internal, structured data. There is much information relevant to the running of the company that comes from sources outside the company.

External data is captured, and information about the metadata is stored in the data warehouse metadata. External data often undergoes significant editing and transformation as the data is moved from the external environment to the data warehouse environment. The metadata that describes the external data and the unstructured data serves as an executive index to information. Much can be done with the index information, such as placing it in both disk storage and near-line storage, creating a link between the data warehouse and unstructured data, doing internal index processing, and so forth. In addition, a "notification" service is often provided whenever a new entry is made into the data warehouse.

External and unstructured data may or may not actually be stored in the data warehouse. By associating external and unstructured data with a data warehouse, the organization precludes the need to store the external and unstructured data in multiple places. Because of the bulk of data that is associated with unstructured data, it is best to store at least part of the unstructured data on a bulk storage medium such as near-line storage.

CHAPTER 9

Migration to the Architected Environment

Any architecture that must be implemented all at once, in a big bang, is doomed to failure in today's world. There simply is too much risk and too long a period to wait until there is a payback. In addition, trying to freeze changes to consider any path that is revolutionary (rather than evolutionary) is unrealistic.

It is very good news indeed that migrating to the architected data warehouse environment is a step-by-step activity that is accomplished one finite deliverable at a time. The most successful implementations of the architected environment have been those in which the data warehouse has been built one iteration at a time. In doing so, the data warehouse can be built for a minimum of employee resources and with absolutely minimal disruption to the existing applications environment. Both the size and the speed of iterative development are important. Results must be delivered quickly.

In this chapter, a generic migration plan and a methodology for development are discussed. The migration plan has been successfully followed by a wide number of companies; it is anything but a fanciful flight. The approach has been gleaned from the experiences of a number of companies. Of course, each company will have its own diversions and permutations. But the migration plan and approach have met with enough success in enough diverse companies to merit the confidence of the general-purpose developer.

A Migration Plan

The beginning point for the migration plan is a corporate *data model*. This model represents the information needs of the corporation. Keep in mind that it represents what the corporation needs, not necessarily what it currently has. In addition, it is built with no consideration of technology.

The corporate data model may be built internally, or it may have been generated from a generic data model. The corporate data model needs to identify, at a *minimum*, the following:

- Major subjects of the corporation
- Definition of the major subjects of the corporation
- Relationships between the major subjects
- Groupings of keys and attributes that more fully represent the major subjects, including the following:
  - Attributes of the major subjects
  - Keys of the major subjects
  - Repeating groups of keys and attributes
  - Connectors between major subject areas
  - Subtyping relationships

In theory, it is possible to build the architected data-warehouse-centric environment without a data model; however, in practice, it is never done. Trying to build such an environment without a data model is analogous to trying to navigate without a map. It can be done, but like a person who has never been outside of Texas landing at New York's La Guardia airport and driving to midtown Manhattan with no map or instructions, it is very prone to trial and error.

Figure 9-1 shows that building or otherwise acquiring a data model is the starting point for the migration process. As a rule, the corporate data model identifies corporate information at a high level. From the corporate data model, a lower-level model is built. The lower-level model identifies details that have been glossed over by the corporate data model. This mid-level model is built from the subject areas that have been identified in the corporate data model, one subject area at a time. It is not built on an all-at-once basis, because doing so takes too long.

Both the corporate data model and its associated mid-level model focus only on the atomic data of the corporation. No attempt is made to include derived data or DSS data in these models. Instead, derived data and DSS are deliberately excluded from the corporate data model and the mid-level models.

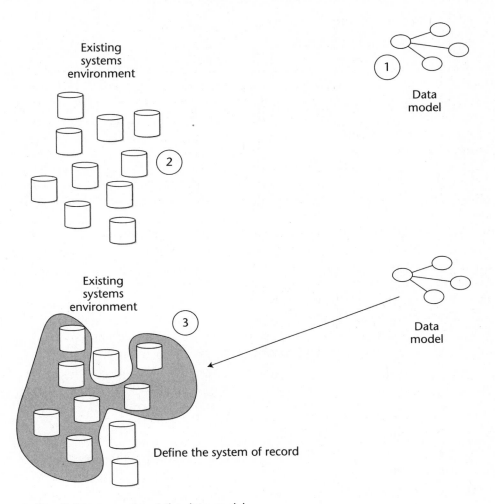

Figure 9-1   Migration to the architected environment.

Some reasons for excluding derived data and DSS data from the corporate data model and the mid-level model include the following:

- Derived data and DSS data change frequently.
- These forms of data are created from atomic data.
- They frequently are deleted altogether.
- There are many variations in the creation of derived data and DSS data.

Because derived data and DSS data are excluded from the corporate data model and the mid-level model, the data model does not take long to build.

After the corporate data model and the mid-level models are in place, the next activity is *defining the system of record*. The system of record is defined in terms of the corporation's existing systems. Usually, these older legacy systems are affectionately known as the "mess."

The system of record is nothing more than the identification of the "best" data the corporation has that resides in the legacy operational or in the Web-based eBusiness environment. The data model is used as a benchmark for determining what the best data is. In other words, the data architect starts with the data model and asks what data is in hand that best fulfills the data requirements identified in the data model. It is understood that the fit will be less than perfect. In some cases, there will be no data in the existing systems environment or the Web-based eBusiness environment that exemplifies the data in the data model. In other cases, many sources of data in the existing systems environment contribute data to the systems of record, each under different circumstances.

The "best" source of existing data or data found in the Web-based eBusiness environment is determined by the following criteria:

- What data in the existing systems or Web-based eBusiness environment is the most complete?
- What data in the existing systems or Web-based eBusiness environment is the timeliest?
- What data in the existing systems or Web-based eBusiness environment is the most accurate?
- What data in the existing systems or Web-based eBusiness environment is the closest to the source of entry into the existing systems or Web-based eBusiness environment?
- What data in the existing systems or Web-based eBusiness environment conforms the most closely to the structure of the data model? In terms of keys? In terms of attributes? In terms of groupings of data attributes?

Using the data model and the criteria described here, the analyst defines the system of record. The system of record then becomes the definition of the source data for the data warehouse environment. Once the system of record is defined, the designer then asks: What are the technological challenges in bringing the system-of-record data into the data warehouse? A short list of the technological challenges includes the following:

- **A change in DBMS** — The system of record is in one DBMS, and the data warehouse is in another DBMS.

- **A change in operating systems** — The system of record is in one operating system, and the data warehouse is in another operating system.

- **The need to merge data from different DBMSs and operating systems** — The system of record spans more than one DBMS and/or operating system. System-of-record data must be pulled from multiple DBMSs and multiple operating systems and must be merged in a meaningful way.

- **The capture of the Web-based data in the Web logs** — Once captured, how can the data be freed for use within the data warehouse?

- **A change in basic data formats** — Data in one environment is stored in ASCII, data in the data warehouse is stored in EBCDIC, and so forth.

Another important technological issue that sometimes must be addressed is the volume of data. In some cases, huge volumes of data will be generated in the legacy environment. Specialized techniques may be needed to enter them into the data warehouse. For example, clickstream data found in the Web logs needs to be preprocessed before it can be used effectively in the data warehouse environment.

There are other issues. In some cases, the data flowing into the data warehouse must be cleansed. In other cases, the data must be summarized. A host of issues relate to the mechanics of the bringing of data from the legacy environment into the data warehouse environment.

After the system of record is defined and the technological challenges in bringing the data into the data warehouse are identified, the next step is to *design the data warehouse*, as shown in Figure 9-2.

If the data modeling activity has been done properly, the design of the data warehouse is fairly simple. Only a few elements of the corporate data model and the mid-level model need to be changed to turn the data model into a data warehouse design. Principally, the following things need to be done:

- An element of time needs to be added to the key structure if one is not already present.

- All purely operational data needs to be eliminated.

- Referential integrity relationships need to be turned into artifacts.

- Derived data that is frequently needed is added to the design.

The structure of the data needs to be altered when appropriate for the following:

- Adding arrays of data
- Adding data redundantly
- Further separating data under the right conditions
- Merging tables when appropriate

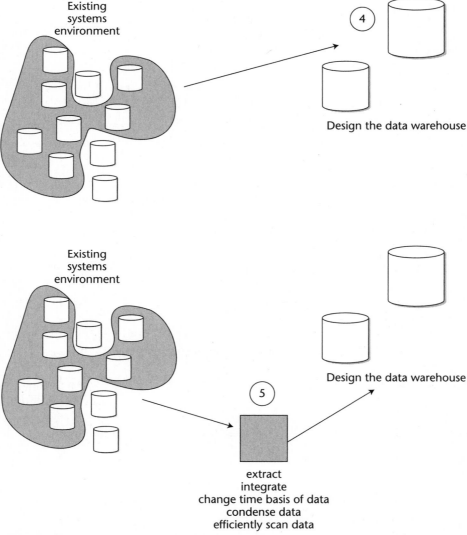

Figure 9-2 Migration to the architected environment.

Stability analysis of the data needs to be done. In stability analysis, data whose content has a propensity for change is isolated from data whose content is very stable. For example, a bank account balance usually changes its content very frequently — as much as three or four times a day. But a customer address changes very slowly — every three or four years or so. Because of the very disparate stability of bank account balance and customer address, these elements of data need to be separated into different physical constructs.

The data warehouse, once designed, is organized by subject area. Typical subject areas are as follows:

- Customer
- Product
- Sale
- Account
- Activity
- Shipment

Within the subject area there will be many separate tables, each of which is connected by a common key. All the customer tables will have CUSTOMER as a key, for example.

One of the important considerations made at this point in the design of the data warehouse is the number of occurrences of data. Data that will have very many occurrences will have a different set of design considerations than data that has very few occurrences. Typically, data that is voluminous will be summarized, aggregated, or partitioned (or all of the above). Sometimes profile records are created for voluminous data occurrences.

In the same vein, data that arrives at the data warehouse quickly (which is usually, but not always, associated with data that is voluminous) must be considered as well. In some cases, the arrival rate of data is such that special considerations must be made to handle the influx of data. Typical design considerations include staging the data, parallelization of the load stream, delayed indexing, and so forth.

After the data warehouse is designed, the next step is to *design and build the interfaces* between the system of record (in the operational environment) and the data warehouses. The interfaces populate the data warehouse on a regular basis.

At first glance, the interfaces appear to be merely an extract process, and it is true that extract processing does occur. But many more activities occur at the point of interface as well:

- Integration of data from the operational, application-oriented environment
- Alteration of the time basis of data

■ Condensation of data

■ Efficient scanning of the existing systems environment

Most of these issues have been discussed elsewhere in this book.

Note that the vast majority of development resources required to build a data warehouse are consumed at this point. It is not unusual for 80 percent of the effort required to build a data warehouse to be spent here. In laying out the development activities for building a data warehouse, most developers overestimate the time required for other activities and underestimate the time required for designing and building the operational-to-data-warehouse interface. In addition to requiring resources for the initial building of the interface into the data warehouse, the ongoing maintenance of the interfaces must be considered. Fortunately, ETL software is available to help build and maintain this interface.

Once the interface programs are designed and built, the next activity is to start the *population of the first subject area,* as shown in Figure 9-3. The population is conceptually very simple. The first of the data is read in the legacy environment; and then it is captured and transported to the data warehouse environment. Once in the data warehouse environment the data is loaded, directories are updated, metadata is created, and indexes are made. The first iteration of the data is now ready for analysis in the data warehouse.

There are many good reasons to populate only a fraction of the data needed in a data warehouse at this point. Changes to the data likely will need to be made. Populating only a small amount of data means that changes can be made easily and quickly. Populating a large amount of data greatly diminishes the flexibility of the data warehouse. Once the end user has had a chance to look at the data (even just a sample of the data) and give feedback to the data architect, then it is safe to populate large volumes of data. But before the end user has a chance to experiment with the data and to probe it, it is not safe to populate large volumes of data.

End users operate in a mode that can be called the "discovery mode." End users don't know what their requirements are until they see what the possibilities are. Initially populating large amounts of data into the data warehouse is dangerous — it is a sure thing that the data will change once populated. Jon Geiger says that the mode of building the data warehouse is "build it wrong the first time." This tongue-in-cheek assessment has a strong element of truth in it.

The population and feedback processes continue for a long period (indefinitely). In addition, the data in the warehouse continues to be changed. Of course, over time, as the data becomes stable, it changes less and less.

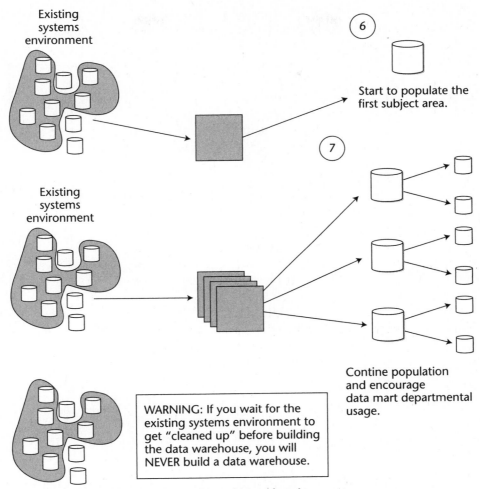

Existing systems environment

6

Start to populate the first subject area.

7

Existing systems environment

Contine population and encourage data mart departmental usage.

WARNING: If you wait for the existing systems environment to get "cleaned up" before building the data warehouse, you will NEVER build a data warehouse.

Figure 9-3   Iterative migration to the architected environment.

A word of caution: If you wait for existing systems to be cleaned up, you will never build a data warehouse. The issues and activities of the existing systems' operational environment must be independent of the issues and activities of the data warehouse environment. One train of thought says, "Don't build the data warehouse until the operational environment is cleaned up." This way of thinking may be theoretically appealing, but in truth it is not practical at all.

One observation worthwhile at this point relates to the frequency of refreshment of data into the data warehouse. As a rule, data warehouse data should be refreshed no more frequently than every 24 hours. By making sure that there is at least a 24-hour time delay in the loading of data, the data warehouse developer minimizes the temptation to turn the data warehouse into an operational environment. By strictly enforcing this lag of time, the data warehouse serves the DSS needs of the company, not the operational needs. Most operational processing depends on data being accurate as of the moment of access (that is, current-value data). By ensuring that there is a 24-hour delay (at the least), the data warehouse developer adds an important ingredient that maximizes the chances for success.

In some cases, the lag of time can be much longer than 24 hours. If the data is not needed in the environment beyond the data warehouse, then it may make sense not to move the data into the data warehouse on a weekly, monthly, or even quarterly basis. Letting the data sit in the operational environment allows it to settle. If adjustments need to be made, then they can be made there with no impact on the data warehouse if the data has not already been moved to the warehouse environment.

But there are cases where rapidly placing data in the warehouse may be what the requirements are. In this case, it helps to have technology suited for what is termed *active data warehousing*. Active data warehousing refers to the technology of being able to support some small amount of online access processing in the data warehouse. (See Teradata for an example of active data warehousing.)

The Feedback Loop

At the heart of success in the long-term development of the data warehouse is the feedback loop between the data architect and the DSS analyst, shown in Figure 9-4. Here the data warehouse is populated from existing systems. The DSS analyst uses the data warehouse as a basis for analysis. On finding new opportunities, the DSS analyst conveys those requirements to the data architect, who makes the appropriate adjustments. The data architect may add data, delete data, alter data, and so forth based on the recommendations of the end user who has touched the data warehouse.

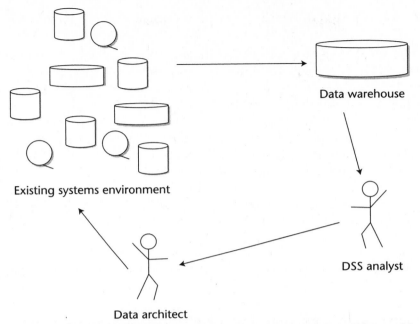

Figure 9-4   The crucial feedback loop between DSS analyst and data architect.

A few observations about this feedback loop are of vital importance to the success of the data warehouse environment:

- The DSS analyst operates — quite legitimately — in a "give me what I want, and then I can tell you what I really want" mode. Trying to get requirements from the DSS analyst before he or she knows what the options are is an impossibility.

- The shorter the cycle of the feedback loop, the more successful the warehouse effort. Once the DSS analyst makes a good case for changes to the data warehouse, those changes need to be implemented as soon as possible.

- The larger the volume of data that has to be changed, the longer the feedback loop takes. It is much easier to change 10GB of data than 100GB of data.

Failing to implement the feedback loop greatly short-circuits the probability of success in the data warehouse environment.

Strategic Considerations

Figure 9-5 shows that the path of activities that have been described addresses the DSS needs of the organization. The data warehouse environment is designed and built for the purpose of supporting the DSS needs of the organization, but there are needs other than DSS needs.

Figure 9-6 shows that the corporation has operational needs as well. In addition, the data warehouse sits at the hub of many other architectural entities, each of which depends on the data warehouse for data.

In Figure 9-6, the operational world is shown as being in a state of chaos. There is much unintegrated data, and the data and systems are so old and so patched they cannot be maintained. In addition, the requirements that originally shaped the operational applications have changed into an almost unrecognizable form.

The migration plan that has been discussed is solely for the construction of the data warehouse. Isn't there an opportunity to rectify some or much of the operational "mess" at the same time that the data warehouse is being built? The answer is that, to some extent, the migration plan that has been described presents an opportunity to rebuild at least some of the less than aesthetically pleasing aspects of the operational environment.

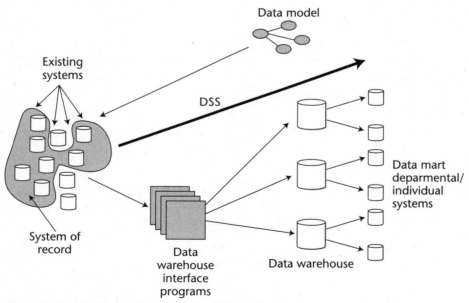

Figure 9-5   The first major path to be followed is DSS.

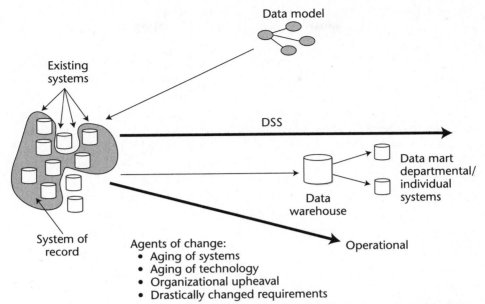

Figure 9-6   To be successful, the data architect should wait for agents of change to become compelling and ally the efforts toward the architected environment with the appropriate agents.

One approach — which is on a track independent of the migration to the data warehouse environment — is to use the data model as a guideline and make a case to management that major changes need to be made to the operational environment. The industry track record of this approach is dismal. The amount of effort, the amount of resources, and the disruption to the end user in undertaking a massive rewrite and restructuring of operational data and systems is such that management seldom supports such an effort with the needed level of commitment and resources.

A better ploy is to coordinate the effort to rebuild operational systems with what are termed the "agents of change":

- The aging of systems
- The radical changing of technology
- Organizational upheaval
- Massive business changes

When management faces the effects of the agents of change, there is no question that changes will have to be made — the only question is how soon and at what expense. The data architect allies the agents of change with the notion of an architecture and presents management with an irresistible argument for the purpose of restructuring operational processing.

The steps the data architect takes to restructure the operational environment — which is an activity independent of the building of the data warehouse — are shown in Figure 9-7.

First a "delta" list is created. The *delta list* is an assessment of the differences between the operational environment and the environment depicted by the data model. The delta list is simple, with very little elaboration.

The next step is the *impact analysis*. At this point an assessment is made of the impact of each item on the delta list. Some items may have a serious impact; other items may have a negligible impact on the running of the company.

Next, the *resource estimate* is created. This estimate is for the determination of how many resources will be required to "fix" the delta list item.

Finally, all the preceding are packaged in a *report that goes to information systems management*. Management then makes a decision as to what work should proceed, at what pace, and so forth. The decision is made in light of all the priorities of the corporation.

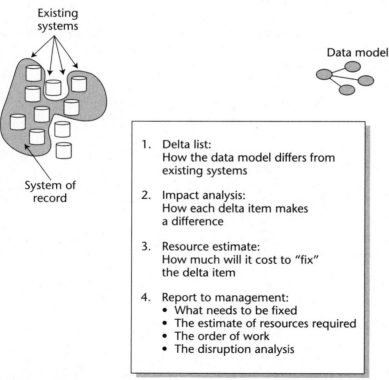

Figure 9-7   The first steps in creating the operational cleanup plan.

Methodology and Migration

The methodology for the building of the data warehouse is called a *spiral development methodology*. A good example of the spiral development methodology is built by J D Welch and sold by Ascential corporation as "Iterations." The spiral methodology is actually much larger than just a development methodology in that it not only contains information about how to build a data warehouse, but also describes how to use the data warehouse.

The spiral development methodology differs from the migration path in several ways. The migration path describes general activities dynamically. The spiral development methodology describes specific activities, deliverables from those activities, and the order of the activities. The iterative dynamics of creating a warehouse are not described, though. In other words, the migration plan describes a sketchy plan in three dimensions, while the spiral development methodology describes a detailed plan in one dimension. Together they form a complete picture of what is required to build the data warehouse.

A Data-Driven Development Methodology

Development methodologies are quite appealing to the intellect. After all, methodology directs the developer down a rational path, pointing out what needs to be done, in what order, and how long the activity should take. However, as attractive as the notion of a methodology is, the industry track record for methodologies has not been good. Across the board, the enthusiasm for methodologies (data warehouse or any other) has met with disappointment on implementation.

Why have methodologies been disappointing? The reasons are many:

- Methodologies generally show a flat, linear flow of activities. In fact, almost any methodology requires execution in terms of iterations. In other words, it is absolutely normal to execute two or three steps, stop, and repeat all or part of those steps again. Methodologies usually don't recognize the need to revisit one or more activities. In the case of the data warehouse, this lack of support for iterations makes a methodology a very questionable subject.

- Methodologies usually show activities as occurring once and only once. Indeed, while some activities need to be done (successfully) only once, others are done repeatedly for different cases (which is a different case than reiteration for refinement).

- Methodologies usually describe a prescribed set of activities to be done. Often, some of the activities don't need to be done at all, other activities need to be done that are not shown as part of the methodology, and so forth.

- Methodologies often tell how to do something, not what needs to be done. In describing how to do something, the effectiveness of the methodology becomes mired in detail and in special cases.

- Methodologies often do not distinguish between the sizes of the systems being developed under the methodology. Some systems are so small that a rigorous methodology makes no sense. Some systems are just the right size for a methodology. Other systems are so large that their sheer size and complexity will overwhelm the methodology.

- Methodologies often mix project management concerns with design and development activities to be done. Usually, project management activities should be kept separate from methodological concerns.

- Methodologies often do not make the distinction between operational and DSS processing. The system development life cycles for operational and DSS processing are diametrically opposed in many ways. A methodology must distinguish between operational and DSS processing and development in order to be successful.

- Methodologies often do not include checkpoints and stopping places in the case of failure. "What is the next step if the previous step has not been done properly?" is usually not a standard part of a methodology.

- Methodologies are often sold as solutions, not tools. When a methodology is sold as a solution, inevitably it is asked to replace good judgment and common sense, and this is always a mistake.

- Methodologies often generate a lot of paper and very little design. Design and development activities are not legitimately replaced by paper.

Methodologies can be very complex, anticipating every possibility that may ever happen. Despite these drawbacks, there still is some general appeal for methodologies. A general-purpose methodology — applicable to the data-driven environment — is described in the spiral development methodology by J D Welch, with full recognition of the pitfalls and track record of methodologies. The data-driven methodology that is outlined owes much to its early predecessors. As such, for a much fuller explanation of the intricacies and techniques described in the methodology, refer to the resources listed in "References" in the back of this book.

One of the salient aspects of a data-driven methodology is that it builds on previous efforts — using both code and processes that have already been developed. The only way that development on previous efforts can be achieved is through the recognition of commonality. Before the developer strikes the first line of code or designs the first database, he or she needs to know what already exists and how it affects the development process. A conscious effort must be made to use what is already in place and not reinvent the wheel. That is one of the essences of data-driven development.

The data warehouse environment is built under what is best termed as an *iterative development approach*. In this approach, a small part of the system is built to completion, and then another small part is completed, and so forth. That development proceeds down the same path repeatedly, which makes the approach appear to be constantly recycling itself. The constant recycling leads to the term *spiral development*.

The spiral approach to development is distinct from the classical approach, which can be called the *waterfall approach*. In the waterfall approach, all of one activity is completed before the next activity can begin, and the results of one activity feed another. Requirements gathering is done to completion before analysis and synthesization commence. Analysis and synthesization are done to completion before design begins. The results of analysis and synthesization feed the process of design, and so forth. The net result of the waterfall approach is that huge amounts of time are spent making any one step complete, causing the development process to move at a glacial speed.

Figure 9-8 shows the differences between the waterfall approach and the spiral approach.

Because the spiral development process is driven by a data model, it is often said to be data driven.

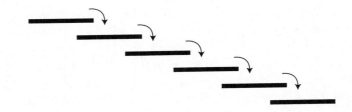

A classical waterfall development approach to development

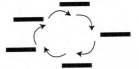

An iterative, or "spiral," approach to development

Figure 9-8   The differences between development approaches, from a high level.

Data-Driven Methodology

What makes a methodology data driven? How is a data-driven methodology any different from any other methodology? There are at least two distinguishing characteristics of a data-driven methodology.

A data-driven methodology does not take an application-by-application approach to the development of systems. Instead, code and data that have been built previously are built on, rather than built around. To build on previous efforts, the commonality of data and processing must be recognized. Once recognized, data is built on if it already exists; if no data exists, data is constructed so that future development may be built on it. The key to the recognition of commonality is the data model.

There is an emphasis on the central store of data — the data warehouse — as the basis for DSS processing, recognizing that DSS processing has a very different development life cycle than operational systems.

System Development Life Cycles

Fundamentally, shaping the data-driven development methodology is the profound difference in the system development life cycles of operational and DSS systems. Operational development is shaped around a development life cycle that begins with requirements and ends with code. DSS processing begins with data and ends with requirements.

A Philosophical Observation

In some regards, the best example of methodology is the Boy Scout and Girl Scout merit badge system, which is used to determine when a scout is ready to pass to the next rank. It applies to both country- and city-dwelling boys and girls, to the athletically inclined and the intellectually inclined, and to all geographical areas. In short, the merit badge system is a uniform methodology for the measurement of accomplishment that has stood the test of time.

Is there is any secret to the merit badge methodology? If so, it is this: The merit badge methodology does not prescribe how any activity is to be accomplished; instead, it merely describes what is to be done with parameters for the measurement of the achievement. The how-to that is required is left up to the Boy Scout or Girl Scout.

Philosophically, the approach to methodology described in the spiral development methodology by J D Welch takes the same perspective as the merit badge system. The results of what must be accomplished and, generally speaking, the order in which things must be done is described. How the results required are to be achieved is left entirely up to the developer.

Summary

In this chapter, a migration plan and a methodology (as found in the spiral development methodology by J D Welch) were described. The migration plan addresses the issues of transforming data out of the existing systems environment into the data warehouse environment. In addition, the dynamics of how the operational environment might be organized were discussed.

The data warehouse is built iteratively. It is a mistake to build and populate major portions of the data warehouse — especially at the beginning — because the end user operates in what can be termed the "mode of discovery." The end user cannot articulate what he or she wants until the possibilities are known.

The process of integration and transformation of data typically consumes up to 80 percent of development resources. In recent years, ETL software has automated the legacy-to-data-warehouse interface development process.

The starting point for the design of the data warehouse is the corporate data model, which identifies the major subject areas of the corporation. From the corporate data model is created a lower "mid-level" model. The corporate data model and the mid-level model are used as a basis for database design. After the corporate data model and the mid-level model have been created, such factors as the number of occurrences of data, the rate at which the data is used, the patterns of usage of the data, and more are factored into the design.

The development approach for the data warehouse environment is said to be an iterative or a spiral development approach. The spiral development approach is fundamentally different from the classical waterfall development approach.

A general-purpose, data-driven methodology was also discussed. The general-purpose methodology has three phases — an operational phase, a data warehouse construction phase, and a data warehouse iterative usage phase.

The feedback loop between the data architect and the end user is an important part of the migration process. Once the first of the data is populated into the data warehouse, the data architect listens very carefully to the end user, making adjustments to the data that has been populated. This means that the data warehouse is in constant repair. During the early stages of the development, repairs to the data warehouse are considerable. But as time passes and as the data warehouse becomes stable, the number of repairs drops off.

The Data Warehouse
and the Web

One of the most widely discussed technologies is the Internet and its associated environment — the World Wide Web. Embraced by Wall Street as the basis for the new economy, Web technology enjoys wide popular support among business people and technicians alike. Although not obvious at first glance, there is a very strong affinity between the Web sites built by organizations and the data warehouse. Indeed, data warehousing provides the foundation for the successful operation of a Web-based eBusiness environment.

The Web environment is owned and managed by the corporation. In some cases, the Web environment is outsourced. But in most cases, the Web is a normal part of computer operations, and it is often used as a hub for the integration of business systems. (Note that if the Web environment is outsourced, it becomes much more difficult to capture, retrieve, and integrate Web data with corporate processing.)

The Web environment interacts with corporate systems in two basic ways. One interaction occurs when the Web environment creates a transaction that needs to be executed — an order from a customer, for example. The transaction is formatted and shipped to corporate systems, where it is processed just like any other order. In this regard, the Web is merely another source for transactions entering the business.

But the Web interacts with corporate systems another way as well — through the collection of Web activity in a log. Figure 10-1 shows the capture of Web activity and the placement of that activity in a log.

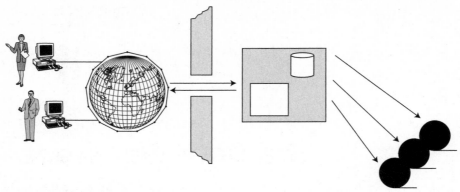

Figure 10-1 The activity of the Web environment is spun off into Web logs in records called clickstream records.

The Web log contains what is typically called *clickstream data*. Each time the Internet user clicks to move to a different location, a clickstream record is created. As the user looks at different corporate products, a record of what the user has looked at, what the user has purchased, and what the user has thought about purchasing is compiled. Equally important, what the Internet user has not looked at and has not purchased can be determined. In a word, the clickstream data is the key to understanding the stream of consciousness of the Internet user. By understanding the mindset of the Internet user, the business analyst can understand very directly how products, advertising, and promotions are being received by the public, in a way much more quantified and much more powerful than ever before.

But the technology required to make this powerful interaction happen is not trivial. There are some obstacles to understanding the data that comes from the Web environment. For example, Web-generated data is at a very low level of detail — in fact, so low that it is not fit for either analysis or entry into the data warehouse. To make the clickstream data useful for analysis and the warehouse, the log data must be read and refined.

Figure 10-2 shows that Web log clickstream data is passed through software that is called a *Granularity Manager (GM)* before entry into the data warehouse environment.

A lot of processing occurs in the Granularity Manager, which reads clickstream data and does the following:

- Edits out extraneous data
- Creates a single record out of multiple, related clickstream log records

- Edits out incorrect data
- Converts data that is unique to the Web environment, especially key data that needs to be used in the integration with other corporate data
- Summarizes data
- Aggregates data

As a rule of thumb, about 90 percent of raw clickstream data is discarded or summarized as it passes through the Granularity Manager. Once it is passed through the manager into the data warehouse, the clickstream data is ready for integration into the mainstream of corporate processing.

In summary, the process of moving data from the Web into the data warehouse involves these steps:

1. Web data is collected into a log.
2. The log data is processed by passing through a Granularity Manager.
3. The Granularity Manager then passes the refined data into the data warehouse.

The way that data passes back into the Web environment is not quite as straightforward. Simply stated, the data warehouse does not pass data directly back into the Web environment. To understand why there is a less-than-straightforward access of data warehouse data, it is important to understand why the Web environment needs data warehouse data in the first place.

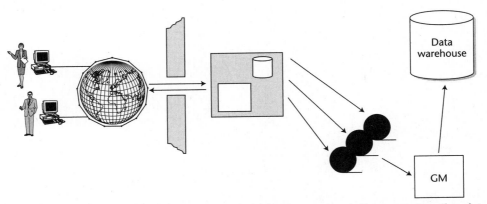

Figure 10-2 Data passes through the Granularity Manager before entering the data warehouse.

The Web environment needs this type of data because it is in the data warehouse that corporate information is integrated. For example, suppose there's a Web site dedicated to selling clothes. Now suppose the business analyst decides that it would be nice for a clothing customer to become a customer for other goods the business sells, such as gardening tools, sports gear, travel accessories, and costume jewelry. The analyst might decide to initiate a special promotion for fancy women's dresses and upscale costume jewelry. But where does the analyst turn to find which women customers have bought costume jewelry in the past? Why, naturally, he or she turns to the data warehouse because that is where the historical information about customers is found.

In another example, suppose the Web site is dedicated to selling cars. The analyst would really like to know who has purchased the brand of car the company is selling. Where is the historical information of this variety found? In the data warehouse, of course.

The data warehouse then provides a foundation of integrated historical information that is available to the business analyst. This affinity between the data warehouse and the Web is shown in Figure 10-3.

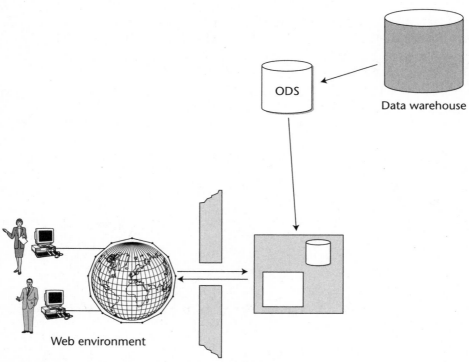

Figure 10-3   Data is passed to the ODS before it goes to the Web.

Figure 10-3 shows that data passes out of the data warehouse into the corporate *operational data store (ODS)*, where it is then available for direct access from the Web. At first glance, it may seem odd that the ODS sits between the data warehouse and the Web. There are some very good reasons for this positioning.

The ODS is a hybrid structure that has some aspects of a data warehouse and other aspects of an operational system. The ODS contains integrated data and can support DSS processing. But the ODS can also support high-performance transaction processing. It is this last characteristic of the ODS that makes it so valuable to the Web.

When a Web site accesses the ODS, the Web environment knows that it will receive a reply in a matter of milliseconds. This speedy response time makes it possible for the Web to perform true transaction processing. If the Web were to directly access the data warehouse, it could take minutes to receive a reply from the warehouse. In the world of the Internet, where users are highly sensitive to response time, this would be unacceptable. Clearly, the data warehouse is not designed to support online response time. However, the ODS is designed for that purpose. Therefore, the direct input into the Web environment is the ODS, as shown in Figure 10-4.

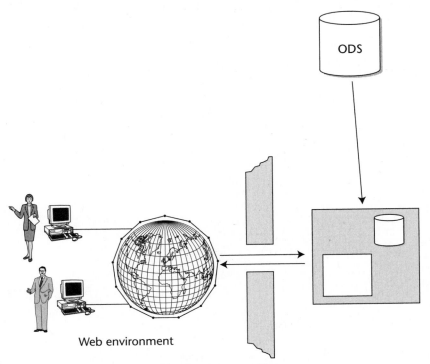

Figure 10-4 The ODS provides fast response time.

At first glance, it may seem that there is a lot of redundant data between the data warehouse and the ODS. After all, the ODS is fed from the data warehouse. Note that the ODS being discussed here is a class IV ODS. For a complete description of the other classes of ODS, refer to my book *Building the Operational Data Store, Second Edition* (Hoboken, N.J.: Wiley, 1999).

In truth, there is very little overlap of data between the data warehouse and the ODS. The data warehouse contains detailed transaction data, while the ODS contains what can be termed "profile" data. To understand the differences between *profile data* and *detailed transaction data*, consider the data seen in Figure 10-5.

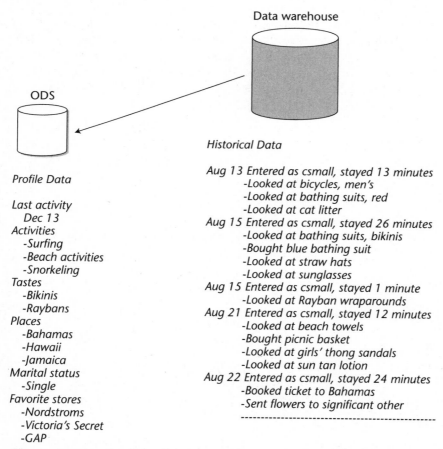

Data warehouse

ODS

Historical Data

Profile Data

Last activity
  Dec 13
Activities
  -Surfing
  -Beach activities
  -Snorkeling
Tastes
  -Bikinis
  -Raybans
Places
  -Bahamas
  -Hawaii
  -Jamaica
Marital status
  -Single
Favorite stores
  -Nordstroms
  -Victoria's Secret
  -GAP

Aug 13 Entered as csmall, stayed 13 minutes
      -Looked at bicycles, men's
      -Looked at bathing suits, red
      -Looked at cat litter
Aug 15 Entered as csmall, stayed 26 minutes
      -Looked at bathing suits, bikinis
      -Bought blue bathing suit
      -Looked at straw hats
      -Looked at sunglasses
Aug 15 Entered as csmall, stayed 1 minute
      -Looked at Rayban wraparounds
Aug 21 Entered as csmall, stayed 12 minutes
      -Looked at beach towels
      -Bought picnic basket
      -Looked at girls' thong sandals
      -Looked at sun tan lotion
Aug 22 Entered as csmall, stayed 24 minutes
      -Booked ticket to Bahamas
      -Sent flowers to significant other

Figure 10-5 The ODS and the data warehouse hold different kinds of data.

The data warehouse contains all sorts of transaction data about past interactions between the customer and the business. Detailed transaction data includes information about the following:

- Searches for men's bicycles
- Searches for women's red bathing suits
- Purchases of a women's blue bathing suits
- Searches for Ray-Ban wraparounds

The data warehouse maintains a detailed log, by customer, of the transactional interactions the customer has had with the business, regardless of the source of the interaction. The interaction could have occurred on the Web, through a catalog order, through a purchase at a retail store, and so forth. Typically, the time the interaction occurred, the place of the interaction, and the nature of the transaction are recorded in the data warehouse.

In addition, the data warehouse contains historical data. The transactions that are found in the data warehouse go back as far as the business analyst thinks is useful — a year, two years, or whatever length of time makes sense. This integrated historical data contains the raw transaction data with no intent to interpret the data.

On the other hand, the ODS is full of interpretive data. Data has been read in the data warehouse, analyzed, and turned into "profile" data, or profile records. The *profile records* reside in the ODS. Figure 10-6 shows that a profile record has been created based on reading all the historical, integrated data found in the data warehouse. The profile record contains all sorts of information that is created as a result of reading and interpreting the transaction data. For example, for the customer shown for Figure 10-6, the profile record shows that the customer is all of the following:

- A beach-oriented person, interested in surfing, sun bathing, and snorkeling
- Likely to travel to places like the Bahamas, Hawaii, and Jamaica
- Single
- An upscale shopper who is likely to frequent places such as Nordstrom, Victoria's Secret, and the Gap

In other words, the customer is likely to have the propensities and proclivities shown in the profile record seen in Figure 10-6. Note that the customer may never have been to Hawaii. Nevertheless, it is predicted that the customer would like to go there.

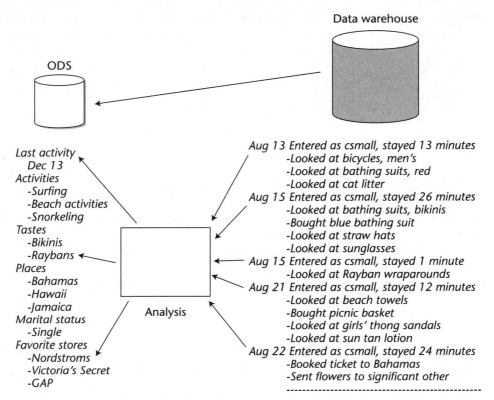

Figure 10-6 Periodically the detailed historical data is read, analyzed, and loaded into the format required for the ODS.

To create the profile data from the transaction data, a certain amount of analysis must be done. Figure 10-6 shows the reading of the transactional data in order to produce profile data.

In Figure 10-6, the detailed integrated historical transaction data is read and analyzed in order to produce the profile record. The analysis is done periodically, depending on the rate of change of data and the business purpose behind the analysis. The frequency of analysis and subsequent update of the profile record may occur as often as once a day or as infrequently as once a year. There is wide variability in the frequency of analysis.

The analytical program is both interpretive and predictive. Based on the past activity of the customer and any other information that the analytical program can get, the analytical program assimilates the information to produce a very personal projection of the customer. The projection is predictive as well as factual. Certain factual information is standard:

- Date of the last interaction with the customer
- Nature of the last interaction
- Size of the last purchase

Other information is not nearly as factual. The predictive aspect of the analysis includes such information as the following:

- Whether the customer is upscale
- The customer's sex
- The customer's age
- Whether the customer is a frequent traveler
- Where the customer is likely to travel

The profile record then contains a thumbnail sketch of the customer that is available in the ODS in an instant. And in that instant, the Web environment is provided with excellent response time and an integrated, interpretive view of the customer base that is being served.

Of course, information other than customer information is available from the data warehouse and the ODS. Typically, vendor information, product information, sales information, and the like are also available for the Web analyst.

Providing good response time and pre-analyzed data are not the only roles the data warehouse environment plays in supporting the Web. Another key role is the management of large amounts of data.

Web processing generates very large amounts of information. Even when a Granularity Manager is used to maximum effectiveness, the Web site still spews forth a mountain of data.

The first impulse of many Web designers is to store Web data in the Web environment itself, but very quickly the Web becomes swamped, and once that happens, nothing works properly. Data becomes entangled in everything — in access queries, in loads, in indexes, in monitors, and elsewhere. Coming to the aid of the Web is the data warehouse itself, as well as the bulk storage overflow component of the data warehouse. Figure 10-7 shows that data is periodically offloaded into the data warehouse from the Web environment. It is then periodically offloaded from the data warehouse to the overflow environment.

The Granularity Manager takes care of loading data from the Web to the data warehouse on a daily or even an hourly basis, depending on the average amount of Web traffic. And data from the data warehouse is loaded monthly or quarterly to the overflow storage environment. In so doing, there never is an unmanageable amount of data at any level of the architecture.

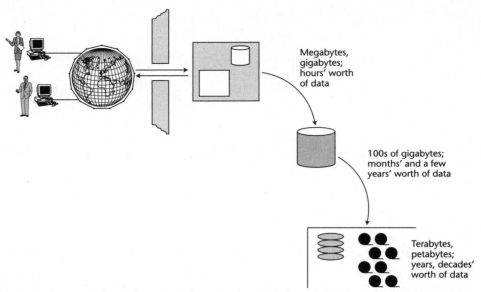

Megabytes,
gigabytes;
hours' worth
of data

100s of gigabytes;
months' and a few
years' worth of data

Terabytes,
petabytes;
years, decades'
worth of data

Figure 10-7 Volumes of data cascade down from the Web to the data warehouse to alternate storage.

Typically, the Web environment holds a day's worth of data, while the data warehouse might hold a year's worth. And typically the overflow storage component holds as much as a decade's worth of data. The data warehouse also supports the Web environment with the integration of data. Figure 10-8 shows that normal operational systems feed data to the data warehouse, where it becomes available for integrated processing. Data comes out of the Granularity Manager to merge with previously integrated business data in the data warehouse. In so doing, the data warehouse becomes the single place where you can get an integrated view of all business data from the Web, from other systems, from anywhere.

Another important aspect of the data warehouse is its ability to support multiple Web sites. For a large corporation, multiple Web sites are a fact of life, and their support is essential for merging and integrating the data from all sites.

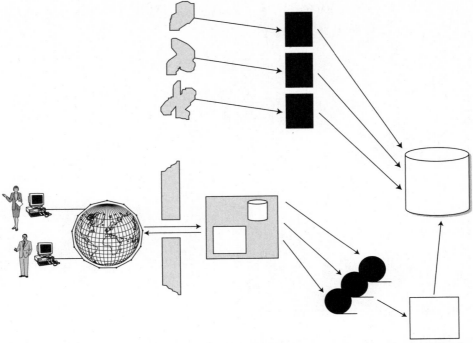

Figure 10-8 The data warehouse is where Web data is integrated with other data from the corporation.

Supporting the eBusiness Environment

A final environment that is supported by the data warehouse is the Web-based eBusiness environment. Figure 10-9 shows the support of the Web environment by the data warehouse.

The interface between the Web environment and the data warehouse is at the same time both simple and complex. It is simple from the perspective that data moved from the data warehouse back and forth to the Web environment. It is complex in that the movement is anything but straightforward.

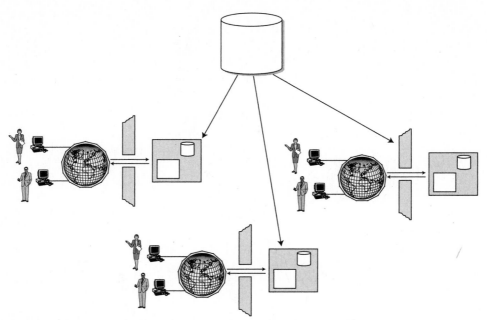

Figure 10-9   The data warehouse can service more than one eBusiness.

Moving Data from the Web to the Data Warehouse

Data in the Web environment is collected at a very, very low level of detail —
too low a level to be of use in the data warehouse. So, as the data passes from
the Web environment to the data warehouse, it must be conditioned and its
level of granularity must be raised. The sorts of things that are done to the data
in the Web environment before becoming useful in the data warehouse are the
following:

- Extraneous data is removed.
- Like occurrences of data are added together.
- Data is resequenced.
- Data is edited.
- Data is cleansed.
- Data is converted.

In short, the Web-based data goes through a rigorous cleansing-conversion-
reduction exercise before it is fit for inclusion into the data warehouse.

The Web-based data usually comes through the Web logs that are created in the Web environment. There is, as a rule of thumb, about a 90 percent reduction of data that occurs as the data from the Web is reduced.

The data coming from the Web passes through software that is often called Granularity Management software. In many ways, the Granularity Management software is akin to the ETL software found in the movement of data from the legacy environment to the data warehouse.

The data coming into the Web environment comes primarily from the clickstream processing that occurs in the Web environment. Clickstream processing is good for telling what has happened in the Web-based user sessions. To be really useful, though, the clickstream data must be connected to the other mainstream data that passes through normal corporate systems. It is only when clickstream data has been distilled and merged with normal corporate data that the full benefit of Web information can be felt.

Moving Data from the Data Warehouse to the Web

The Web environment is very sensitive to response time; it cannot be kept waiting more than a millisecond or two when it needs information. If the Web environment must wait longer than that, performance will be impacted. In many regards, the Web environment is very similar to the OLTP environment; at least as far as response-time sensitivity is concerned. It is for these reasons that there is no direct interface between the data warehouse and the Web environment.

Instead, the interface between the two environments passes through the corporate ODS residing in the same environment as the data warehouse. The ODS is designed to provide millisecond response time; the data warehouse is not. Therefore, data passes from the data warehouse to the ODS. Once in the ODS, the data waits for requests for access from the Web environment. The Web then makes a request and gets the needed information very quickly and very consistently.

The ODS contains profile information, unlike the data warehouse, which contains detailed historical information. In addition, the ODS contains truly corporate-wide information.

Once the data from the ODS passes into the Web environment, it can be used in any number of ways. The data can be used to shape the dialogues the Web has with its users, for personalization, or for direct dialogue. In short, the data coming from the ODS data warehouse can be used as the creativity of the Web designer demands.

Web Support

What exactly is it that the data warehouse provides for the Web-based eBusiness environment? The data warehouse provides several important capabilities:

- **The ability to absorb huge amounts of data** — Once the data warehouse is equipped with an overflow storage mechanism such as alternate or near-line storage and once the Web data passes through a Granularity Manager, the data warehouse is equipped to effectively handle an infinite amount of data. The data is quickly moved through the Web environment into the data warehouse. In doing so, the volumes of data generated by the Web environment are not an impediment to performance or availability in the Web environment.

- **Access to integrated data** — Web data by itself is naked and fairly useless. But once Web-generated data is combined with other corporate data, the mixture is very powerful. Web data once put into the data warehouse is able to be integrated, and once it is integrated, very useful information is created.

- **The ability to provide very good performance** — Because the Web accesses the ODS, not the data warehouse, good performance is consistently achieved.

These then are the important features that the data warehouse provides to the Web-based eBusiness environment. The data warehouse provides the important background infrastructure that the Web needs to be successful.

Summary

We have seen that the Web environment is supported by the data warehouse in a variety of ways. The interface for moving data from the Web to the data warehouse is fairly simple. Web data is trapped in logs. The logs feed their clickstream information to the Granularity Manager. The Granularity Manager edits, filters, summarizes, and reorganizes data. The data passes out of the Granularity Manager into the data warehouse.

The interface for moving data from the warehouse to the Web is a little more complex. Data passes from the data warehouse into an ODS. In the ODS, a profile record is created. The ODS becomes the sole point of contact between the Web environment and the data warehouse for purposes of data flow from the data warehouse to the Web environment. The reason for this is simple: The ODS is able to ensure that online transactions are processed quickly and consistently, which is essential for efficient Web processing.

In addition, the data warehouse provides a place where massive amounts of data can be downloaded from the Web environment and stored.

The data warehouse also provides a central point where corporate data can be merged and integrated with data coming in from one or more Web sites into a common single source.

CHAPTER 11

Unstructured Data and the Data Warehouse

For years, there have been two worlds that have grown up side-by-side — the world of unstructured data and related processing, and the world of structured data and related processing. It is a shame that these worlds have had very little intersection, because a plethora of business opportunities opens up when an interface between the two worlds is created.

The world of *unstructured data* is one that is dominated by casual, informal activities such as those found on the personal computer and the Internet. The following are typical of the data formats for unstructured data:

- Emails
- Spreadsheets
- Text files
- Documents
- Portable Document Format (.PDF) files
- Microsoft PowerPoint (.PPT) files

Figure 11-1 shows the world of unstructured data.

The polar opposite of unstructured data is structured data. *Structured data* is typified by standard DBMSs, reports, indexes, databases, fields, records, and the like. Figure 11-2 depicts the structured world.

The unstructured environment is aptly named because it contains practically no format, records, or keys. People get on the Internet and say what they want with no guidance from anyone else. People build and change spreadsheets with no instructions from anyone. People write reports and memos to their satisfaction alone. In short, there is no structure whatsoever to the unstructured environment. Furthermore, there is a lot of what can be called "blather" in the unstructured environment. Blather is simply communications and other information that has no business connection or use. When a person writes, "Let's do dinner," in an email to his or her friend, there is no business information that can be gleaned out of that message.

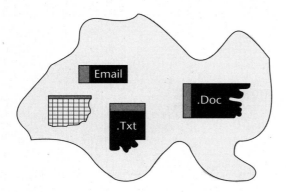

Figure 11-1 There is a world of unstructured data.

	Order number	Description	Amount	Date	Agent	U/m
Record 1						
Record 2						
Record 3						
Record 4						
Record 5						
Record 6						
Record 7						
Record 8						
Record 9						
Record 10						

Figure 11-2 Structured data.

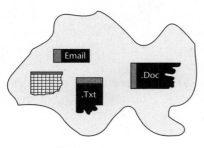 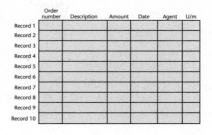

- Text   - Numbers
- Communications   - Transactions

Figure 11-3   Some of the fundamental differences between unstructured data and structured data.

Unstructured data can be roughly divided into two broad categories — communications and documents. *Communications* tend to be relatively short and are for very limited distribution. Communications tend to have a short life. *Documents* tend to be for a wider audience and are typically larger than communications. Documents tend to live a lot longer than communications. The essence of both documents and communications is text. Text forms the most basic substance of what is found in the unstructured environment.

The world of structured data is one that is dominated by numbers. The world of structured data has keys, fields, records, databases, and so forth. There is a high degree of order found in the world of structured systems. In almost every case, structured systems are created as a byproduct of transactions. A person makes a bank withdrawal. A person reserves an airline seat. A person buys an insurance policy. A company takes an order, and so forth. All of these transactions result in one or more structured records being created. Each record contains a key or identifier, some information about the transaction, and the numbers associated with the transaction (the amount of money withdrawn, the cost of the airline ticket, the terms of the insurance policy, the amount and cost of an order, and so forth).

Figure 11-3 shows the primary differences between structured data and unstructured data.

Integrating the Two Worlds

You can introduce a whole new world of possibilities by combining structured data and unstructured data. For example, consider customer relationship management (CRM). CRM freely gathers demographic data from the structured world, such as the age of the customer, the gender of the customer, the education of the customer, the address of the customer, and so forth. What

CRM lacks are communications. From the unstructured world, it is possible to add the emails from and/or to the customer, the letters and other communications from the customer, and so forth. But matching the two worlds of unstructured data and structured data is a difficult task.

One way to think about the difficulties of matching these two worlds is to think of matching different formats of electricity — alternating current (AC) and direct current (DC). The unstructured world operates on AC and the structured world operates on DC. If you put an appliance or tool that operates in AC in a DC system, either the tool or appliance will simply not work, or a fire will start. Simply put, things that work on AC do not work on DC, and vice versa. For the most part, mixing the two environments is just a mismatch at a very basic level.

Text — The Common Link

So, what is required to match these worlds? The common link between the two worlds is *text*. Without text, it is not possible to form a linkage. But even with text, a linkage may be fraught and full of misleading information.

Suppose you attempt a raw match between text found in the two worlds? Figure 11-4 shows such a match.

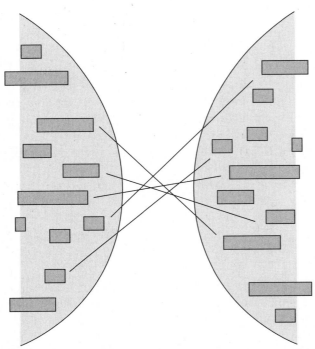

Figure 11-4　Merely matching a few words from one environment to another is random and confusing.

If all that is done is a raw match between two worlds based on text, then plenty of problems arise, including the following:

■ **Misspelling** — What if two words are found in the two environments — Chernobyl and Chernobile? Should there be a match made between these two worlds? Do they refer to the same thing or something different?

■ **Context** — The term "bill" is found in the two worlds. Should they be matched? In one case, the reference is to a bird's beak and in the other case, the reference is to how much money a person is owed.

■ **Same name** — The same name, "Bob Smith," appears in both worlds. Are they the same thing? Do they refer to the same person? Or, do they refer to entirely different people who happen to have matching names?

■ **Nicknames** — In one world, there appears the name "Bill Inmon." In another world there appears the name "William Inmon." Should a match be made? Do they refer to the same person?

■ **Diminutives** — Is 1245 Sharps Ct the same as 1245 Sharps Court? Is NY, NY, the same as New York, New York?

■ **Incomplete names** — Is Mrs. Inmon the same as Lynn Inmon?

■ **Word stems** — Should the word "moving" be connected and matched with the word "moved"?

When it comes to a random matching of text across the two environments, there are relatively few valid matches compared to the false positives and the false negatives that occur.

There are plenty of reasons why making a match between two separate environments is a risky proposition. Figure 11-5 illustrates one of those reasons.

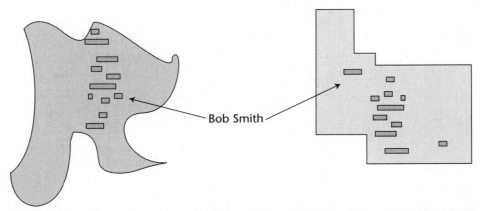

Bob Smith

Figure 11-5 How do you know that the Bob Smith in one environment is the same as Bob Smith in the other environment?

A Fundamental Mismatch

While grammatically there are many differences between the two environments, perhaps the biggest reasons why matching raw data from one environment to the next is so fraught with misleading conclusions is that there is a fundamental mismatch between the environments represented between the two worlds. The unstructured environment represents documents and communications. The structured environment represents transactions.

In the structured environment, the minimum amount of textual data is captured. The textual data in the transaction environment serves only to identify and clarify the transaction. Any more text than that serves to clog the data communications lines of the transaction-processing environment. In the unstructured environment, there is nothing but text. Text can be verbose, text can be cryptic, and/or text can be eloquent in the unstructured environment. Text can also be confusing.

The different environments in which text is found and stored greatly influence the content, usage, and style of the text, which in turn greatly influences the capability of the text to be matched in a meaningful manner across different environments.

Despite the difficulties of matching text across the two environments, it still is the key to the integration of data and the placement of unstructured data (or data whose source is unstructured) in the data warehouse environment.

Matching Text across the Environments

So, how can a match of text across the two environments be made? How can data meaningfully arrive in the data warehouse environment from an unstructured source? There are many ways a meaningful match can be made.

In order for a meaningful match to be made, basic edits of the unstructured data must be done. The first kind of edit is that of the removal of extraneous stop words. A *stop word* is a word that occurs so frequently as to be meaningless to the document. Typical stop words include the following:

- a
- an
- the
- for
- to
- by from
- when
- which

- that
- where

An index on the word "the" produces a completely meaningless index. It simply is not useful.

The second basic edit that must be done is the reduction of words back to their stem. For example, the following words all have the same *grammatical stem:*

- moving
- moved
- moves
- mover
- removing

Each of these words has the root "move." If there is to be a meaningful comparison of words, word comparisons are best done at the stemmed level.

A Probabilistic Match

One of the ways that a meaningful match of data across the two environments can be made is through related data being included in the matching process. For example, consider the matching of the name "Bob Smith" between the unstructured environment and the structured environment. The name "Bob Smith" is a common American name and appears in many telephone books. So, how can a match between one "Bob Smith" and another "Bob Smith" be made? In other words, what can be done to determine if a "Bob Smith" appearing in one place is the same "Bob Smith" appearing elsewhere?

The classical way to make this determination is to create what can be termed a *probabilistic match*. In a probabilistic match, as much data that might be used to indicate the "Bob Smith" that you're looking for is gathered and is used as a basis for a match against similar data found where other "Bob Smiths" are located. Then, all the data that intersects is used to determine if a match on the name is valid. Figure 11-6 shows such a match.

Figure 11-6 shows that in the unstructured environment other types of information are gathered along with the name "Bob Smith." In particular, Bob's Social Security number and Bob's employee ID are gathered and stored with the name "Bob Smith." Then, in the structured environment, information other than the name "Bob Smith" is also collected. In this case, Bob's address, phone number, and employee ID are collected.

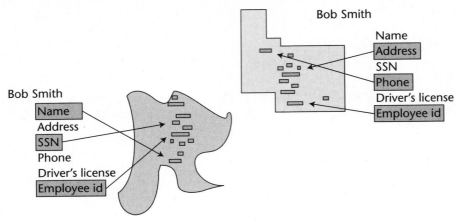

Figure 11-6   Likely data is gathered from each environment.

Matching All the Information

So, now there are two sets of information. In the unstructured environment, you have the name, Social Security number, and employee ID. In the structured environment, you have the name, address, telephone number, and employee ID. Fortunately, there is an intersection on something other than the name. The data element employee ID is collected in both places. Now, when there is a match on name there must be a match on employee ID as well in order to determine whether they are the same person. This is a simple form of a probabilistic match.

A probabilistic match is not a perfect thing in the best of circumstances. A probabilistic match assigns a probability of matching based on the strength of the match. For example, a match between two people with the name "Bob Smith" is a weak match. A match on two people named "Bob Smith" who both reside in Colorado is a slightly stronger match. A match based on two people named "Bob Smith" who live in Westminster, Colorado, is a stronger match. And a match on two people named "Bob Smith" who live at 18 Juniper Circle, Westminster, Colorado, is an even stronger match. But even a match on an address is not a perfect thing. There may, in fact, be a "Bob Smith" and a "Bob Smith, Junior" who both reside at the same address, and the son may not have included the "Junior" in his name.

One technique for visualizing the strength of a probabilistic match is to assign a numeric value from 1 to 10 as a description of the match. For example, a match on name would be a 1. A match on name and state would be a 2. A match on name, state, and city would be a 3. A match on name state, city, and address would be a 4, and so forth. The more variables that match, the greater the number assigned to the match. By using such a numerical ranking, an analyst can tell at a glance what the strength of the match might be.

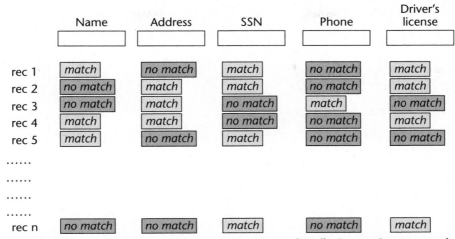

Figure 11-7   A probabilistic match is one way to handle integration across the two environments.

Figure 11-7 shows a kind of index that can be created to depict the data available for matching in a probabilistic manner.

A Themed Match

A probabilistic matching of data is not the only way there is to match text between the structured and the unstructured environments. Another way of creating a match, or at least a relationship of text between the structured and the unstructured environments, is through a technique that can be called an "industrially recognized" grouping or theme of data.

Suppose there is a body of unstructured text. This text can be a variety of documents taken together to form a library or the text can be collection of communications, such as a body of emails taken over time from a variety of sources. In any case, there is a lot of unstructured text that has been gathered together.

There needs to be a way of looking at and organizing these unstructured collections of data.

Industrially Recognized Themes

One way to organize the unstructured data is by *industrially recognized themes*. In this approach, the unstructured data is analyzed according to the existence of words that relate to industrialized themes. For example, suppose there are two industrially recognized themes — accounting and finance. The industrially recognized themes contain words that are related to the topical theme. For example, the accounting theme would contain words and phrases such as the following:

- receivable
- payable
- cash on hand
- asset
- debit
- due date
- account

The finance theme would contain such information as the following:

- price
- margin
- discount
- gross sale
- net sale
- interest rate
- carrying loan
- balance due

There can be many industrially recognized themes for word collections. Some of the word themes might be the following:

- sales
- marketing
- finance
- human resources
- engineering
- accounting
- distribution

Figure 11-8 shows the usage of industrially recognized themes as a basis for organizing data in the unstructured environment.

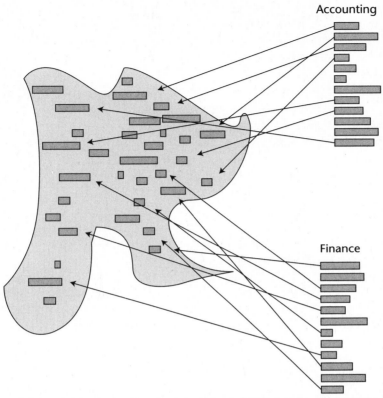

Figure 11-8   One way of organizing libraries of information is to take industrially recognized groupings of data and locate those words or phrases in the unstructured environment.

Once the collections of industrially recognized themes have been gathered, the unstructured data is passed against the themes. Any time a word or the root of a word exists in the unstructured environment, a tally is made. At the end of the analysis, there is a tally made of how the unstructured document measures up to the themes under which it has been analyzed.

This technique of passing unstructured text against industrially recognized themes allows the documents to be organized. A set of documents that has a strong orientation against accounting will have many "hits" against the industrially recognized list of words. A document that does not have a strong orientation to accounting will have few or even no hits when matched against the words found in the accounting industrially recognized words theme.

Not only are industrially recognized themes useful for determining the contents and the demeanor of the data found in the unstructured environment, the matching of industrially recognized themes and unstructured data is good for determining exactly where in the unstructured environment certain references are.

One of the commercial uses of this approach is in the determination of what communications are in compliance with regulations such as Sarbanes Oxley, HIPAA, and BASEL II. The communications are passed against the words and phrases that Sarbanes Oxley, HIPAA, and BASEL II hold important. Once the words or phrases are discovered, a match is made and management knows they need to be cognizant of the communication that is being made.

Naturally Occurring Themes

Another way to organize unstructured data is through naturally occurring themes. Figure 11-9 shows this organization.

In an organization by "natural" themes, the unstructured data is collected on a document-by-document basis. Once the data is collected, the words and phrases are ranked by number of occurrences. Then, a theme to the document is formed by ranking the words and phrases inside the document based on the number of occurrences.

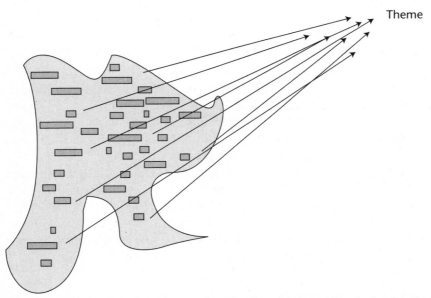

Figure 11-9 Another way to organize libraries of information is to identify themes of information that are built from the information found inside the documents.

For example, suppose a document had the following words and phrases that have been ranked:

- fire — 296 occurrences
- fireman — 285 occurrences
- hose — 277 occurrences
- firetruck — 201 occurrences
- alarm — 199 occurrences
- smoke — 175 occurrences
- heat — 128 occurrences

The conclusion could be drawn that the theme of the document had something to do with fire or putting out a fire.

Suppose the document also contained the following words:

- Rock Springs, WY — 2
- alabaster — 1
- angel — 2
- Rio Grande river – 1
- beaver dam — 1

Because these words occurred so infrequently, it would be assumed that the theme of this document had little or nothing to do with Rock Springs, alabaster, or angels.

The theme of a document can then be established by looking at the occurrence of words and their frequency of occurrence.

Linkage through Themes and Themed Words

Linkage can be formed to the structured environment through the data that forms the theme of a document, as shown in Figure 11-10.

One way to relate the themed data found in the unstructured environment to the data found in the structured environment is through a *raw match of data*. In a raw match of data, if a word is found anywhere in the structured environment and the word is part of the theme of a document, the unstructured document is linked to the structured record. But such a matching is not very meaningful and may actually be misleading.

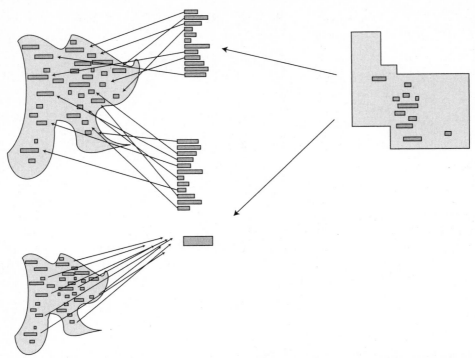

Figure 11-10   Linkage from libraries to structured data can be accomplished through themes or industrially recognized relationships to the library.

Linkage through Abstraction and Metadata

Instead, another way to link the two environments is by the metadata found in the structured environment. To see how such linkage can occur, refer to the data found in Figure 11-11.

In Figure 11-11, data in the unstructured environment includes such people as Bill Jones, Mary Adams, Wayne Folmer, and Susan Young. All of these people exist in records of data that have a data element called "Name."

Put another way, data exists at two levels in the structured environment — the abstract level and the actual occurrence level. Figure 11-12 shows this relationship of data.

In Figure 11-12, data exists at an abstract level — the metadata level. In addition, data exists at the occurrence level — where the actual occurrences of data reside.

Based on this set of relationships, data in the unstructured environment based on themes can best be related to the abstraction of data in the structured environment. Stated differently, data in the structured environment at the occurrence level does not easily relate to data in the unstructured environment.

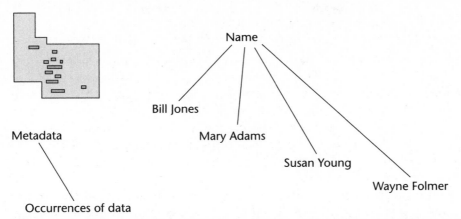

Figure 11-11   The structuring of data that is common in the structured environment is that of metadata and occurrences of metadata.

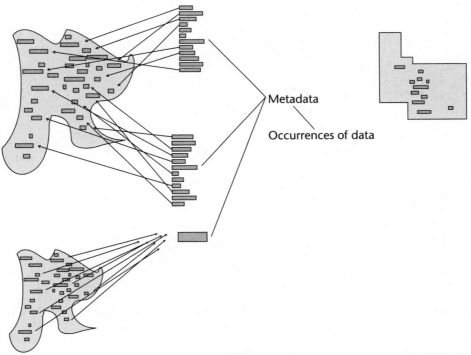

Figure 11-12   One way that structured data can be related to unstructured data is through metadata relating to themes or industrially recognized relationships.

A Two-Tiered Data Warehouse

There are two basic approaches to the usage of unstructured data in the data warehouse environment. One approach is to access the unstructured environment and pull data over into the structured environment. This approach works well for certain kinds of unstructured data. Another approach to unstructured data and the data warehouse environment is to create a *two-tiered data warehouse*. One tier of the data warehouse is for unstructured data and another tier of the data warehouse is for structured data. Figure 11-13 shows this approach.

In Figure 11-13, there are two related but separate components of a data warehouse. There may be either a tight or a casual relationship of data between the two environments, or there may be no relationship at all. There is nothing implied about the data in that regard.

The data found in the unstructured data warehouse is in many ways similar to the data found in the structured data warehouse. Consider the following when looking at data in the unstructured environment:

- It exists at a low level of granularity.
- It has an element of time attached to the data.
- It is typically organized by subject area or "theme."

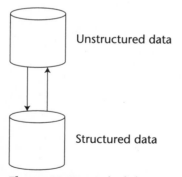

Unstructured data

Structured data

Figure 11-13 A dual data warehouse where part of the data warehouse is unstructured and the other part of the warehouse is structured.

Dividing the Unstructured Data Warehouse

There are some major differences between the structured data warehouse and the unstructured data warehouse. Data in the unstructured data warehouse is divided into one of the two following categories:

- Unstructured communications
- Documents and libraries

Figure 11-14 shows the division of data inside the unstructured data warehouse.

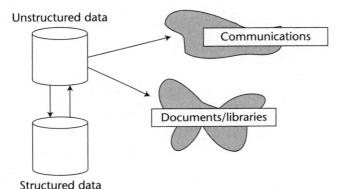

Figure 11-14 The unstructured data warehouse is made up of documents, libraries, and communications.

Communications found in the unstructured data warehouse are usually short (relative to documents found in the other part of the unstructured data warehouse). Communications almost always have a date of the communication and a key attached to the data found in the unstructured communications warehouse. Communications are divided up into two classes — business relevant communications and "blather" (those communications that have no business value). Typical blather might be, "Let's do dinner," or "I just met the cutest guy. He has brown eyes and curly hair." Usually, blather is eliminated from the communications held in the data warehouse.

Communications have keys that typically are such things as the following:

- Email address
- Telephone number
- Fax number

The relationship between communications and structured data is formed on the basis of identifiers.

Documents are found in the unstructured data warehouse as well. As a rule, documents are much larger than communications. And documents are intended for a much wider audience than the communications. A third difference between documents and communications is that documents have a much longer useful life than communications.

Documents are grouped into *libraries*. A library is merely a collection of documents, all of which relate to some subject. Subjects for a library might be almost anything, such as the following:

- Oil and gas accounting
- Terrorism and hijacking
- Explosives, mines, and artillery
- Insurance tables and calculations

Whereas communications are organized by identifiers, documents and libraries are organized according to words and themes. The themes can be developed from the documents, as has been described. Once developed, the themes and the contents of the documents form the basis for storage in the data warehouse.

Documents in the Unstructured Data Warehouse

Depending on quite a few variables, it may be desirable to store the actual document in the unstructured data warehouse, or it may make sense to store only references to the location of the document in the data warehouse. Following are some of the factors that determine whether or not the actual document is stored in the data warehouse:

- How many documents are there?
- What is the size of the documents?
- How critical is the information in the document?
- Can the document be easily reached if it is not stored in the warehouse?
- Can subsections of the document be captured?

An intermediate solution between having the document in storage or out of storage is storing the sentence before and after where the themed word lies. In other words, suppose the word "kill" is used as a themed word. The following information may be stored along with "kill":

■■ "The test at mid-term was a real killer. Only 2 students out of 30 passed."

■ "He was a real lady killer. The women just fell over when he came in the room."

■ "The best quarterback out of the northwest this year is Sonny Sixkiller. He can pass and run with the best."

■ "Ants find that this pesticide is an effective killer. It works on contact and lasts for a week."

By storing text found before and after the themed word, it is possible for an individual to preview a document without actually having to retrieve it.

Visualizing Unstructured Data

Once the unstructured data has been captured and organized into a data warehouse, it is possible to visualize the unstructured data.

Unstructured visualization is the counterpart to structured visualization. *Structured visualization* is known as Business Intelligence. There are many commercial products that are used to embody structured visualization, including Business Objects and MicroStrategy. Figure 11-15 shows the different kinds of visualization for the different data warehouses.

The essence of structured visualization is the display of numbers. Numbers can be added and subtracted. Numbers can be formed into bar charts, Pareto charts, and pie charts. In other words, there are many ways to display numerical data.

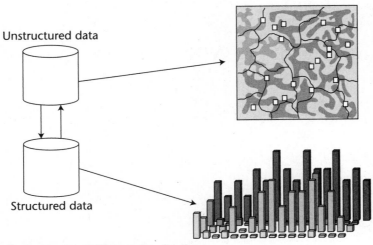

Figure 11-15   Different visualizations.

Visualization can also be done for textual-based data. Textual-based data forms the foundation of unstructured technology. A commercial example of unstructured visualization is Compudigm. To create a textual visualization, documents and words are collected. Then the words are edited and prepared for display. The words are then fed to a display engine where they are analyzed, clustered, and otherwise prepared for visualization.

A Self-Organizing Map (SOM)

The result is a *self-organizing map (SOM)*. The SOM produces a display that appears to be a topographical map. The SOM shows how different words and the documents are clustered, and displayed according to themes.

Figure 11-16 shows a visualization for the unstructured environment.

The SOM has different features. One feature is the clustering of information based on the data found in different documents. In this feature, data that shares like characteristics and relationships are clustered together. By looking at clusters, data that has common characteristics and relationships can be grouped for easy reference. Another feature of a SOM is the ability to do drill-down processing. In drill-down processing, data is arranged in layers so that access and analysis of one layer can lead to another layer.

Figure 11-17 shows that once the SOM is created, the data can be further analyzed.

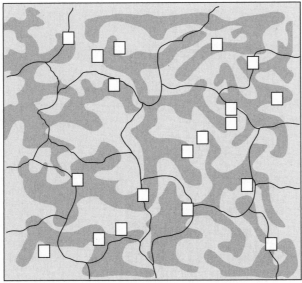

Figure 11-16　A self-organizing map (SOM).

Figure 11-17   Analyzing text in an SOM.

One important aspect of an SOM is the ability to quickly relate documents. Once the analyst has examined the SOM, if you want to look at a document, then direct access of the document can be allowed.

By using an SOM, an organization can look at the information contained in thousands of documents and can examine the data and the relationships intuitively and immediately.

The Unstructured Data Warehouse

What exactly does the structure of the unstructured data warehouse look like? Figure 11-18 shows a high-level view of the unstructured data warehouse.

In Figure 11-18, the unstructured data warehouse is divided into two basic organizations — one part for documents and another part for communications. The documents section is for long treatises such as those found in research, science, and engineering. In addition, books, articles, and reports may all be found in the documents section.

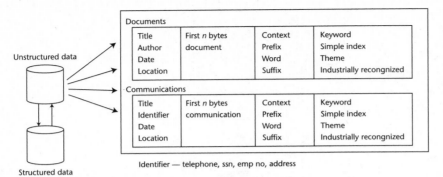

Figure 11-18   What the unstructured data warehouse looks like.

The communications section is for shorter messages. Communications include email, memos, letters, and other short missives.

The data that can be stored in each section includes the following:

- The first n bytes of the document
- The document itself (optional)
- The communication itself (optional)
- Context information
- Keyword information

Volumes of Data and the Unstructured Data Warehouse

In every data warehouse of every kind, volumes of data are an issue. Unstructured data warehouses are no exception. Fortunately there are some basic things the data warehouse developer can do to mitigate the effects of huge volumes of data. Whereas volumes of data in the structured data warehouse environment are an issue, volumes of data in the unstructured environment are an order of magnitude more important simply because there is so much more unstructured data than structured data.

Following are some of the approaches used to mitigate the volumes of data that can collect in the unstructured data warehouse:

- Remove communications blather. Up to 90 percent of communications may be blather. All blather does is to take up space. Blather contributes nothing toward the information base of the organization.
- Do not store all of the documents. Store simple indexes to where those documents can be found, or at least their last know address. Store only documents that are important.

- Create an area where the documents or communications are stored separately, if they have to be stored at all. Keep the identifiers (first n bytes, dates, and so forth) separate. (Identifiers are discussed in detail in the following section, "Fitting the Two Environments Together.")

- Age data off by date wherever possible.

- Monitor the usage of the unstructured data warehouse to determine what the patterns of usage are.

- Do not store too many context references. Keep track of the usage of the context references to determine which can be discarded or archived.

These are some of the ways the storage requirements of the unstructured data warehouse can be minimized.

Fitting the Two Environments Together

For all practical purposes, the unstructured environment contains data that is incompatible with data from the structured environment. Unstructured data might as well be running AC, and structured data might as well be DC. The two types of current just don't mix easily, or at all. However, despite the major differences between the contents of the two environments, there are ways that the two environments can be related.

It is text that relates the two environments, a shown in Figure 11-19.

Figure 11-19 shows that the structured environment consists of several components, including the following:

- At an abstract level — metadata and a repository
- At a record level — raw data, identifiers, and close identifiers

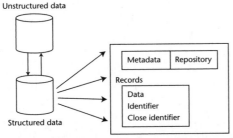

Figure 11-19   The data found in the operational environment.

An *identifier* is an occurrence of data that serves to specifically identify a record. Typical of identifiers are Social Security number, employee number, and driver's license number. An identifier is specific about its identification. Once identification is made, there is a very strong possibility that the identified record is, in fact, identified properly.

Close identifiers are identifiers where there is a good probability that a solid identification has been made. Close identifiers include names, addresses, and other identifying data. The difference between an identifier and a close identifier is the sureness of the identification. When a person has been identified by Social Security number, there is a very high probability that the person is who he or she really is. But close identifiers are not the same. Consider name.

There is a person named "Bill Inmon." Does that mean that the person is the same person who wrote this book? The answer is maybe. There aren't many Bill Inmon's in the world, but there are several. So, when you refer to "Bill Inmon," you are probably referring to the person who wrote this book, but there is a legitimate chance that it may be another person.

Narrowing down the opportunity for identification, suppose we know that the "Bill Inmon" being referred to was born in San Diego, California, in 1945. Now, do we know who we are talking about? Probably, but there is a chance that two Bill Inmon's may have been born in San Diego in 1945. So, we are not perfectly sure we have the right person. We are pretty sure, but not absolutely sure.

Close identifiers are used to provide linkage between different data where there is a probabilistic match being made.

Now, how does structured data relate to unstructured data?

Figure 11-20 shows the data types that are found in the structured environment and the unstructured environment. On the top are the data types from the structured environment. On the bottom are the data types from the unstructured environment.

The unstructured environment is divided into two basic categories — documents and communications. In the documents category are found document-identifying information such as title, author, data of document, and location of document. Also found are the first *n* bytes of the document. Context, prefix, word, and suffix are found. There are also keywords. The keywords have a simple index. In addition, the relationship of the keyword to the document is found. The keyword can be related to the document by means of being a part of a theme or by coming from an industrially recognized list of words.

The communications part of unstructured data is similar to the document part except that the communications part contains identifiers and close identifiers. But other than that difference, the information about communications is the same.

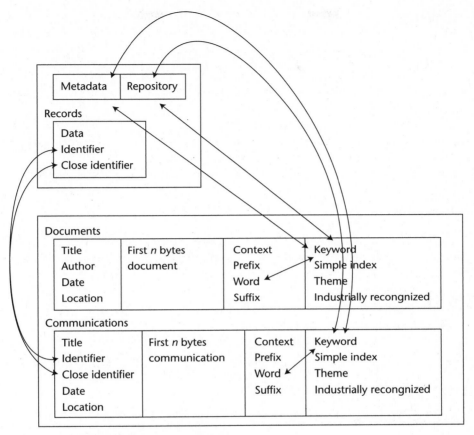

Figure 11-20   How data in the different environments relate.

Figure 11-20 shows that identifiers from the structured environment can be matched with identifiers from the unstructured environment. Close identifiers from the structured environment can probabilistically be matched with close identifiers from the unstructured environment. Keywords can be matched from the unstructured environment with either metadata or repository data from the structured environment.

While other matches can be done in theory, usually those matches are almost random (or, at best, sporadic) in nature.

Summary

The world of information technology is really divided into two worlds — structured data and unstructured data. Many opportunities open up when those two worlds are connected and integrated. The common bond between the two worlds is text.

Text in the unstructured environment comes in two basic flavors — communications and documents. Text in the structured world comes in two basic flavors — abstractions (or metadata) and occurrences.

Merely matching text is a random and almost meaningless thing to do. There are many problems with matching text that must be resolved before a match can be deemed useful. Some of the problems with matching text are false positives and false negatives.

A useful technique for solving some of the problems of matches is to use probabilistic matching. Another way of organizing documents is by alignment with industrially recognized themes. And a third way of resolving matches is by using occurrence-derived themes from a document.

A two-tiered data warehouse can be formed where one tier is unstructured data and the other tier is structured data.

Once the two-tiered data warehouse is built, it can be visualized. Business intelligence is used to visualize structured data, while self-organizing maps (SOMs) can be used to visualize unstructured data.

The structured environment and the unstructured environment can be matched at the identifier level, at the close identifier level using a probabilistic match, and at the keyword to metadata or repository level. Any other type of matching between the two environments is random.

CHAPTER 12

The Really Large
Data Warehouse

Data warehouses entail large amounts of data. As testimony to the volumes of data that come with data warehouses, consider the vocabulary of capacity planning. In the days before data warehousing, capacity was measured in kilobytes (KB), megabytes (MB), and occasionally, gigabytes (GB). But data warehouses appeared and soon there were new words in the vocabulary, including "hundreds of gigabytes," "terabytes," and even "petabytes." Thus, volumes of data have increased in multiples of orders of magnitude with the advent of data warehouses. Figure 12-1 shows the increase as it has typically occurred.

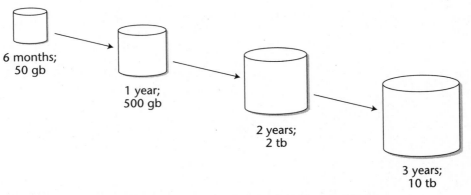

6 months;
50 gb

1 year;
500 gb

2 years;
2 tb

3 years;
10 tb

Figure 12-1 The growth of the data warehouse over time is explosive.

As shown in Figure 12-1, at the beginning of a data warehouse, there were a few gigabytes of data. These volumes were not surprising and caused no one any particular anguish. Then, a short time passed and there were hundreds of gigabytes of data. This volume was a minor concern, but not a large one. Time passed and soon there were several terabytes (trillions of bytes) of data. Now some genuine concerns were starting to be raised. There was the budget to think about. There was database design and administration. There was response time. And more time passed and the organization woke up to 10 or more terabytes of data. The worries of yesterday became the crises of today. Data kept accumulating almost of its own volition. And with each new byte that accumulated, problems began to mount.

Why the Rapid Growth?

So, why was it that large volumes of data began to show up in the data warehouse? There were several good reasons why data in the data warehouse grew at such a rapid rate. Figure 12-2 shows some of the reasons for the rapid growth of data in the data warehouse.

Figure 12-2 shows that the data warehouse contains history. Nowhere else in the information-technology environment is there such a store of historical data. Indeed, in the OLTP environment, historical data was jettisoned as fast as possible because historical data negatively impacted performance. The more historical data there was, the worse performance was. So, naturally, the systems programmer and the applications developer removed historical data as quickly as possible to get good response time.

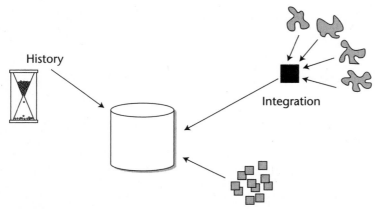

Figure 12-2   The reasons why data warehouses grow large.

But historical data plays an important role in understanding the customer. Since customers around the world are creatures of habit, it makes sense that understanding the customer over time becomes the key to being able to predict what the customer will do in the future. But, because OLTP programmers abhor historical data, there is no other place than the data warehouse to collect historical data.

The second reason why data warehouses grow so large is that data warehouses collect data at the most granular level. If a data warehouse is to be flexible (and that, after all, is one of the main reasons for even having a data warehouse), then the data warehouse must collect detailed data. The reason for the detail should be obvious. With detail, a developer or analyst can look at data in a manner that no one has ever done before. When the data is summarized, the data cannot be broken down and reformed or reshaped in a different manner. Summarized data is very inflexible and is not versatile.

If a foundation of data that is reusable is to be created, then that foundation must be created at a low level of granularity.

The third reason for the large volumes of data that congregate inside a data warehouse is because of the need to bring lots of different kinds of data together. In a data warehouse, the sources of data are normally very diverse. The data warehouse represents the point of integration of data for the corporation. Stated differently, the data warehouse is the true embodiment of the enterprise database.

There are common keys, common reference tables, common definitions of data, common encoding schemes, common structures, and so forth. The data warehouse represents the one place where there is a lowest common denominator of data in the corporation.

These, then, are the reasons why a lot of data creeps into the data warehouse. There is another simplistic way to state the same thing:

Historical data _ Detailed data _ Diverse data = Lots of data

The Impact of Large Volumes of Data

It simply is a fact of life that data warehouses collect large volumes of data. But so what? Why should that matter?

It turns out that there are a lot of reasons why having a large collection of data matters, including the following:

- **Cost** — A lot of data costs a lot of money.
- **Usefulness** — Is the corporation actually using all the collected data?
- **Data management** — The rules of data management change as the volume of data rises.

Of these important reasons, perhaps the most interesting is that the rules of data management change as data volumes grow. To understand why this is so, consider a few basic activities of data management, such as those depicted in Figure 12-3.

Basic Data-Management Activities

Figure 12-3 shows that with a modest amount of data — 50 gigabytes (GB) — most basic data-management activities are done with little thinking and little preparation. With 50GB of data, loading data takes about an hour or less. Indexing the data can be done in a short amount of time — say, 15 minutes. Access to data is fast, measured in milliseconds. But with 10 terabytes of data, these basic data-management activities change. To load 10 terabytes (TB) takes 12 hours or more. To index 10TB may take 72 hours or longer, depending on the indexing being done. To access 10TB, response time is measured in seconds, not milliseconds. In addition, the space needed for an index becomes a consideration.

To make an analogy, managing 50GB is like steering a rowboat in a lake while managing terabytes is like steering the Queen Elizabeth II in the North Atlantic during a winter storm. Both tasks can be done, but there are completely different considerations and complexities surrounding the tasks.

For these reasons alone, examining and managing the volumes of data that crop up in a data warehouse bears a deep examination of the environment, the practices, and the budget associated with the data warehouse.

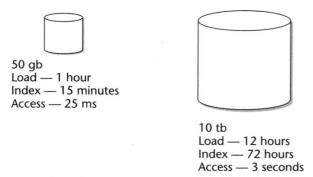

50 gb
Load — 1 hour
Index — 15 minutes
Access — 25 ms

10 tb
Load — 12 hours
Index — 72 hours
Access — 3 seconds

Figure 12-3   As data volumes grow large, normal database functions require increasingly larger amounts of resources.

The Cost of Storage

One factor that often goes unaccounted for is the cost of the storage for the data warehouse. Figure 12-4 shows that as the data warehouse increases in size, the budget for the data warehouse also increases, in some cases exponentially.

Figure 12-4 shows that when the data warehouse is in its infancy, the data warehouse costs pennies, relatively speaking. In fact, in many environments, the data warehouse costs so little initially that the data warehouse is begun on a "skunk works" budget. In a *skunk works budget*, there are dollars allocated for something other than a data warehouse. But, because the data warehouse initially costs so little, the data warehouse can be slipped into the budget under the guise of something else. So, the initial rendition of the data warehouse can be started with a very small budget.

As time passes and the volume of data in the data warehouse grows, the budget for the data warehouse starts to accelerate. By this time, the data warehouse has already proved its worth to the corporation, so no one really pays a lot of attention to the cost of the data warehouse.

But one day, the organization wakes up and finds that the data warehouse eats resources like a ravenous bear in March, just fresh out of winter hibernation. The data warehouse starts to eat up budget right and left, at an unprecedented rate.

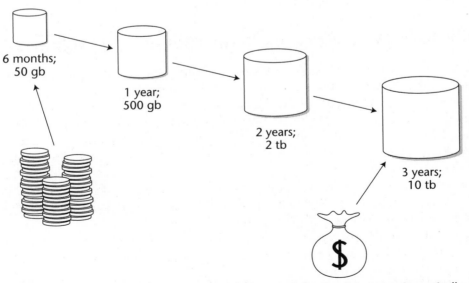

6 months; 50 gb

1 year; 500 gb

2 years; 2 tb

3 years; 10 tb

Figure 12-4 As the volume of data grows, the cost of the data increases dramatically.

In theory, the disk vendors tell you this shouldn't happen. They tell you that disk capacity is getting cheaper all the time. And, as far as they are looking, they are right. The problem is that the disk vendor is not telling a completely accurate truth. What they are not telling you is that the disk storage component is only a part (a relatively small part) of the total cost of storage in general.

The Real Costs of Storage

Figure 12-5 shows a more accurate picture of the costs of disk storage.

Figure 12-5 shows that there are lots of components to disk storage aside from the storage device itself. There is the disk controller. There are the communications lines. There is the processor (or processors) that are required to control the usage of the data. Then there is the software that is required to make the processor operate properly. There is data base software, operating system software, and business intelligence software, to name a few types of software. *All* of these components go up in cost when your volume of data increases. The actual cost per megabyte of storage is only one expense in a much larger picture. For these reasons, then, there is a profound effect on the IT cost when the volumes of storage increase. Looking merely at the cost per megabyte and seeing that it is decreasing is terribly misleading.

Another way to look at the decreasing cost of storage at the megabyte level is to understand that the rate of consumption of storage is increasing at a far faster rate than that of the decrease of storage costs.

The Usage Pattern of Data in the Face of Large Volumes

There is another related factor to the increasing budget for hardware: the usage of the data that has been captured, as shown in Figure 12-6.

When an organization has only 50GB of storage in its data warehouse, it is a good bet that all or most of all of the data found in the data warehouse is being used. Most queries can afford to access all the data in the data warehouse as needed. But, as the volume of data in the data warehouse grows, that basic practice ceases to be a possibility.

As the volume of data ratchets upward, the percentage of data that is actually used ratchets downward. Stated differently, as the volume of data increases, the percentage of the data actually being used decreases.

To prove that the percentage of volume of data in a data warehouse that is being used decreases over time as the data warehouse grows large, it is instructive to do a simple exercise.

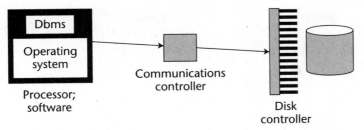

Figure 12-5   The cost of storage is not the megabyte cost. Instead, the cost of storage is about the infrastructure surrounding the data.

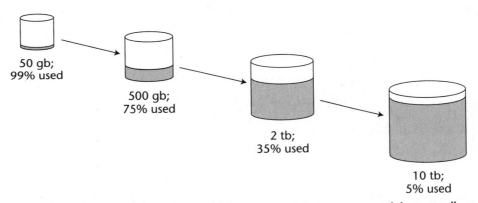

Figure 12-6   Over time, as the volume of data grows, the percentage of data actually used drops.

A Simple Calculation

Take the number of end users you have using your data warehouse. Determine how many queries on an average day they are doing. Then, find out on the average how many bytes of data a query uses. Now, for 200 days a year (roughly the number of working days in a year) calculate how much data is being accessed:

Number of users _ Queries per day _ Bytes per query _ 200 days

Now factor in overlap. *Overlap* is a factor because there will be some amount of data that is queried more than once. Estimate the overlap factor and use the inverse. For example, if 50 percent of the data is overlap, divide by 2.

Divide the amount of data by the overlap factor, and you will find out how many bytes of data are required to service your organization for a year. Typical numbers are 250GB of data servicing 600 users, where the data warehouse is 2TB of data.

Now calculate a ratio:

Usage ratio = Actual bytes used / Total data warehouse bytes

It is not unusual to find that you are using only 5 percent or less of your actual data. In one large shop that had a very large data warehouse, it was estimated that in a year's time, the organization used less that 1 percent of the data found in its data warehouse.

There is a case to be made for the type of user that is being considered. If your organization is made up mostly of "farmers," then your number of bytes used will be predictable and low. But if you have a lot of "explorers," then your percentage of data used will probably be very high. (*Farmers* are those users who use data in a predictable manner; *explorers* are those users who use data in an unpredictable manner.)

In any case, as the volume of data found in your data warehouse goes up, the actual percentage used goes down.

Two Classes of Data

As your shop approaches a large warehouse, it is common to look at the data in the data warehouse as residing in one of two classes. In a large data warehouse, data is either frequently used or infrequently used. Infrequently used data is often called *dormant data* or *inactive data*. Frequently used data is often called *actively used data*.

Figure 12-7 shows this way of looking at data in a large data warehouse.

Over time, data gravitates to one of two states — frequently used data or infrequently used data. The larger the data warehouse, the less frequently used data there is and the more infrequently used data there is.

A unit of frequently used data may be used two or three times a month. Infrequently used data may be accessed less than 0.5 times per year. Of course, these numbers are all relative to your environment.

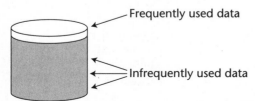

Frequently used data

Infrequently used data

Figure 12-7 Over time, there is a clear division in the way that data is used.

Implications of Separating Data into Two Classes

The phenomenon of the separation of data into one of two classes as the volumes of data grow in a data warehouse carries with it a lot of implications. One such implication is in the fitfulness of disk storage for a data warehouse. In other words, if data divides into two classes as the volumes of data grow, is disk storage the ideal storage medium on which to place a data warehouse? To consider the case for a data warehouse residing on storage other than disk, consider the access of data in different environments, as depicted in Figure 12-8.

Figure 12-8 shows that there is OLTP data and there is data warehouse DSS data. The two types of data are placed on disk storage.

There is a roughly equal probability of access of data for the OLTP environment. In the OLTP environment, a transaction comes into the system and one unit of data needs to be accessed. Then, another transaction enters the system and another unit of data needs to be accessed. Then, a third transaction enters the system and yet another unit of data needs to be accessed. For all practical purposes, there is no order to the transactions that enter the system. Transactions enter the OLTP system in a completely random manner. A consequence of this random entry of OLTP transactions is that there is no predictable pattern of disk access when accessing OLTP data. OLTP data is accessed randomly and there is roughly an equal probability of access for each unit of data in the OLTP environment. For this pattern of random access, disk storage is ideal.

Now, consider the pattern of access for data warehouse DSS data. A report must be written and all data from 2004 is used. Next, an analysis is done of data from 2004 to 2005. Then a multidimensional load of data is requested for data from mid 2003 to 2005. In short, data from 2000, 2001, and 2002 is hardly noticed or ever accessed. No one accesses the older data and everyone accesses the newest data.

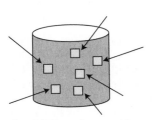

The OLTP environment—
random access to any
given unit of data

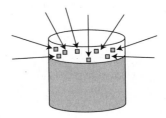

The DSS environment—
a sharp division between
frequently used data and
infrequently used data

Figure 12-8   There is a dramatic difference between the different patterns of usage of OLTP data and DSS data warehouse data.

As a consequence, in the data warehouse DSS environment, there is not a random pattern of access, as was seen in the OLTP environment. In truth, most DSS processing is qualified by date. The fresher the data, the more likely it is to be used. The older the data, the less likely it is that it will be accessed. So, there is definitely a pattern of access for the data warehouse DSS environment that is decidedly not random.

Disk Storage in the Face of Data Separation

When the pattern of access is as skewed as it is for data warehouse DSS data, it is questionable whether or not disk storage is optimal. Disk storage is expensive. The hardware vendor does not charge any less for data that is not being used than the vendor charges for storage that is being used.

Because of this fact, it makes sense to split the data in a data warehouse over multiple forms of storage. Actively used data goes on high-performance storage and inactively used data goes on bulk-storage media.

Figure 12-9 shows the division of data over multiple forms of storage based on the differences in the probability of usage.

Figure 12-9 shows that frequently used data is placed in high performance disk storage. Infrequently used data is placed in bulk storage. Bulk storage is slower, less expensive, and capable of holding a lot of data securely for a long period of time. Often bulk storage is called *near-line storage*, which (depending on the vendor) is sequential storage.

The disk storage vendors always argue that all data should be placed on disk storage because of performance. And, if all data had an equal probability of access, then the disk storage vendor would be correct. But data warehouse DSS data does not have an equal probability of access. Placing infrequently used data on near-line storage actually enhances performance in the data warehouse DSS environment as opposed to hurting it.

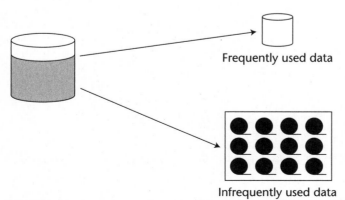

Frequently used data

Infrequently used data

Figure 12-9 Splitting data over multiple storage media based on frequency of usage.

Near-Line Storage

Figure 12-10 shows some of the features of near-line storage. Near-line storage is sequential. The sequential cartridges are robotically controlled — human hands never touch the units of sequential storage. Near-line storage is inexpensive compared to disk storage. Over a long time, near-line storage has cost about an order of magnitude less than disk storage. The disk vendor is fond of saying that disk storage is getting cheaper all the time. In truth, near-line storage has been getting cheaper as well. So, the ratio between the costs of the different forms of storage has remained constant (or close to constant) for a long time.

Near-line storage is suited for storing very large amounts of data. Tens and hundreds of terabytes of data can be stored near-line. Near-line storage is reliable for a long period of time. When it comes time to back up, near-line storage is cheap enough that data can be backed up onto another unit of near-line storage.

The performance penalty of going to near-line storage is paid for only the first record that is sought. All other records in a block are accessed in electronic, nanosecond time once the first record has been retrieved. Only the first record in the block is accessed in mechanical time. All other records in the block are accessed in electronic times.

Figure 12-11 shows the access of data in a near-line block.

Figure 12-11 shows that once the block is placed in memory, all rows in the block other than the first row are accessed as if they had always been in main memory. Given that sequential access is common in the data warehouse environment, such efficient access of sequential data becomes an important factor.

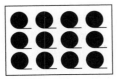

- Robotically controlled
- Inexpensive
- Bulk amounts of data
- Reliable over a long period of time
- Seconds to access first record

Figure 12-10 Near-line storage

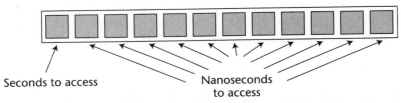

Seconds to access   Nanoseconds to access

Figure 12-11 Once the first row is accessed, the remaining accesses are done at electronic speeds.

Access Speed and Disk Storage

Disk vendors like to make a big issue of the loss of speed that occurs when an organization goes to a split-storage media. When you have to go from electronic speeds to mechanical speeds as you do when you access data on near-line storage, there is a performance price to pay. But placing all your warehouse data on disk storage incurs a performance penalty of another kind. In fact — much to the disbelief of the disk storage vendors — placing all of your data in a data warehouse where the data warehouse is large on disk storage is *slower* than placing your data on split-storage media.

In order to understand why data is slowed up by placing all of it on disk storage, consider the analogy depicted in Figure 12-12.

Figure 12-12 shows two scenarios. In one scenario, all data is placed on disk storage. In another scenario, all the data — the same data — is placed on split-storage media, based on the probability of access of the data. All actively used data is placed on disk storage and all inactively used data is placed on near-line storage.

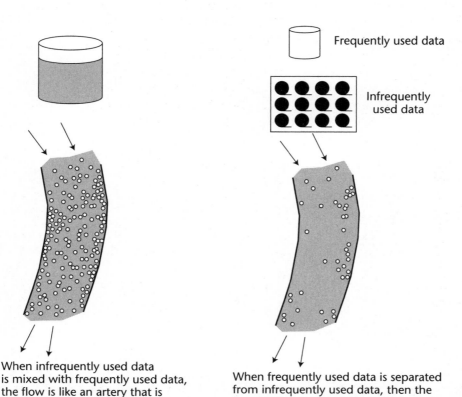

Frequently used data

Infrequently used data

When infrequently used data is mixed with frequently used data, the flow is like an artery that is clogged with cholesterol

When frequently used data is separated from infrequently used data, then the flow of data is like a blood system that is free of cholesterol

Figure 12-12   The difference between freely flowing blood and blood with many restricting components

Consider the flow of data throughout the system. In many ways, data flows like blood through the arteries. When there is a lot of unused data in the disk-only environment, the unused data acts like cholesterol. The more cholesterol there is, the less efficient the blood system. And, the less efficient the blood system is, the slower the system response time.

Now, consider the environment where data is split by probability of usage. In this case there is a very efficient flow of data throughout the system. Using our same analogy, there is very little cholesterol in the system and, as a consequence, the heart has to work a lot less to get the same amount of pumping accomplished. There indeed is good performance because the system pumps only data that is needed through its veins.

For this very fundamental reason, then, performance improves when data warehouse DSS data is placed on a split-storage media. (This is much to the chagrin of the disk-storage vendor, who wishes all data had the characteristics of OLTP processing. Indeed, if all data had the same patterns of usage as the OLTP environment, there would be no need for anything but disk storage.)

Archival Storage

There are needs for split storage other than the mere management of large amounts of data. In addition to needing to manage large amounts of data, there is a need to manage data in an archival manner. Figure 12-13 shows that, in addition to disk storage and near-line or bulk storage, that there is a need for archival storage.

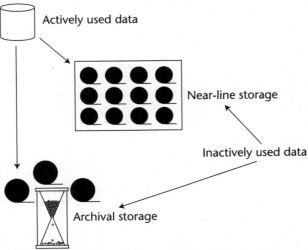

Figure 12-13   There are different forms of inactively used data.

Archival storage is very similar to near-line storage, except that in archival storage, the probability of access drops very low. To put the probability of access in perspective, consider the following simple chart:

High performance disk storage	Access a unit of data once a month
Near-line storage	Access 0.5 units of data every year
Archival storage	Access 0.1 units of data every decade.

It is seen that the probability of access for archival data drops significantly, almost to 0 (zero). Indeed, there is a case to be made for storing data in an archive even if the probability of access drops to 0. On occasion, there will be a law that mandates the storage of data. In this case, it is mandatory to store data whether the data is ever accessed or not. Or, in another case, data is stored in an archive in the event that a legal issue arises relating to the data. In the best and normal case, there will never be a need to go back and look at the data. But if a lawsuit ever arises where the data is in question, then it will be convenient for the organization to have the data to stand in defense of the organization.

There are cases where data needs to migrate down the chain from the near-line environment to the archival environment.

Despite the similarities between the near-line environment and the archival environment, there are some significant differences as well. One significant difference is that of the notion of the data being extended from the data warehouse. Consider Figure 12-14.

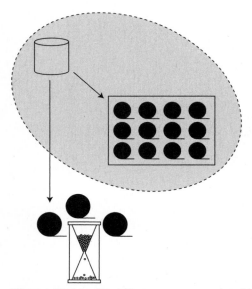

Figure 12-14 Near-line storage can be thought of as a logical extension of the data warehouse. Archival storage cannot be thought of as a logical extension.

Figure 12-14 shows that, logically speaking, the near-line storage environment is seen to be merely an extension of the data warehouse. Indeed, in some cases the location of the data may be transparent to the end user. In this case, when the end user makes a query, he or she does not know whether the data is located in high-performance storage or the data is located in near-line storage. However when the data is in archival storage, the end user always knows that the data is not in high performance storage. This is what is meant by the location of the data being *transparent* in near-line storage and not in archival storage.

Implications of Transparency

The implications of this transparency are rather profound. The very first implication is that if there is to be transparency of data, a row of data in the near-line environment must look identical in format to a row of data in the data warehouse high-performance storage environment. Figure 12-15 shows this need.

But there are other implications as well. If transparency is to be achieved, it is necessary to have the near-line system available to the database system. In addition, there must be compatibility between the two environments in terms of technology.

Of course, there are no such requirements between the data warehouse environment and the archival environment. The archival environment can hold data in any format desired and the archival environment may or may not be compatible with the database environment chosen for the data warehouse.

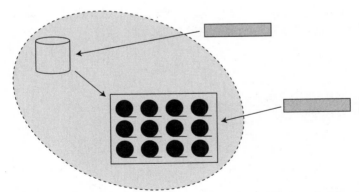

Figure 12-15 A record or row in the data warehouse is identical to a record or row in near-line storage.

Moving Data from One Environment to Another

Moving data from the near-line and the disk-based data warehouse environment can be accomplished in many ways. Figure 12-16 shows some of the ways.

Figure 12-16 shows that there are three ways to manage the flow of data to and from the data warehouse to the near-line environment. One way to manage the flow is to have a database administrator manually move data. This approach is very flexible, and it works surprisingly well. The administrator takes requests for the movement of data from near-line storage and "tees up the data." The administrator can move whole data sets or subsets of a table, as desired. The administrator runs a monitor against the data warehouse to determine what data should be moved to near-line storage. This approach — the manual one — is a viable option and should not be overlooked. It is certainly the most low-tech option and is available to anyone.

A second approach is the hierarchical storage management (HSM) approach. In the HSM approach, whole data sets are moved to and from the data warehouse and the near-line environment. This approach can be implemented automatically so that no human interaction is required. All in all this approach is fairly simple. The problem with the HSM approach is that it operates on the basis of the movement of entire sets of data. Moving entire sets of data is a viable alternative for some environments such as the personal computing environment. But for the data warehouse environment, moving entire sets of data back and forth from the data warehouse to the near-line environment is usually not a good thing to do. The migration of data to and from the data warehouse and the near-line environment needs to be done on the basis of a finer granularity than the data set level used by the HSM approach.

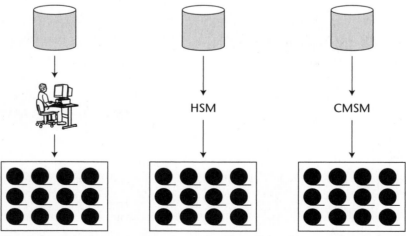

Figure 12-16   Three ways to manage the flow of data from one level of storage to another.

The third alternative is the cross-media storage management (CMSM) option. The CMSM option is fully automated. The CMSM option operates at the row level of granularity so that rows of data can be migrated to and from the data warehouse and the near-line environment. The CMSM option solves many of the problems of the other two approaches. However, the CMSM option is complex to implement and is expensive.

There are then three approaches to the management of the movement of the data to and from the data warehouse and near-line storage environment. Each approach has its advantages and disadvantages, as shown in Table 12-1.

However it is done, there is a need for managing the flow of data to and from the near-line environment.

The CMSM Approach

The CMSM technology is fully automated. The CMSM is software that makes the physical location of the data transparent. Stated differently, with the CMSM the end user does not need to know where data is — in the data warehouse or on near-line storage.

To see how CMSM software works, look at Figure 12-17 and follow a user request through the system.

First a request is received from the system. Then the request is parsed to determine what data is needed. If the request needs data that is already in the data warehouse (that is, already on disk storage), then the system merely lets the query proceed. However, if the system sees that data stored in near-line storage is needed, then the system queues the query and goes to the near-line environment. The system then finds the near-line data that is needed and gathers it. Once gathered, the data is sent to the data warehouse environment. After the data is in the data warehouse environment, it is added to the data warehouse tables where it belongs. Once the data has been loaded into the data warehouse, the query is dequeued and sent into execution. At that point, it looks to the query as if the data had been in the data warehouse all along.

Table 12-1 Options for Moving Data

	ADVANTAGES	DISADVANTAGES
Manual	Very simple; available immediately; operates at the row level	Prone to error; requires human interaction
HSM	Relatively simple; not too expensive; fully automated	Operates at the data set level
CMSM	Fully automated; operates at the row level	Expensive; complex to implement and operate

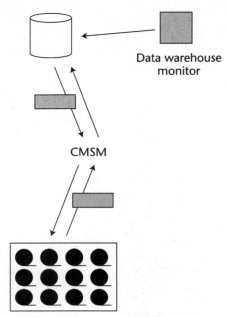

Figure 12-17   A cross-media storage manager (CMSM).

The end user sees no difference in a query against data found in a data warehouse and a query going against data found in the data warehouse and near-line storage. The only difference is in the time the query takes to execute. When a query goes against data found in the near-line environment, it takes longer to execute. But other than that, no action is required on the part of the end user.

Of course, if the environment operates properly, only an occasional query will pay the penalty for data residing in near-line storage since, by definition, near-line storage contains infrequently accessed data.

A Data Warehouse Usage Monitor

The operations of the CMSM environment can be streamlined by the usage of a *data warehouse monitor*. Figure 12-18 shows a data warehouse monitor.

Figure 12-18 shows that SQL calls going into the data warehouse are monitored and the result set coming out of those calls are monitored as well. The system administrator can tell what data *is* and *is not* being used in the data warehouse. The monitor can look at data usage at the row level and the column level. By using a data monitor, the system administrator can be much more finely tuned than the classical approach of merely putting 24-month-old data in the data warehouse.

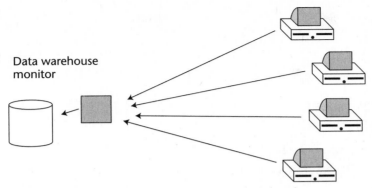

Figure 12-18   SQL calls are intercepted and analyzed.

There are two types of data warehouse monitors — those that are supplied by the DBMS vendor and those supplied by third-party monitors. As a rule, the third-party monitors are much better because the monitors supplied by the DBMS vendors require far more resources than those supplied. In fact, the DBMS vendor-supplied monitors require so many overhead resources to run that they have to be turned off at peak periods of traffic — exactly the moment when you don't want them to be turned off. The data warehouse monitors that are supplied by the third-party vendors require only a tiny amount of resources and are specifically geared for data warehouse usage.

On occasion, an administrator will attempt to use a *transaction monitor* in the data warehouse environment. A transaction monitor is designed for optimizing the smooth flow of transactions in the OLTP environment. Trying to use a transaction monitor for managing data usage in the data warehouse is like trying to use the mechanic tools for a car while working on an airplane or a boat. It simply is an uncomfortable fit, if it works at all.

The Extension of the Data Warehouse across Different Storage Media

With the extension of the data warehouse from disk storage to near-line and archival storage, the data warehouse can be extended to a very large volume of data. Figure 12-19 shows this extension.

The data warehouse can grow to *petabytes* (equivalent to a quadrillion bytes) of data and can still be effective and still be managed.

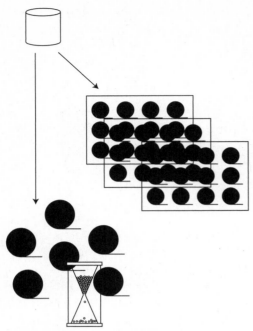

Figure 12-19 Growth to infinity.

Inverting the Data Warehouse

When alternate forms of storage are entered into the equation, it is possible to "invert the data warehouse." With a data warehouse inversion, there is the possibility of managing any amount of data.

So what is an *inverted data warehouse*? Consider a normal data warehouse. The way that almost all companies build a data warehouse is to put data first into disk storage. Then, after the data ages, the data is placed on near-line or archival storage. There is a rather natural flow of data across the different storage media.

But there is an alternative. The alternative is to first enter data into near-line storage, not disk storage. Then, when a query is done, the data is "staged" from the near-line environment to the disk environment. Once in the disk environment, the data is accessed and analyzed as if the data resided there permanently. Once the analysis is over, the data is returned to near-line storage.

In a normal data warehouse, current data is thought to reside on disk storage. In an inverted data warehouse, current data is thought to reside on near-line storage.

There is, of course, a price to pay for inverting the data. Every request must be staged, and staging takes time. But (depending on the analysis being done) staging may not be an onerous penalty. If there are a lot of explorers accessing and analyzing the data, then staging may simply be part of the price to be paid for satisfying irregular requests.

Of course, some of the performance penalty can be mitigated by running more than one instance of the disk-based DBMS. In such a fashion more than one query can be accommodated at the same time. In other words, with two disk-based DBMSs running, two queries and analyses can be accommodated, thereby mitigating some of the time needed for queuing the data waiting for staging. By using more than one instance of the disk based DBMS, a certain amount of parallelism can be achieved.

Total Cost

There is another way to look at the management of very large amounts of data: as the data grows, so grows the budget required for the data warehouse. But with the introduction of near-line and archival storage, the growing costs of a data warehouse can be mitigated. Figure 12-20 shows the total cost curve over a long period of time for the implementation of a data warehouse.

On the left-hand side, the cost curve is for the data warehouse that is a disk-only data warehouse. On the right-hand side, the cost curve is for a data warehouse where near-line and archival storage have been introduced. The inflection of the curve on the right-hand side comes when the introduction of near-line storage and archival storage is made.

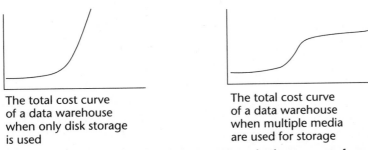

The total cost curve of a data warehouse when only disk storage is used

The total cost curve of a data warehouse when multiple media are used for storage

Figure 12-20   The difference in the long term budgetary costs for organizations that have near-line storage and organizations that do not have near-line storage.

Maximum Capacity

In many places, you might hear, "XYZ machine can handle up to *nnn* terabytes of data." This statement is usually said in an attempt to shock, as if a machine handling a large number of bytes were an impressive feat. In actuality, measuring the number of bytes a machine can handle is almost meaningless. The fact is that measuring the capacity of a machine must be done in combination with a fair number of other parameters.

Figure 12-21 shows that there are three parameters that must be measured in tandem with each other in order to make a meaningful measurement of a machines capacity. Those parameters are:

- Volumes of data
- Number of users
- Workload complexity

These three measurements taken in combination give a good measurement of a machine's capabilities.

For any parameter, the parameter can be maximized at the expense of the other parameters. Figure 12-22 shows that a lot of data can be loaded onto a machine if there are very few users and if the workload is very simple.

Another possibility is to have a very complex workload at the expense of the number of users and the volumes of data. Figure 12-23 shows this case.

Yet another possibility is that there are a large number of users, a very simple workload, and a small volume of data. Figure 12-24 shows this case.

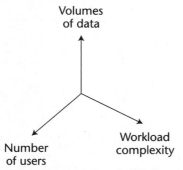

Figure 12-21   The three parameters of capacity management.

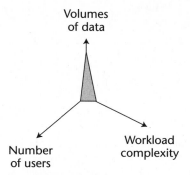

Figure 12-22   Capacity optimized on volumes of data.

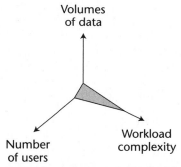

Figure 12-23   Capacity optimized on workload complexity.

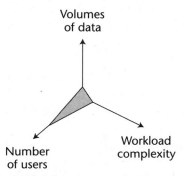

Figure 12-24   Capacity optimized on number of users.

The balanced case is where there is a fair amount of data, a fair number of users, and a reasonably complex workload. This case is seen in Figure 12-25.

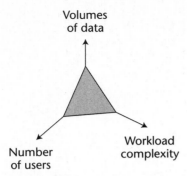

Figure 12-25 Balanced capacity.

After examining Figure 12-25 and the other figures, you could conclude that any one parameter can be stretched at the expense of the other parameters. Indeed, a large amount of data can be loaded onto a machine. It's just that if enough data is loaded, there can be no workload and no users. That is why looking at just the volume of data that can be loaded onto a machine is almost a meaningless thing to do.

Summary

Data warehouses grow large explosively. In a few short years, it is typical for a data warehouse to grow from a few gigabytes to terabytes of data. Data warehouses grow large because they contain historical data, detailed data, and data from a diverse set of sources. As data warehouses grow large, the everyday activities of data management become challenging to execute, for no other reason than the amount of time needed to handle large volumes of data.

As data warehouses grow large, the data inside the warehouse separates into one of two classes — frequently used data or infrequently used data. Infrequently used data is often called dormant data. The separation of data warehouse data into two classes means that disk storage is not optimal for all the data in a data warehouse. Infrequently used data belongs on slower, less-powerful storage such as near-line storage. By placing infrequently used data in near-line storage, the cost of the data warehouse is mitigated and the performance that is possible is greatly enhanced. Performance is enhanced because when infrequently used data is separated from frequently used data, the efficiency of processing is greatly accelerated.

Near-line storage is sequential technology put in the framework of robotics and modern electronics. There is a price of performance to be paid for accessing the first record in a block. But once the block has been located and placed in the processor, all other accesses within the block are done quickly.

Another form of storage similar to near-line storage is known as archival storage. In near-line storage, the data residing in near-line storage is logically an extension of the data warehouse. In archival storage, the data in archival storage is not considered to be a direct extension of the data warehouse. In addition, the probability of access of data found in the near-line environment is higher than the probability of access of the data found in the archival environment.

There are three approaches to the management of the flow of data to and from the data warehouse and near-line storage. Those approaches are the manual approach, the HSM approach, and the CMSM approach. Each of the approaches has their own set of advantages and disadvantages.

The CMSM technology allows data to be accessed and managed transparently from its storage location. The end user does not know whether the data being accessed is on disk storage or near-line storage when CMSM technology is being used.

For really large volumes of data there is the possibility of inverting the data warehouse. When a data warehouse is inverted, data enters the near-line environment, and is staged from there when access is required. The inverted approach is ideal for really large amounts of data or for the case where there are a lot of explorers who must be satisfied.

The total cost of ownership for a large data warehouse over the long haul is temporized by the introduction and usage of near-line and archival storage. Without near-line and/or archival storage, the costs of the data warehouse skyrocket as the data warehouse grows large.

CHAPTER 13

The Relational and the Multidimensional Model as a Basis for Database Design

One of the issues facing data warehousing professionals is that of the basic model for data warehouse database design. There are two basic models for database design that are widely considered — the relational model and the multidimensional model. The *relational model* is widely considered to be the "Inmon" approach, while the *multidimensional model* is considered to be the "Kimball" approach to design for the data warehouse.

This chapter addresses what the different approaches are and how they apply to data warehousing. Both approaches have their advantages and disadvantages. Those advantages and disadvantages are discussed, and the conclusion is drawn that the relational foundation for database design is the best long-term approach for the building of the data warehouse and for the case where a true enterprise approach is needed. The multidimensional model is good for short-term data warehouses, where there is a limited scope for the data warehouse.

The Relational Model

The relational approach to database design begins with the organization of data into a table. Different columns are in each row of the table. Figure 13-1 shows a simple table.

NOTE For the definitive work on the relational model and relational database design, refer to the books and articles by Ted Codd and Chris Date.

The relational table can have different properties. The columns of data have different physical characteristics. Different columns can be indexed and can act as identifiers. Certain columns may be null upon implementation. The columns are all defined in terms of a data definition language (DDL) statement.

The relational approach to database design has been around since the 1970s and is well established through the relational implementation of technologies such as IBM's DB2, Oracle's Oracle DBMS product, and Teradata's DBMS product, among others. Relational technology uses keys and foreign keys to establish relationships between rows of data. Relational technology carries with it the structured query language (SQL), which is widely used as an interface language from program to data.

Figure 13-2 shows a classical relational database design.

| Column a |
| Column b |
| Column c |
| Column d |
| Column e |
| Column f |

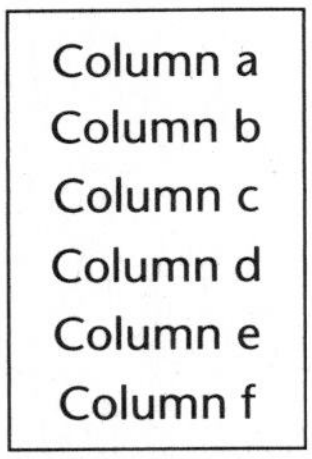

Figure 13-1   A simple table.

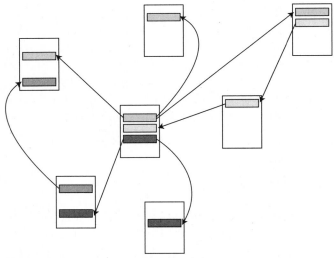

Figure 13-2   A relational database design.

Figure 13-2 shows that there are different tables, and the tables are connected by means of a series of key-foreign key relationships. The key-foreign key relationship is a basic relationship where an identical unit of data resides in both tables, as seen in Figure 13-3.

It is through the identical unit of data that any two or more rows of data are related. For example, suppose two rows have the value "Bill Inmon" in a column. The two rows are related by the occurrence of a common value.

The data in the relational model exists in a form that is termed the "normalized" level. *Normalization of data* implies that the database design has caused the data to be broken down into a very low level of granularity. Data in a normalized form exists in an insular mode where data relationships within the table are very disciplined. When normalized, the data inside a table has a relationship with only other data that resides in the table. Normalization is said to typically exist at three levels — first normal form, second normal form, and third normal form.

The value of the relational model for database design for the data warehouse is that there is discipline in the way the database design has been built, clarity of the meaning, and use of the detailed level of normalized data. In other words, the relational model produces a design for the data warehouse that is very flexible. Databases based on the design can be looked at first one way, and then another when the design has been based on the relational model. Data elements can be shaped and reshaped in many different ways. Flexibility, then, is the great strength of the relational model. Versatility is the second great strength. Because the detailed data is collected and can be combined, many different views of the data can be supported when the design for the data warehouse is based on the relational model.

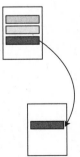

Figure 13-3   A key-foreign key relationship.

The Multidimensional Model

The other database design approach for the building of a data warehouse that is commonly considered is termed the *multidimensional approach*. The multidimensional approach is also sometimes called the *star join approach*. The multidimensional approach has been championed by Dr. Ralph Kimball. At the center of the multidimensional approach to database design there is the star join, as shown in Figure 13-4.

> **NOTE** For a more detailed explanation of the Kimball approach to multidimensional database design, refer to the books and articles by Dr. Kimball.

The star join data structure is so-called because its representation depicts a "star" with a center and several outlying structures of data.

There are different components of the star join, as shown in Figure 13-5.

Figure 13-5 shows that at the center of the star join is a fact table. A *fact table* is a structure that contains many occurrences of data. Surrounding the fact table are *dimensions*, which describe one important aspect of the fact table. There are fewer number of occurrences of a dimension table than the number of occurrences of fact tables.

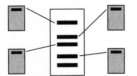

Figure 13-4   A star join.

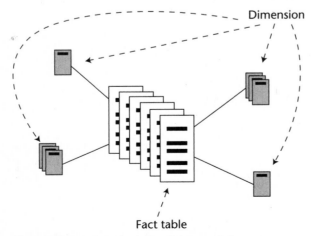

Figure 13-5   Components of the star join.

Typical of the many occurrences that might appear in a fact table might be the orders for a part. Or, the fact table might contain occurrences for a customer. Or, the fact table might represent a banking transaction. In any case, the fact table represents data that occurs many times. The dimension table contains relevant, yet separate, information (such as the corporate calendar, the corporate pricing tables, the locations of stores, the means of shipment for an order, and so forth). The dimension table defines important, yet ancillary, information that relates to the fact table. The fact table and the dimension table are related by the existence of a common unit of data. For example, the fact table might contain the data "week 21." In the dimension table, there is a reference to "week 21." Week 21 may be "April 19–26" in the dimension table, for example. And the dimension table would go on to say that week 21 had no holidays and was the third week in the corporate reporting period.

Snowflake Structures

As a rule, in a star join there is one fact table. But more than one fact table can be combined in a database design to create a composite structure called a *snowflake structure*. Figure 13-6 depicts a snowflake structure.

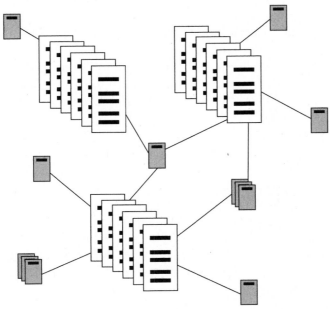

Figure 13-6   A snowflake structure.

In a snowflake structure, different fact tables are connected by means of sharing one or more common dimensions. Sometimes these shared dimensions are called *conformed dimensions*. The thought behind a snowflake structure is that the different fact and dimension tables combine to form a shape similar to a snowflake.

The great advantage of the multidimensional design is its efficiency of access. When designed properly, the star join is very efficient in delivering data to the end user. To make the delivery of information efficient, the end-user requirements must be gathered and assimilated. The processes the end user has that will use the data are at the heart of defining what the multidimensional structure will look like. Once the end-user requirements are understood, the end-user requirements are used to shape the star join into its final, most optimal structure.

Differences between the Models

The differences between the star join and the relational structure as a basis for data warehouse design are many. The single most important difference is in terms of flexibility and performance. The relational model is highly flexible, but is not optimized for performance for any user. The multidimensional model is highly efficient at servicing the needs of one user community, but it is not good at flexibility.

Another important difference in the two approaches to database design is in the scope of the design. Of necessity, the multidimensional design has a limited scope. Since processing requirements are used to shape the model, the design starts to break down when many processing requirements are gathered. In other words, the database design can be optimized for one and only one set of processing requirements. When an entirely different set of processing requirements is added to a design, the optimization becomes a moot issue. A database design can be optimized for performance only one way.

When the relational model is used, there is no particular optimization for performance one way or the other. Since the relational model calls for data to be stored at the lowest level of granularity, new elements of data can be added ad infinitum. There simply is no end to the data that can be added to the relational model. For this reason the relational model is appropriate to a very large scope of data (such as an enterprise model), while the multidimensional model is appropriate to a small scope of data (such as a department or even a sub-department).

The Roots of the Differences

The roots of the differences between the multidimensional model and the relational model go back to the original shaping of the models themselves. Figure 13-7 shows how the models are shaped.

Figure 13-7 shows that the relational environment is shaped by the corporate or enterprise data model. The star join or multidimensional model is shaped by the end-user requirements. In other words one model — the relational model — is shaped by a pure data model and the other model — the multidimensional model — is shaped by processing requirements. This difference in the shaping of the models leads to several subtle, but very important, consequences.

The first consequence is in terms of serviceability. The relational model is shaped around an abstraction of data. Because of this, the model itself is very flexible. But for all the flexibility of the relational model, the relational model is not terribly optimal for the performance of the direct access of data. If you want to get good performance out of the relational model, it is optimal to pull data out of the model and recast it into a form that is suitable for fast access. Despite the performance limitations, since the relational model supports the reshaping of data, the relational model is good for the indirect access of data.

The multidimensional model, on the other hand, is good for speedy and efficient direct access to data. The multidimensional model supports direct access to data, as opposed to the indirect access to data supported by the relational data model.

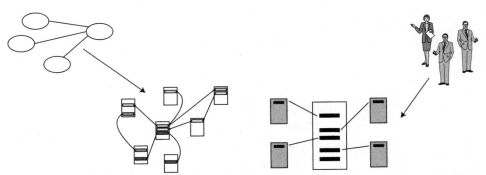

Figure 13-7   The relational model is shaped from a data model. A star join is shaped from user requirements.

The differences between the direct access of data and the indirect access of data may not seem important, but they are. From an architectural standpoint, the differences mean that the relational model is the much better model for the support of the data warehouse. The reason that the relational model is better for the basis of design for the data warehouse is that the data warehouse needs to support many different sets of users with many different agendas with many different ways of looking at the data. In other words, the data warehouse is not optimized for the access of any one given user. Instead, the data warehouse supports many different users in many different ways.

The second subtle difference between the origins of the relational model and the origins of the multidimensional model are that the data model behind the relational model is at a fairly high level of abstraction, while the process model that is behind the multidimensional model is not at an abstract level at all. Because of its level of abstraction, the relational model is able to support many uses. Because of its specific processing requirements orientation, the multidimensional model is able to support only a few specific requirements. However, the multidimensional model (if done well) supports those processing requirements well.

Reshaping Relational Data

How is it that the relational model supports the shaping and reshaping of many different forms of data? Figure 13-8 shows a basic relational structuring of data.

In the structuring of data, new files are created from the base data found in the relational database. The essence of the relational data is that it is non-redundant, bedrock data organized in its simplest form. Because of the granular level of detail found in the relational files, it is easy to pull data from other related relational tables and create a customized table. The customized table is created around the specific needs of a single set of users. The customized table — once designed and populated — is then ready for use and is efficient to access.

If another customized table is required, then the relational tables are accessed once again and a new customized table is created. The same relational tables can be used over and over again to form different customized tables.

The merging of relational tables to create a new relational table is easy for several reasons:

- Data is stored at the most granular, normalized level.

- Relationships between relational tables are already identified and have a key-foreign key manifestation.

- New tables can contain new summaries, new selection criteria for those summaries, and aggregations of the base data found in the relational table.

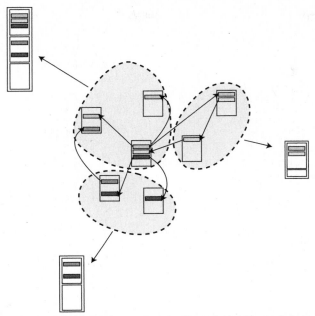

Figure 13-8 The base data in the relational model can be shaped and reshaped in as many ways as desired.

For these basic reasons, it is easy to use relational data and tables as a form of information putty. Relational tables are easily shaped one way and reshaped another way, which is ideal for the data warehouse environment.

Indirect Access and Direct Access of Data

For the reasons that have been discussed, it is apparent that the relational model is good for indirect access of data and the multidimensional model is good for direct access of data. Figure 13-9 shows this relationship.

While the star join, multidimensional approach is good for the optimal access of data by one group of people, the optimization comes at an expense. Anyone who is not a member of the group for which optimization has been done pays the price of less-than-optimal performance. And, of course, there is the issue of having the data available that is needed to service a group of people other than the original group of people for whom the star join was created. Stated differently, there is no guarantee that the star join that is optimal for one group of users will contain the data needed for another group of users. Figure 13-10 shows the inability of a star join to serve multiple diverse groups of users.

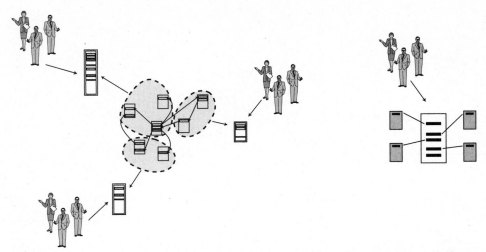

Figure 13-9 The star join is good for direct end-user access. The relational model is good for indirect user access.

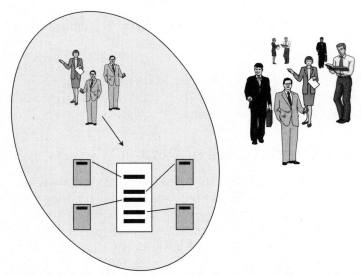

Figure 13-10 The star join optimizes the access of data for one group of people at the expense of all other groups of people.

Servicing Future Unknown Needs

Servicing existing groups of users is not the only issue that there is. There is also the issue of servicing future unknown needs and future unknown users. The granular data inside the relational model is like atoms. Atoms, we are told, can be combined to create many different things. One of the secrets of atoms is their granularity. Because atoms are so fine, they can be used in an almost infinite number of ways. Similarly, the granular data in the relational model is used to service unknown future needs for information. Figure 13-11 shows this capability.

Servicing the Need to Change Gracefully

There is yet another advantage of the relational model as a basis for the data warehouse — the ability to change gracefully. The relational model is designed to be used in an indirect fashion. This means that the direct users of the data warehouse data access data that comes from the relational model, not data in the relational model itself. When it comes time for change, the impact is minimal because the different users of the data warehouse are accessing different databases.

In other words, when user A wants to make a change to data, the change is made for the database servicing user A's needs. The relational foundation may not be touched at all. The odds of impacting user B, C, and D are absolutely minimal when a change has to be made on the behalf of user A. Figure 13-12 shows this effect.

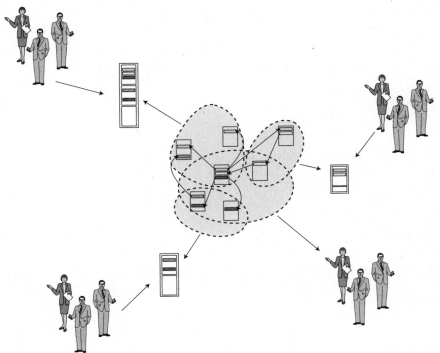

Figure 13-11   When a new set of requirements appears, the relational model provides a foundation of reusability.

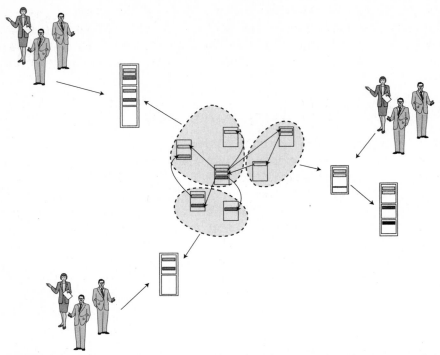

Figure 13-12 When it comes time to make a change of data for one set of users, that change can be made with no disruption to other users.

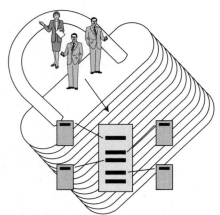

Figure 13-13 Once the data is designed and developed into the star join format, the data is "locked up" and becomes difficult to change or adapt as new requirements are created or discovered.

The ability to change gracefully is not one of the characteristics of the star join, multidimensional approach to database design. The design of a multidimensional database is fragile and is a result of many processing requirements taken together. When the processing requirements change, the design of the multidimensional database may or may not be able to be gracefully changed. Once the data has been set in the form of a multidimensional database, change is not easy. Figure 13-13 shows the cement that multidimensional data is mired in once the design is finalized.

For all of the reasons that have been discussed, the relational model forms the proper basis for the data warehouse design. Figure 13-14 reinforces this point.

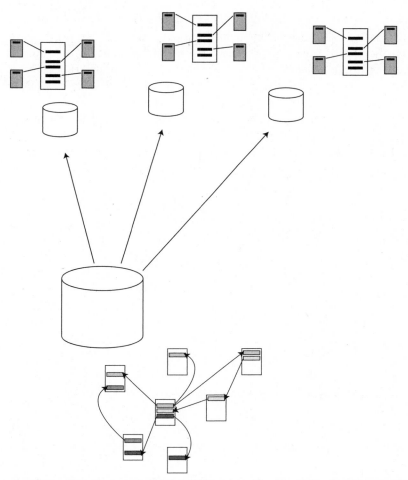

Figure 13-14   The relational model forms an ideal basis for the data warehouse, while the star join forms the ideal basis for the data mart.

Independent Data Marts

Another aspect of the multidimensional model is the alignment of the multidimensional model with what is referred to as the *independent data mart approach*. (A *data mart* is a data structure that is dedicated to serving the analytical needs of one group of people, such as the accounting department or the finance department.) The independent data mart is a data mart that is built directly from the legacy applications. Figure 13-15 shows an independent data mart.

Independent data marts are appealing because they appear to be a direct solution to solving the information problem. An independent data mart can be created by a single department with no consideration to other departments or without any consideration to a centralized IT organization. There is no need to "think globally" when building an independent data mart. The independent data represents a subset of the entire DSS requirements for an organization. An independent data mart is a relatively inexpensive thing to build, and it allows an organization to take its own information destiny in its own hands. These are just a few of the reasons why independent data marts are popular.

Looking back at Figure 13-15 you can see that multidimensional technology strongly suggests that independent data marts be built.

The architectural counterpoint to the independent data mart is the dependent data mart. Figure 13-16 shows a dependent data mart.

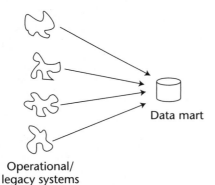

Operational/
legacy systems

Figure 13-15   Independent data marts.

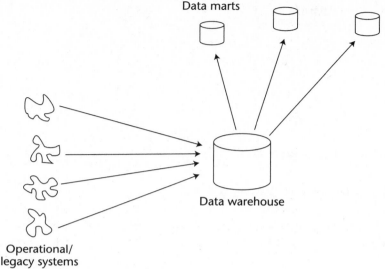

Figure 13-16 Dependent data marts.

The opposite of an independent data mart is a dependent data mart. A *dependent data mart* is one that is built from data coming from the data warehouse. The dependent data mart does not depend on legacy or operational data for its source. It depends on only the data warehouse for its source data. The dependent data mart requires forethought and investment. It requires that someone "think globally." The dependent data mart requires multiple users to pool their information needs for the creation of the data warehouse. In other words, the dependent data mart requires advance planning, a long-term perspective, global analysis, and cooperation and coordination of the definition of requirements among different departments of an organization.

Building Independent Data Marts

To show the long-term difficulties with the independent data mart approach, consider the following progression. In the beginning an organization builds an independent data mart, as shown in Figure 13-17.

Upon building the independent data mart, the end users are delighted. The end users get their information, have their own data and analysis, and have information like they have never seen it before. They wonder what could have ever been the criticism of independent data marts. As long as there is only one independent data mart, there is absolutely no problem.

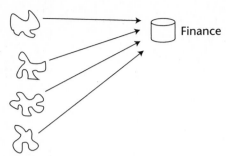

Figure 13-17   The first independent data mart is successful.

But there never is only one data mart.

Other users hear of the success of the independent data mart, and one of the user departments that does not have a data mart starts to build their own independent data mart. Figure 13-18 shows the arrival of the second independent data mart.

The second set of users is also delighted with their independent data mart. Someone notices that the information between the two data marts is not integrated and is not synchronized. But that hardly seems an issue in the face of all of the happiness the new data mart has brought.

The success of the first few independent data marts has brought a lot of momentum. Now another department wishes to build their own independent data mart. So a new, third independent data mart is created (Figure 13-19). The end user is delighted once the data mart is built. Then someone notices that there is yet a third irreconcilable opinion as to what data values are. And it is also noticed that the same detailed data is being collected by each new independent data mart. In truth, with each of the independent data marts, there is an increasing redundancy of detailed data.

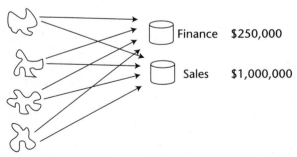

Figure 13-18   The second independent data mart is also successful. But someone notices that the answer to similar questions is not coordinated.

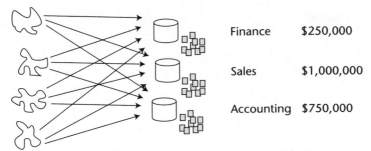

Finance $250,000

Sales $1,000,000

Accounting $750,000

Figure 13-19   The third data mart is added. Now there are three opinions on everything and the same detailed data appears every time a new data mart is added.

The momentum for independent data marts is now firmly established. A new department adds their independent data mart to the collection of existing independent data marts (Figure 13-20). Now there is yet one more irreconcilable opinion as to the state of the business. Even more redundant detailed data is added. And now the number of interface programs grows beyond a reasonable number. Not only are a lot of resources required for the building of the interface programs, but the maintenance of those programs becomes a burden. And to top it off, the online resources for the execution of the interface programs start to become difficult to manage because so many programs have to execute in a finite amount of time.

Despite all the shortcomings of the independent data mart approach, the momentum continues. Now engineering wants to build their own data mart, as shown in Figure 13-21. But when they start the process, they find that none of the work done by any of the departments that have previously built a data mart is reusable. The new department has to build a data mart from scratch. And they make yet one more copy of the same detailed data that has been extracted by previous data mart owners. The owners of the new data mart add one more opinion as to the state of the business. The new department adds one more set of interface programs that have to be written and maintained. And the new department competes for resources to get their load programs executed.

After a number of independent data marts have been built, the issues of what is wrong with the independent data mart approach becomes apparent. Independent data marts are good for short, fast solutions, but when the longer-term perspective is taken, independent data marts are simply inadequate to solve the problems of information across the organization.

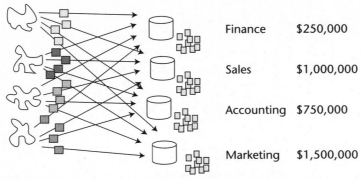

Figure 13-20   The fourth data mart is added. There is yet one more option that cannot be correlated with any other opinion. There is more detailed data that is gathered and is redundant. There are a whole host of interface programs that have to be built and maintained.

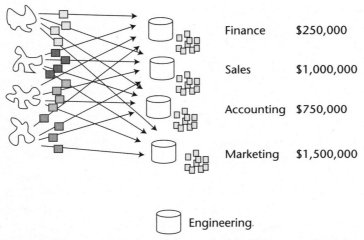

Figure 13-21   Engineering wishes to build a data mart. There is no foundation on which to build and there is no historical data to access. All integration must be redone (one more time), and there is no coordination with any previous efforts at integration.

Of course, if the organization had adopted the dependent data mart approach and had first built a data warehouse before building any of the data marts, then the architectural problems inherent to the independent data mart approach would never have arisen. If there had been dependent data marts emanating from a data warehouse, there would have been reusability of data and a limited numbers of interface programs written. There still would have been different opinions, but they would be reconcilable. Figure 13-22 shows that if there had been dependent data marts and a data warehouse, the architectural problems of independent data marts would never have arisen.

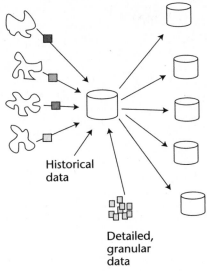

Historical data

Detailed, granular data

Figure 13-22 With dependent data marts, all problems of independent data marts are solved.

In other words, independent data marts represent a short-term, limited scope solution where it is not necessary to look at the global, long-term picture. Dependent data marts, on the other hand, require a long-term and a global perspective. But independent data marts do not provide a firm foundation for corporate information, while dependent data marts indeed do provide a sound long-term foundation for information decisions.

Summary

There are two basic models that are used for database design for the data warehouse: the relational model and the multidimensional (star join) model. The relational model is a superior choice for the design of the data warehouse for many reasons. The primary reason is that the relational model is flexible and is capable of servicing the information needs of many organizations. The multidimensional model is good for servicing the needs of only one set of users at the expense of all other users.

The relational model is ideal for serving indirect access to the data warehouse, while the multidimensional model is ideal for serving the needs of the direct use of the data warehouse.

Another characteristic of the multidimensional model is the direct access of legacy and operational data for analytical purposes in a data mart. There are two types of data marts: independent data marts and dependent data marts. Independent data marts produce many problems. However, the problems associated with independent data marts do not become apparent until several of the independent data marts have been built.

The problems with the independent data marts are that the independent data marts

- Do not provide a platform for reusability
- Do not provide a basis for reconciliation of data
- Do not provide a basis for a single set of legacy interface programs
- Do require that every independent data mart create its own pool of detailed data, which is, unfortunately, massively redundant with the pools of detailed data created by other independent data marts

Fortunately, dependent data marts that take data from a data warehouse do not have to have the same set of architectural problems.

CHAPTER 14

Data Warehouse Advanced Topics

In this chapter, many different topics will be addressed. The purpose of this chapter is to tie together many of the concepts that are required to make the data warehouse successful.

The subject of data warehousing — at the heart of the corporate information factory (CIF) and business intelligence — is a complex subject with many facets. This chapter addresses some of the topics that do not comfortably fit with other topics that have been addressed elsewhere.

End-User Requirements and the Data Warehouse

One of the questions frequently asked and often misunderstood is where do the requirements for the building of the data warehouse come from? In truth, the requirements for the building of the data warehouse come from a data model. End-user requirements are a part of the picture, although the end-user requirements enter the picture indirectly. To understand how end-user requirements enter into the usage of data found in the data warehouse, consider the following design considerations for the data warehouse.

The Data Warehouse and the Data Model

The data warehouse is shaped by a data model. The data model has different levels. The data model typically has the high-level data model, the midlevel data model, and the low-level data model.

The high-level data model shows how the major subject areas of the data warehouse should be divided. Typical high-level subject areas are customer, product, shipment, order, part number, and so forth.

The midlevel data model identifies keys, attributes, relationships, and other aspects of the details of the data warehouse. The mid-level model "fleshes out" the details of the high-level data model.

The low-level model is where physical database design is done. The low-level model is the place where partitioning is done, foreign key relationships are defined to the DBMS, indexes are defined, and other physical aspects of design are completed.

Figure 14-1 shows the different relationships of the data model and how the data model relates to the data warehouse.

The Relational Foundation

Now consider how the data warehouse is used. The relational components of the data warehouse are used for the purpose of supporting other views of the data. Figure 14-2 shows that the relational foundation of the data warehouse is used as a basis for creating other views and combinations of the data.

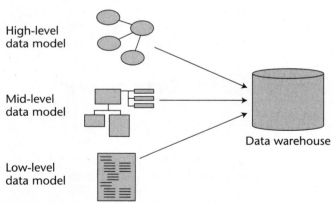

Figure 14-1   How the data model is shaped.

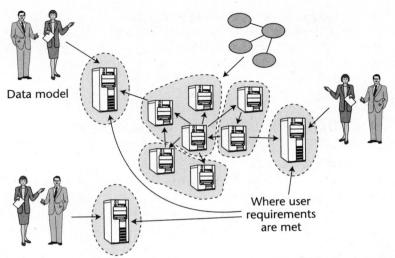

Data model

Where user
requirements
are met

Figure 14-2 End-user requirements are not met directly in the data warehouse.

Once the relational database is created (forming the nucleus of the data warehouse), end-user requirements are used to show how data must be reshaped. So, end-user requirements do shape the data warehouse, at least indirectly. The granular, base data that is needed to support end-user requirements must be in the data warehouse to support the end-user needs.

The Data Warehouse and Statistical Processing

Consider this. What happens to a machine when a heavy amount of statistical analysis hits it (such as when an explorer makes a request)? Suppose a machine is being used to service a normal data warehouse workload where people (farmers) are pulling snippets of data off of the machine periodically. Then, one day the machine gets a request to look at 100 million rows of data and do a heavy statistical analysis. In this heavy request, there is a need to sort the data, look at each row, create some calculations, and then pass the calculations against the base data once again. Once this request is finished, a different set of parameters is entered and the process is repeated.

What happens to normal data warehouse processing when such a request is received? Under normal conditions, normal processing comes to a dead halt. And what happens when normal processing comes to a dead halt? End users become dissatisfied quickly.

The truth is normal access of data and heavy statistical processing do not mix well. Someone suffers when there is significant contention for machine resources.

However much suffering might be going on, there is still no doubt that there is a valid need for both regular analytical processing and statistical analysis of data found in a data warehouse. The problem is that the regular mixing of the two types of processing creates a contention for resources on the machine that holds the data.

Resource Contention in the Data Warehouse

If the resource contention occurs once a year, the statistical processing can be cleverly scheduled so as to avoid a problem. If the contention occurs once a quarter, then there probably will be moments in time where the statistical analysis can be done, but care must be taken not to overextend the machine. If the contention occurs once a month, then the statistical processing will be really difficult to schedule. If the contention occurs once a week, it will be almost impossible to schedule the statistical analysis for a convenient time. If the contention occurs daily, it is effectively impossible to schedule to avoid conflict.

The issue of contention then is one that all depends on the frequency of the periods of contention. If contention occurs infrequently, then the problem is minimal. If the contention occurs frequently, then contention for resources becomes a big problem.

The Exploration Warehouse

In the cases where contention for resources becomes an issue, it is wise to investigate a special form of a data warehouse. That form of a data warehouse is called an *exploration warehouse* or a *data mining warehouse*.

Figure 14-3 shows an exploration warehouse being built from a data warehouse.

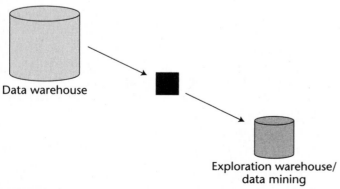

Data warehouse

Exploration warehouse/
data mining

Figure 14-3   Exploration processing is done outside the data warehouse.

The purpose of an exploration warehouse is to provide a foundation for heavy statistical analysis. Once the exploration warehouse has been built, there will be no more contention problems with the data warehouse. Statistical analyses can be run all day long and there will be no contention issues because the processing that is occurring is happening on separate machines. The statistical processing occurs one place and the regular data warehouse processing occurs elsewhere.

But there are reasons other than contention for creating an exploration warehouse.

Another reason for the creation of an exploration warehouse is that the technology of statistical analysis is so different from other styles of analysis that it makes sense to try to separate the environments. With separate environments, the communities that want to do statistical processing are very different communities from those that want to do more normal analytical processing.

Database design is another reason for building a separate exploration warehouse. The exploration warehouse is seldom a direct copy of the data found in the data warehouse. Instead, the exploration warehouse starts with a subset of the data found in the data warehouse. Then the data that is taken from the data warehouse is recast.

A typical recast of the data warehouse data is the creation of what can be termed "convenience" fields. A *convenience field* is one that is created for the purpose of streamlining statistical analysis. As an example, suppose that the following data elements are found in the data warehouse environment:

- Gross sales price

- Tax

- Commission

- Shipping charge

Now, suppose that, in the exploration environment, you want to do an analysis on net sales. When the data is being entered into the exploration environment, it is advisable to enter the data as a result of a calculation, not enter the data literally as found in the data warehouse:

Net sale = Gross sale price – (Tax + Commission + Shipping charge)

By creating a value (net sale) in the exploration warehouse, several positive objectives are met:

- The data has to be calculated only once, thereby saving resources.

- The data is consistent. The calculation is made the same way every time it is needed.

- Space is saved by having one data element, not four data elements.

Exploration warehouses are usually focused on projects. This means that when the results of the project are obtained, the exploration warehouse goes away. This is in contrast to the data warehouse that is built for permanent purposes. Under normal circumstances, data warehouses are not built and then discarded.

Figure 14-4 shows some of the characteristics of an exploration warehouse.

The Data Mining Warehouse

Exploration warehouses are similar to a data mining warehouse. But there is a shade of difference between an exploration warehouse and a data mining data warehouse.

The primary purpose for an exploration warehouse is the creation of assertions, hypotheses, and observations. A data mining warehouse has the purpose of proving the strength of the truth of the hypotheses. For example, in an exploration warehouse, an analyst may look at some of the data in the exploration warehouse and proclaim that "most large sales are made on Wednesdays." For the number of cases viewed by the user in the exploration warehouse, this observation may have appeared to be true.

Now, suppose the data mining warehouse is used to analyze the size of sales made on different days. In the data mining warehouse, many, many examples of sales are researched. The result of the analysis is to prove or disprove the hypothesis that large sales are made mostly on Wednesdays.

The exploration warehouse must have a wide diversity of data types to provide a breadth of information. The data mining warehouse needs to have depth. It needs to have on-hand as many occurrences as possible of whatever is being analyzed.

One difference between the exploration warehouse and the data mining warehouse then is this: *The exploration warehouse is optimized on breadth while the data mining warehouse is optimized on depth.*

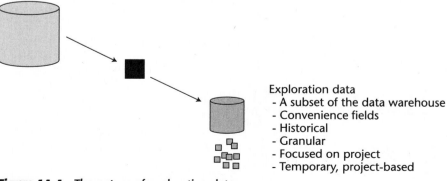

Exploration data
 - A subset of the data warehouse
 - Convenience fields
 - Historical
 - Granular
 - Focused on project
 - Temporary, project-based

Figure 14-4   The nature of exploration data.

Because the differences between an exploration warehouse and a data mining warehouse are so subtle, it is only very sophisticated companies that make this distinction. In most companies, the exploration warehouse serves both exploration and mining purposes.

Freezing the Exploration Warehouse

There is one characteristic of an exploration warehouse that is entirely different from a data warehouse: The exploration warehouse on occasion *cannot* be refreshed with the most current detailed data. On the other hand, the data warehouse is normally and regularly refreshed with detailed data as soon as the data is ready. Figure 14-5 shows the case for not refreshing the exploration warehouse with detailed data.

In Figure 14-5, the exploration warehouse is not refreshed regularly and quickly with current detailed data because heuristic processing is occurring in the exploration warehouse. On Day 1, an analysis is done showing that women spend $25.00 per month on shoes. The next day, fresh data is fed into the exploration warehouse. Another analysis is done showing that women under 40 spend $20.00 per month on new shoes. Now the question is asked: Is the difference in the analysis caused by a change in the calculations and selection of data, or is the change in analysis somehow a byproduct of the data that has just been fed into the exploration warehouse? The answer is — no one knows.

To achieve a precise analysis, it is necessary to hold the data that is being analyzed constant, while the algorithms being tested change when doing heuristic analysis. If the data changes, there can be no certainty about the changes in results that are obtained. Therefore, on occasion it is important to *not* refresh new and current data into the exploration warehouse.

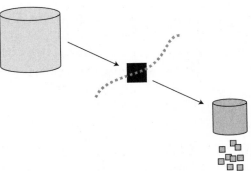

Figure 14-5 Oftentimes, exploration warehouses are not updated on a timely basis to accommodate heuristic analysis.

External Data and the Exploration Warehouse

One other major difference exists between the data warehouse and the exploration warehouse: External data fits nicely into the exploration warehouse, while external data often has a hard time fitting into the data warehouse. This fit is shown in Figure 14-6.

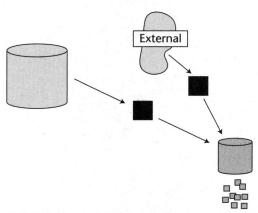

Figure 14-6   External data can go into the exploration warehouse without passing through the data warehouse.

Often it makes sense to use external data in the exploration warehouse. In many cases, comparing external results versus internal results yields very interesting insights. For example, if you see that corporate revenue has fallen, then that may be taken as a bad omen. But if it happens that industry revenue has fallen in the same period at a steeper rate, then things don't look nearly so bleak. So, contrasting internally generated numbers against externally generated numbers is often very enlightening.

But fitting external data into a data warehouse is often a difficult thing to do because of the tight integration that is required. In many cases, external data simply does not have the depth of information that allows it to be blended meaningfully inside the data warehouse. Therefore, the treatment of external data is quite different in an exploration warehouse than it is in a data warehouse.

Data Marts and Data Warehouses in the Same Processor

On occasion, there is the issue of whether a data mart or data marts should be placed in the same processor as the data warehouse. Figure 14-7 shows this instance.

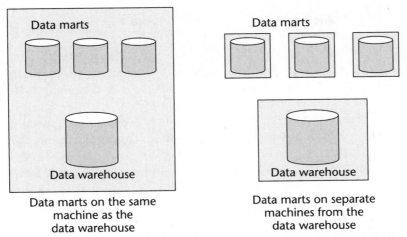

Figure 14-7   In every case, it is recommended that the data marts be placed on a separate machine from the data warehouse. In fact, placing the data marts on separate machines from each other is a good idea.

It is almost always possible to place one or more data marts in the same processor as the data warehouse. But it almost never makes sense to do so.

There are several very good reasons why placing data marts on a separate machine from a data warehouse makes sense:

- The larger the processor, the more expensive it is. By placing data marts on separate and smaller machines, the cost of processing goes down.

- When the data mart workloads are separated from the data warehouse work load, the processing becomes a lot more manageable.

- Capacity planning becomes more predictable and manageable when there is a separation of data marts and the data warehouse.

- When the data marts are separated from the data warehouse, different departments can take ownership of the data marts. The idea of departmental ownership of data marts is a very powerful concept. The idea of departmental ownership of data marts is organizationally pleasing.

Not only is separating data marts off of the same processor a good idea, but separating data marts onto their own separate machine is a good idea as well. In this case, data mart ABC goes on machine 123, data mart BCD goes on machine 234, data mart CDE goes on machine 345, and so forth. In doing this, there is a further reduction of cost of the basic processing cycle for a data warehouse DSS environment.

The Life Cycle of Data

There is a life cycle of data as it enters the corporation and then is used there. It makes sense to match the life cycle of data to the different technologies found in the corporation. Figure 14-8 shows the life cycle of data within the corporation.

Figure 14-8 shows that data enters the corporation or is otherwise captured. Usually, an event occurs or a transaction happens that triggers the initial capture of data. Next, the data that has been captured undergoes some basic edits and range checks. The data is loaded into an application and then made available to online access. Typical online access of data might be a teller checking a balance, an ATM verifying an account, an airline reservation clerk verifying a flight, and so forth.

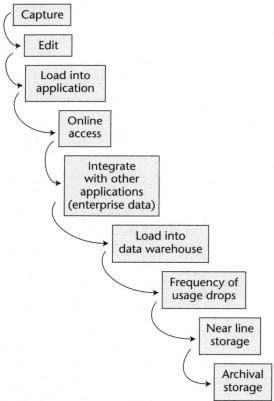

Figure 14-8 The life cycle of data

Time passes and the online data must be integrated. The data passes through an ETL process and into a data warehouse. At this point, the data is transformed into enterprise data. When passed into the data warehouse, the frequency of use of the data is high. But as time passes, the use of the data drops off as well. After awhile, the data passes into near line storage. Once in near-line storage, the data is occasionally used. When it is decided the data should be put into archival processing, it is then removed from near-line storage and placed into archives.

Mapping the Life Cycle to the Data Warehouse Environment

This is a brief rendition of the life cycle of data. It makes sense to map the life-cycle of data to the data warehouse and the components of information architecture that surround the data warehouse. Figure 14-9 shows this mapping.

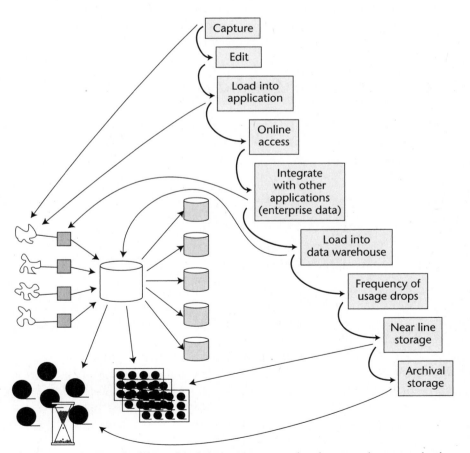

Figure 14-9 How the life cycle of data maps onto the data warehouse and other architectural components.

Figure 14-9 shows that, as data is captured, it goes into an operational application. From the operational application, the data is accessed online. After awhile, the data passes from the online application to an ETL component. From the ETL component, the data passes into the data warehouse. The data resides in the data warehouse for awhile — 2 or 3 years — and then passes into the near-line storage component. From the near-line storage component, data then passes into the archival environment.

An interesting question to ponder is what if the flow of data throughout the information life cycle does not follow work as described? The answer is that data becomes bloated and clogged up. For example, what if data does not flow into the data warehouse? The answer is that the operational environment becomes bloated and the organization wakes up to find that it cannot do business intelligence. Or, what if the data warehouse does not allow data to pass into the near-line storage environment? The answer is that the data warehouse becomes bloated and that analysis of older data becomes difficult and expensive.

Throughout the life cycle of data, as the probability of access of data changes and as the need for an enterprise view of data changes, data must pass from one component of the architecture to another.

Testing and the Data Warehouse

An important question in the data warehouse environment is this: Is there a need for a formal test environment in the data warehouse DSS environment? Figure 14-10 poses this question.

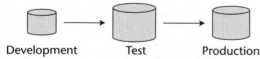

Development   Test   Production

Figure 14-10 The classical operations environment.

It is a standard practice in the operational world to have a separate test environment and production environment. Indeed, in many operational environments it is normal to have a separate development environment as well. But when you go to the data warehouse environment, many organizations merely have a data warehouse. So, what is different about a data warehouse environment and a production environment?

The primary difference between the two environments is that of expectations. In the operational environment, it is expected that when code arrives in production that the code is correct. When a new banking transaction is put into production, if the code is faulty, the bank could lose a lot of money fast. Furthermore, the money may be irretrievably lost. There may not be any recourse for the bank since it was its mistake that lost the money. Therefore, the computer code had better be right once it meets the public.

But there is a different set of expectations for a data warehouse. The essence of a data warehouse is constant adjustment and readjustment. In the data warehouse, it is a fact of life that data is subject to adjustment.

Figure 14-11 shows that the end user provides a constant feedback loop when it comes to the accuracy and completeness of the data found in the data warehouse.

Now, does this mean that a data warehouse professional deliberately places bad data in a data warehouse? Absolutely not. A professional does his or her best to place the best data in the data warehouse at all times. But does this mean that data in the data warehouse is perfect? The answer is absolutely not. The data placed in the data warehouse is the best data that can be placed there, but no one guarantees the perfection of the data in the data warehouse.

There is, then, a different standard and a different set of expectations as to what data is to be found in a data warehouse versus the data found in the operational environment. Part of the reason for the different expectations of data in the different environments is the type of decision made with the data.

In the case of the operational environment, data must be precise down to a detailed level. When a bank tells me that I have $512.32 in my account, that number had better be accurate. But when a number is calculated from a data warehouse, there can be some leeway as to the accuracy of the number. For example, suppose an organization calculates that the inventory on hand is worth $1,337,290.12. What if the real summarization is $1,336,981.01? Does the inaccurate information really make a difference to the business? Is the inaccuracy of the information going to be central to a business decision? The answer is that it is a strange business decision that is affected by this inaccuracy.

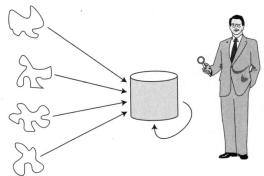

Figure 14-11   Testing in the data warehouse environment.

Therefore, if a data warehouse is 99 percent accurate, there is probably no drop-off in the effectiveness of the data warehouse. Of course, if a data warehouse is only 50 percent accurate, then there is a real drop-off in the usefulness of the data warehouse.

Tracing the Flow of Data through the Data Warehouse

For many purposes, it becomes worthwhile to trace the flow of data through the data warehouse and its related components. Figure 14-12 shows this tracing capability.

Once the tracing is done, a map can be created depicting the flows of data.

Of the many reasons for tracing the flow of data through the data warehouse and its related components is the support of the end user doing analysis. When an analyst is looking at an element of data ("revenue," for example), the end user has no idea what the data really means. It is dangerous to simply use the data element "revenue" without knowing what kind of revenue is on hand. Is it recognizable revenue? Projected revenue? Lost revenue? Committed revenue? These are all forms of revenue and each one is quite different from other forms of revenue. To blindly starting using the data element "revenue" is usually a very misleading thing to do.

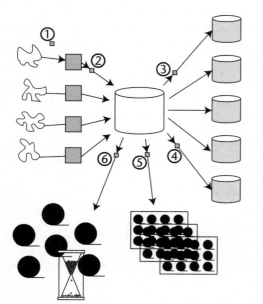

Tracing the flow of data
through the data warehouse

1. Initial capture
2. ETL enterprise integration
3. Data mart transformation
4. Exploration warehouse/data mining
5. Near line storage
6. Archival storage

Figure 14-12 Tracing the flow of data through the data warehouse.

The way the analyst can determine what the data really means is to trace the lineage of the data. What are the origins of the data, all the way back to the initial capture of the data? By tracing the data through the data warehouse, through the transformations the data goes through, through the recalculations, and so forth, the analyst can know precisely what the data means.

One of the issues of tracing data throughout the data warehouse and its related components is that of the mutation of data. *Data mutation* occurs in at least two ways: by the changing names (that is, the alteration of metadata) and by the transformation of the value itself.

Name changes occur frequently. For example, in one system, the name of a unit of data may be "abc." The data moves to another system and in the new system the data is named "bcd." The data is moved again and in the third system the data is named "xyz." Keeping track of the name changes is one important aspect of the tracing of data throughout the data warehouse environment.

The other aspect of tracing data is more complex, but occurs less frequently. On occasion, a unit of data will be recalculated as it moves. As a simple example of recalculation, in one environment a unit of data is captured under one chart of accounts, then, as the data is moved, it is entered into another system where there is a different chart of accounts. In this case, the data is recalculated. Part of the data value is entered into one account and another part of the data is entered into another account. While the total value of the data remains the same, the detailed value is quite different and is spread over more than one place. As data is traced, it is important to keep track of the value transformations as well as the metadata changes.

The tracing of data is important to more than just the end-user analyst. The tracing of the lineage of data is also important to the data warehouse administrator and the maintenance programmer. These types of people need the information that is obtained by creating a trace of data.

A final observation is that when the map is created as a result of the tracing of information, it is not a static thing. The map is constantly changing. Every time a new unit of data is added to the data warehouse, every time a calculation changes, and every time an old source of data goes away and a new source of data is added, there is the potential for a change to the map that is created by tracing all of the data in the data warehouse and its related components.

Data Velocity in the Data Warehouse

Related to the tracing of the data in the data warehouse is the notion of data velocity through the data warehouse. *Data velocity through the data warehouse* refers to the speed with which data passes from initial capture to the point of use by the analyst. Figure 14-13 depicts data velocity.

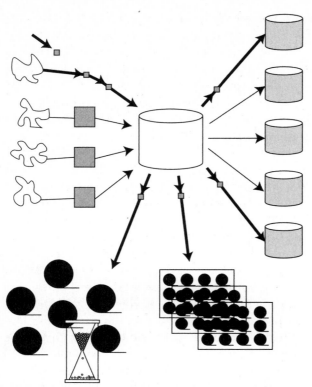

Figure 14-13   The velocity of data as it passes through the data warehouse.

Data velocity can be calculated by looking at the average time of entry into the system until the data is ready for use by the end-user analyst. This means that the time from entry to passage into applications, to passage into ETL and into the data warehouse, to passage into the data mart analytical environment determines the velocity of data.

There are certain factors that impede velocity. One factor is the need for integration. The more integration that must be done, the less the velocity. Conversely, the less integration that needs to be done, the greater the velocity.

There are some things that an organization can do to speed up the velocity. In some cases, the movement of data through the ETL component can be done very quickly. In fact, it is possible to move data into the data warehouse in millisecond speed using data-moving software. And there is the Class I ODS in which data moves almost instantaneously into the ODS from the operational application. (See Chapter 3 for more information on the four classes of ODS.) So, expediency of data movement into the data warehouse can be accomplished. The faster the movement into the data warehouse, the less integration can be done on the data.

"Pushing" and "Pulling" Data

The rate of speed of moving data out of the data warehouse into the data mart and analytical environment is another story altogether. Whereas data being moved into the data warehouse can be considered to be a "push" process (that is, where the data is being pushed from the operational environment into the data warehouse), data going from the data warehouse going into the data marts is a "pull" process. In a *pull process*, data is moved only as needed. In a *push process*, data is moved as it is available. There is, then, an entirely different set of technologies and objectives for data velocity going from the data warehouse than for data entering the data warehouse.

As an example of the pull process, consider two data marts. One data mart needs to see data as quickly as possible. The instant data is available in the data warehouse, the data is moved to the data mart. But the next data mart is quite different. The next data mart needs to see data only when the end of the month rolls around, at which time the data mart collects data out of the data warehouse. There is no sense of urgency to load data into the data mart in mid-month because the data is incomplete and effectively unusable at that point in time.

There is the philosophy in some circles that the greater the velocity of data, the better. In many cases, this philosophy is true. But there are cases where data velocity actually is not desirable. One such case is that of exploration systems where heuristic analysis is being done. In the case of an exploration environment supporting heuristic processing, there is a need from time to time for cutting off the flow of data altogether. Data flowing into the exploration environment under these circumstances is not welcome and potentially damages the integrity of the heuristic processing environment.

Data Warehouse and the Web-Based eBusiness Environment

One of the potentially most powerful uses of a data warehouse is in conjunction with the eBusiness environment. The *eBusiness environment* is Web-based, where business is conducted with the public over the Internet.

In the early days of eBusiness, it was popular to state that eBusiness should be kept separate from corporate systems. There was a certain snobbery as the eBusiness community looked with disdain on the standard, older, "bricks and mortar" corporate information systems. Then the Dot Com Bust hit and the organizations that insisted on a separation of the eBusiness environment and corporate systems went out of business.

Indeed, those organizations that made a success of eBusiness found that the secret to successful eBusiness was tying eBusiness and the Web to corporate systems, quite the opposite of what was being stated by the early proponents of the eBusiness environment.

So, how exactly should eBusiness and the Web be tied to corporate systems? The answer is that the data warehouse and the ODS form the best basis for interfacing the Web and corporate information.

The Interface between the Two Environments

Figure 14-14 shows the interface between the Web and corporate environments.

Figure 14-14 shows that data flows from the Web environment to the Granularity Manager. From the Granularity Manager, data flows to the data warehouse. Once the direction is reversed, data flows from the data warehouse to the ODS. Then data flows from the ODS to the Web environment.

In order to understand these dynamics, consider the following.

The Granularity Manager

The Web environment generates huge amounts of data. The data that is generated is called *clickstream data* and is typically located in the Web logs.

Clickstream data is generated as part of every Internet user's session. Every time a new page is accessed, every time the mouse is moved, and every time a selection is made or a hyperlink is followed, a clickstream record is created. There is a tremendous amount of data that is created as a byproduct of Web processing. In truth, most of the data placed in the clickstream has little or no business usefulness. Indeed, it is estimated that only 5 percent or less of the clickstream data is useful. As a consequence, it is necessary to reduce the volume of data found in the clickstream. To this end there is a component known as a Granularity Manager, as shown in Figure 14-15.

The Granularity Manager is a piece of software whose job it is to understand what clickstream data is important and useful and which clickstream data is not useful. The Granularity Manager does such tasks as the following:

- Removes extraneous clickstream data
- Summarizes clickstream data
- Aggregates clickstream data
- Merges clickstream data when appropriate
- Compacts clickstream data when appropriate

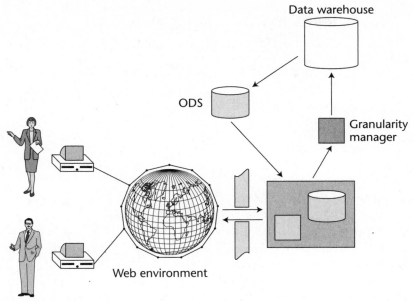

Figure 14-14   The data warehouse and eBusiness.

Clickstream data is useful for preparing a massive volume of data for entry into the data warehouse. A reduction of at least 95 percent is the expectation when passing data into a Granularity Manager.

Once data passes out of the Granularity Manager, the data is ready for entry into the data warehouse and is useful to the business of the corporation. The Granularity Manager is treated as just another feed of data going into the data warehouse.

Once data in the data warehouse is needed in the Web environment, the journey starts with movement from the data warehouse to the ODS. There is no direct link from the data warehouse to the Web environment. A good reason for the lack of a direct link is because the Web environment needs subsecond response time. The data warehouse is not geared for supporting subsecond response time. Under no circumstances should any process ever expect subsecond response time out of a data warehouse. Therefore, the data that is needed by the Web environment is passed to the ODS. Once in the ODS, subsecond response time can indeed be supported.

Because of this indirect connection, the data analyst must anticipate what data is needed in the Web environment. Usually this is easy to do. The data that is needed by the Web environment that passes through the ODS is the data that supports the business related to the Web environment.

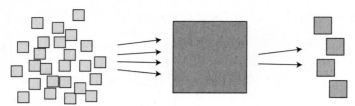

Figure 14-15 The Granularity Manager.

Profile Records

Once the data is moved into the ODS from the data warehouse to support the Web environment, the data is typically arranged in what can be called a "profile" record format. A *profile record* is a form of data where a composite picture of something is formed based on many observations. A profile is created from the many observations that are reported.

A typical profile record might be one that exists for a customer. The profile record might look like this:

```
Customer name
Customer address
Customer gender
Customer telephone
Customer income level
Customer hobbies
Customer children
Customer birth date
Customer automobile
Customer paying habits
Customer browsing habits
Customer past purchases
Customer reading habits
Customer musical preferences
Last customer interaction
```

All of this disparate information is gathered for each customer from a wide variety of records and sources. Some records that contribute are from past purchases, some records are from customer history, some affect browsing habits, and so forth. When the detailed records come over from the data warehouse, they are condensed into a profile record. Now, when the Web environment needs to see information, it can efficiently go to the customer profile record and can quickly get the information it needs.

The ODS, Profile Records, and Performance

To see the value of the profile record in the ODS, consider what happens when the Web site needs to see a value. If there were no profile record, the Web site would have to go to the data warehouse. Once there, the Web site would have to wait its turn for service, which, given the traffic going through the Web site, might be a considerable amount of time. Once the Web site gets its turn for looking at information, it has to find and rummage through a lot of records. Then it has to have those records analyzed.

All of this processing takes time. Without the profile record existing in the ODS, the response time back to the Web site might be minutes or even hours. The Internet user will be long gone if he or she has to wait that long. Therefore, to support the need for immediate information, the Web site accesses the ODS, not the data warehouse.

For these reasons, creating the profile record and placing the profile record in the ODS makes sense. Once created and in the ODS, the access time to the profile record is measured in terms of milliseconds. The Internet user will be served in a very efficient and expeditious manner.

The Financial Data Warehouse

Every data warehouse must have some starting point. In many organizations the starting point is a data warehouse for financials. Certainly, financials is close to the business, or at least close to the heart of the business. Financials usually involve a relatively small amount of data. Financials have data that is surrounded by discipline. So, in many respects, financial data seems to be a good starting point for many data warehouses.

But there is a drawback related to financial data warehouses. Most finance people do not understand the difference between application data and corporate data. Most financial analysts have grown so used to their day-to-day reports that they have no concept of corporate data as opposed to application data. This difference in perception makes the financial data warehouse hard to swallow.

To understand this difference and why it is important, consider the simple data warehouse shown in Figure 14-16.

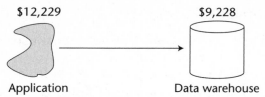

$12,229 $9,228

Application   Data warehouse

Figure 14-16 There is a difference in values as data is moved into the data warehouse.

Figure 14-16 shows that in the application there is one dollar amount and in the data warehouse there is another dollar amount. The financial analyst looks at this difference and proclaims that the data warehouse is not trustworthy. The financial analyst feels that the application environment and the data warehouse environment must agree in dollar value down to the penny. Anything else is untrustworthy.

But there is absolutely nothing wrong with the scenario depicted in Figure 14-16. There can be many valid explanations why there is a discrepancy. Following are some of the possible reasons why there is a discrepancy of data found in the application and the data found in the data warehouse:

- The data in the data warehouse is measured in a common currency. The data in the application is measured in U.S. dollars, while the data in the data warehouse is measured in Canadian dollars.

- The data in the application has been collected on the basis of a calendar month. The data in the data warehouse is collected on the basis of a corporate month, which is not the same as a calendar month. To make the data in the data warehouse consistent, there must be an adjustment made to the data.

- Accounting classifications have changed. Data in the application has been classified according to one set of accounting classifications, but data in the data warehouse has been classified according to another set of classifications. To make the data consistent, the data in the data warehouse must be adjusted to a single accounting classification.

Indeed there may be *many* other reasons why values have to be adjusted as they pass from the application foundation to the data warehouse. Indeed, it would be surprising if the values actually remained the same.

Unfortunately, the financial analyst needs more education than other communities about the architecture that is at the foundation of the data warehouse.

Figure 14-17 shows the need for integration.

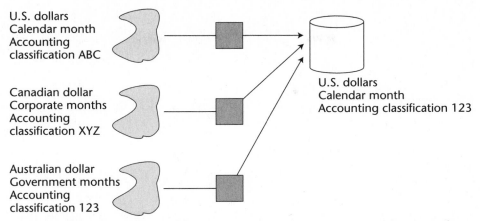

Figure 14-17   Why there is a difference between application data and corporate data.

The System of Record

An essential aspect of the data warehouse environment is that called the "system of record." The *system of record* is the definitive source of information for any given value of information. To understand the importance of the system of record, consider how it is that banks manage lots of data. Consider the data value for a bank account. The record for a bank account is a field called the "amount" field. The account amount field can be found in many places throughout the bank. But there is only one place in the bank that is the system of record. In the bank, the system of record means the one place where data is updated. All other places where the field account amount occurs are copied from the system of record.

The bank is in trouble if there ever is any place where an update of the account amount occurs. Furthermore, if there is ever a discrepancy between different occurrences of the account amount, the place that has been designated the system of record is the correct value by default. The system of record then establishes the integrity of data in an environment where the same data element can appear any number of times.

To understand the system of record in the data warehouse environment, consider the relationship between the supporting applications and the applications, as shown in Figure 14-18.

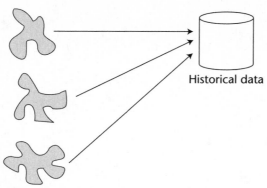

Current valued data

Figure 14-18 There is a fundamental difference in the type of data found in the application environment and the data found in the data warehouse.

Figure 14-18 shows that the applications hold current value data and the data warehouse contains historical data. *Current value* refers to the accuracy of data as of the moment of access. If someone wants to know how much money is in an account right now, the current value data is accessed. If someone wants to know the history of data movement throughout an account, the proper place to go is the historical record. Thus, the applications and the data warehouse environment contain different kinds of data.

The system of record for current value data resides — not surprisingly — in the application environment, as shown in Figure 14-19.

Figure 14-19 shows that different data from different applications serves as the system of record for current value data. Note that one application may contain some system of record data and another application may contain another system of record data. The system of record data for the application environment is selected based on many criteria, such as the following:

- What data is the most accurate?
- What data is the most current?
- What data is the most detailed?
- What data is the most complete?
- What data is the most up-to-date?

The system of record for the application environment then is the best source of data.

Note that in some cases a unit of data in the data warehouse will have more than one unit of data as a system of record. In such a case, multiple sources exist for the same unit of data. There needs to be logic to separate out which unit of data is the best source under which conditions.

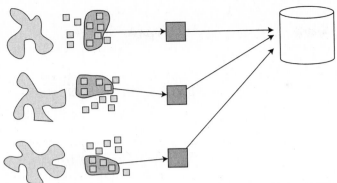

Figure 14-19   The system of record for current value data feeds the data warehouse.

But the system of record does not end in the application environment. As data is passed to the data warehouse environment, data changes from current value data to historical data. As such, a system of record for historical data is created. Figure 14-20 shows the system of record for historical data.

The system of record that has been established within the data warehouse in turn becomes a source of data for all sorts of DSS processing. The data warehouse system of record serves the following environments:

- Data mart environment
- ODS environment
- DSS applications environment
- Exploration/data mining environment

There is, then, an extended system of record for the application and the data warehouse environment.

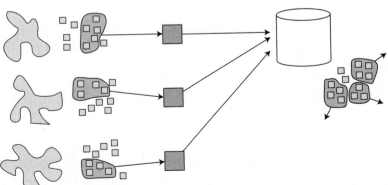

Figure 14-20   The data warehouse becomes the system of record for historical and DSS data.

A Brief History of Architecture — Evolving to the Corporate Information Factory

The world of technology is in its infancy. Compared to other, more mature professions, we are still in diapers. Roads and walls in Rome that are used today were built by engineers 2000 years ago. The hieroglyphics on the tombs in Egypt contain proclamations from accountants saying how much grain was owed the Pharaoh. Excavations of Clovis man from caves in Chile show that mankind practiced medicine in at least a crude form as long as 16,000 years ago. A historical comparison of the IT profession to the engineering, accounting, and medical professions shows that the IT profession is barely out of the womb. The origins of the IT profession go back to 1950 or so. Other professions go back to the dawn of civilization.

But the IT profession has come a long way fast. As evidence of how far we have come, look at IT architecture, or at least architecture as perceived by the IT professional.

Prior to 1983, there were applications. Accounts payable, accounts receivable, online, and batch were all types of applications that dominated the landscape. But around 1983, someone looked up and decided that there was a need for information, not data. There arose a need to look across the corporation, not just at a tiny application area. In addition, it was noticed that there was no historical data to speak of. Applications jettisoned historical data as quickly as they could to accommodate performance.

Thus borne in 1983 was the early form of the data warehouse — *atomic data*. The need for granular, integrated, historical data opened up the doors to styles of processing never before possible. With the data warehouse, business intelligence became a possibility. Without the data warehouse, business intelligence was just a theory. But it quickly was discovered that the legacy systems in their moribund state needed more than programmers to create the data warehouse. The legacy environment was so frozen — so tightly bound — that a way to automatically access and integrate data was needed. In 1990, there appeared ETL. And with ETL, data could be accessed and integrated coming from the legacy application environment.

ETL opened up the floodgates for business intelligence. From about 1994, there appeared all sorts of extensions to the data warehouse. There appeared the miltidimensional OLAP data marts, the exploration warehouse, and the ODS. Soon people were doing all sorts of business intelligence. With the ODS, it was possible to do real-time processing where updates and transactions could be run against integrated data. With data marts, star schemas and fact tables found their home. With the exploration warehouse, the statisticians had the foundation of data that emancipated the data miner from data administrator to statistical analyst.

It is at this time that the data warehouse evolved into the corporate information factory (CIF).

Around 2000 came the Web explosion. Organizations started to use the Web environment as a separate arm for marketing and sales. At first, the Web professionals wanted to remain separate from corporate systems. But quickly it was discovered that, to be successful in the Web environment, integration with corporate systems was mandated. The connection with the corporate environment was made by straining data through a Granularity Manager that then placed data into the data warehouse. For data coming from the corporate environment going to the Web environment, data flowed through the ODS. In addition, at this time, DSS applications were being built. Corporate performance management began to be a reality. In addition, changed data capture began to emerge. In addition, the *adaptive data mart* was added to the world of business intelligence. The adaptive data mart is a temporary structure that has some of the characteristics of a data mart and an exploration data warehouse.

At approximately the same time, the volumes of data found in the data warehouse were growing explosively. Placing all data found in a data warehouse on disk storage began to be very unappealing because of the fact that massive amounts of data in the data warehouse were being used very infrequently. At this point, placing data on multiple physical storage media became attractive.

Enterprise application integration (EAI) made its appearance as a back-end mechanism for transporting application data from one application to another. EAI focused on the speed of transmission and the volumes of data being transmitted. Little or no integration of data was accomplished by EAI.

In 2004, more refinements to the information factory were added. The two most prominent features were the *virtual operational data store (VODS)* and the addition of unstructured data. The VODS was a feature that allowed organizations to access data on the fly, without building an infrastructure. The VODS is very flexible and very fast to construct. But the VODS offers answers to queries that are valid only as of the moment the query is made. Unstructured data began to be combined with structured data and an entirely new world of applications was possible. For the first time, corporate communications could be combined with corporate transactions. The picture that was painted was much more complete than anything previously created.

Other additions to the information factory included archival data. Archival data complemented near-line storage and allowed organizations to manage far more data than ever before. Managing the traffic between the data warehouse and the near-line, archival environment was the cross media storage manager (CMSM). As the probability of access of data fluctuated, the movement of rows of data was accomplished by the CMSM.

Supplementing the unstructured environment was the *unstructured visualization* technology. Unstructured visualization was the equivalent of business intelligence, except that unstructured visualization was for textual data, while business intelligence was for numeric data.

In addition, it became apparent that a monitor for the data warehouse environment was needed. The monitor for data warehousing was fundamentally different than the monitor for transaction processing.

The world of data exploration began to mature into a world of data mining and data exploration, where there are subtle, yet real, differences between data mining and data exploration.

All of this architecture came under the name of the information factory or the CIF. The CIF, then, is a living organism that is constantly growing and changing. Each new advance in technology causes some change to the CIF.

Looking at the growth of the CIF from 1980 to 2005 is like watching man evolve from creatures swinging in the trees to today's modern family — with cars, TVs, homes, hot and cold running water, and fresh food readily available at the marketplace. The only thing that is certain is that the evolution of the information will not stop where it is today.

Evolving from the CIF

The CIF emerged from the data warehouse. Then, the September 11 (9/11) disaster occurred and the *government information factory (GIF)* was created.

The GIF is in many ways similar to the CIF. The GIF basic architecture is very similar to the CIF architecture. There is no question that the two architectures are related. First came the CIF, and then came the GIF. But there are significant differences between the two architectures.

The first significant difference between the architectures is the need for wide integration of data in government systems. Consider corporate systems. When you ask a corporate data warehouse professional why he or she is building the data warehouse, the response is never, "We are building the data warehouse for someone else." Chevron does not build its data warehouse for sharing data with Levi's; ATT does not build its data warehouse for sharing of data with Shell Oil; Wells Fargo does not build its data warehouse for sharing data with Burlington Northern; and so forth. The corporate motivation for a data warehouse includes only the corporation.

But the government has a different set of problems. After 9/11, there was a mandate from Congress and the president to share data. Within the boundaries of the law, data must be shared among the FBI, the U.S. Citizen and Immigration Service, the CIA, and many others. If the United States is to be serious about defeating terrorism, data sharing must become a reality. But the different government organizations over the years have created their own fiefdoms of data.

The GIF is an architecture that is designed to address the infrastructure and the technology of sharing across the government. The political issues of data sharing are still up to the politicians.

So, the first difference between the CIF and the GIF is *the scope of data sharing and integration.*

The second difference is one that at first glance appears to be mundane. That difference is the recognition that *data lives longer in government systems than in corporate systems.* In the corporation, the argument is made that the business was so different five years ago that any data reflecting business conditions greater than five years may actually be harmful because old data may be misleading. In practice, a few commercial organizations collect and manage data greater than five years old. But most corporations do not.

However, in the government, data lives a very long time. The reasons for the longevity of data in governmental circles are many. Sometimes the reasons for holding onto data are mandated by law. Other times common business practice dictates the longevity of data. On one project I worked on years ago, the Army was collecting data that went back to the Civil War. But even the smallest agency collects data and holds on to it for a long time. It simply is not true in government circles that data lives for five years or less. It lives a lot longer.

As a consequence, because data lives longer in the government environment, there are even greater volumes of data to be managed than found in the commercial sector. Among other things this means that archival storage and bulk processing of data is very important in the world of government, while those topics are of lesser importance in the commercial world.

The third difference between architectures for the government and for the commercial world is that of *security.* In the commercial world, security for data warehouses is lax (and this is probably an understatement). Very little emphasis is put on the security of a commercial warehouse. The commercial impetus is to get the warehouse up and running and to start to use the warehouse. Most organizations think of warehouse security as an afterthought.

This is not so in government circles. Because of the nature of the business and because of legislation, government agencies cannot afford to take a blasé attitude toward security. Security must be built into the architecture from the very beginning when it comes to government data warehouses.

Those then are the main differences between the GIF and the CIF. There are undoubtedly more differences, but the ones listed here are the most important differences between the CIF and the GIF:

- The need for widespread integration and data sharing well beyond the agency
- The need to accommodate data for very long periods of time
- The need for security from the outset of design

Obstacles

One of the obstacles the GIF faces is the "not invented here" (nih) syndrome. The government never sponsored the GIF. There is no mandate. And it is not in any agency's charter to build systems according to the GIF. Furthermore, the GIF is trademarked intellectual property, so system integrators have a problem when they want to start to use the GIF. System integrators cannot repackage and resell the GIF because it is not public domain intellectual property.

On the other hand, the GIF does not compete with other architectural approaches found in the government. The other architectural approaches are more "paper and pencil" exercises to ensure that requirements have been gathered completely and properly. When it comes to the nuts and bolts of implementation — how architecture meets technology — there is only the GIF. In this regard, the GIF is complementary to the other government-sponsored architectures. By aligning with the GIF, other government architectures have a road map to achieve implementation.

Despite these obstacles, the GIF is seeping into the government consciousness. Large contracts are being let that specify that they have to align with the GIF. If the government contractors are resistant to the GIF, their stubbornness melts when contract specifications are let.

CIF — Into the Future

From heresy a few short years ago to conventional wisdom today, the CIF and data warehousing have come a long way in a short amount of time. But is the journey complete? The answer is that things are just now getting rolling. The future is as likely to hold new and exciting adventures as yesterday did.

There are (at least) four directions for the CIF and data warehousing on the immediate horizon:

- Analytics
- ERP/SAP business intelligence
- Unstructured business intelligence
- The capturing and management of massive volumes of data

Analytics

Once the data warehouse is built, or at least as soon as the first population of data is made into the data warehouse, the question arises: How can I get maximum value from my investment? The answer turns to analytics. *Analytics* are the information generated from looking at and analyzing the data in the data warehouse. The detailed, historical data found in the data warehouse can be examined in many ways. Business patterns emerge. The business is able to get a look at itself as it has never looked before. The result is business insight. The business insight is useful in many ways — to marketing, sales, and management, to name a few. In some cases, the business insight is a look over time. In other cases, the business insight is a look at segments of customers never before perceived. In yet other cases, the business insight is from a financial or a product standpoint.

One of the most promising forms of analytics is that of *forward-looking analytics*. Whereas most analytics in the business intelligence environment are backward-looking because the data found in the data warehouse is historical, there are analytics that use the data found in the data warehouse as a baseline and then do forward projections (forecasts).

Analytics brings information and information capabilities into the world of business where such information has never before been possible. And there are as many forms of analytics as there are stars in the sky. The future of analytics is limited only by the imagination of the analyst and the developer.

Most analytics are built in the form of a vendor-supplied package. Very few analytics are built as a homegrown application. And (not surprisingly) the analytics that are built are peculiar to the strengths of the technology of the vendor building the analytics.

ERP/SAP

The world of CIF and the data warehouse is enhanced immeasurably by the support of the *enterprise resource planning* (*ERP*) vendors. The ERP vendors have found that building operational applications is a good business to be in until the market becomes saturated. Then, CIF and data warehousing become a natural annexation of the traditional ERP business. Leading the way is a company called SAP. Not only does SAP lead in terms of market share, but SAP leads in terms of extending the meaning of CIF.

Some of the recent innovations from SAP BW include the following:

- The ability to support massive sizes of data through the extension of the data warehouse to near-line storage.

- The advancement of analytics on a wide front. Indeed, in terms of breadth of offerings, SAP eclipses any other vendor.

- The access and analysis of data through portal technology.

- The extension of business intelligence beyond the world of R/3. Building an SAP data warehouse means including non-SAP transactional data in the data warehouse as well.

- Offering ETL alternatives. In addition to the Ascential alternative, SAP offers its own burgeoning ETL capabilities native to the SAP BW product.

Given the number of worldwide customers and the energy and innovation put into the product line, SAP far outstrips any competition and is making a very real contribution to the world of CIF and data warehousing.

Unstructured Data

For years, data warehousing and the CIF have concentrated solely on structured data. And there has been a wealth of information to be gleaned from examining structured data. But there is a world apart from structured systems. There is the world of emails, telephone conversations, spreadsheets, and documents. An entirely different kind of decision-making takes place in the unstructured world.

The future of the CIF encompasses both the structured and the unstructured world. The most challenging and interesting aspect of this form of business intelligence is the bridging of the gap between structured and unstructured data. Unfortunately, this gap is a fundamentally difficult gap to bridge. Data on one side of the gap is like an electrical alternating current (AC) and data on the other side of the gap is like an electrical direct current (DC). Because of the very fundamental differences between the two worlds, bridging the gap is very challenging.

But the gap can be breached in a meaningful manner. And when the gap is bridged, many business intelligence opportunities suddenly pour out.

Following are some of the business intelligence opportunities that emerge from the bridging of unstructured and structured data:

- **CRM enhancement** — When the unstructured or structured bridge is breached, a true 360 degree view of the customer can be created, when messages and communications are added to customer demographics.

- **Compliance** — Sarbanes-Oxley, HIPAA, and Basel II (and others) require that ongoing proposals, commitments, and other relationships with customers and prospects be monitored. By looking at messages and communications in a methodical way and bringing them into the structured world, a new level of compliance can be reached.

- **Visualization** — To date, visualization has been for numeric data. But there is no reason why textual data cannot be visualized as well. And, in doing so, whole new vistas of information can be achieved.

Indeed these few applications merely scratch the surface for the data warehouse and CIF possibilities for unstructured information.

Volumes of Data

The history of data warehousing and the CIF has been one where there are ever-increasing volumes of data. Following are some of the reasons for the massive volumes of data in the data warehouse:

- Data warehouses contain granular, detailed data.
- Data warehouses contain historical data.
- Data warehouses contain data from a wide variety of sources.

And there is a simple equation:

Detail _ History _ Many sources = Lots of data

The data that we have today is small compared to the volumes of data we are going to have tomorrow.

For a variety of reasons (economics, use of the data, and management of the data), the storage media for data warehouses will grow beyond mere disk storage. Today, it is acceptable to place data on disk storage. In the future, it is going to be insufficient to place data on only disk storage. In the future, the placement of data on storage media that is less expensive, capable of holding massive amounts of data, and holding that data with a high degree of integrity over time will become common. When that happens, data warehouses will be able to grow to infinity without breaking the budget of the organization owning the data warehouse.

While economics are the first and most powerful argument against the placement of data on only disk storage, in the long run, economics are not the only valid argument. Another powerful argument for the placement of data warehouse data on other than disk storage is the fact that with the data warehouse, there is a distinct pattern of access not found in the classical OLTP environment. In the OLTP environment, there is usually a random and equal probability of access for each unit of data. Under these circumstances, disk storage is ideal. But in the data warehouse environment, data divides itself into two broad classifications: actively used data and inactively used data. It makes no sense to place inactively used data on disk storage.

Furthermore, by placing inactively used data on bulk storage, the ongoing cost of disk storage operation and maintenance is mitigated.

But disk-storage vendors do not like the idea of other technology becoming prevalent in the marketplace. The disk-storage vendors will do almost anything to deny the validity of the placement of data on a form of storage other than disk. But disk storage vendors are an anachronism. Economics, time, and the unique usage characteristics of a data warehouse will prevail in the long term.

These, then, are the trends for the immediate future of data warehousing and the CIF.

Summary

The data warehouse is directly shaped from the corporate data model and indirectly shaped from end-user requirements. At the heart of the data warehouse is a relational database. The relational database is directly shaped by the data model. The relational data model serves as a basis for data that is reshaped. The reshaped data is patterned directly from the end-user's requirements for information.

If a lot of heavy statistical analysis is to be done, it is advised that a separate exploration warehouse be created. If only an occasional statistical process needs to be done, then it is possible to do the statistical processing on the data warehouse.

The exploration warehouse has some interesting properties:

- It is a subset of the data warehouse, often containing convenience fields.
- It can have external data directly entered into it.
- It can be cut off from refreshment periodically.

The exploration warehouse is usually project-based. This means that the life of the exploration warehouse is temporary — only for as long as the project lives.

Data marts almost never should be placed on the same machine as the data warehouse. Placing the data marts there is wasteful and runs contrary to organizational needs for the control of data.

There is a life cycle of data as data enters the corporation, as data ages, and as the data is used in different ways. The life cycle of data should be carefully matched to the data warehouse and the related components in support of the data warehouse.

Testing in the data warehouse environment is far different from testing in the classical operational environment. The primary reason for the differences in testing stem from the expectations related to the use of the data.

It is useful to trace the flow of data throughout the data warehouse environment. Data needs to be traced at the metadata level and the content level. The tracing is useful to many types of people (such as the end user, the data warehouse administrator, and the maintenance programmer).

There is a velocity of data as it passes through the warehouse environment. The velocity is measured from the time data initially enters the environment until the data is available for end-user analysis. There are two kinds of motivations that affect the velocity. There is the "pushing" of data and there is the "pulling" of data. Pushing of data occurs to ensure that data is available whenever it is ready. Pulling of data occurs when data is needed for use, not when the data is ready and available.

Data warehouse serves as the appropriate connection between the corporate information systems environment and the Web-based eBusiness environment. The interface is formed by data flowing from the Web into a Granularity Manager. From the Granularity Manager, the data flows into the data warehouse. For the reverse flow of data, data passes from the data warehouse into an ODS. Once in the ODS, a profile record is formed. The Web site then can access the ODS and get at the profile record in an efficient manner.

While many organizations start their data warehouse efforts with the financial organization, one drawback is that financial organizations often expect data to be reconcilable down to the penny between the two environments. In fact, data is transformed from an applications environment to a corporate environment as it passes from the application to the data warehouse.

From the data warehouse, there has evolved the corporate information factory (CIF). The center of the CIF is the data warehouse. Surrounding the CIF are architectural entities such as data marts, exploration warehouses, ODS, and so forth. From the CIF evolved the government information factory (GIF). The GIF is suited for government's needs. There are many similarities between the CIF and the GIF, but there are some fundamental differences as well. Some of the differences are in the need for cross architecture integration, security, and the time horizon of data.

Cost-Justification and Return on Investment for a Data Warehouse

The question "Am I getting my money's worth?" inevitably arises during the building of a data warehouse. The infrastructure surrounding a data warehouse is not inexpensive. The first time a data warehouse is built in an organization, no one knows for sure what to expect. Because of these reasons, it is absolutely normal for an organization to question whether they should be doing a data warehouse.

Copying the Competition

A quick and simple way to justify a data warehouse is to point out how many other data warehouses have been built in the industry. In many ways, building a data warehouse is merely a reaction to remaining competitive in the marketplace. The argument, "Well, company ABC, our competitor, has a data warehouse so we need one, too," is a surprisingly powerful argument. And it is true that built and used properly, a data warehouse leads to greater market share, increased revenue, and increased profitability.

But sometimes management wants more in the way of a cost justification. Management wants to see in black and white exactly why it is building a data warehouse.

The Macro Level of Cost-Justification

One way to approach the justification of building a data warehouse is at the macro level. Another way to approach the justification of building a data warehouse is at the micro level. Figure 15-1 shows these two perspectives.

The macro level refers to a discussion at a high level. Typical of such discussions might be, "We built the data warehouse and corporate profits rose by 15 percent." Or, "We built the data warehouse and our stock went up by $6.00." Unfortunately, arguments about the corporation and data warehouse at this level are always specious. Figure 15-2 illustrates the advent of a data warehouse matched against the stock price of a corporation.

Figure 15-2 shows that a data warehouse was implemented and the stock price began to climb. The argument might be, "We implemented a data warehouse and the stock price took off." The problem with this macro justification is that it is not credible. There are many reasons why the stock price might have gone up other than the implementation of a data warehouse. A new product might have been introduced at the same time. The stock market may have decided to rise on its own, as it occasionally does. Competition may have slacked off. Operations may have become more efficient. In truth, there are many reasons why a stock price rises or falls. Building a data warehouse — as strategically important as that may be — is only one of many factors affecting the rise or fall of a stock price.

Because there are so many competing and legitimate factors at the macro level, it is really difficult to use a macro argument for the cost-justification of a data warehouse.

For these reasons, then, a micro argument for the cost-justification of a data warehouse is much more believable and much more powerful.

The macro approach   The micro approach

Figure 15-1   Two approaches to looking at cost justification of the data warehouse.

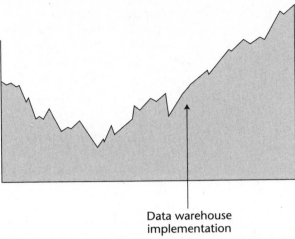

Figure 15-2 Matching the advent of a data warehouse against the stock price of a corporation.

A Micro Level Cost-Justification

To build a foundation for a micro argument for a data warehouse cost-justification, consider two companies — company A and company B, as shown in Figure 15-3.

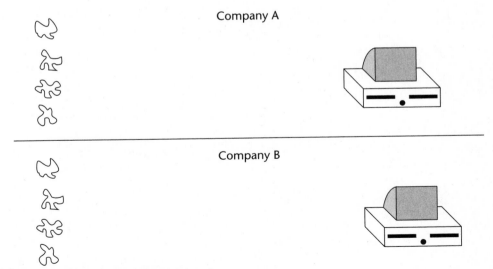

Figure 15-3 Consider two companies.

Company A and company B both have a foundation of operational applications, or legacy systems. The operational applications are shown to the left in Figure 15-3. On the right of Figure 15-3 is the symbol of a personal computer. This symbol refers to the fact that there is a need for information in each company. When it comes to a basis of operational applications and a need for information, company A and company B are identical.

There is one important difference between company A and company B. Company B has a data warehouse, as seen in Figure 15-4.

Now, consider how the need for new information is supported in each environment. Figure 15-5 shows the way company A responds to a need for new information.

Figure 15-5 shows that, in order to respond to the need for new information, company A needs to go back to the operational source systems and find the information needed to support the new information requirement.

So, what exactly does company A have to do? What is involved in going back to the operational environment to support a new requirement for information? Figure 15-6 shows what is required.

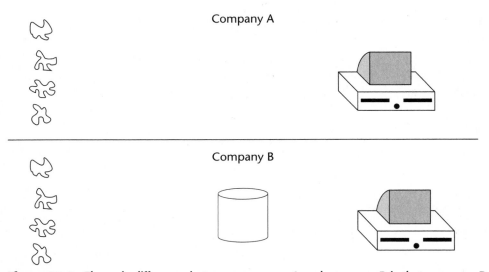

Figure 15-4 The only difference between company A and company B is that company B has the data warehouse.

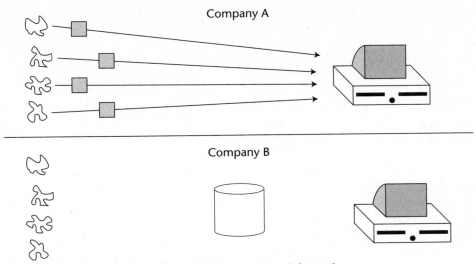

Figure 15-5   Company A wishes to have some new information.

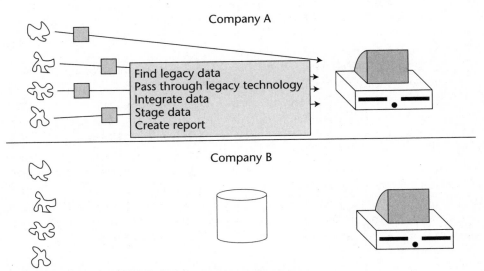

Figure 15-6   What's required to create the new report.

Information from the Legacy Environment

To support a new information requirement, company A must go back to the operational or legacy environment. The first step in going back to the operational or legacy environment is that of finding the legacy data needed to support the information requirement. Finding legacy data can be difficult because the legacy data is often undocumented or partially documented. Even looking for the proper data is a risky proposition. In many cases, guesses have to be made. And whenever guesses are made, some guesses will be right and some guesses will be wrong. It may even be necessary to go back into old source code in order for guesses to be made properly. In some cases, even source code doesn't exist. So, looking backward in time at operational or legacy systems is never an easy or straightforward process.

But even if source code and documentation exists, the old operational and legacy environments are framed in technology of yesteryear. It is normal for legacy applications to be written in Integrated Database Management System (IDMS), Information Management System (IMS), Virtual Storage Access Management (VSAM), Customer Information Control System (CICS), Adabas, and Model 204. In today's world, even finding someone with the technical skills to decipher these older technologies is difficult to do. And as time passes, there are fewer people with these skills. So, even if the documentation is in order, having to go back and traipse through older technologies is no picnic.

Then there's the really difficult task of dealing with multiple technologies as a foundation for operational or legacy processing. Once the data has been located in the operational or legacy environment, the data must be integrated. Integration of multiple sources of data is difficult because old legacy systems in most cases were never designed to be merged together. Physical data characteristics, encoding values, and data structures are all different. But perhaps the worst aspect of integration is in rectifying data definitions. In one system, "customer" means all current customers. In another system, "customer" means all current and past customers from Latin America. In another system, "customer" means potential customers from the commercial marketplace. Merely adding the customers together produces a polyglot that is almost nonsensical.

Assuming that there is documentation, that older technology can be interpreted, and that integration can be done, the next step is to stage the data. Data from one source is ready immediately. Data from another source is ready on Wednesdays after 9:00 a.m. And data from yet another source is ready after the first of the month. To accommodate all these schedules, it is necessary to have a staging area.

Once data is in the staging area, it is now ready for reporting. Now the report can be created. At last!

The process that has been described in one form or the other is what company A must go through to create a new foundation of information. In some cases, the process can be gone through without much difficulty. In other cases, the process is tortuous.

The Cost of New Information

So how much money does it cost to do all of this manipulation? Depending on the number of legacy applications, the documentation of those applications, the technology those applications are wrapped in, and the complexity of the request, it might take from $500,000 to $2 million to fulfill the request. And how long does this process take to go through? The answer is that it may take from 6 months to 2 years, or even longer, depending on the particulars.

Gathering Information with a Data Warehouse

Now let's consider what is required to create a new report for company B. Figure 15-7 shows the information environment of company B.

Figure 15-7 shows that building a report from the data warehouse is a simple and efficient thing to do. To build a report from the data warehouse may take from $1,000 to $25,000. And how long does such a report take to build? The answer is from 30 minutes to maybe 10 days in the worst case.

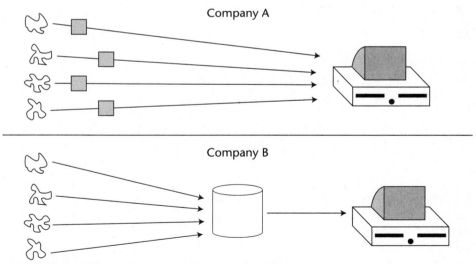

Figure 15-7 Getting new data when there is a data warehouse.

Comparing the Costs

The difference in the cost of information, then, is the basis for the cost justification of the data warehouse.

Consider the following for a new analysis of information:

- No data warehouse — $500,000 to $2 million; 6 months to 2 years
- Data warehouse — $1,000 to $25,000; 30 minutes to 10 days

It is this differential that explains why data warehouses significantly lower the price of information.

In looking at these figures, the difference is almost too good to be true. Sure enough, the cost of building the data warehouse in company B has not been accounted for. If a proper cost comparison is to be made, it is unfair to not account for the cost of building the data warehouse.

To understand what must be done to build a data warehouse, consider the activities shown in Figure 15-8.

Building the Data Warehouse

To build the data warehouse, the developer must do the following:

- Go back and search for data in the legacy or operational environment
- Go back and wrestle with older technology
- Integrate the data once it is found
- Stage the data

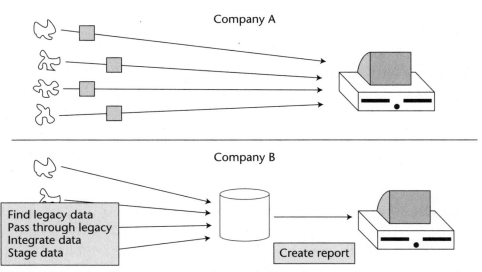

Figure 15-8   What happens when you have a data warehouse.

In other words, the developer must do the same activities as the person working for company A had to do. With the exception of the reporting activity, the activities for building a data warehouse are the same as if a simple new report or an analysis is needed. When it comes to doing a proper comparison of costs, the cost of building a data warehouse has to be thrown in if the comparison is to be a fair one.

So, how much does it cost to build a data warehouse? The answer is entirely dependent on the source systems, the size and the complexity of the information, the technology the base source systems are in, how well documentation has been done, and so forth. For the purposes of this discussion, the value ($1 million) will be assigned to a data warehouse development effort. That number is in line with the scale of the other numbers being used in this discussion.

To do a true cost comparison in the justification of a data warehouse, it is necessary to factor in one more consideration. That consideration is that no corporation or organization operates on the basis of a single report or analysis. The larger the corporation, the more demands for information there are. Finance wants to look at data one way. Accounting wants to look at data another way. Sales wants to look at data yet another way. Practically everyone in the corporation wants their own way of looking at data and no two people share exactly the same perspective. Therefore, there is no such thing as a corporation having one way to look at information. There are many ways a corporation needs to look at information. Furthermore, those ways of looking at data change as business conditions change. And business conditions are changing all the time.

A Complete Picture

Once the cost of the data warehouse and the need for looking at the same information in multiple fashions are factored into the equation, a true set of cost tradeoffs is created. That set of tradeoffs is seen in Figure 15-9.

Figure 15-9 shows that there are multiple needs for information. It also shows that there is a cost of the data warehouse. Then there is the differential for the cost of information. In company A, the same gruesome infrastructure must be built and rebuilt every time there is a need for information. This drives up the cost of information when there is no data warehouse. But once the data warehouse is built, the cost of information drops dramatically. With a data warehouse, the cost of information is the cost of reporting, whereas without a data warehouse, an entire infrastructure must be built before reporting can be done.

Stated differently, the infrastructure for information must be built only once when there is a data warehouse, instead of every time there is a need for information when there is no data warehouse. And that is the real cost-justification for a data warehouse. Figure 15-9 shows the important costs of information with and without a data warehouse.

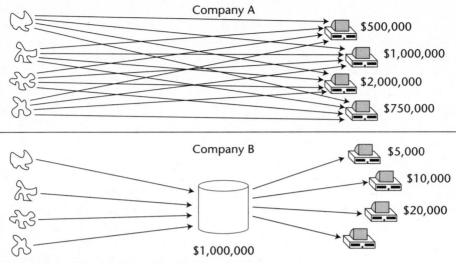

Figure 15-9 Cost-justifying the data warehouse.

Information Frustration

There is one other aspect of Figure 15-9 that is worthy of discussion. Do organizations without a data warehouse — such as company A — really spend the amounts of money that are shown? The answer is that they may spend money for a few important views of information. But not many organizations have the money or the patience to build the infrastructure shown in Figure 15-9. What happens is that the sources of information never get built and that leads to what can be termed "information frustration." Major parts of the organization have only scraps of information. In these environments, it is common to hear, "I know the information is there if only I could get at it."

Since organizations don't really build a massive infrastructure as was shown in Figure 15-9 when there is no data warehouse, it becomes clear that a data warehouse becomes an enabler. With a data warehouse, it is cheap to be able to get information. Therefore, a data warehouse enables an organization to get information it otherwise would not be able to afford.

The Time Value of Data

There is another very important thing that data warehousing does that is not quantified by the dollar. Data warehouses greatly reduce the time required to get information. In order to see this phenomenon, take a look at Figure 15-10.

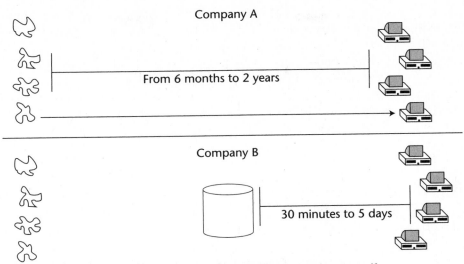

Figure 15-10   The time factor is very important, but is hard to quantify.

Figure 15-10 shows that without a data warehouse, it takes a long time to get new information out of an IT environment. But with a data warehouse, it takes only a short amount of time to get new information. Depending on what you want and depending on the data that resides in the data warehouse, it may take from 30 minutes to 5 or 10 days to get new information.

The Speed of Information

One day a business executive walks into an office and asks the IT individual for some new information. Without a data warehouse, the IT person takes a year to get the information. A year later, the IT person walks into the executive's office and displays the new reports. By this time, the executive has forgotten all about the reports and why they were ever needed. The executive can't even remember why he or she wanted the information in the first place. Because of the length of time that it has taken to get the new information, the value of the information has greatly diminished.

Now, consider the same scenario where the organization has a data warehouse. The business executive walks into the office of the IT person. The request for new information is made. In a half hour, the IT person has an answer for the executive. The IT person walks into the executive's office and hands the information to him or her the same day that they asked for it. The information that is given to the executive is still relevant. Whatever prompted the executive to ask for the information is still a burning business issue. With the new information, the executive can give an informed opinion.

There is then the issue of the time value of information. It is intuitively obvious that the faster information can be calculated or retrieved, the more the information is worth. There is a point in time after which information is worthless. With a data warehouse, data can be accessed very quickly. Without a data warehouse, data is accessed slowly.

Data warehousing greatly enhances and accelerates the time value of information. In some instances, the time value is more important than the raw costs of information. Unfortunately, it is often difficult to assign a dollar value to the time value of information.

Integrated Information

While the raw cost of information and the time value of information are two very important reasons for the cost justification of a data warehouse, there are other, indirect justifications as well. Consider the value of integrated information.

Figure 15-11 shows that data is integrated in a data warehouse and is not integrated inside the operational environment.

Figure 15-11 shows that there is no integration of information inside the operational or legacy environment. Organizations find that there is tremendous value in integrating data and that integrated data is found in the data warehouse.

Consider customer data, for example. Once customer data is integrated, there are all sorts of possibilities:

- Cross-selling to the customer
- Looking at the life cycle of the customer and selling based on the position of the customer and anticipated needs of the customer
- Selling to the customer based on relationships with other customers
- Selling to the customer as a part of a household

In short, there are all sorts of opportunities for approaching the customer base when there is a lot of integrated data that can be centered around a customer.

When the data is in the operational or legacy environment, it simply is not as accessible. The end user must become a data administrator and a database administrator to find the data in the operational or legacy environment. Very few end-user analysts wish to add these skills to an already challenging job.

Because of the business opportunities that exist, and because of the value of integration, there is another value-based dimension to the world of data warehousing — historical data.

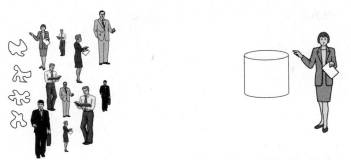

Figure 15-11   With legacy systems, there is no integrated data. With the data warehouse, there is an integrated view of the data.

The Value of Historical Data

Consider what happens to historical data in the operational or legacy environment, as shown in Figure 15-12. In many places in the operational environment, transaction performance is of the utmost importance. When operational transactions do not perform adequately, the end user considers the system to be a failure. Therefore, in the operational environment system, transaction performance is at a premium.

So, how does the systems programmer go about improving transaction performance? The answer is that the systems programmer does many things. But one of the most fundamental things the system programmer does is to remove historical data from the transaction processing system. Historical data is removed because it hinders performance. The more historical data there is, the less efficient the transaction processing system. Therefore, one of the primary objectives of the systems programmer is to remove historical data as quickly as possible from the operational transaction processing system.

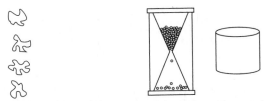

Figure 15-12   With legacy data, there is no place for history. With the data warehouse, there is a place for historical data.

Historical Data and CRM

Historical data then has a real value to the information processing world. As just one value of historical data, consider the role of historical data in the context of CRM. In CRM, information centers around the customer. CRM exists to better understand the customer.

Consider this fact about customers. Customers around the world are creatures of habit. The habits formed early in life stick with the customer throughout their life. Habits include practically everything about the customer. The habits that are formed early include the following:

- The food that is eaten
- The clothes that are worn
- The place where one lives
- The car one drives
- The education of the person
- The income of the person
- The way a person pays bills
- The way a person invests
- The way a person takes vacations
- The way a person marries and has children
- The way a person saves money
- The way a person works, and so forth.

The habits set in early life are a powerful indicator of the way a person will conduct his or her life in the future. So, there is real value to historical data because it is historical data that sets the stage for the future. Stated differently, when a corporation understands the history of a customer, the corporation is in a position to be proactive in offering products and services. And the data warehouse is the ideal place for the storing of historical data.

Historical data then becomes another important part of the value dimension of the data warehouse.

Summary

The cost-justification of a data warehouse at a macro level is very difficult to do because of other large external factors that have an effect on the organization. A better way to proceed with a data warehouse cost-justification is at a micro level.

To do a micro cost-justification, consider two companies — one that does not have a data warehouse and one that does have a data warehouse. The cost of information in the company without a data warehouse is extraordinarily high as compared to the cost of information in the company with a data warehouse. In addition, the data warehouse greatly accelerates the time value of information as well as providing a platform for integration. And finally, data warehousing provides a convenient place for historical data. Historical data adds another value dimension to information.

CHAPTER 16

The Data Warehouse and the ODS

A data warehouse can never be accessed on a millisecond basis. Because of the nature of the data, the volume of the data, and the mixed workload that uses data from the data warehouse, the data warehouse is not geared to support OLTP types of processes. Guaranteed subsecond response for an access to the data warehouse is architecturally not a viable option.

But subsecond response time is, in fact, very valuable in many operations. Many businesses require very fast response time, and those businesses cannot have access to the data warehouse. When subsecond response time is required and integrated DSS data must be accessed, there is a structure known as an *operational data store* (*ODS*) that is the place to go to when high-performance processing must be done.

Unlike the data warehouse, the ODS is optional. Some organizations have an ODS and other organizations do not have an ODS. The need for an ODS depends entirely on the organization and the processing that is being done.

Complementary Structures

In many ways, the ODS and the data warehouse are complementary structures. Both reside outside of the operational environment. Both support DSS processing. Both use integrated data. For these reasons, the ODS and the data warehouse are often considered to be complementary. Data flows between the ODS and the data warehouse in a bidirectional manner. On some occasions, the ODS feeds the data warehouse. On other occasions, the data warehouse feeds the ODS. In any case, the ODS is a physically different structure than the data warehouse. Under no circumstances does an ODS reside inside a data warehouse.

Unlike the data warehouse environment, the ODS is designed for high-performance, real-time processing. Figure 16-1 shows this difference between the two environments.

The ODS is designed to support consistent 2- to 3-second response-time transactions. The ODS has several features that enable this fast response time, including the following:

- Segregation of the workload into different modes of processing. Sometimes the ODS supports high-performance processing where transactions use very little data. At other times, the ODS supports large transactions that use large amounts of data and take a long time to execute.

- Some data in the ODS is designed for high-performance transaction processing. Other data is designed for flexible, integrated access.

- When update processing is done, it uses small transactions, each of which consume a small amount of resources.

Updates in the ODS

One of the distinctive features of the data warehouse is that of not having updates performed. The data warehouse consists of many finite snapshots of data. Once the snapshot is recorded properly, the data in the data warehouse doesn't change. If the data in the real world changes, a new snapshot of the data is taken and is placed inside the data warehouse.

Data in the ODS environment does not act this way. Updates of data in the ODS are normal and there is no reason why updates in the ODS cannot be done. Suppose there is a record of data in the ODS that has a value of $5,970.12. That value can be changed to $6,011.97 if business conditions warrant. No snapshot is taken. The value is simply changed in the ODS.

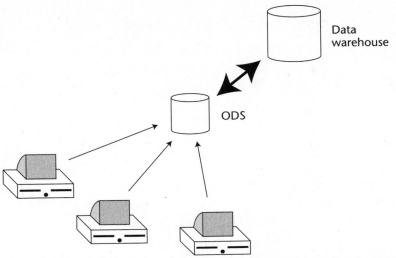

Figure 16-1   The ODS is where high-performance response time is available.

Another way of stating this fundamental difference in data characteristics is that data in the ODS is said to be "current-valued," while data in the data warehouse is said to be "historical." In other words, when you go to the ODS, you get the most current information about whatever topics you are searching for. But when you go to the data warehouse, you get the historical record of the information about whatever topic you are searching for.

Historical Data and the ODS

Because of this basic difference between the two environments, only a very limited amount of historical data is found in the ODS, while the data warehouse contains an almost unlimited amount of historical data. Figure 16-2 shows this differentiation between the two environments.

As a result of the differences in historical data versus current data, applications that need current-value data run on the ODS rather than the data warehouse. Typically, the ODS contains no more than a month's worth of historical data. On the other hand, the data warehouse may contain a decade of historical data.

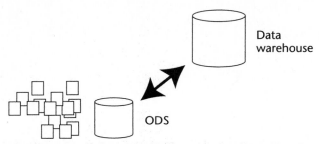

Figure 16-2   Only a limited amount of historical data is found in the ODS

Data that is found in the data warehouse is stored in terms of historical records of an event. For example, a data warehouse may typically include the following:

- A record of each purchase made by an individual
- A record of each shipment made by a manufacturer
- A record of each check written by each bank customer
- A record of each phone call made by a telephone customer
- A record of each movie shown in each theatre across the United States

The data warehouse, then, is a place where historical, detailed records are kept.

Profile Records

Often the ODS stores records in what are termed "profile records." A *profile record* is a record made from many observations about a customer. A profile record is made from looking at and creating a synopsis of lots of occurrences of data.

For example, consider a profile record that might be created for a customer, Lynn Inmon:

- Buys clothes once a month
- Shops throughout the week
- Prefers blue silky blouses
- Shops for groceries occasionally
- Usually buys in bulk

- Does not buy alcohol
- Spends about $200 per trip when shopping for groceries
- Goes to a chiropractor every three weeks
- Visits an eye doctor once a year
- Buys a car every 5 years
- Has her car fixed every 5 months
- Does not smoke
- Prefers white wine
- Pays bills on time

The profile record in the ODS is constructed by looking at many, many detailed historical records contained in the data warehouse.

The value of the ODS profile record is that it can be accessed very quickly. There is no need to go and look at hundreds of detailed historical records to get information about Lynn Inmon. Furthermore, information of different types can be placed in the profile record. Some information is about buying habits, some information is about paying habits, and other information is about preferences. In other words, the profile record is a place where massive amounts of data can be concisely captured. Once captured, the information can be quickly and conveniently accessed.

Figure 16-3 shows that profile records are created from many detailed observations taken from the data warehouse.

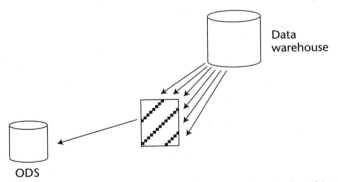

Figure 16-3   Profile records are often created and placed in the ODS.

Different Classes of ODS

There are four classes of ODS (see Figure 16-4): class I, class II, class III, and class IV. The ODS class is determined by how fast data arrives in the ODS — the length of time from the occurrence of a transaction until the moment the transaction arrives in the ODS.

The different ODS classes are defined as follows:

- **Class I** — There are milliseconds from the time an operational update is made until the data arrives in the ODS. In a Class I ODS, the length of time from an operational transaction executing and the ODS being altered is transparent. The change happens so fast the end user doesn't know that there are milliseconds that have elapsed between the two environments being kept in sync.

- **Class II** — There are several hours from the time an operational transaction has executed and the time that the ODS is updated. The end user can definitely know that there is a difference between the data in the ODS and the same data in the operational environment.

- **Class III** — There is an overnight gap or longer between the coordination of the data in the data warehouse and the data in the ODS.

- **Class IV** — There is a long period of time — months and perhaps even years — between the coordination of data in the ODS and its source. Typically, in a Class IV ODS, the source of data is the data warehouse, although it can be from other sources.

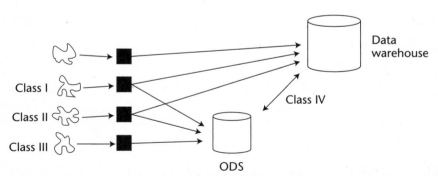

Figure 16-4 There are different classes of ODS based on the speed of refreshment.

Class I of the ODS is very rare. There is seldom a real business justification for a Class I ODS. The Class I ODS is expensive and is technologically challenging. An example of the Class I ODS is the airline reservation environment. The problem with the Class I ODS (other than complexity and cost) is that it does not have the time needed for integration. There is so much emphasis on the speed of update and synchronization that there is no time left for integration. Because of this, a Class I ODS applies primarily to simple transactions that are shuffled from one environment to another.

Class II of the ODS is common. In a Class II ODS, there is ample time for integration of data before the data goes from the operational environment to the ODS environment. An example of a Class II ODS is the name and address of a customer. The name and address of a customer change very infrequently. When the change of address is discovered, it rarely hurts the business if the change is made on a three- or four-hour basis. The Class II ODS can be built using conventional technology and is not terribly challenging. Relative to a Class I ODS, a Class II ODS is inexpensive.

Class III of the ODS represents the ODS that has a slower update cycle than a Class II ODS. The Class III ODS has an overnight or longer cycle of refreshment. An example of a Class III ODS is the sale of insurance policies, which occurs at a very gradual rate. There may be as much as a week that goes by between coordinating the ODS environment with the operational environment. The Class III ODS can be built using conventional technology and is relatively inexpensive.

Class IV of the ODS represents a special ODS that has a very long frequency of coordination. The Class IV ODS may be created from the output of special reports or special projects. In many cases, the creation of a Class IV ODS is a one-time event. In other cases, the Class IV ODS can be coordinated on an annual basis. There is no expectation of a close coordination of a Class IV ODS and a data warehouse or any other source. An example of a Class IV ODS is a survey of customer buying habits made from data found in the data warehouse and transferred to the ODS twice a year.

While most ODS records are Class I, II, III, or IV, it is possible to have an ODS record where part of the data in the ODS record is one class and another part of the ODS record is another class. Such a record is not uncommon at all.

Database Design — A Hybrid Approach

The ODS is designed in a hybrid manner. Figure 16-5 shows that part of an ODS design is relational and another part of the ODS design is multidimensional.

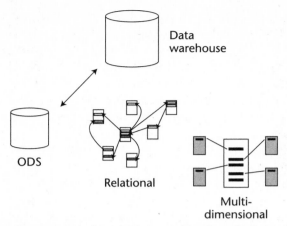

Figure 16-5 The ODS is a combination of relational design and multidimensional design.

The relational portion of the ODS database design is the portion where flexibility is the most important parameter. The multidimensional portion of the ODS design is the part where performance is the most important parameter.

This dichotomy of design presents the database designer with a dilemma. It is like painting one part of a wall black and another part of the wall white, and calling the finished product gray. Of necessity, the design of an ODS is a compromise between flexibility and performance. Because of this compromise (which is part of every ODS design), ODS design is more of an art than a science. Not coincidentally, the development of an ODS takes considerable time. Making design tradeoffs consumes considerable time and effort. It requires an experienced designer to be able to make the tradeoffs judiciously.

Drawn to Proportion

When the ODS and the data warehouse are shown together, usually the ODS is drawn somewhat smaller than the data warehouse. But, in fact, if the ODS and the data warehouse are drawn to scale, a much different proportion results. Figure 16-6 shows the proportional differences between the ODS and the data warehouse.

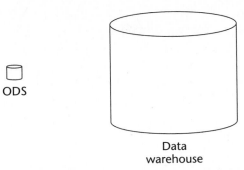

Figure 16-6 The ODS and the data warehouse drawn to proportion.

Figure 16-6 shows that the data warehouse is *much* larger than the ODS. Following are some reasons why the data warehouse is so much larger:

- The data warehouse contains historical data. The ODS contains only a smattering of historical data.

- The data warehouse is dedicated to serving all users. As a consequence, the data warehouse contains a wide variety of data. The ODS is dedicated to serving one type of processing. Therefore, the data in the ODS is much less diversified than the data in the data warehouse,

- The data in the data warehouse is completely granular and relational. The data in the ODS is summarized and much more compact, since only one audience of users needs the ODS.

For these reasons, then, the ODS is significantly smaller than the data warehouse.

Transaction Integrity in the ODS

Another significant difference between the data warehouse and the ODS is that the data warehouse and the ODS have different requirements when it comes to the basic DBMS. The data warehouse DBMS does not need to have transaction integrity since the data warehouse is not updated and since the data warehouse does not serve high-performance transaction processing. This means that the overhead of running a data warehouse DBMS is much lower than the DBMS that runs with transaction integrity.

On the other hand, the DBMS that is suited for the ODS does require transaction integrity. This means that real-time back-out and recovery from database updates is required if a transaction fails. The ODS requires transaction integrity because the ODS supports high-performance processing and updates into the ODS. The overhead required for transaction integrity is considerable, even if updates are not occurring. Transaction integrity is needed if there is the potential for updates occurring, as there is for the processing that occurs within the ODS.

Time Slicing the ODS Day

The ODS processing day is divided into slices of time that are dedicated to different kinds of processing. This time slicing is the secret to the ODS being able to offer high performance. Figure 16-7 shows how the typical day is sliced into different modes of processing.

Figure 16-7 shows that at the early hours of the day, the ODS has its processing workload dedicated to one kind of processing — large sequential batch jobs that load data, edit data, monitor data, and so forth. Then, as the regular daily working hours start, the ODS turns into a machine dedicated to high performance. During these periods, the workload consists of many fast-running activities. Large sequential activities are not allowed to run during peak daytime hours. Then, in the late afternoon, the ODS turns into a machine that can have a mixed workload running.

By time slicing, the ODS can support multiple kinds of activities and can guarantee good performance during peak processing hours.

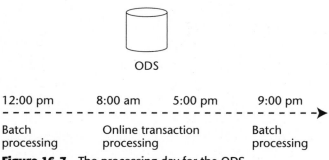

Figure 16-7   The processing day for the ODS.

Multiple ODS

The ODS is dependent on processing requirements. There can be many different kinds of processing requirements in an organization, including financial processing requirements, engineering processing requirements, marketing processing requirements, and so forth. Because of this diversity of processing requirements, there can be multiple ODSs in an organization. There can be one ODS for each of the different processing requirements an organization has.

While there may be multiple ODSs, there is only one enterprise data warehouse.

ODS and the Web Environment

One special use of an ODS is worthy of mention. That use of the ODS is in conjunction with the interfacing of the Web environment to the data warehouse. This interface is shown in Figure 16-8.

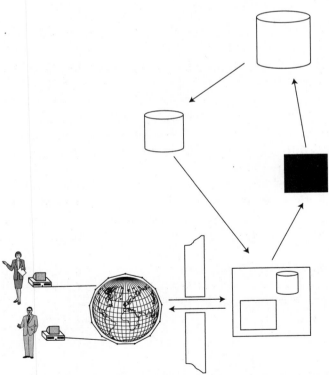

Figure 16-8 How the Web environment communicates with the Web based on an eBusiness environment.

Figure 16-8 shows that the Web environment interfaces with the data warehouse indirectly. Web data (that is, clickstream data) comes from the Web environment through a Granularity Manager. After the processing of the Granularity Manager is completed, the data then passes into the data warehouse. When data coming from the data warehouse to the Web environment is needed, it passes from the data warehouse into the ODS. Once the data is in the ODS, usually a profile record is created. The Web environment then accesses the ODS to find the data needed. There is no direct access from the Web environment to the data warehouse. The data warehouse is shielded from the large amounts of data generated by the Web environment. And the data warehouse is shielded from the need for high-performance requests generated by the Web environment. The Granularity Manager shields the data warehouse from the massive volumes of data and the ODS shields the data warehouse from the high performance requests coming from the Web environment. The Granularity Manager and the ODS act as shock absorbers for the data warehouse.

An Example of an ODS

As a final example of the use of an ODS, consider the arrangement shown in Figure 16-9.

Figure 16-9 shows a data warehouse created for telephone calls. There is a record of millions of telephone calls found in the data warehouse. The telephone calls are organized by customer and a profile record is created for each customer. The calling habits of each customer are synopsized into a profile record recording such things as how many phone calls a customer makes, where those phone calls go, how many long distance phone calls there are, and so forth.

The ODS is opened up to the operators of the organization. Now, when an operator gets a phone call, the operator knows all sorts of information about the person who is calling. The operator can do promotions on the spot. The operator can know whether the person is high-profile, whether the person is a big spender, and so forth.

The information coming from the ODS is available in terms of milliseconds. This means that when the operator answers the phone call, a screen with all the information about the customer is available as soon as the operator and the caller engage in conversation.

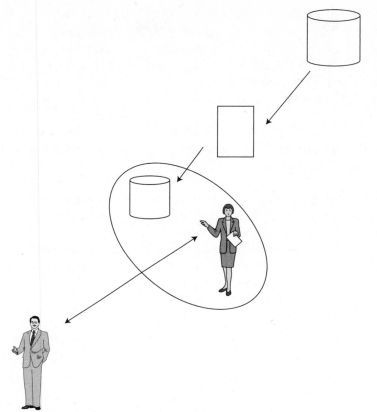

Figure 16-9   An example of using an ODS. ·

Summary

The ODS is a companion architectural structure with the data warehouse. The ODS is geared for fast response time and updating, unlike the data warehouse. The ODS contains only a limited amount of historical data, whereas the data warehouse contains massive amounts of historical data.

A normal form of database design for the ODS is a profile record. The profile record is a synopsis of many of the historical records found in the data warehouse.

There are different classes of ODS, including Class I, Class II, Class III, and Class IV. The different classes are determined by the speed with which the ODS is refreshed. A Class I ODS is refreshed in milliseconds. A Class II ODS is refreshed in hours. A Class III ODS is refreshed in overnight cycles. A Class IV ODS is refreshed on a very infrequent basis.

The design of an ODS is a mixture of relational structures and multidimensional structures.

Drawn proportionately, the ODS is much smaller than the data warehouse. The data warehouse does not require that a DBMS have transaction integrity capabilities, while the ODS does require that the DBMS have transaction integrity capabilities.

The time of day for different kinds of processing is divided for the ODS. Some of the day is dedicated to high-performance processing and other parts of the day are dedicated to long sequential processing.

There can be multiple ODSs in a shop, depending on the processing requirements. The ODS plays a special role in interfacing the data warehouse and the Web environment. The data warehouse sends data to the ODS, and the ODS directly interfaces with the Web environment.

CHAPTER 17

Corporate Information Compliance and Data Warehousing

Corporate information compliance has become the law of the land, at least in the United States and for companies wishing to trade securities in the United States. Some of the more prominent compliance standards are Sarbanes Oxley, Basel II, and HIPAA. These compliance standards have come about for a variety of reasons.

Probably the best-known set of circumstances is that of Sarbanes Oxley. Around the year 2000, certain corporations were caught in public scandal. The officers of the company were trying to inflate the stock price of the company fraudulently. In doing so, investors would be paying for corporate stock at a higher price that the company really warranted. The corporations inflated these stock prices through accounting "smoke and mirrors." Some of the companies caught inflating stock prices were Enron, MCI/WorldCom, and Global Crossings.

In response to the artificial accounting and deceiving transactions that were being foisted off on the public, the Sarbanes Oxley Act was enacted. Sarbanes Oxley (among other things) caused the corporation to do their accounting in a proper and honest manner. In addition, Sarbanes Oxley made executives criminally responsible for their corporation's books. Prior to Sarbanes Oxley, it was difficult to hold top management criminally responsible for corporate reporting and financial transactions. After the enactment of Sarbanes Oxley, it became possible to send executives to jail for willful disobedience of corporate accounting and reporting standards.

Prior to this, information compliance had been an informal issue. The Financial Accounting Standards Board (FASB) and Generally Accepted Accounting Principles (GAAP) have governed corporate information for years. FASB and GAAP address the issues of auditing and accounting opinions as to the corporate financial picture. FASB and GAAP are rules and procedures by which accountants measure corporate finances. Prior to Sarbanes Oxley, corporations that had unusual financial dealings and reporting were subject to adverse opinions and civil penalty. In addition, the news of adverse opinions from an accounting firm almost always led to price adjustments of the publicly traded stock. Since Sarbanes Oxley, there are now criminal penalties for corporate mismanagement and misstatement of corporate finances for publicly traded corporations.

And there were other standards as well. For the financial community there was Basel II. For the healthcare community there was the Health Insurance Portability and Accountability Act (HIPAA). It is predictable that in the future there will be other corporate compliance standards for information and information processing.

It may not be apparent, but data warehousing plays a prominent role in required compliance with Sarbanes Oxley and other information compliance standards. Figure 17-1 shows the "20,000 foot view" of what corporations need to do in order to comply with information standards such as Sarbanes Oxley, as well as the role data warehousing plays with regard to compliance.

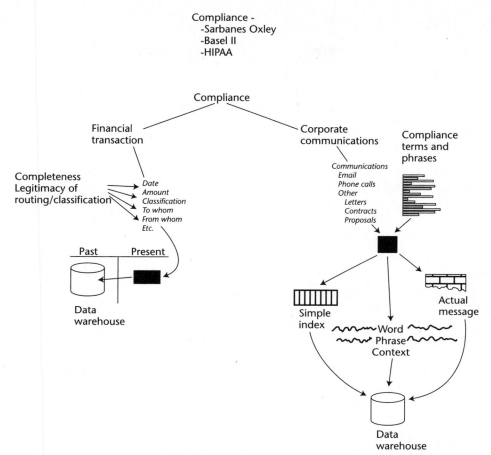

Figure 17-1   Compliance and data warehousing.

Two Basic Activities

There are two basic activities that an organization must do in order to meet compliance standards:

- Comply with financial requirements and controls
- Comply with the organizational communications aspect of regulation

These activities are related, yet distinctly different.

Financial Compliance

Financial compliance deals with the recording, procedures, and reporting of financial transactions. In some regards, financial compliance is nothing more than adherence to the GAAP and FASB standards that have been published for years. The Sarbanes Oxley standards are for large publicly traded corporations. The sorts of financial activities that are governed by compliance standards include the following:

- Recording the date of a transaction
- Recording the amount of the transaction
- Recording the participants in the transaction
- Classification of the transaction

There are a whole series of approvals and formalization of procedures that most corporations were never before confronted with. In many ways, these standards require all businesses to be brought up to the level of banking and financial compliance. The world of banking and finance has always had a high degree of compliance to data-integrity standards. This high degree of compliance is required because each customer account (savings account, checking account, loans, and so forth) requires minute attention to detail. If so much as one transaction is not handled properly, the bank or financial institution or their customer base suffers. Therefore, banks and financial institutions have always had strict procedures and controls to ensure that funds are handled properly.

With Sarbanes Oxley, all organizations are being asked to take the same care with their information as banks, whether the business of the organization warrants it or not, and whether or not the organization has honestly and successfully done business for a hundred years.

In addition to looking at financial transactions at the detailed level, financial transactions are examined at the macro level. Some of the ways that a macro inspection of financial transactions is done is to see if all financial transactions are included. One easy way to "cook the books" is to not include all financial transactions. Or, another technique is to trundle whole classes of transactions to an account or subsidiary that is inappropriate. The financial transactions must be cared for at both the micro and the macro levels.

There are two aspects to financial transactions — the past and the present. Most implementations of Sarbanes Oxley concentrate on the current transactions in which the organization is engaged. This means that when a transaction occurs, it is subject to a series of audits. These "mini audits" ensure — up front — that the financial transaction is in compliance. So, there is the up-front financial audit and procedures that each transaction is subject to.

Upon finishing the audit and procedures, the financial data eventually finds its way to the data warehouse.

Most corporations begin their Sarbanes Oxley journey with the present transaction audit.

The second aspect of Sarbanes Oxley is looking back at financial data over time. In this case, examining older financial data is the focus. Naturally, the data warehouse becomes the focus here. The data warehouse is the natural place to start because the data warehouse holds the following:

- Historical data
- Granular data
- Integrated data

The data warehouse, then, becomes an enabler for financial auditing — for Sarbanes Oxley, Basel II, HIPAA, and other standards. When looked at broadly, there are two aspects to corporate finance — the "what" and the "why."

The "What"

The "what" of financial affairs is the record of what financial transactions have occurred. It tracks the details of all financial transactions. Typical of the data found in tracking the "what" of financial affairs is the information shown in Figure 17-2.

Looking at the corporate financial transactions from the standpoint of compliance, there are several important perspectives:

- Are all the transactions included?
- Are the transactions recorded at the lowest level of granularity?
- Is all of the relevant information for each financial transaction recorded properly?
- Is the recording of information accurate?
- Have the transactions been classified properly?

These aspects of the recording of financial transactions are essential to the compliance of what transactions have occurred.

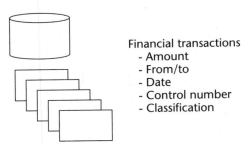

Financial transactions
 - Amount
 - From/to
 - Date
 - Control number
 - Classification

Figure 17-2   Financial transactions.

A byproduct of keeping financial transactions at a historical detailed level is having to store massive volumes of data. Whereas data warehouses store massive volumes of data on a regular basis, there are some substantial differences in the storing of financial data for the purpose of compliance.

One of the substantive differences between a standard data warehouse and the storing of data for the purpose of compliance is the *probability of access*. The probability of access for data in a standard data warehouse is reasonably high. If, in fact, data in a data warehouse has its probability of access drop, then the data is placed in near-line or alternate storage. So, data in a data warehouse has a reasonably high probability of access.

But data stored for the purpose of compliance has a very, very low probability of access. Data stored for the purpose of compliance may never be accessed. In fact, in most circumstances, the corporation is quite happy when the data stored for compliance is never accessed.

So, one major difference between data in the data warehouse and data stored for compliance is that data stored for compliance is hardly ever (if ever) accessed, while data in the data warehouse is accessed on a reasonably frequent basis.

Another difference between data stored in a data warehouse and data stored for the purpose of compliance is the *sensitivity to loss*. If data in a data warehouse is lost, there are problems but no catastrophes. In other words, it is important to keep data in a data warehouse, but if the data becomes lost, the consequences are usually not catastrophic.

But in a store of data serving compliance needs, losing financial data can be disastrous. If financial data is lost, the corporation is open to the charges of wrongdoing, whether the charges are founded are not. Therefore, backup for data stored for compliance is even more important than data stored in a data warehouse.

Another difference between the data warehouse and the data stored for the purposes of compliance is the *speed of queries*. As a rule, unless the analyst is doing statistical processing, there must be a reasonable response time for the data warehouse query. Reasonable response time is an entirely relative thing — in some cases reasonable is a 10-second query, and in other cases reasonable may be a 30-minute query. Of course, in the case of heavy statistical analysis, reasonable may be measured in terms of days.

But in the case of queries going against data stored for the purpose of compliance, a reasonable response time may be measured in terms of days or even weeks. So, the response expectations in the two environments are very different.

Yet another major difference between data warehouse data and data stored for the purpose of compliance is *content*. Data warehouse data covers just about every kind of data that there is, whereas data stored for compliance is limited to financial data, for the most part.

The *length of time* that compliance data needs to be stored is a product of several factors:

- How long storage is legislated
- How long the company feels comfortable, regardless of the legislated length of time
- How long data can be physically stored in any media

One of the factors in the storage of data for the purpose of compliance is the storage and preservation of relevant metadata, as well as the data itself. It does little good for the corporation to store data for compliance over a long period of time if the corporation cannot interpret the data once it is read. In other words, if the metadata is lost, the data stored for compliance has little worth.

The "Why"

As important as financial transactions are, they are only one side of the coin. The equally important aspect of financial transactions is that of the "why." The "why" of financial transactions deals with the activities that take place before the transactions occur. In every financial transaction, there is some amount of what can be termed a "prefinancial" activity. A *prefinancial activity* is the negotiation that occurs before the transaction can be consummated.

In some cases, the prefinancial negotiation is simple — you see a bar of candy for sale for $.50 and you buy it. There is effectively no prefinancial transaction negotiation here. But, in other cases, there is a lot of prefinancial negotiation. For example, a building is to be constructed. Who owns the land? How tall is the building to be? What kind of elevators will there be? What terms will be created for the repayment of the loan for the building? What exterior will the building have? How much will a lease cost?

In a large undertaking, there is always negotiation — usually considerable. Figure 17-3 shows the prefinancial negotiations that occur.

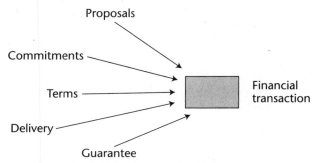

Figure 17-3   Prefinancial activities.

There are many aspects to a negotiation. There are proposals, offers, counteroffers, commitments, deliveries, terms, guarantees, warranties, and so forth. Each negotiation is slightly different from each other negotiation.

The prefinancial activities are as important as the financial activities to the process of compliance because the prefinancial activities explain why the financial activity occurred. From the standpoint of financial compliance, the prefinancial activities are as important, or even more important, than the financial activities.

But capturing and interpreting prefinancial activities is a difficult chore simply because prefinancial activities are unstructured and open to interpretation. In other words, prefinancial activities are subjective.

And where do prefinancial activities take place? Prefinancial activities take place in the unstructured email or telephone-conversation environment. Prefinancial activities are (for the most part) free-form discussion and conversation.

Figure 17-4 shows where prefinancial activities occur.

The prefinancial negotiations occur in the unstructured environment. Typically, the prefinancial negotiations occur in the email or conversational environment. In other cases, there are memos, proposals, "straw man" contracts, and written terms.

These prefinancial negotiations are as relevant and important to compliance as the actual financial transaction itself. They show intent, which is at the heart of compliance.

But prefinancial negotiations are hard to capture and track simply because they are informal and because they occur in different forms.

Figure 17-5 shows how these informal, unstructured negotiations can be captured and analyzed.

Figure 17-5 shows that the unstructured messages and communications are passed through a filter. The filter consists of words and phrases important to Sarbanes Oxley and other forms of compliance. Upon passing through the filter, the messages and communications are aligned with their content relative to compliance. A message that is very important to compliance will be marked as such, and a message irrelevant to compliance will be not marked at all.

In such a fashion, the messages and communications that are relevant and important to compliance are plucked out of the many different places where the messages are recorded.

Once the messages and communications have been processed, they are made available to the standard analytical tools, such as Business Objects, Cognos, MicroStrategy, or Crystal Reports. Figure 17-6 shows how the results of passing through the filter are obtained.

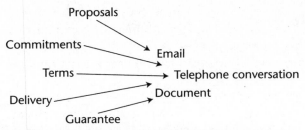

Figure 17-4   Where prefinancial activities are found.

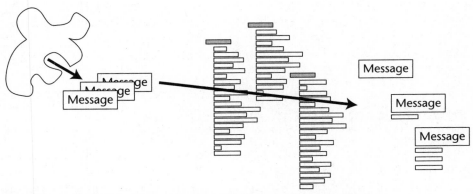

Figure 17-5   Filtering information from messages and communications.

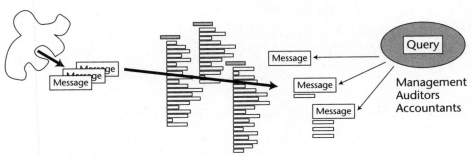

Figure 17-6   Analyzing the compliance data.

Once the results are obtained, they can be accessed by many different parties, such as management, auditors, accountants, and other interested parties.

One interesting aspect of passing messages and communications through a filter is that the results are good for both historical reporting and for ongoing up-to-date processing.

There are essentially two major aspects to compliance — audits of past activities and ongoing audits. Audits of past activities can take place for data that is 5 to 10 years old, and even older. There are few limits for past historical audits.

But there is also a need for ongoing up-to-the-second audits. An ongoing audit is an examination of prefinancial activity *before* the financial activity is completed. In other words, the contracts and proposals which are in the process of being completed need to be audited as well. The filtering infrastructure that has been described is good for both kinds of audits.

Management is asked to sign off on deals that are in progress according to Sarbanes Oxley.

Auditing Corporate Communications

While financial auditing is of the essence in compliance to Sarbanes Oxley, it is not the only issue. In order to completely fulfill the intent of Sarbanes Oxley, it is necessary to look at activity that has happened before the transaction occurred. Stated differently, in most regards a financial transaction is the end result of a long negotiation. Before the financial transaction is consummated, a lot of other activities have transpired:

- A selection of goods or services has been made.

- A price has been agreed upon.

- A delivery date has been negotiated.

- Customization or changes to the product or service have been discussed.

- Grouping of multiple goods or services has been done.

In other words, the financial transaction only represents the end result of a lot of other activities that have preceded the transaction. And Sarbanes Oxley is as interested in the activities leading up to the financial transaction as it is in the financial activities themselves.

As an example of the kind of prefinancial transaction activities that Sarbanes Oxley is interested in, consider the practice of contingent sales. A *contingent sale* is one where a sale may or may not have been made, but where the corporation has booked the sale in any case. Consider the following. A software company, ABC, has a hot prospect. To push the prospect into signing a purchase order, ABC asks the sales prospect to install the software, use it for 90 days, and then determine whether a sale will be made or not. So, the sales prospect does exactly that. The sales prospect installs the software. In the meantime, ABC declares that a sale has been made. And indeed, in 90 days the prospect may sign the agreement. But the prospect may also throw the product out or throw part of the product out. Or, the sales prospect may combine the product purchase with another product, receiving a large discount.

In the meantime, the stock of ABC is riding high because it looks as if sales are blossoming. Never mind that all or some of the sales price may have to be renegotiated and revenue will have to be taken off the books. If in the next quarter there are enough new sales prospects that can have the sales booked, the booking of the next quarter's revenue will more than offset the adjustments that have to be made for last quarter's contingent sales.

In such a manner, a corporation's revenues can be artificially boosted and the stock price will be artificially high.

There are several more circumstances that Sarbanes Oxley looks for. Some of these circumstances are for promises to deliver, loans to executives, and so forth.

One of the issues with monitoring prefinancial activities and discussions is the volume of data that must be filtered. Only in theory is it possible to manually look in every message or communication. In a modern corporation, there may be millions of emails each day. It simply is not practical to ask anyone to read and monitor that many messages in a day's time.

The question, then, is where are these prefinancial transactions found? Where are the negotiations and the promises and commitments to customers found? The answer is that these prefinancial activities are captured in the unstructured environment. The unstructured environment includes emails, letters, agreements, proposals, transcribed telephone conversations, and so forth. In one form or the other, these unstructured activities contain the information that is relevant to Sarbanes Oxley.

To effect an audit on unstructured data, first the unstructured data is captured. In truth, unstructured data is found in many places and in many forms. In the case of telephone conversations, the conversation has to be transcribed into a textual format. In the case of emails, the ones that are relevant must be separated from those that are irrelevant.

However they are captured, they are placed in a form and location where they can be edited. Now the messages and communications are passed against a screen of predetermined words and phrases that are sensitive to Sarbanes Oxley (or Basel II, or HIPAA, and so forth). The messages and communications are passed — word for word — against the compliance words and phrases. If no word or phrase is found, nothing happens. The next message or communication is processed.

But if a word or phrase is found, then it is classified into one of three categories:

- An ordinary word or phrase
- A critical word or phrase
- A "red hot" word or phrase

Depending on the criticality of the word or phrase that has been encountered, the results are placed in one of three places. Following are the three destinations of the "hit" that has been made:

- A simple index
- A context index
- A copy of the message or communication

The *simple index* holds the reference back to the word or phrase. Suppose the word "account" has been encountered. The simple index merely points back to the document or email where the word was encountered. Sarbanes Oxley does not require any special action, but Sarbanes Oxley does require that a reference be made to the place where the mention was found.

The *context index* is for those words and phrases where there is a perceived criticality of information. For example, suppose the phrase "contingent sale" is found. In a context reference, the text before and after the phrase is captured. The context reference might look like "...whereupon there shall be a contingent sale made for the multi line task server 5800...." In this case, the entire textual string is captured and indexed. Now the auditor can look at the context to see if the document is worth investigating.

A *copy of the actual message or communication* can be made if it is determined that the discovery of a word or phrase is very important. Suppose the following message was received: "We have plans to embezzle the company." In this case, the entire message is captured and stored. If someone in the organization discovers that a monitoring of communications is occurring, then even if the person erases his or her email, the email in its entirety has already been captured.

In such a manner, the messages and communications of the corporation can be monitored for compliance with Sarbanes Oxley or one of the other compliance standards.

Once the results have been collected, they can be placed in the data warehouse. Once in the data warehouse, the results become a permanent record of the auditing of the prefinancial activities of the organization.

Summary

Compliance is an activity that has been forced on most organizations whether they like it or not. Different forms of compliance include Sarbanes Oxley, HIPAA, Basel II, and others.

Sarbanes Oxley compliance is concerned with two forms of compliance: financial transaction compliance and communications compliance. Financial transaction compliance relates to the accuracy of each financial transaction. Communications compliance refers to the activities and discussions leading up to the consummation of the financial transaction. The auditing of financial activities requires that detailed, historical data be kept. The auditing of prefinancial activities requires that messages and communications be audited.

An effective way to audit messages and communications is to pass the messages and communications through a filter, where words and phrases are picked out. Once the messages and communications are passed through a filter, the results are put in a database that can be used for auditing.

One of the issues of auditing messages and communications is the volumes of data that are entailed. In some corporations, millions of messages must be screened each day.

To monitor communications, each communication is passed against a list of words and phrases relevant to Sarbanes Oxley. Then, based on the results of the screening, all hits are classified into one of three categories:

- Normal
- Critical
- "Red hot"

CHAPTER 18

The End-User Community

Data warehouses and their ultimate use are shaped profoundly by the end user. But there is no "end user" per se for the data warehouse environment. In fact, there is an entire community of end users and in that community there is great diversity.

The end-user community can be characterized by looking at the type of individual who constitutes the community. In general, there are four types of end users:

- Farmers
- Explorers
- Miners
- Tourists

Each of these classifications of end user has his or her own set of unique characteristics.

The Farmer

The *farmer* is the most predominant type of user found in the data warehouse environment. The farmer is a predictable person. He or she does the same activity on a routine basis. The types of queries the farmer submits vary only by the type of data that the query is submitted for. The same type of query is run repeatedly by the farmer.

The queries submitted by the farmer tend to be short. Since the farmer knows what he or she wants, the farmer goes directly to where the data is. The queries that the farmer submits have a similar pattern of access. If the farmer submits lots of queries on Mondays one week, then it is a good bet that the farmer will submit lots of queries on Monday next week.

The farmer has a high "hit rate" on finding whatever he or she wants. If the farmer were a baseball player, the farmer would be a batter that hits for average. Seldom does the farmer hit home runs, but seldom does the farmer strike out.

The Explorer

The second kind of end user is the *explorer*. The explorer is a person that does not know what he or she wants. The explorer operates in a mode of complete unpredictability. He or she will go six months and submit no queries and then in the next week will submit 10 of them. The explorer has the habit of looking at large volumes of data. The explorer does not know what he or she wants before the exploration process is begun. The explorer looks for patterns in data that may or may not exist. If the explorer were a baseball player, he or she would hit many home runs and would also strike out a lot. The batting average of the explorer would be low.

The explorer operates in what is termed a "heuristic mode." In a *heuristic mode,* the explorer does not know what the next step of analysis is going to be until the results of the current step are complete. The explorer operates in a project basis. When the project is finished, the exploration process ceases.

In many cases, the explorer looks for something and never finds it. But on other occasions, the explorer finds a gem that has been overlooked.

The Miner

The *miner* is the individual who digs into piles of data and determines whether the data is saying something or not. A miner is one who is presented an assertion and is asked to determine the validity and the strength of the assertion. The miner usually uses statistical tools. The miner operates on a project basis. The miner creates queries that are enormous in size. The miner operates in a heuristic manner. The miner often operates closely in tandem with the explorer. The explorer creates assertions and hypotheses, while the miner determines the strength of those assertions and hypotheses.

The miner has special skills (usually mathematical) that set the miner apart from other technicians.

The Tourist

The *tourist* is an individual who knows where to find things. The tourist has a breadth of knowledge, as opposed to a depth of knowledge. The tourist is familiar with both formal and informal systems. The tourist knows how to use the Internet. The tourist is familiar with metadata, in its many forms. The tourist knows where to find indexes and how to use them. The tourist is as familiar with structured data as he or she is with unstructured data. The tourist is familiar with source code and how to read and interpret it.

The Community

All of these user types make up the end-user community. Collectively, they constitute all of the requests made on the behalf of DSS processing and data warehousing. But individually, they have very different sets of needs.

Demographically, there are probably more farmers than there are any other types of end user. But ironically, an end user may change types on the fly. One minute an end user may be behaving as a farmer and the next minute the end user behaves as an explorer. So, depending on the task at hand, the same person at different moments in time may appear to be a different type of user.

Different end users answer different kinds of questions. The following are typical of the kinds of questions that an end user may be faced with:

- **Farmer** — On a weekly basis, how many problem loans are there and is the status of the loans getting better or worse?

- **Explorer** — Perhaps we need to categorize problem loans differently. What are the different ways a problem loan can be categorized?

- **Miner** — Now that we have a new categorization of problem loans, how many of these loan types do we have and what exposure amount is there?

- **Tourist** — Where can I find more information about problem loan account 12345?

Different Types of Data

It may not be obvious that there are indeed different types of end users and that those end users have a profound effect on the design and use of the data warehouse. As one example, consider this. Data exists in different bands of probability of use in the data warehouse. Figure 18-1 shows this separation of data based on its use.

Figure 18-1 shows that some data is used actively and other data is used inactively. As data volumes grow large, this separation occurs naturally.

However, from the perspective of the different end users, farmers access the actively used data whereas explorers access data from all over the data warehouse — actively used data and inactively used data.

The reason why this scattering of data use is important is that if no explorers are going to be served, then the distribution of data becomes very easy to do. When only farmers are being served, there is not a lot of need for accessing inactively used data. When that is the case, there is no need for near-line storage or archival storage. But when the explorer community must be served, there is a real need for access of data that is infrequently being used.

In addition, different user types access different parts of the CIF. Farmers typically access data marts, explorers access the data warehouse and the exploration warehouse, data miners access the data mining or exploration warehouse, and tourists access metadata.

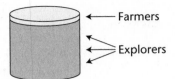

Figure 18-1   Farmers are very predictable in their use of the data warehouse. Explorers are not predictable at all.

Cost-Justification and ROI Analysis

Another place where the difference between user types becomes relevant is in the cost-justification of a data warehouse. The value proposition for farmers is almost always used for return on investment (ROI) and cost-justification for the data warehouse. Following are the reasons why farmers are used:

- The value of the work done by farmers is obvious and familiar. People see the work done by farmers on a day-by-day basis.

- The probability of success for a farmer is high. On a day-to-day basis, there is a good chance that the information found by the farmer is going to help in the decision process.

Stated differently, given that explorers strike out (or fail) a high percentage of time, it is risky to justify a data warehouse effort on the basis of the contributions of an explorer. In truth, the explorer might find nothing, at which point the whole data warehouse effort becomes circumspect.

There is a train of thought that farmers find little flakes of gold while explorers find diamonds. The farmer can be counted on to find endless amounts of small flakes of gold. Explorers, on the other hand, often find nothing. But when an explorer does find something, it is a nugget of great value.

Most management is risk-aversive. Therefore, when selling the capabilities of the data warehouse, it is often best to concentrate on the results that the farmer will obtain, not the explorer.

Summary

It is difficult to talk about the DSS end user. In fact, the DSS end user has very different characteristics that depend on the information needs of the end user. Following are the four different categories of the DSS end user:

- Farmers
- Explorers
- Miners
- Tourists

The differences between the end users show up in many places, such as the use of data across actively used data and inactively used data, and in terms of ROI analysis and cost justification.

CHAPTER 19

Data Warehouse Design Review Checklist

One of the most effective techniques for ensuring quality in the operational environment is the design review. Through a design review, errors can be detected and resolved prior to coding. The cost benefit of identifying errors early in the development life cycle is enormous.

In the operational environment, a design review is usually done on completion of the physical design of an application. The types of issues around which an operational design review centers are the following:

- Transaction performance
- Batch window adequacy
- System availability
- Capacity
- Project readiness
- User requirements satisfaction

Done properly in the operational environment, a design review can save significant resources and greatly increase user satisfaction. Most importantly, when a design review has been properly executed, major pieces of code do not have to be torn up and rewritten after the system has gone into production.

A design review is as applicable to the data warehouse environment as it is to the operational environment, with a few provisos.

One proviso is that systems are developed in the data warehouse environment in an iterative manner, where the requirements are discovered as a part of the development process. The classical operational environment is built under the well-defined system development life cycle (SDLC). Systems in the data warehouse environment are not built under the SDLC. Other differences between the development process in the operational environment and the data warehouse environment are the following:

- Development in the operational environment is done one application at a time. Systems for the data warehouse environment are built a subject area at a time.

- In the operational environment, there is a firm set of requirements that form the basis of operational design and development. In the data warehouse environment, there is seldom a firm understanding of processing requirements at the outset of DSS development.

- In the operational environment, transaction response time is a major and burning issue. In the data warehouse environment, transaction response time had better not be an issue.

- In the operational environment, the input from systems usually comes from sources external to the organization, most often from interaction with outside agencies. In the data warehouse environment, it usually comes from systems inside the organization where data is integrated from a wide variety of existing sources.

- In the operational environment, data is nearly all current-value (that is, data is accurate as of the moment of use). In the data warehouse environment, data is time-variant (that is, data is relevant to some one moment in time).

There are, then, some substantial differences between the operational and data warehouse environments, and these differences show up in the way the design review is conducted.

When to Do a Design Review

A design review in the data warehouse environment is done as soon as a major subject area has been designed and is ready to be added to the data warehouse environment. It does not need to be done for every new database that goes up. Instead, as whole, new major subject areas are added to the database, a design review becomes an appropriate activity.

Who Should Be in the Design Review?

The attendees at the design review include anyone who has a stake in the development, operation, or use of the DSS subject area being reviewed. Normally, this includes the following parties:

- The data administration (DA)
- The database administration (DBA)
- Programmers
- The DSS analysts
- End users other than the DSS analysts
- Operations
- Systems support
- Management

Of this group, by far the most important attendees are the end users and the DSS analysts.

One important benefit from having all the parties in the same room at the same time is the opportunity to short-circuit miscommunications. In an everyday environment where the end user talks to the liaison person who talks to the designer who talks to the programmer, there is ample opportunity for miscommunication and misinterpretation. When all the parties are gathered, direct conversations can occur that are beneficial to the health of the project being reviewed.

What Should the Agenda Be?

The subject for review for the data warehouse environment is any aspect of design, development, project management, or use that might prevent success. In short, any obstacle to success is relevant to the design review process. As a rule, the more controversial the subject, the more important it is that it be addressed during the review.

The questions that form the basis of the review process are discussed later in this chapter.

The Results

A data warehouse design review has three results:

- An appraisal to management of the issues, and recommendations as to further action

- A documentation of where the system is in the design, as of the moment of review

- An action item list that states specific objectives and activities that are a result of the review process

Administering the Review

The review is led by two people — a facilitator and a recorder. The facilitator is never the manager or the developer of the project being reviewed. If, by some chance, the facilitator is the project leader, the purpose of the review — from many perspectives — will have been defeated.

To conduct a successful review, the facilitator must be someone removed from the project for the following reasons:

- As an outsider, the facilitator provides an external perspective — a fresh look — at the system. This fresh look often reveals important insights that someone close to the design and development of the system is not capable of providing.

- As an outsider, a facilitator can offer criticism constructively. The criticism that comes from someone close to the development effort is usually taken personally and causes the design review to be reduced to a very base level.

A Typical Data Warehouse Design Review

1. Who is missing in the review? Is any group missing that ought to be in attendance? Are the following groups represented?
   - DA
   - DBA
   - Programming
   - DSS analysts
   - End users
   - Operations
   - Systems programming
   - Auditing
   - Management

Who is the official representative of each group?

ISSUE: The proper attendance at the design review by the proper people is vital to the success of the review regardless of any other factors. Easily, the most important attendee is the DSS analyst or the end user. Management may or may not attend at its discretion.

2. Have the end-user requirements been anticipated at all? If so, to what extent have they been anticipated? Does the end-user representative to the design review agree with the representation of requirements that has been done?

ISSUE: In theory, the DSS environment can be built without interaction with the end user — with no anticipation of end-user requirements. If there will be a need to change the granularity of data in the data warehouse environment, or if EIS or artificial intelligence processing is to be built on top of the data warehouse, then some anticipation of requirements is a healthy exercise to go through. As a rule, even when the DSS requirements are anticipated, the level of participation of the end users is very low, and the end result is very sketchy. Furthermore, a large amount of time should not be allocated to the anticipation of end-user requirements.

3. How much of the data warehouse has already been built in the data warehouse environment?

- Which subjects?
- What detail? What summarization?
- How much data — in bytes? In rows? In tracks or cylinders?
- How much processing?
- What is the growth pattern, independent of the project being reviewed?

ISSUE: The current status of the data warehouse environment has a great influence on the development project being reviewed. The very first development effort should be undertaken on a limited-scope, trial-and-error basis. There should be little critical processing or data in this phase. In addition, a certain amount of quick feedback and reiteration of development should be anticipated.

Later efforts of data warehouse development will have smaller margins for error.

4. How many major subjects have been identified from the data model? How many are currently implemented? How many are fully implemented? How many are being implemented by the development project being reviewed? How many will be implemented in the foreseeable future?

ISSUE: As a rule, the data warehouse environment is implemented one subject at a time. The first few subjects should be considered almost as experiments. Later subject implementation should reflect the lessons learned from earlier development efforts.

5. Does any major DSS processing (that is, data warehouse) exist outside the data warehouse environment? If so, what is the chance of conflict or overlap? What migration plan is there for DSS data and processing outside the data warehouse environment? Does the end user understand the migration that will have to occur? In what time frame will the migration be done?

ISSUE: Under normal circumstances, it is a major mistake to have only part of the data warehouse in the data warehouse environment and other parts out of the data warehouse environment. Only under the most exceptional circumstances should a "split" scenario be allowed. (One of those circumstances is a distributed DSS environment.)

If part of the data warehouse, in fact, does exist outside the data warehouse environment, there should be a plan to bring that part of the DSS world back into the data warehouse environment.

6. Have the major subjects that have been identified been broken down into lower levels of detail?

- Have the keys been identified?
- Have the attributes been identified?
- Have the keys and attributes been grouped together?
- Have the relationships between groupings of data been identified?
- Have the time variances of each group been identified?

ISSUE: There needs to be a data model that serves as the intellectual heart of the data warehouse environment. The data model normally has three levels — a high-level model where entities and relationships are identified; a midlevel where keys, attributes, and relationships are identified; and a low level, where database design can be done. While not all of the data needs to be modeled down to the lowest level of detail in order for the DSS environment to begin to be built, at least the high-level model must be complete.

7. Is the design discussed in question 6 periodically reviewed? (How often? Informally? Formally?) What changes occur as a result of the review? How is end-user feedback channeled to the developer?

ISSUE: From time to time, the data model needs to be updated to reflect changing business needs of the organization. As a rule, these changes are incremental in nature. It is very unusual to have a revolutionary change. There needs to be an assessment of the impact of these changes on both existing data warehouse data and planned data ware-house data.

8. Has the operational system of record been identified?

   - Has the source for every attribute been identified?
   - Have the conditions under which one attribute or another will be the source been identified?
   - If there is no source for an attribute, have default values been identified?
   - Has a common measure of attribute values been identified for those data attributes in the data warehouse environment?
   - Has a common encoding structure been identified for those attributes in the data warehouse environment?
   - Has a common key structure in the data warehouse environment been identified? Where the system of record key does not meet the conditions for the DSS key structure, has a conversion path been identified?
   - If data comes from multiple sources, has the logic to determine the appropriate value been identified?
   - Has the technology that houses the system of record been identified?
   - Will any attribute have to be summarized on entering the data warehouse?
   - Will multiple attributes have to be aggregated on entering the data warehouse?
   - Will data have to be resequenced on passing into the data warehouse?

   ISSUE: After the data model is built, the system of record is identified. The system of record normally resides in the operational environment. The system of record represents the best source of existing data in sup-port of the data model. The issues of integration are very much a factor in defining the system of record.

9. Has the frequency of extract processing — from the operational system of record to the data warehouse environment — been identified? How will the extract processing identify changes to the operational data from the last time an extract process was run?

   - By looking at time-stamped data?
   - By changing operational application code?
   - By looking at a log file? An audit file?
   - By looking at a delta file?
   - By rubbing "before" and "after" images together?

ISSUE: The frequency of extract processing is an issue because of the resources required in refreshment, the complexity of refreshment processing, and the need to refresh data on a timely basis. The usefulness of data warehouse data is often related to how often the data warehouse data is refreshed.

One of the most complex issues — from a technical perspective — is determining what data is to be scanned for extract processing. In some cases, the operational data that needs to pass from one environment to the next is straightforward. In other cases, it is not clear at all just what data should be examined as a candidate for populating the data warehouse environment.

10. What volume of data will normally be contained in the DSS environment? If the volume of data is large:

- Will multiple levels of granularity be specified?
- Will data be compacted?
- Will data be purged periodically?
- Will data be moved to near-line storage? At what frequency?

ISSUE: In addition to the volumes of data processed by extraction, the designer needs to concern himself or herself with the volume of data actually in the data warehouse environment. The analysis of the volume of data in the data warehouse environment leads directly to the subject of the granularity of data in the data warehouse environment and the possibility of multiple levels of granularity.

11. What data will be filtered out of the operational environment as extract processing is done to create the data warehouse environment?

ISSUE: It is very unusual for all operational data to be passed to the DSS environment. Almost every operational environment contains data that is relevant only to the operational environment. This data should not be passed to the data warehouse environment.

12. What software will be used to feed the data warehouse environment?

- Has the software been thoroughly shaken out?
- What bottlenecks are there or might there be?
- Is the interface one-way or two-way?
- What technical support will be required?
- What volume of data will pass through the software?
- What monitoring of the software will be required?
- What alterations to the software will be periodically required?
- What outage will the alterations entail?

- How long will it take to install the software?
- Who will be responsible for the software?
- When will the software be ready for full-blown use?

ISSUE: The data warehouse environment is capable of handling a large number of different types of software interfaces. The amount of break-in time and "infrastructure" time, however, should not be underestimated. The DSS architect must not assume that the linking of the data warehouse environment to other environments will necessarily be straightforward and easy.

13. What software interface will be required for the feeding of DSS departmental and individual processing out of the data warehouse environment?

- Has the interface been thoroughly tested?
- What bottlenecks might exist?
- Is the interface one-way or two-way?
- What technical support will be required?
- What traffic of data across the interface is anticipated?
- What monitoring of the interface will be required?
- What alterations to the interface will there be?
- What outage is anticipated as a result of alterations to the interface?
- How long will it take to install the interface?
- Who will be responsible for the interface?
- When will the interface be ready for full-scale utilization?

14. What physical organization of data will be used in the data warehouse environment? Can the data be directly accessed? Can it be sequentially accessed? Can indexes be easily and cheaply created?

ISSUE: The designer needs to review the physical configuration of the data warehouse environment to ensure that adequate capacity will be available and that the data, once in the environment, will be able to be manipulated in a responsive manner.

15. How easy will it be to add more storage to the data warehouse environment at a later point in time? How easy will it be to reorganize data within the data warehouse environment at a later point in time?

ISSUE: No data warehouse is static, and no data warehouse is fully specified at the initial moment of design. It is normal to make corrections in design throughout the life of the data warehouse environment. To construct a data warehouse environment either where midcourse corrections cannot be made or are awkward to make is to have a faulty design.

16. What is the likelihood that data in the data warehouse environment will need to be restructured frequently (that is, columns added, dropped, or enlarged, keys modified, and so on)? What effect will these activities of restructuring have on ongoing processing in the data warehouse?

    ISSUE: Given the volume of data found in the data warehouse environment, restructuring it is not a trivial issue. In addition, with archival data, restructuring after a certain moment in time often becomes a logical impossibility.

17. What are the expected levels of performance in the data warehouse environment? Has a DSS service-level agreement been drawn up either formally or informally?

    ISSUE: Unless a DSS service-level agreement has been formally drawn up, it is impossible to measure whether performance objectives are being met. The DSS service-level agreement should cover both DSS performance levels and downtime. Typical DSS service-level agreements include such information as the following:

    ■ Average performance during peak hours per units of data

    ■ Average performance during off-peak hours per units of data

    ■ Worst performance levels during peak hours per units of data

    ■ Worst performance during off-peak hours per units of data

    ■ System availability standards

    One of the difficulties of the DSS environment is measuring performance. Unlike the operational environment, where performance can be measured in absolute terms, DSS processing needs to be measured in relation to the following:

    ■ How much processing the individual request is for

    ■ How much processing is going on concurrently

    ■ How many users are on the system at the moment of execution

18. What are the expected levels of availability? Has an availability agreement been drawn up for the data warehouse environment, either formally or informally?

    ISSUE: (See the issue for question 17.)

19. How will the data in the data warehouse environment be indexed or accessed?

    ■ Will any table have more than four indexes?

    ■ Will any table be hashed?

- Will any table have only the primary key indexed?
- What overhead will be required to maintain the index?
- What overhead will be required to load the index initially?
- How often will the index be used?
- Can or should the index be altered to serve a wider use?

ISSUE: Data in the data warehouse environment needs to be accessed efficiently and in a flexible manner. Unfortunately, the heuristic nature of data warehouse processing is such that the need for indexes is unpredictable. The result is that the accessing of data in the data warehouse environment must not be taken for granted. As a rule, a multitiered approach to managing the access of data warehouse data is optimal:

- The hashed or primary key should satisfy most accesses.
- Secondary indexes should satisfy other popular access patterns.
- Temporary indexes should satisfy the occasional access.
- Extraction and subsequent indexing of a subset of data warehouse data should satisfy infrequent or once-in-a-lifetime accesses of data.

In any case, data in the data warehouse environment should not be stored in partitions so large that they cannot be indexed freely.

20. What volumes of processing in the data warehouse environment are to be expected? What about peak periods? What will the profile of the average day look like? The peak rate?

    ISSUE: Not only should the volume of data in the data warehouse environment be anticipated, but the volume of processing should be anticipated as well.

21. What level of granularity of data in the data warehouse environment will there be?

    - A high level?
    - A low level?
    - Multiple levels?
    - Will rolling summarization be done?
    - Will there be a level of true archival data?
    - Will there be a living-sample level of data?

    ISSUE: Clearly, the most important design issue in the data warehouse environment is that of granularity of data and the possibility of multiple levels of granularity. In other words, if the granularity of the data warehouse environment is done properly, then all other issues become straightforward. If the granularity of data in the data warehouse environment is not designed properly, then all other design issues become complex and burdensome.

22. What purge criteria for data in the data warehouse environment will there be? Will data be truly purged, or will it be compacted and archived elsewhere? What legal requirements are there? What audit requirements are there?

   ISSUE: Even though data in the DSS environment is archival and of necessity has a low probability of access, it nevertheless has some probability of access (otherwise, it should not be stored). When the probability of access reaches zero (or approaches zero), the data needs to be purged. Given that volume of data is one of the most burning issues in the data warehouse environment, purging data that is no longer useful is one of the more important aspects of the data warehouse environment.

23. What total processing capacity requirements are there?

   - For initial implementation?
   - For the data warehouse environment at maturity?

   ISSUE: Granted that capacity requirements cannot be planned down to the last bit, it is worthwhile to at least estimate how much capacity will be required, just in case there is a mismatch between needs and what will be available.

24. What relationships between major subject areas will be recognized in the data warehouse environment? Will their implementation:

   - Cause foreign keys to be kept up-to-date?
   - Make use of artifacts?

   What overhead is required in the building and maintenance of the relationship in the data warehouse environment?

   ISSUE: One of the most important design decisions the data warehouse designer makes is that of how to implement relationships between data in the data warehouse environment. Data relationships are almost never implemented the same way in the data warehouse as they are in the operational environment.

25. Do the data structures internal to the data warehouse environment make use of:

   - Arrays of data?
   - Selective redundancy of data?
   - Merging of tables of data?
   - Creation of commonly used units of derived data?

ISSUE: Even though operational performance is not an issue in the data warehouse environment, performance is nevertheless an issue. The designer needs to consider the design techniques listed previously when they can reduce the total amount of I/O consumed. The techniques listed previously are classical physical denormalization techniques. Because data is not updated in the data warehouse environment, there are very few restrictions on what can and can't be done.

The factors that determine when one or the other design technique can be used include the following:

- The predictability of occurrences of data
- The predictability of the pattern of access of data
- The need to gather artifacts of data

26. How long will a recovery take? Is computer operations prepared to execute a full data warehouse database recovery? A partial recovery? Will operations periodically practice recovery so that it will be prepared in the event of a need for recovery? What level of preparedness is exhibited by:

- Systems support?
- Applications programming?
- The DBA?
- The DA?

For each type of problem that can arise, is it clear whose responsibility the problem is?

ISSUE: As in operational systems, the designer must be prepared for the outages that occur during recovery. The frequency of recovery, the length of time required to bring the system back up, and the domino effect that can occur during an outage must all be considered.

Have instructions been prepared, tested, and written? Have these instructions been kept up-to-date?

27. What level of preparation is there for reorganization or restructuring of:

- Operations?
- Systems support?
- Applications programming?
- The DBA?
- The DA?

Have written instructions and procedures been set and tested? Are they up-to-date? Will they be kept up-to-date?

ISSUE: (See the issue for question 26.)

28. What level of preparation is there for the loading of a database table by:
    - Operations?
    - Systems support?
    - Applications programming?
    - The DBA?
    - The DA?

    Have written instructions and procedures been made and tested? Are they up-to-date? Will they be kept up-to-date?

    ISSUE: The time and resources for loading can be considerable. This estimate needs to be made carefully and early in the development life cycle.

29. What level of preparation is there for the loading of a database index by:
    - Operations?
    - Systems support?
    - Applications programming?
    - The DBA?
    - The DA?

    ISSUE: (See issue for question 28.)

30. If there is ever a controversy as to the accuracy of a piece of data in the data warehouse environment, how will the conflict be resolved? Has ownership (or at least source identification) been done for each unit of data in the data warehouse environment? Will ownership be able to be established if the need arises? Who will address the issues of ownership? Who will be the final authority as to the issues of ownership?

    ISSUE: Ownership or stewardship of data is an essential component of success in the data warehouse environment. It is inevitable that at some moment in time the contents of a database will come into question. The designer needs to plan in advance for this eventuality.

31. How will corrections to data be made once data is placed in the data warehouse environment? How frequently will corrections be made? Will corrections be monitored? If there is a pattern of regularly occurring changes, how will corrections at the source (that is, operational) level be made?

    ISSUE: On an infrequent, nonscheduled basis, changes made need to be made in the data warehouse environment. If there appears to be a pattern to these changes, then the DSS analyst needs to investigate what is wrong in the operational system.

32. Will public summary data be stored separately from normal primitive DSS data? How much public summary data will there be? Will the algorithm required to create public summary data be stored?

    ISSUE: Even though the data warehouse environment contains primitive data, it is normal for there to be public summary data in the data warehouse environment as well. The designer needs to have prepared a logical place for this data to reside.

33. What security requirements will there be for the databases in the data warehouse environment? How will security be enforced?

    ISSUE: The access of data becomes an issue, especially as the detailed data becomes summarized or aggregated, where trends become apparent. The designer needs to anticipate the security requirements and prepare the data warehouse environment for them.

34. What audit requirements are there? How will audit requirements be met?

    ISSUE: As a rule, a system audit can be done at the data warehouse level, but this is almost always a mistake. Instead, detailed record audits are best done at the system-of-record level.

35. Will compaction of data be used? Has the overhead of compacting and decompacting data been considered? What is the overhead? What are the savings in terms of DASD for compacting and decompacting data?

    ISSUE: On one hand, compaction or encoding of data can save significant amounts of space. On the other hand, both compacting and encoding data require CPU cycles as data is decompacted or decoded on access. The designer needs to make a thorough investigation of these issues and a deliberate trade-off in the design.

36. Will encoding of data be done? Has the overhead of encoding and decoding been considered? What, in fact, is the overhead?

    ISSUE: (See the issue for question 35.)

37. Will metadata be stored for the data warehouse environment?

    ISSUE: Metadata needs to be stored with any archival data as a matter of policy. There is nothing more frustrating than an analyst trying to solve a problem using archival data when he or she does not know the meaning of the contents of a field being analyzed. This frustration can be alleviated by storing the semantics of data with the data as it is archived. Over time, it is absolutely normal for the contents and structure of data in the data warehouse environment to change. Keeping track of the changing definition of data is something the designer should make sure is done.

38. Will reference tables be stored in the data warehouse environment?

ISSUE: (See the issue for question 37.)

39. What catalog or dictionary will be maintained for the data warehouse environment? Who will maintain it? How will it be kept up-to-date? To whom will it be made available?

ISSUE: Not only is keeping track of the definition of data over time an issue, but keeping track of data currently in the data warehouse is important as well.

40. Will update (as opposed to loading and access of data) be allowed in the data warehouse environment? (Why? How much? Under what circumstances? On an exception-only basis?)

ISSUE: If any updating is allowed on a regular basis in the data warehouse environment, the designer should ask why. The only update that should occur should be on an exception basis and for only small amounts of data. Any exception to this severely compromises the efficacy of the data warehouse environment.

When updates are done (if, in fact, they are done at all), they should be run in a private window when no other processing is done and when there is slack time on the processor.

41. What time lag will there be in getting data from the operational to the data warehouse environment? Will the time lag ever be less than 24 hours? If so, why and under what conditions? Will the passage of data from the operational to the data warehouse environment be a "push" or a "pull" process?

ISSUE: As a matter of policy, any time lag less than 24 hours should be questioned. As a rule, if a time lag of less than 24 hours is required, it is a sign that the developer is building operational requirements into the data warehouse. The flow of data through the data warehouse environment should always be a pull process, where data is pulled into the warehouse environment when it is needed, rather than being pushed into the warehouse environment when it is available.

42. What logging of data warehouse activity will be done? Who will have access to the logs?

ISSUE: Most DSS processing does not require logging. If an extensive amount of logging is required, it is usually a sign of a lack of understanding of what type of processing is occurring in the data warehouse environment.

43. Will any data other than public summary data flow to the data warehouse environment from the departmental or individual level? If so, describe it.

ISSUE: Only on rare occasions should public summary data come from sources other than departmental or individual levels of processing. If much public summary data is coming from other sources, the analyst should ask why.

44. What external data (that is, data other than that generated by a company's internal sources and systems) will enter the data warehouse environment? Will it be specially marked? Will its source be stored with the data? How frequently will the external data enter the system? How much of it will enter? Will an unstructured format be required? What happens if the external data is found to be inaccurate?

    ISSUE: Even though there are legitimate sources of data other than a company's operational systems, if much data is entering externally, the analyst should ask why. Inevitably, there is much less flexibility with the content and regularity of availability of external data, although external data represents an important resource that should not be ignored.

45. What facilities will exist that will help the departmental and the individual user to locate data in the data warehouse environment?

    ISSUE: One of the primary features of the data warehouse is ease of accessibility of data. And the first step in the accessibility of data is the initial location of the data.

46. Will there be an attempt to mix operational and DSS processing on the same machine at the same time? If so:

    - Why?
    - How much processing?
    - How much data?

    ISSUE: For a multitude of reasons, it makes little sense to mix operational and DSS processing on the same machine at the same time. Only where there are small amounts of data and small amounts of processing should there be a mixture. But these are not the conditions under which the data warehouse environment is most cost-effective. See my previous book, *Data Architecture: The Information Paradigm* (Wellesey, MA: QED/Wiley, 1992) for an in-depth discussion of this issue.

47. How much data will flow back to the operational level from the data warehouse level? At what rate? At what volume? Under what response time constraints? Will the flowback be summarized data or individual units of data?

    ISSUE: As a rule, data flows from the operational to the warehouse level to the departmental to the individual levels of processing. There are some notable exceptions. As long as not too much data "backflows," and as long as the backflow is done in a disciplined fashion, there usually is no problem. If there is a lot of data engaged in backflow, then a red flag should be raised.

48. How much repetitive processing will occur against the data warehouse environment? Will precalculation and storage of derived data save processing time?

     ISSUE: It is absolutely normal for the data warehouse environment to have some amount of repetitive processing done against it. If only repetitive processing is done, however, or if no repetitive processing is planned, the designer should question why.

49. How will major subjects be partitioned? (By year? By geography? By functional unit? By product line?) Just how finely does the partitioning of the data break the data up?

     ISSUE: Given the volume of data that is inherent to the data warehouse environment and the unpredictable use of the data, it is mandatory that data warehouse data be partitioned into physically small units that can be managed independently. The design issue is not whether partitioning is to be done. Instead, the design issue is how partitioning is to be accomplished. In general, partitioning is done at the application level rather than the system level.

     The partitioning strategy should be reviewed with the following in mind:

     - Current volume of data
     - Future volume of data
     - Current use of data
     - Future use of data
     - Partitioning of other data in the warehouse
     - Use of other data
     - Volatility of the structure of data

50. Will sparse indexes be created? Would they be useful?

     ISSUE: Sparse indexes created in the right place can save huge amounts of processing. By the same token, sparse indexes require a fair amount of overhead in their creation and maintenance. The designer of the data warehouse environment should consider their use.

51. What temporary indexes will be created? How long will they be kept? How large will they be?

     ISSUE: (See the issue for question 50, except as it applies to temporary indexes.)

52. What documentation will there be at the departmental and individual levels? What documentation will there be of the interfaces between the data warehouse environment and the departmental environment? Between the departmental and the individual environment? Between the data warehouse environment and the individual environment?

ISSUE: Given the free-form nature of processing in the departmental and the individual environments, it is unlikely that there will be much in the way of available documentation. Documentation of the relationships between the environments is important for the reconcilability of data.

53. Will the user be charged for departmental processing? For individual processing? Who will be charged for data warehouse processing?

ISSUE: It is important that users have their own budgets and be charged for resources used. The instant that processing becomes "free," it is predictable that there will be massive misuse of resources. A chargeback system instills a sense of responsibility in the use of resources.

54. If the data warehouse environment is to be distributed, have the common parts of the warehouse been identified? How are they to be managed?

ISSUE: In a distributed data warehouse environment, some of the data will necessarily be tightly controlled. The data needs to be identified up-front by the designer and metadata controls put in place.

55. What monitoring of the data warehouse will there be? At the table level? At the row level? At the column level?

ISSUE: The use of data in the warehouse needs to be monitored to determine the dormancy rate. Monitoring must occur at the table level, the row level, and the column level. In addition, monitoring of transaction needs to occur as well.

56. Will Class IV ODS be supported? How much performance impact will there be on the data warehouse to support Class IV ODS processing?

ISSUE: Class IV ODS is fed from the data warehouse. The data needed to create the profile in the Class IV ODS is found in the data warehouse.

57. What testing facility will there be for the data warehouse?

ISSUE: Testing in the data warehouse is not the same level of importance as in the operational transaction environment. But occasionally there is a need for testing, especially when new types of data are being loaded and when there are large volumes of data.

58. What DSS applications will be fed from the data warehouse? How much volume of data will be fed?

ISSUE: DSS applications, just like data marts, are fed from the data warehouse. There are the issues of when the data warehouse will be examined, how often it will be examined, and what performance impact there will be for the analysis.

59. Will an exploration warehouse and/or a data mining warehouse be fed from the data warehouse? If not, will exploration processing be done directly in the data warehouse? If so, what resources will be required to feed the exploration and/or data mining warehouse?

ISSUE: The creation of an exploration warehouse and/or a data mining data warehouse can greatly alleviate the resource burden on the data warehouse. An exploration warehouse is needed when the frequency of exploration is such that statistical analysis starts to have an impact on data warehouse resources.

The issues here are the frequency of update and the volume of data that needs to be updated. In addition, the need for an incremental update of the data warehouse occasionally arises.

60. What resources are required for loading data into the data warehouse on an ongoing basis? Will the load be so large that it cannot fit into the window of opportunity? Will the load have to be parallelized?

    ISSUE: Occasionally there is so much data that needs to be loaded into the data warehouse that the window for loading is not large enough. When the load is too large, there are several options:

    ■ Creating a staging area where much preprocessing of the data to be loaded can be done independently

    ■ Parallelizing the load stream so that the elapsed time required for loading is shrunk to the point that the load can be done with normal processing

    ■ Editing or summarizing the data to be loaded so that the actual load is smaller

61. To what extent has the midlevel model of the subject areas been created? Is there a relationship between the different midlevel models?

    ISSUE: Each major subject area has its own midlevel data model. As a rule, the midlevel data models are created only as the iteration of development needs to have them created. In addition, the midlevel data models are related in the same way that the major subject areas are related.

62. Is the level of granularity of the data warehouse sufficiently low enough to service all the different architectural components that will be fed from the data warehouse?

    ISSUE: The data warehouse feeds many different architectural components. The level of granularity of the data warehouse must be sufficiently low to feed the lowest level of data needed anywhere in the corporate information factory (CIF). This is why it is said that the data in the data warehouse is at the lowest common denominator.

63. If the data warehouse will be used to store eBusiness and clickstream data, to what extent does the Granularity Manager filter the data?

    ISSUE: The Web-based environment generates a huge amount of data. The data that is generated is at much too low a level of granularity. To summarize and aggregate the data before entering the data warehouse, the data is passed through a Granularity Manager. The Granularity

Manager greatly reduces the volume of data that finds its way into the data warehouse.

64. What dividing line is used to determine what data is to be placed on disk storage and what data is to be placed on alternate storage?

    ISSUE: The general approach that most organizations take in the placement of data on disk storage and data on alternate storage is to place the most current data on disk storage and to place older data on alternate storage. Typically, disk storage may hold two years' worth of data, and alternate storage may hold all data that is older than two years.

65. How will movement of data to and from disk storage and alternate storage be managed?

    ISSUE: Most organizations have software that manages the traffic to and from alternate storage. The software is commonly known as a cross-media storage manager (CMSM).

66. If the data warehouse is a global data warehouse, what data will be stored locally and what data will be stored globally?

    ISSUE: When a data warehouse is global, some data is stored centrally and other data is stored locally. The dividing line is determined by the use of the data.

67. For a global data warehouse, is there assurance that data can be transported across international boundaries?

    ISSUE: Some countries have laws that do not allow data to pass beyond their boundaries. The data warehouse that is global must ensure that it is not in violation of international laws.

68. For ERP environments, has it been determined where the data warehouse will be located — inside the ERP software or outside the ERP environment?

    ISSUE: Many factors determine where the data warehouse should be placed:

    - Does the ERP vendor support the data warehouse?
    - Can non-ERP data be placed inside the data warehouse?
    - What analytical software can be used on the data warehouse if the data warehouse is placed inside the ERP environment?
    - If the data warehouse is placed inside the ERP environment, what DBMS can be used?

69. Can alternate storage be processed independently?

    ISSUE: Older data is placed in alternate storage. It is often quite useful to be able to process the data found in alternate storage independently of any consideration of data placed on disk storage.

70. Is the development methodology that is being used for development a spiral development approach or a classical waterfall approach?

    ISSUE: The spiral development approach is always the correct development approach for the data warehouse environment. The waterfall SDLC approach is never the appropriate approach.

71. Will an ETL tool be used for moving data from the operational environment to the data warehouse environment, or will the transformation be done manually?

    ISSUE: In almost every case, using a tool of automation to transform data into the data warehouse environment makes sense. Only where there is a very small amount of data to be loaded into the data warehouse environment should the loading of the data warehouse be done manually.

72. Will unstructured data be entered into the data warehouse?

    ISSUE: Unstructured data can be very valuable in the data warehouse. But integrating unstructured data is difficult to do. To be useful, unstructured data must be edited and organized before it can be entered into the data warehouse. The editing includes the removal of stop words and the stemming of words. In addition, identifiers must be found. There are two kinds of useful identifiers: identifiers and close identifiers. *Identifiers* are those terms which serve to specifically identify an account. Typical identifiers are Social Security number, license number, and employee number. Typical *close identifiers* are name, address, and other descriptive information.

    In addition to text being edited, unstructured data needs to be screened. Much of text is what can be termed "blather." Blather does not contribute to the business intelligence and does not belong in the data warehouse.

73. Will corporate communications be organized before being placed in the data warehouse?

    ISSUE: Corporate communications can be very valuable to the data warehouse. Typically, corporate communications are useful for the purpose of complementing CRM data. However, in order for corporate communications to be useful, it must be edited and organized according to identifiers. In addition, it helps to sort through the communications, identifying which ones are critical and which ones are non-critical.

74. Is there ever a need for referring back to the unstructured environment?

    ISSUE: On occasion, there is the need to refer back to the unstructured environment. The problem is that there is no guarantee that the data found in the unstructured environment will be there when referenced. Emails are deleted. Text files are erased. Data changes location. What is the contingency plan for finding data once displaced in the unstructured environment?

75. Unstructured data in the data warehouse environment can take up large amounts of space. How can the space required for unstructured data in the structured environment be minimized?

    ISSUE: Data warehouses grow large with no help from anyone. But when unstructured data is added to a data warehouse, the potential for very large volumes of data grows. Several techniques can be employed to minimize the space required for unstructured data, including the following:

    ▪ The use of simple indexes. If a unit of unstructured data is not required online, simply create an index that points to where the unstructured data is found.

    ▪ Use the first n bytes of an unstructured document to allow the user to look at what the document look like from the beginning. In doing so, it may not be necessary to store the entire document.

    ▪ Carry context surrounding keywords. The context surrounding key words tells the user little about the document and a lot about the context within which keywords are found and used.

76. Is the data warehouse regularly monitored in terms of use?

    ISSUE: As data warehouses grow large, the volumes of data contained inside them starts to exhibit different patterns of use. Some data is used infrequently; other data is used frequently. It is very important that the data administrator knows when this division in the patterns of use of data starts to occur.

77. Is data monitored by column for use?

    ISSUE: It is not enough to monitor the use of data by rows. Occasionally, columns of data that are never used will be included in a data warehouse. It makes sense to remove those columns.

78. How many resources does the data monitor consume?

    ISSUE: Typically, the monitor provided by the DBMS vendor uses huge amounts of resources. A common practice is to turn off the monitor during peak-period processing. Unfortunately, the peak period is the very moment when you want the monitor to be turned on. Third-party software is usually much more efficient in monitoring the data warehouse than vendor-supplied software.

79. Is data monitored by row for use?

    ISSUE: The most common way of measuring use is by row. Rows of data that are not being accessed should be removed from the data warehouse to near-line storage or archival storage.

80. How will data be managed in terms of transmitting the data from disk storage to near-line storage or from disk storage to archival storage?

    ISSUE: Will a CMSM be used? Will the transportation be done by hand? How long will the transportation be done by hand? What sort of operating window is required?

81. What signals the system that a query may be accessing data from near-line storage or archival storage?

    ISSUE: If the system waits until a query goes into execution, then the system has only awkward choices as to accessing data from near-line storage or archival storage. It is much better if the end user submits a queuing request before the query is submitted. An alternative is to parse and queue requests that will look at data from the near-line environment.

82. What rate of growth will there be for the data?

    ISSUE: Not only is a large amount of data needed for the data warehouse, but the data's growth is an issue as well. It is wise to anticipate growth and make sure that there is space enough before the space is needed.

83. Will a miltidimensional database design be used for the data warehouse?

    ISSUE: Miltidimensional design is for data marts and other analytical structures. Miltidimensional design does not fit with the data warehouse.

84. Will statistical analysis be done to any extent in the data warehouse?

    ISSUE: If statistical analysis will be done to any extent in a data warehouse, strong consideration should be given to an exploration warehouse.

85. Will external data be entered into the data warehouse for the purpose of use in statistical analysis?

    ISSUE: If external data is being placed in the data warehouse for the purpose of statistical analysis, it may make sense to build a separate exploration warehouse and put the external data in the exploration warehouse.

86. Are data marts being placed on the same physical processor as the data warehouse?

    ISSUE: For a variety of reasons, it makes almost no sense to place data marts on the same physical processor as the data warehouse. Because of the differences in work load, the cost of the machine cycles, and the volumes of data that are collected there, moving data marts to a separate processor always makes sense.

    In fact, moving data marts to separate processors from other data marts usually makes sense. By moving data marts to separate processors, different organizational units can be assigned to a processor and can take ownership of the data and the processing that occurs inside the data mart.

87. Has the data velocity been calculated for a data warehouse? Does there need to be a higher velocity?

    ISSUE: Data has velocity as it passes through the data warehouse. On occasion, it is necessary to push the data through the data warehouse as quickly as possible. When that is the case, the cost of high velocity can be quite high. The business case for high velocity needs to be examined. On occasion, the need for high velocity may be a symptom of the building of operational systems in the data warehouse environment. If that is the case, the operational processing needs to be placed elsewhere.

88. Is clickstream data being entered into the data warehouse? If so, is the clickstream data being passed through the Granularity Manager?

    ISSUE: Clickstream data is data that is generated by the Web environment. Approximately 90 percent of clickstream data needs to be eliminated or consolidated before it is entered into the data warehouse.

89. Is clickstream data entered directly into the data warehouse without first passing through a Granularity Manager?

    ISSUE: Data should never enter the data warehouse directly from the Web environment without first passing through the Granularity Manager. There is enough data in the data warehouse without contaminating the data there with massive amounts of irrelevant detailed data.

90. Does data flow directly from the data warehouse to the Web environment?

    ISSUE: The proper flow of data is from the data warehouse to the ODS environment. Once in the ODS environment, data is collected and then is available to the Web-based environment. In almost every case, the flow of data from the data warehouse environment to the Web is a very bad idea. The data warehouse is not geared to support the response times needed by the Web environment.

91. Is "real-time" data warehousing being done in the data warehouse?

    ISSUE: Real-time data warehousing is best done in the ODS environment. The ODS environment is physically separate from the data warehouse environment. While it is true that the data warehouse environment can withstand some small amounts of real-time processing at certain slow periods of the day, to make a real-time processing environment out of the data warehouse is a strategic mistake.

92. Are profile records being collected and created in the ODS environment?

    ISSUE: One of the best uses of the ODS environment is to collect detailed transaction data in the data warehouse and then use that detailed data for the creation of a profile record in the ODS. Once the profile record is created in the ODS, the profile data is ready in milliseconds for access, from the Web environment or elsewhere.

93. Is data being used directly from the data warehouse?

ISSUE: Over time, the use of data from the data warehouse shifts from direct use to indirect use. If, after five years, there is still a lot of direct use of data from the data warehouse, then it may be time to ask the question, "Should we build some data marts of other analytical applications?"

94. Are end users being prevented from using data in the data warehouse?

ISSUE: While it is true that data from the data warehouse has few users, it is a bit extreme to say that no one should directly use the data in the data warehouse. Even in the mature days of a data warehouse, there will be a few cases where direct access to the data warehouse is needed and is a good thing to do.

95. Is data being monitored to see if patterns of use are starting to appear?

ISSUE: If patterns of use are starting to appear in the data warehouse, it is time to ask the question, "Should data marts or other forms of analytical processing be created?"

96. What kind of training are your end users receiving in the usage data warehouse?

ISSUE: In many cases, training your user on the capabilities of the data warehouse can pay very big dividends

97. How are your users being kept abreast of the changes that are being made in the data warehouse?

ISSUE: The data warehouse changes over time. New data and new features of the data warehouse may produce big benefits for your users, but not if your users don't know about what's new.

98. Is the data warehouse being used primarily by farmers or by explorers?

ISSUE: In the well-rounded data warehouse environment, there normally is a mixture of both farmers and explorers who use the data warehouse. If you are not using the data warehouse in multiple ways, then you are not getting your full money's worth from your data warehouse.

Summary

Design review is an important quality-assurance practice that can greatly increase the satisfaction of the user and reduce development and maintenance costs. Thoroughly reviewing the many aspects of a warehouse environment prior to building the warehouse is a sound practice. The review should focus on both detailed design and architecture.

Glossary

access the operation of seeking, reading, or writing data on a storage unit.

access method a technique used to transfer a physical record from or to a mass storage device.

access pattern the general sequence in which the data structure is accessed (for example, from tuple to tuple (row to row), from record to record, from segment to segment, and so forth).

accuracy a qualitative assessment of freedom from error or a quantitative measure of the magnitude of error, expressed as a function of relative error.

ad hoc processing one-time-only, casual access and manipulation of data on parameters never before used, usually done in a heuristic, iterative manner.

after image the snapshot of data placed on a log on the completion of a transaction.

agent of change   a motivating force large enough not to be denied, usually aging of systems, changes in technology, radical changes in requirements, and so forth.

algorithm   a set of statements organized to solve a problem in a finite number of steps.

alternate storage   storage other than disk-based storage used to hold bulk amounts of relatively inactive storage.

analytical processing   using the computer to produce an analysis for management decision, usually involving trend analysis, drill-down analysis, demographic analysis, profiling, and so forth.

application   a group of algorithms and data interlinked to support an organizational requirement.

application database   a collection of data organized to support a specific application.

archival database   a collection of data containing data of a historical nature. As a rule, archival data cannot be updated. Each unit of archival data is relevant to a moment in time, now passed.

artifact   a design technique used to represent referential integrity in the DSS environment. *See also* **decision-support system (DSS)**.

atomic   (1) data stored in a data warehouse; (2) the lowest level of process analysis.

atomic database   a database made up of primarily atomic data; a data warehouse; a DSS foundation database. *See also* **decision-support system (DSS)**.

atomic-level data   data with the lowest level of granularity. Atomic-level data sits in a data warehouse and is time-variant (that is, accurate as of some moment in time now passed).

attribute   a property that can assume values for entities or relationships. Entities can be assigned several attributes (for example, a tuple in a relationship consists of values). Some systems also allow relationships to have attributes as well.

audit trail   data that is available to trace activity, usually update activity.

backup   a file serving as a basis for the activity of backing up a database; Usually a snapshot of a database as of some previous moment in time.

batch   computer environment in which programs (usually long-running, sequentially oriented) access data exclusively, and user interaction is not allowed while the activity is occurring.

batch environment   a sequentially dominated mode of processing. In the batch environment, input is collected and stored for future processing. Once collected, the batch input is transacted sequentially against one or more databases.

before image   a snapshot of a record prior to update, usually placed on an activity log.

bitmap   a specialized form of an index indicating the existence or nonexistence of a condition for a group of blocks or records. Bitmaps are expensive to build and maintain, but provide very fast comparison and access facilities.

blocking   the combining of two or more physical records so that they are physically located together. The result of their physical colocation is that they can be accessed and fetched by a single execution of a machine instruction.

cache   a buffer usually built and maintained at the device level. Retrieving data out of a cache is much quicker than retrieving data out of a cylinder.

cardinality (of a relation)   the number of tuples (that is, rows) in a relation.

CASE   computer-aided software engineering.

checkpoint   an identified snapshot of the database or a point at which the transactions against the database have been frozen or have been quiesced.

checkpoint/restart a means of restarting a program at some point other than the beginning (for example, when a failure or interruption has occurred). *N* checkpoints may be used at intervals throughout an application program. At each of those points, sufficient information is stored to permit the program to be restored to the moment in time the checkpoint has been taken.

CLDS the facetiously named system development life cycle for analytical, DSS systems. CLDS is so named because, in fact, it is the reverse of the classical *systems development life cycle (SDLC)*.

clickstream data data generated in the Web environment that tracks the activity of the users of the Web site.

column a vertical table in which values are selected from the same domain. A row is made up of one or more columns.

commonality of data similar or identical data that occurs in different applications or systems. The recognition and management of commonality of data is one of the foundations of conceptual and physical database design.

Common Business Oriented Language (COBOL) a computer language for the business world. A very common language.

compaction a technique for reducing the number of bits required to represent data without losing the content of the data. With compaction, repetitive data is represented very concisely.

condensation the process of reducing the volume of data managed without reducing the logical consistency of the data. Condensation is essentially different from compaction.

contention the condition that occurs when two or more programs try to access the same data at the same time.

continuous time span data data organized so that a continuous definition of data over a span of time is represented by one or more records.

convenience field a field created in analytics for the convenience of the analyst. The convenience field consists of detailed data elements coming from a non-analytical source.

corporate information factory (CIF)   the framework that surrounds the data warehouse. Typically, it contains an ODS, a data warehouse, data marts, DSS applications, exploration warehouses, data mining warehouses, alternate storage, and so forth. *See also* **decision-support system (DSS)** and **operational data store (ODS)**.

CPU   central processing unit.

CPU-bound   the state of processing in which the computer can produce no more output because the CPU portion of the processor is being used at 100 percent capacity. When the computer is CPU-bound, typically the memory and storage processing units are less than 100 percent utilized. With modern DBMS, it is much more likely that the computer is I/O-bound, rather than CPU-bound. *See also* **database management system (DBMS)**.

CRM   customer relationship management, a popular DSS application designed to streamline customer and/or corporate relationships. *See also* **decision-support system (DSS)**.

cross-media storage manager (CMSM)   software whose purpose is to move data to and from disk storage and alternate storage.

current-value data   data whose accuracy is valid as of the moment of execution, as opposed to time-variant data.

DASD   *see* **direct access storage device**.

data   a recording of facts, concepts, or instructions on a storage medium for communication, retrieval, and processing by automatic means and presentation as information that is understandable by human beings.

data administrator (DA)   the individual or organization responsible for the specification, acquisition, and maintenance of data management software and the design, validation, and security of files or databases. The data model and the data dictionary are classically the charge of the DA.

database   a collection of interrelated data stored (often with controlled, limited redundancy) according to a schema. A database can serve single or multiple applications.

database administrator (DBA)   the organizational function charged with the day-to-day monitoring and care of the databases. The DBA function is more closely associated with physical database design than the DA is. *See also* **data administrator (DA)**.

database key   a unique value that exists for each record in a database. The value is often indexed, although it can be randomized or hashed.

database management system (DBMS)   a computer-based software system used to establish and manage data.

data-driven development   the approach to development that centers around identifying the commonality of data through a data model and building programs that have a broader scope than the immediate application. Data-driven development differs from classical application-oriented development.

data element   (1) an attribute of an entity; (2) a uniquely named and well-defined category of data that consists of data items and that is included in a record of an activity.

data item set (DIS)   a grouping of data items, each of which directly relates to the key of the grouping of data in which the data items reside. The data item set is found in the midlevel model.

data mart   a departmentalized structure of data feeding from the data warehouse where data is denormalized based on the department's need for information.

data mining   the process of analyzing large amounts of data in search of previously undiscovered business patterns.

data model   (1) the logical data structures, including operations and constraints provided by a DBMS for effective database processing; (2) the system used for the representation of data (for example, the ERD or relational model). *See also* **entity-relationship diagram (ERD)**.

data structure   a logical relationship among data elements that is designed to support specific data manipulation functions (trees, lists, and tables).

data velocity   the speed with which data passes through and populates an architecture.

data warehouse   a collection of integrated, subject-oriented databases designed to support the DSS function, where each unit of data is relevant to some moment in time. The data warehouse contains atomic data and lightly summarized data. *See also* **decision-support system (DSS)**.

data warehouse monitor   a monitor of the use of the data in a data warehouse.

decision-support system (DSS)   a system used to support managerial decisions. Usually DSS involves the analysis of many units of data in a heuristic fashion. As a rule, DSS processing does not involve the update of data.

decompaction   the opposite of compaction. Once data is stored in a compacted form, it must be decompacted to be used.

delta list   a list of the differences of data from one file to another.

denormalization   the technique of placing normalized data in a physical location that optimizes the performance of the system.

derived data   data whose existence depends on two or more occurrences of a major subject of the enterprise.

derived data element   a data element that is not necessarily stored, but that can be generated when needed (age, current date, and date of birth, for example).

design review   the quality-assurance process in which all aspects of a system are reviewed publicly prior to the striking of code.

dimension table   the place where extraneous data that relates to a fact table is placed in a miltidimensional table.

direct access   retrieval or storage of data by reference to its location on a volume. The access mechanism goes directly to the data in question, as is generally required with online use of data. Also called *random access* or *hashed access*.

direct access storage device (DASD) a data storage unit on which data can be accessed directly without having to progress through a serial file (such as a magnetic tape file). A disk unit is a direct-access storage device.

dormant data data that is very infrequently used.

download the stripping of data from one database to another based on the content of data found in the first database.

drill-down analysis the type of analysis where examination of a summary number leads to the exploration of the components of the sum.

DSS application an application whose foundation of data is the data warehouse.

dual database the practice of separating high-performance, transaction-oriented data from decision-support data.

dual database management systems the practice of using multiple database management systems to control different aspects of the database environment.

dumb terminal a device used to interact directly with the end user where all processing is done on a remote computer. A dumb terminal acts as a device that gathers data and displays data only.

eBusiness commerce conducted based on Web interactions.

encoding a shortening or abbreviation of the physical representation of a data value (for example, male = "M," female = "F").

enterprise resource planning (ERP) application software for processing transactions.

entity a person, place, or thing of interest to the data modeler at the highest level of abstraction.

entity-relationship diagram (ERD) a high-level data model; the schematic showing all the entities within the scope of integration and the direct relationship between those entities.

event   a signal that an activity of significance has occurred. An event is noted by the information system.

Executive Information Systems (EIS)   systems designed for the top executive, featuring drill-down analysis and trend analysis.

explorer   an individual who does not know what he or she wants at the outset of analysis.

extract/load/transformation (ELT)   the process of taking legacy application data and integrating it into the data warehouse.

exploration warehouse   a structure specifically designed for statistical processing that searches for business patterns.

external data   (1) data originating from other than the operational systems of a corporation; (2) data residing outside the central processing complex.

extract   the process of selecting data from one environment and transporting it to another environment.

extract/transform/load (ETL)   the process of finding data, integrating it, and placing it in a data warehouse.

fact table   the center of a star join table where data that has many occurrences will be located. *See also* **star join**.

Farmer   an individual who knows what he or she wants at the outset of analysis.

flat file   a collection of records containing no data aggregates, nested repeated data items, or groups of data items.

foreign key   an attribute that is not a primary key in a relational system, but whose values are the values of the primary key of another relation.

fourth-generation language   language or technology designed to allow the end user unfettered access to data.

functional decomposition   the division of operations into hierarchical functions (activities) that form the basis for procedures.

global data warehouse   a warehouse suited to the needs of the headquarters of a large corporation.

government information factory (GIF)   an architecture for the information systems of the government.

granularity   the level of detail contained in a unit of data. The more detail there is, the lower the level of granularity. The less detail there is, the higher the level of granularity.

Granularity Manager   the software or processes that edit and filter Web data as it flows into the data warehouse. The data that flows into the data warehouse environment from the Web environment is usually clickstream data that is stored in a Web log.

heuristic   the mode of analysis in which the next step is determined by the results of the current step of analysis. Used for decision-support processing.

identifier   an attribute used to pick out a row from a list of other rows.

image copy   a procedure in which a database is physically copied to another medium for the purposes of backup.

independently evolving distributed data warehouse   a data warehouse that evolves according to a set of local requirements.

index   the portion of the storage structure maintained to provide efficient access to a record when its index key item is known.

information   data that human beings assimilate and evaluate to solve a problem or make a decision.

integrity   the property of a database that ensures that the data contained in the database is as accurate and consistent as possible.

interactive   a mode of processing that combines some of the characteristics of online transaction processing (OLTP) and batch processing. In interactive processing, the end user interacts with data over which he or she has exclusive control. In addition, the end user can initiate background activity to be run against the data. *See also* **online transaction processing (OLTP).**

Internet   a network of users who have access to data and Web addresses around the world.

"is a type of"   an analytical tool used in abstracting data during the process of conceptual database design (for example, a cocker spaniel is a type of dog).

iterative analysis   the mode of processing in which the next step of processing depends on the results obtained by the existing step in execution; heuristic processing.

joint application design (JAD)   an organization of people, usually end users, who create and refine application system requirements.

judgment sample   a sample of data where data is accepted or rejected for the sample based on one or more parameters.

key   a data item or combination of data items used to identify or locate a record instance (or other similar data groupings).

key, primary   a unique attribute used to identify a single record in a database.

key, secondary   a non-unique attribute used to identify a class of records in a database.

living sample   a representative database typically used for heuristic, statistical, analytical processing in place of a large database. Periodically, the very large database is selectively stripped of data so that the resulting living sample database represents a cross-section of the very large database as of some moment in time.

load   to insert data values into a database that was previously empty.

local data warehouse   a data warehouse holding geographically local data in support of a global data warehouse.

lock manager   a part of technology that guarantees integrity of update of data as of some one moment in time.

log   a journal of activity.

logging   the automatic recording of data with regard to the access of the data, the updates to the data, and so forth

loss of identity   occurs when data is brought in from an external source and the identity of the external source is discarded (a common practice with microprocessor data).

magnetic tape   (1) the storage medium most closely associated with sequential processing; (2) a large ribbon on which magnetic images are stored and retrieved.

master file   a file that holds the system of record for a given set of data (usually bound by an application). *See also* **system of record.**

metadata   (1) data about data; (2) the description of the structure, content, keys, indexes, and so forth, of data.

microprocessor   a small processor serving the needs of a single user.

migration   the process by which frequently used items of data are moved to more readily accessible areas of storage and infrequently used items of data are moved to less readily accessible areas of storage.

million instructions per second (mips)   the standard measurement of processor speed for minicomputers and mainframe computers.

miner   an individual who uses statistical techniques for analysis of data.

miltidimensional processing   data mart processing based on a star join structuring of data. *See also* **star join.**

near-line storage   data that is not stored on disk but is nevertheless still accessible; used to hold very large amounts of relatively inactive data.

online analytical processing (OLAP)   departmental processing for the data mart environment.

online storage   storage devices and storage media where data can be accessed in a direct fashion.

online transaction processing (OLTP)   the high-performance transaction-processing environment.

operational data   data used to support the daily processing a company does.

operational data store (ODS)   a hybrid structure designed to support both operational transaction processing and analytical processing.

operations   the department charged with running the computer.

optical disk   a storage medium using lasers as opposed to magnetic devices. Optical disk is typically write-only, is much less expensive per byte than magnetic storage, and is highly reliable.

overflow   (1) the condition in which a record or a segment cannot be stored in its home address because the address is already occupied, in which case, the data is placed in another location referred to as overflow; (2) the area of DASD where data is sent when the overflow condition is triggered. *See also* **direct access storage device (DASD)**.

ownership   the responsibility for updating operational data.

page   (1) a basic unit of data on DASD; (2) a basic unit of storage in main memory.

parameter   an elementary data value used as a criterion for qualification, usually of data searches or in the control of modules.

partition   a segmentation technique in which data is divided into physically different units. Partitioning can be done at the application or the system level.

populate   to place occurrences of data values in a previously empty database. *See also* **load**.

primary key   an attribute that contains values that uniquely identify the record in which the key exists.

primitive data   data whose existence depends on only a single occurrence of a major subject area of the enterprise.

processor   the hardware at the center of execution of computer programs. Generally speaking, processors are divided into three categories: mainframes, minicomputers, and microcomputers.

processor cycles   the hardware's internal cycles that drive the computer (for example, initiate I/O, perform logic, move data, perform arithmetic functions).

production environment   the environment where operational, high-performance processing is run.

punched cards   an early storage medium on which data and input were stored. Today, punched cards are rare.

query language   a language that enables an end user to interact directly with a DBMS to retrieve and possibly modify data held under the DBMS. *See also* **database management system (DBMS).**

record   an aggregation of values of data organized by their relation to a common key.

record-at-a-time processing   the access of data a record at a time, a tuple (row) at a time, and so forth.

recovery   the restoration of the database to an original position or condition, often after major damage to the physical medium.

redundancy   the practice of storing more than one occurrence of data. In the case where data can be updated, redundancy poses serious problems. In the case where data is not updated, redundancy is often a valuable and necessary design technique.

referential integrity   the facility of a DBMS to ensure the validity of predefined relationships. *See also* **database management system (DBMS)**.

reorganization   the process of unloading data in a poorly organized state and reloading the data in a well-organized state. Reorganization in some DBMSs is used to restructure data. Reorganization is often called "reorg," or an "unload/reload" process.

repeating groups   a collection of data that can occur several times within a given record occurrence.

rolling summary   a form of storing archival data where the most recent data has the most details stored, and data that is older has fewer details stored.

Sarbanes Oxley a law passed ensuring the integrity of information in publicly traded corporations.

scope of integration the formal definition of the boundaries of the system being modeled.

SDLC *see* **system development life cycle (SDLC).**

self-organizing map (SOM) a method of organizing and displaying textual information according to the frequency of occurrence of text and the relationship of text from one document to another.

sequential file a file in which records are ordered according to the values of one or more key fields. The records can be processed in this sequence starting from the first record in the file, continuing to the last record in the file.

serial file a sequential file in which the records are physically adjacent, in sequential order.

set-at-a-time processing access of data by groups, each member of which satisfies a selection criterion.

snapshot a database dump or the archiving of data out of a database as of some moment in time.

snowflake structure the result of joining two or more star joins.

solutions database the component of a DSS environment where the results of previous decisions are stored. Solutions databases are consulted to help determine the proper course of action in a current decision-making situation.

spiral development iterative development, as opposed to waterfall development. *See also* **waterfall development.**

staging area a place where data in transit is placed, usually coming from the legacy environment prior to entering the ETL layer of processing. *See also* **extract/transform/load (ETL).**

star join a data structure where data is denormalized to optimize the access of the data; the basis of miltidimensional data mart design.

storage hierarchy   storage units linked to form a storage subsystem, in which some units are fast but small and expensive, and other units are large but slower and less expensive.

structured data   data whose content is organized into a predictable format.

subject database   a database organized around a major subject of the corporation. Classical subject databases are for customer, transaction, product, part, and vendor.

system development life cycle (SDLC)   the classical operational system development life cycle that typically includes requirements gathering, analysis, design, programming, testing, integration, and implementation.

system log   an audit trail of relevant system events (for example, transaction entries, database changes, and so forth).

system of record   the definitive and singular source of operational data. If data element ABC has a value of 25 in a database record but a value of 45 in the system of record, by definition, the first value is incorrect and must be reconciled. The system of record is useful for managing redundancy of data.

table   a relation that consists of a set of columns with a heading and a set of rows (that is, tuples).

technologically distributed data warehouse   a data warehouse whose distribution is managed by technology.

theme   the basic message of a document.

time stamping   the practice of tagging each record with some moment in time, usually when the record was created or when the record was passed from one environment to another.

time-variant data   data whose accuracy is relevant to some moment in time. The three forms of time-variant data are continuous time span, event discrete, and periodic discrete data. *See also* **current-value data**.

tourist   an individual who knows where to find lots of things.

transition data   data possessing both primitive and derived characteristics; usually very sensitive to the running of the business. Typical transition data are interest rates for a bank, policy rates for an insurance company, retail sale rates for a manufacturer and/or distributor, and so forth.

transparency   the property of a structure to be examined synthetically.

trend analysis   the process of looking at homogeneous data over a spectrum of time. See also **Executive Information System (EIS)**.

true archival data   data at the lowest level in the atomic database, usually stored on bulk-storage media.

unstructured data   data whose content has no format (typically textual data).

update   to change, add, delete, or replace values in all or selected entries, groups, or attributes stored in a database.

user   a person or process issuing commands and messages to the information system.

waterfall development   the classical approach to development where all development activity of one type is completed before the next development phase begins. The classical SDLC or structured approach to development. *See also* **system development life cycle (SDLC)**.

Web   the network of Internet users.

Web log   the place in the Web site where detailed clickstream data is accumulated.

Zachman framework   a framework for information blueprints developed by John Zachman.

References

Articles

Adelman, Sid. "The Data Warehouse Database Explosion." *DMR* (December 1996). A very good discussion of why volumes of data are growing as fast as they are in the data warehouse environment and what can be done about it.

Geiger, Jon. "Data Element Definition." *DMR* (December 1996). A good description of the definitions required in the system of record.

———. "What's in a Name." *Data Management Review* (June 1996). A discussion of the implications of naming structures in the data warehouse environment.

Gilbreath, Roy, M.D. "Informational Processing Architecture for Outcomes Management." A description of data warehouse as it applies to health care and outcomes analysis. Under review.

Gilbreath, Roy, M.D., Jill Schilp, and Robert Pickton. "Towards an Outcomes Management Informational Processing Architecture." *HealthCare Information Management* 10, No. 1 (Spring 1996). A discussion of the architected environment as it relates to healthcare.

Graham, Stephen. "The Financial Impact of Data Warehousing." *Data Management Review* (June 1996). A description of the cost benefit analysis report done by IDC.

———. "The Foundations of Wisdom." IDC Special Report (April 1996). International Data Corporation (Toronto, Canada). The definitive study on the return on investment for data warehouse, as well as the measurement of cost effectiveness.

Hackney, Doug. "Vendors Are Our Friends." *Data Management Review* (June 1996). Doug Hackney talks about beneficial relationships with vendors.

Hufford, Duane, A.M.S. "A Conceptual Model for Documenting Data Synchronization Requirements." *Data Management Review* (January 1996) Data synchronization and data warehouse.

———. "Data Warehouse Quality, Part 1." *Data Management Review* (January 1996). A description of data warehouse quality.

———. "Data Warehouse Quality, Part II." *Data Management Review* (March 1996). The second part of the discussion on data quality.

Imhoff, Claudia. "End Users: Use 'Em or Lose 'Em." *DMR* (November 1996). An excellent discussion of the ways to manage the end-user data warehouse effort.

Imhoff, Claudia, and Jon Geiger. "Data Quality in the Data Warehouse." *Data Management Review* (April 1996). A description of the parameters used to gauge the quality of warehouse data.

Inmon, W.H. "Choosing the Correct Approach to Data Warehousing: 'Big Bang' vs. Iterative." *Data Management Review* (March 1996). A discussion of the proper strategic approach to data warehousing.

———. "Commentary: The Migration Path." *ComputerWorld* (July 29, 1996). A brief description of some of the issues of migrating to the data warehouse.

———. "Cost Justification in the Data Warehouse." *Data Management Review* (June 1996). A discussion of how to justify DSS and a data warehouse on the cost of reporting.

———. "Data Warehouse Lays Foundation for Bringing Data Investment Forward." *Application Development Trends* (January 1994). A description of data warehouse and the relation to legacy systems.

———. "Data Warehouse Security: Encrypting Data." *Data Management Review* (November 1996). A description of some of the challenges of data warehouse security and industrial-strength security.

———. "The Future in History." *DMR* (September 1996). A discussion of the value of historical information.

———. "Knowing Your DSS End-User: Tourists, Explorers, Farmers." *DMR* (October 1996). A description of the different categories of end users.

———. "Managing the Data Warehouse: The Data Content Card Catalog." *DMR* (December 1996). An introduction to the notion of a data content card catalog, that is, the stratification of data content.

———. "Managing the Data Warehouse Environment." *Data Management Review* (February 1996). Defining who the data warehouse administrator is.

——. "Measuring Capacity in the Data Warehouse." *Enterprise Systems Journal* (August 1996). A discussion of how capacity should be measured in the data warehouse and DSS environment.

——. "Monitoring the Data Warehouse Environment." *Data Management Review* (January 1996). What a data monitor for the data warehouse environment is and why you would need it.

——. "Rethinking Data Relationships for Warehouse Design." *Sybase Server* 5, No. 1 (Spring 1996). A discussion of the issues data warehouse data relationships.

——. "SAP and the Data Warehouse." *DMR* (July/Aug 1996). A description of why the data warehouse is still needed in the face of SAP.

——. "Security in the Data Warehouse: Data Privatization." *Enterprise Systems Journal* (March 1996). A data warehouse requires a very different approach to security than the traditional VIEW-based approach offered by DBMS vendors.

——. "Summary Data: The New Frontier." *Data Management Review* (May 1996). A description of the different types of summary data, including dynamic summary data, static summary data, lightly summarized data, and highly summarized data.

——. "User Reaction to the Data Warehouse." *DMR* (December 1996). A description of the different user types in data warehousing.

——. "Virtual Data Warehouse: The Snake Oil of the '90s." *Data Management Review* (April 1996). A discussion of the virtual data warehouse and how the concept tries to attach itself to the legitimacy of the data warehouse.

"In the Words of Father Inmon." *MIS* (February 1996) An interview with Bill Inmon in November of 1995 in Australia.

Jordan, Arthur. "Data Warehouse Integrity: How Long and Bumpy the Road?" *Data Management Review* (March 1996). A discussion of the issues of data quality inside the data warehouse.

Kalman, David. "The Doctor of DSS." *DBMS Magazine* (July 1994). An interview with Ralph Kimball.

Lambert, Bob. "Break Old Habits to Define Data Warehousing Requirements." *Data Management Review* (December 1995). A description of how the end user should be approached to determine DSS requirements.

——. "Data Warehousing Fundamentals: What You Need to Know to Succeed." *Data Management Review* (March 1996). Several significant strategies for data warehousing to guide you through a successful implementation.

Laney, Doug. "Are OLAP and OLTP Like Twins?" *DMR* (December 1996). A comparison of the two environments.

Myer, Andrea. "An Interview with Bill Inmon." *Inside Decisions* (March 1996). An interview discussing the start of data warehousing, the use of data warehousing for competitive advantages, the origins of Prism Solutions, and building the first data warehouse.

Rudin, Ken. "Parallelism in the Database Layer." *DMR* (December 1996). An excellent discussion of the differences between DSS parallelism and OLTP parallelism.

———. "Who Needs Scalable Systems?" *DMR* (November 1996). A good discussion of the issues of scalability in the data warehouse environment.

Swift, Ron. "Creating Value through a Scalable Data Warehouse Framework." *DMR* (November 1996). A very nice discussion of the data warehousing issues scale.

Tanler, Richard. "Data Warehouses and Data Marts: Choose Your Weapon." *Data Management Review* (February 1996). A description of the differences between data marts and the current level detail of the data warehouse.

———. "Taking Your Data Warehouse to a New Dimension on the Intranet." *Data Management Review* (May 1996). A discussion of the different components of the data warehouse as they relate to the intranet.

Winsberg, Paul. "Modeling the Data Warehouse and the Data Mart." *INFODB* (June 1996). A description of architecture and modeling as it relates to different types of data warehouses.

Wright, George. "Developing a Data Warehouse." *DMR* (October 1996). A very good discussion of snapshots and the basic structures of a data warehouse.

Books

Adamson, Christopher, and Michael Venerable. *Data Warehouse Design Solutions*. New York: John Wiley & Sons, 1998.

Adelman, Sid, and Larissa Moss. *Data Warehouse Project Management*. Reading, MA: Addison Wesley, 2000.

Berry, Michael, and Gordon Linoff. *Data Mining Techniques*. New York: John Wiley & Sons, 1997.

Brackett, Mike. *The Data Warehouse Challenge*. New York: John Wiley & Sons, 1996.

Devlin, Barry. *Data Warehouse: From Architecture to Implementation*. Reading, MA: Addison Wesley, 1997.

Dodge, Gary, and Tim Gorman. *Oracle8i Data Warehousing*. New York: John Wiley & Sons, 2000.

Dyche, Jill. *The CRM Handbook*. Reading, MA: Addison Wesley, 2001.

———. E-data: Turning Data into Information with Data Warehousing. Reading, MA: Addison Wesley, 2000.

English, Larry. *Improving Data Warehouse and Business Information Quality*. New York: John Wiley & Sons, 1999.

Hackathorn, Richard. *Web Farming for the Data Warehouse*, San Francisco: Morgan Kaufman, 1998.

Imhoff, Claudia, Lisa Loftis, and John Geiger. *Building the Customer-Centric Enterprise*. New York: John Wiley & Sons, 2001.

Inmon, W.H. *Building the Data Warehouse*. New York: John Wiley & Sons, 1996.

——. *Building the Data Warehouse*. Second Edition. New York: John Wiley & Sons, 1996.

——. *Building the Operational Data Store*. Second Edition. New York: John Wiley & Sons, 1999.

——. *Data Architecture: The Information Paradigm*. New York: QED, 1993.

——. *Third Wave Processing: Database Machines and Decision Support Systems*. New York: John Wiley & Sons, 1993.

Inmon, W.H., and Richard Hackathorn. *Using the Data Warehouse*. New York: John Wiley & Sons, 1994.

Inmon, W.H., Jon Geiger, and John Zachman. *Data Stores, Data Warehousing and the Zachman Framework*. New York: McGraw Hill, 1997.

Inmon, W.H., Katherine Glassey, and J.D. Welch. *Managing the Data Warehouse*. New York: John Wiley & Sons, 1996.

Inmon, W.H., Claudia Imhoff, and Ryan Sousa. *Corporate Information Factory: Third Edition*. New York: John Wiley & Sons, 2000.

Inmon, W.H., and Jeff Kaplan. *Information Systems Architecture: Development in the 90s*. New York: John Wiley & Sons, 1993.

Inmon, W.H., and Chuck Kelley. *RDB/VMS: Developing the Data Warehouse*. Boston. QED Pub Group, 1993.

Inmon, W.H., Joyce Montanari, Bob Terdeman, and Dan Meers. *Data Warehousing for E-Business*. New York: John Wiley & Sons, 2001.

Inmon, W.H., and Sue Osterfelt. *Understanding Data Pattern Processing*. New York: QED, 1993.

Inmon, W.H., Ken Rudin, Christopher Buss, and Ryan Sousa. *Data Warehouse Performance*. New York: John Wiley & Sons. 1998.

Inmon, W.H., and R.H. Terdeman. *Exploration Warehousing*. New York: John Wiley & Sons, 2000.

Kachur, Richard. *Data Warehouse Management Handbook*. Englewood Cliffs, NJ: Prentice Hall, 2000.

Kelly, Sean. *Data Warehousing: The Key to Mass Customization*. New York: John Wiley & Sons, 1996.

Kimball, Ralph, and Richard Merz. *The Data Webhouse Toolkit*. New York: John Wiley & Sons, 2000.

Kimball, Ralph, Laura Reeves, Margy Ross, and Warren Thornthwaite. *The Data Warehouse Lifecycle Toolkit*. New York: John Wiley & Sons, 1998.

Kimball, Ralph, and Margy Ross. *The Data Warehouse Toolkit: Practical Techniques for Building Dimensional Data Warehouses*. New York: John Wiley & Sons, 2002.

Love, Bruce. *Enterprise Information Technologies*. New York: John Wiley & Sons, 1993.

Marco, David. *Meta Data Repository*. New York: John Wiley & Sons. 2000.

Parsaye, Kamran, and Marc Chignell. *Intelligent Database Tools and Applications*. New York: John Wiley & Sons, 1989.

Silverston, Len. *The Data Model Resource Book Volume I*. New York: John Wiley & Sons, 2001.

Sullivan, Dan. *Document Warehousing and Text Mining*. New York: John Wiley & Sons, 2001.

Swift, Ron. *Accelerating Customer Relationships*. Englewood Cliffs, NJ: Prentice Hall, 2000.

Tannenbaum, Adrienne. *Metadata Solutions*. Reading, MA: Addison Wesley. 2002.

White Papers

NOTE **For more white papers, refer to the Web site,** www.inmoncif.com.

"Accessing Data Warehouse Data from the Operational Environment." Most data flow is from the operational environment to the data warehouse environment, but not all. This Tech Topic discusses the "backward" flow of data.

"Building the Data Mart or the Data Warehouse First?" Although the data mart is a companion to the data warehouse, data mart vendors try to encourage people to build the data mart without building the data warehouse. This Tech Topic addresses the issues relevant to this important design decision.

"Capacity Planning for the Data Warehouse." This Tech Topic discusses the issue of capacity planning and projection for both disk storage and processor resources for the data warehouse environment.

"Changed Data Capture." The resources required for repeatedly scanning the operational environment for the purpose of refreshing the data warehouse can be enormous. This briefing addresses an alternative way to accomplish the same thing.

"Charge Back in the Data Warehouse DSS Environment." Charge back is an extremely useful way to get the end user to take responsibility for the resources that are being consumed. This Tech Topic addresses the issues of charge back.

"Client/Server and Data Warehouse." Client/server processing is quite able to support data warehouse processing. This Tech Topic addresses the issues of architecture and design.

"Creating the Data Warehouse Data Model from the Corporate Data Model." This paper outlines the steps you need to take to create the data warehouse data model from the corporate data model.

"Data Mining: An Architecture." Using the data warehouse is an art. This Tech Topic relates the underlying architecture of the data warehouse to the sophisticated way in which the data warehouse can be used.

"Data Mining: Exploring the Data." Once the data is gathered and organized and the architecture for exploitation has been built, the task remains to use the data. This Tech Topic addresses how data can be mined once the architecture is built.

"Data Stratification in the Data Warehouse." How do you tell someone what is inside a 1-terabyte data warehouse? How many customers? Of what type? Of what age? Living where? Buying how much per year? This Tech Topic addresses the technique of stratifying data in order to create a library "table of contents" that describes the actual data content inside a data warehouse.

"Data Warehouse Administration." With DSS and data warehouses comes the need to manage the environment. A new organizational function has arisen: data warehouse administration. This Tech Topic addresses the charter of data warehouse administration and other important data management issues.

"Data Warehouse Administration in the Organization." Once the need for data warehouse administration is recognized, there is the question, Where should the DWA function be placed in the organization? This Tech Topic addresses the issues of the organization placement of the DWA function.

"The Data Warehouse Budget." This Tech Topic addresses the different patterns of spending and the rate at which funds are spent. In addition, some suggestions for minimizing expenses are included.

"Data Warehouse and Cost Justification." A priori cost justification is a difficult thing to do for a data warehouse. This topic discusses the issues.

"Defining the System of Record." The design considerations of identifying and defining the system of record.

"EIS and Data Warehouse." EIS under a foundation of legacy systems is very shaky, but EIS under a data warehouse foundation is very solid, as detailed in this Tech Topic.

"Explaining Metadata to the End User." When the layman first encounters metadata, the first reaction usually is, "What in the world is metadata and why would I ever need it?" This Tech Topic addresses metadata in very plain, straightforward terms.

"Getting Started." The data warehouse is built iteratively. This Tech Topic describes the first steps you need to take in a detailed manner.

"Information Architecture for the '90s: Legacy Systems, Operational Data Stores, Data Warehouses." This paper defines the role of operational data stores and includes a description of these stores, along with a description of the architecture that results when you mix an operational data store and a data warehouse.

"Information Engineering and the Data Warehouse." The data warehouse architecture is extremely compatible with the design and modeling practices of information engineering. This Tech Topic describes that relationship.

"Iterative Development Using a Data Model." Data modeling is an essential part of the data warehouse design process. This Tech Topic explains how iterative development can be done and at the same time how the data model is incorporated into the development process.

"Loading the Data Warehouse." At first glance, loading data into the data warehouse seems to be an easy task. It is not. This discussion is on the many different considerations of loading data from the operational environment into the data warehouse.

"Managing Multiple Data Warehouse Development Efforts." When the organization starts to build multiple data warehouse efforts simultaneously, a new set of design and development issues arise. This Tech Topic identifies and addresses those issues.

"Managing the Refreshment Process." Data periodically needs to be refreshed from the legacy environment into the data warehouse. The refreshment process is much more complex than one would ever imagine. This Tech Topic addresses the issues of data warehouse refreshment.

"Metadata in the Data Warehouse: A Statement of Vision." Metadata is an important part of the data warehouse environment. Metadata has a dual, conflicting role. In some cases, metadata must be shared. In other cases, metadata needs to be managed autonomously. This Tech Topic addresses the distributed metadata architecture that enables metadata to be simultaneously distributed and managed autonomously.

"Monitoring Data Warehouse Activity." Activity in the data warehouse needs to be monitored for a variety of reasons. This Tech Topic describes monitoring techniques and considerations, and includes a description of why activity monitoring needs to be done.

"Monitoring Data Warehouse Data." Although activity monitoring is very important, so is the monitoring of data itself in the data warehouse. The growth of the data, the quality of the data, and the actual content of the data are all at stake in this issue.

"OLAP and Data Warehouse." Lightly summarized data has always been an integral part of the data warehouse architecture. Today this construct is known as OLAP or a data mart. This Tech Topic addresses the relationship of OLAP and the detailed data found in the data warehouse.

"The Operational Data Store." The operational counterpoint of the data warehouse is the operational data store (the ODS). The ODS is defined and described in detail in this tech topic.

"Operational and DSS Processing from a Single Database: Separating Fact and Fiction." An early notion was that a single database should serve as the basis for both operational processing and DSS analytical processing. This Tech Topic explores the issues and describes why a data warehouse is the appropriate foundation for DSS informational processing.

"Parallel Processing in the Data Warehouse." The management of volumes of data is the first and major challenge facing the data architect. Parallel technology offers the possibility of managing much data. This Tech Topic is on the issues of parallel technology in the data warehouse environment.

"Performance in the Data Warehouse Environment." Performance is as important in the DSS data warehouse environment as it is in the OLTP environment. However, performance plays a very different role. This Tech Topic is all about performance in the DSS data warehouse environment.

"Reengineering and the Data Warehouse." Many organizations are not aware of the strong and positive relationship between reengineering and the data warehouse. This topic identifies the relationship and discusses the ramifications.

"Representing Data Relationships in the Data Warehouse: Artifacts of Data." Design issues for the building of data relationships in the data warehouse

"Security in the Data Warehouse." Security takes on a different dimension in the data warehouse than in other data processing environment. This Tech Topic describes the issues. Tech Topics are available from PRISM Solutions.

"Service Level Agreements in the Data Warehouse Environment." One of the cornerstones of online operations is the service level agreement. Service level agreements are applicable to the data warehouse, but are implemented quite differently.

"Snapshots of Data in the Warehouse." A description of the different types of snapshots and the advantages and disadvantages of each.

"Summary Data in the Data Warehouse/Operational Data Store." Summary data has its own set of unique considerations. There are, for example, dynamic summary data and static summary data. Both types of summary data require very different treatment from the designer and the end user. This Tech Topic creates a taxonomy for summary data and relates the different types of summary data to the data warehouse and the operational data store.

"Telling the Difference Between Operational and DSS." In every shop, the issue arises: What is operational and what is DSS? This Tech Topic tells you how to tell the difference between the two environments.

"Time-Dependent Data Structures." A discussion of the different types of data structures and their advantages and disadvantages

"Using the Generic Data Model." Some corporations have a data model as a point of departure for the design of their data warehouse; others do not. The generic data model jump-starts the data warehouse design and development effort.

"What Is a Data Mart?" Data marts are a natural emanation from the data warehouse. This Tech Topic outlines the salient characteristics of the data mart.

"What Is a Data Warehouse?" This Tech Topic defines what a data warehouse is and what its structure looks like. This is a basic discussion appropriate to anyone investigating the world of data warehouse.

Index

Index

NUMBERS

4GLs (fourth generation languages), 4

9/11, effects on IT architecture, 404

A

activity-based organization, 38

activity-generated events, 112–113

adaptive data marts, 403

aggregating data, 291

airline commission calculation example, 119–121

algorithmic differential of data, 8

analytics, 406–407

architected environment. *See also* data warehouse environment.

architectural environment, 16–18

atomic environment, 16–18

CASE tools, 22

CLDS cycle, 21

data example, 17–18

data integration, 18–19

data warehouse environment, 16–18, 25–28

departmental environment, 16–18

DSS analysts, 20

ETL (Extract/transform/load), 18–19

individual environment, 16–18

levels of data, 16–18

migration from production environment, 23–24

operational environment, 16–18, 22

patterns of hardware utilization, 22

primitive *versus* derived data, 14–15

removing bulk data, 23–24

SDLC (system development life cycle), 20–22

spiral development, 21

transforming legacy systems, 23–24

waterfall development, 21

architected environment, migrating to. *See also* legacy data.

agents of change, 281–282

cleansing operational data, 280–282

delta lists, 282

differences from the operational environment, 282

architected environment, migrating
  to *(continued)*
  feedback loop, 278–279
  impact analysis, 282
  methodology
    Boy/Girl Scout analogy, 286
    data driven, 286
    drawbacks, 283–285
    iterative development, 285
    spiral development, 285
    system development life cycles,
      286
    waterfall development, 285
  motivation for, 281–282
  planning
    corporate data model, 270–271
    data arrival rate, 275
    data occurrences, 275
    data refreshment frequency, 278
    data volume, 273
    defining the system of record,
      272–273
    designing and building interfaces,
      275–276
    designing the data warehouse,
      273–275
    excluding derived data, 272
    identifying the best data, 272–273
    iterative migration, 277
    populating subject areas, 276
    resource requirements, 276
    stability analysis, 275
    starting point, 270
    technological challenges, 273
    typical subject areas, 275
  from the production environment,
    23–24
  report to IS management, 282
  resource estimation, 282
  spiral development, 282
  strategic considerations, 280–282

architectural environment, 16–18
architecture, IT. *See* IT architecture.
archival disk storage, 343–345
Ascential corporation, 283
atomic data, 402
atomic environment, 16–18
auditing
  corporate communications,
    452–454
  data warehouse environment, 61
"average day" comparisons, 27

B
books and publications
  Building the Operational Data Store,
    294
  *The Corporate Information
    Factory*, 16
  *Information Systems Architecture:
    Development in the 90s*, 82
Boy/Girl Scout analogy, 286
Building the Operational Data Store,
  294
business intelligence, 402. *See also*
  structured visualization.
business metadata, 165

C
calculated (derived) data
  excluding, 272
  illustration, 98
  I/O reduction, 96
  versus primitive data, 14–15
CASE tools, 22
CDC (changed data capture), 189
change frequency requirements, 114
CIF (corporate information factory)
  analytics, 406–407
  CRM enhancement, 408
  data volume, 409
  description, 403

ERP (enterprise resource planning), 407–408
future of, 406–409
SAP, 407–408
standards compliance, 408
unstructured data, 408
visualization, 408
CLDS cycle, 21
cleaning data, 109, 300
clickstream data, 290–291, 394–396
clickstream logs, 149
close identifiers, 328
CMSM (cross-media storage manager), 347–348
communications, as unstructured data, 307, 328–329
compacting data, 169
compliance with standards. *See* standards compliance.
compound keys, 60, 169
connectors, data models, 85
contention for resources. *See* resource contention.
context indexes, corporate communications, 454
contextual data, 185–188
contingent sales, 452–453
continuous files, 58–60
continuous organization, 38
convenience fields, 381
converting data, Web environment, 290, 300. *See also* migrating.
corporate data models
  data migration, 270–271
  developing distributed warehouses, 219–223
The Corporate Information Factory, 16
corporate information factory (CIF). *See* CIF (corporate information factory).
cost, data volume, 335–336, 351

cost justification
  CRM (customer relationship management), 425–426
  data integration, 424–426
  DSS analysts, 461
  information overload, 422
  keeping up with competition, 413
  macro level, 414–415
  micro level, 415–417
  recovering legacy information
    building the warehouse, 420–421
    cost of recovery, 419, 420
    description, 418–419
    value of historical data, 425–426
  ROI (return on investment), 461
  speed of data, 423–424
  time value of data, 422–424
  tradeoffs, 421–422
creative indexes, 97–99
creative profiles, 97–99
credit scoring example, 123–125
CRM (customer relationship management)
  cost justification for warehouses, 425–426
  description, 307–308
  enhancement, 408
cross-media storage manager (CMSM), 347–348
cubes, 177–178
cumulative structure, 56–57
current-value data, 33
cyclicity of data, 105–108

D
DASD (direct access storage device), 4, 37. *See also* disk storage; storage.
data
  algorithmic differential, 8
  application-oriented. *See* operational data.

data *(continued)*
  arrival rate, 275
  cleansing, 109
  compacting, 169
  converting to information, 12–14
  correcting, 67–69
  credibility, 7–9
  current-value, 33
  cyclicity of, 105–108
  derived (calculated)
    excluding, 272
    versus primitive, 14–15
    warehouse design, 96, 98
  explorers, 458
  external
    archiving, 267
    capturing, 260
    comparing to internal, 267–268
    components of, 264–265
    frequency of availability, 260
    internal to corporations, 260
    lack of discipline, 260
    metadata, 261–263
    modeling, 265
    in naturally evolving
        architecture, 9
    notification data, 261–263
    problems with, 257–258, 260–261
    secondary reports, 266
    sources of, 259
    storing, 263–264
    types of, 258
    unpredictability, 260
    in warehouses, 260–261
  extraction, 108
  farmers, 458
  format conversion, 111
  heterogeneity, 61–64
  homogeneity, 61–64
  identifying the best, 272–273
  indexing, 162

  integration. *See* integrating data.
  level of detail. *See* granularity.
  life cycles
    description, 386–387
    mapping to warehouse
        environment, 387–388
  loading
    efficiency, 166–168
    en masse, 168
    with a language interface, 168
    for migration, 74–76
    staging, 168
    with a utility, 168
  longevity, 405
  management, 164–165
  metadata
    business, 165
    in data warehousing, 182–185
    designing for, 102–105
    developing distributed
        warehouses, 223, 234–235
    external data, 261–263
    linking unstructured data with
        structured data, 318–319
    managing, 165
    mapping operational data to data
        warehouses, 183–184
    technical, 165
    tracking structural changes,
        184–185
  miners, 459
  monitoring, 162
  occurrences, 275
  organized. *See* structured data.
  overlapping. *See* redundancy.
  placement, 163–164
  primitive. *See* naturally evolving
      architecture; operational data.
  profiles, data warehouse
      environment, 25–28
  purging, 64

refreshing data warehouses, 188–190
refreshment frequency, 278
relationships, 110
replication, refreshing data warehouses, 189
selection, 108
sharing, scope of, 405
speed of, 423–424
summarization, 110
time value of, 422–424
tourists, 459
triggering population of, 112–113
unorganized. *See* unstructured data.
variable length, 169–170
velocity, 391–392
Web environment
  aggregating, 291
  cleaning and converting, 300
  clickstream, 290–291
  converting, 290
  editing, 290, 291
  flow, warehouse to Web, 291–293, 301
  flow, Web to warehouse, 291, 300–310
  historical, 295
  integrating, 302
  interpretive, 295
  profile *versus* detailed transaction, 294–295
  redundant, 294
  summarizing, 291
  user movements, 290–291
  volume, 298, 302
data, levels
  atomic environment, 16–18
  departmental environment, 16–18
  individual environment, 16–18

operational environment
  description, 16–18
  patterns of hardware utilization, 22
  time horizon, 66
  window of opportunity, 65–67
data, operational
  cleansing, 280–282
  from data warehouses
    airline commission calculation example, 119–121
    credit scoring example, 123–125
    description, 117–118
    direct access, 118–119
    examples, 119–126
    indirect access, 119–126
    retail personalization example, 121–123
  to data warehouses
    format inconsistencies, 74
    integration, 72–74
    limiting, 75–77
    loading, 74–76
    semantic field transformation, 74
    transferring from legacy systems, 72
  description, 16–18
  global distributed warehouses, 210–211
data, volume
  cost, 351
  disk storage
    access speed, 342–343
    archival, 343–345
    description, 340
    media transparency, 345
    near-line storage, 341
    performance, 342–343
  financial compliance, 453
  growth over time, 331–333

data, volume *(continued)*
impact of
active data, 338
cost of storage, 335–336
data management activities, 334
data usage patterns, 336–338
dormant data, 338
inactive data, 338
separating data by usage,
339–340
inverting data warehouses,
350–351
managing, 115–116, 159–161
maximum capacity, 352–354
migration issues, 273
moving between environments
across media, 349–350
CMSM (cross-media storage
manager), 347–348
description, 346
usage monitoring, 348–349
reasons for, 409
staging data, 350–351
storage media, 409
technological issues, 273
unstructured data, 326–327
in warehouse design, 111
Web environment, 298, 302
data flow
warehouses
data velocity, 391–392
pushing and pulling data, 393
to/from data marts, 393
tracing, 390–393
Web environment
warehouse to Web, 291–293, 301
Web to warehouse, 291, 300–310
data item set (DIS), 84–88
data mart level. *See* departmental
environment.

data marts
building, 371–375
data to/from warehouses, 393
data velocity, 391–392
versus data warehouses, 127–133
dependent, 371
independent, 370–375
multidimensional model, 370–375
pushing and pulling data, 393
separating from warehouses,
384–385
tracing data, 390–393
data mining, 50, 382
data models
connectors, 85
customizing, 79–81
data warehouse, 81–84
definition, 78–79
description, 79–81
DIS (data item set), 84–88
ERD (entity relationship diagram),
81–84
iterative development, 91–94
JAD (Joint Application Design)
sessions, 83–84
modeling constructs, 84–88
output of, 94
physical model, 88–91
primary data grouping, 84
relational tables, 88
scope of integration, 82
secondary data grouping, 85
stability analysis, 80–81
"Type of" data, 85, 87
user view sessions, 83–84
data passage problem, developing
distributed warehouses, 234
data types, and DSS analysts,
460–461
data warehouse data models, 81–84

data warehouse environment. *See also* architected environment; Web environment.
  activity-based organization, 38
  auditing, 61
  characteristics of, 29–33
  continuous organization, 38
  current-value data, 33
  data mining, 50
  day 1 to day *n* phenomenon, 39–41
  description, 16–18
  design issues. *See* granularity; partitioning.
  exploration, 50
  extended storage. *See* near-line storage; overflow storage.
  heuristic analysis, 52
  individual date organization, 38
  integration, 30–31
  judgment samples, 50–53
  level of detail. *See* granularity.
  living sample database, 50–53
  monitoring, 25–28
  near-line storage, 33
  overflow storage, 33
  partitioning data, 53–56
  storage devices
    DASD (direct access storage device), 37
    fiche, 37
    magnetic tape, 37
    optical disk, 37
  structure of, 33–34
  structuring data
    compounded keys, 60
    continuous files, 58–60
    cumulative structure, 56–57
    simple direct files, 58–59
    storage of rolling summary data, 56–58
  subject orientation, 29–30, 34–38

  time horizons, 33
  time variance, 32–33
  typical subject areas, 34–35
  volatility, 31–32
data warehouses. *See also* DSS (decision support systems).
  combining structured data with unstructured. *See* two-tiered warehouse.
  growth over time, 331–333. *See also* data, volume.
  size. *See* data, volume.
  space requirements, calculating, 140–141
  two-tiered
    definition, 320
    description, 320
    documents, 321–322, 322–323
    keys, 321–322
    libraries, 321–322
    structured tier *versus* unstructured, 321–322
    unstructured communications, 321–322
    visualizing unstructured data, 323–324. *See also* business intelligence.
  users. *See* DSS analysts.
data warehouses, cost justification
  CRM (customer relationship management), 425–426
  data integration, 424–426
  DSS analysts, 461
  information overload, 422
  keeping up with competition, 413
  macro level, 414–415
  micro level, 415–417
  recovering legacy information
    building the warehouse, 420–421
    cost of recovery, 419, 420

data warehouses, cost justification
  (continued)
    description, 418–419
    value of historical data, 425–426
  ROI (return on investment), 461
  speed of data, 423–424
  time value of data, 422–424
  tradeoffs, 421–422
data warehouses, distributed
  developing
    across distributed locations,
      218–219
    coordinating development
      groups, 226–231
    corporate data models, 219–223
    data passage problem, 234
    leaving detailed data, 234
    metadata, 223, 234–235
    on multiple levels, 223–226
    multiple platforms, common
      detail data, 235–236
    multiple platforms, same data
      type, 232–234
    redundancy, 228–231
    related warehouses, 217–223
    requirements, by level, 228–231
    typical cases, 213–215
    unrelated warehouses, 215–217
  global
    accessing, 207–211
    assessing need for, 194–197
    definition, 193–194
    description, 198–201
    mapping to local, 201–205
    moving data into, 208–210
    operational data, 210–211
    redundancy, 206–207
  independently evolving, 213
  local
    accessing, 207–211
    assessing need for, 194–197

    definition, 193–194
    description, 197–198
    mapping to global, 201–205
    moving data to global, 208–210
  technological distribution, 211–213
  types of, 193–194
databases, designing. *See*
    designing databases; designing
    warehouses.
data-driven methodology, 286
day 1 to day *n* phenomenon, 39–41
DBMS (database management
  system)
  for data warehouses
    changing for existing data
      warehouses, 174–175
    cubes, 177–178
    data-warehouse specific, 172–174
    freespace, 174
    indexing, 174
    load-and-access processing, 172
    multidimensional processing,
      175–181
    OLAP foundation, 177–178
    problems, 179–181
    required facilities, 173
  history of DSS (decision support
    systems), 4
decision support systems (DSS). *See*
    DSS (decision support systems).
default values, designing, 109
delta lists, 282
denormalization, 94–102
departmental environment, 16–18
dependent data marts, 371. *See also*
    data marts.
derived (calculated) data
  excluding, 272
  illustration, 98
  I/O reduction, 96
  versus primitive data, 14–15

designing databases. *See also*
 designing warehouses.
dimensions, 360–361
fact tables, 360–361, 361–362
multidimensional model
 description, 360–361
 independent data marts, 370–375
multidimensional model *versus*
 relational
 direct *versus* indirect data access,
  364, 365–366
 graceful change, 367–369
 meeting future needs, 366–367
 model shape, 363
 overview, 362
 reshaping relational data, 364–365
 roots of differences, 363–364
 serviceability, 363
ODS (operational data store),
 435–436
relational model
 description, 357–359
 granularity, 359
 normalizing data, 359
review checklist
 administering the review, 466
 agenda, 465
 description, 463–464
 example, 466–488
 participants in reviews, 465
 results, 465–466
 timing of reviews, 464
snowflake structures, 361–362
star join approach, 126–133
designing warehouses. *See also*
 designing databases.
activity-generated events, 112–113
aggregate records. *See* profile
 records.
change frequency requirements,
 114

corporate data model conformance,
 111
creative indexes, 97–99
creative profiles, 97–99
data
 cleansing, 109
 cyclicity of, 105–108
 extraction, 108
 format conversion, 111
 large volumes of, 111, 115–116
 relationships, 110
 selection, 108
 summarization, 110
 triggering population of, 112–113
data marts *versus* data warehouses,
 127–133
data migration, 273–275
data models
 connectors, 85
 customizing, 79–81
 data warehouse, 81–84
 definition, 78–79
 description, 79–81
 DIS (data item set), 84–88
 ERD (entity relationship
  diagram), 81–84
 high level. *See* ERD.
 iterative development, 91–94
 JAD (Joint Application Design)
  sessions, 83–84
 low level. *See* physical model.
 mid level. *See* DIS.
 modeling constructs, 84–88
 output of, 94
 physical model, 88–91
 primary data grouping, 84
 relational tables, 88
 scope of integration, 82
 secondary data grouping, 85
 stability analysis, 80–81

designing warehouses *(continued)*
   "Type of" data, 85, 87
   user view sessions, 83–84
default values, 109
denormalization, 94–102
derived (calculated) data, 96, 98
design issues. *See* granularity;
   partitioning.
distributed warehouses. *See*
   developing distributed
   warehouses.
ETL (extract/transform/load
   software), 111–112
events, 112–113
integration, 108–112
merging multiple inputs, 109
metadata, 102–105
multidimensional approach. *See*
   star joins.
multiple outputs, 109
nonkey data, 109
nonstandard input formats, 110
normalization, 94–102
ODS support, 133–134
operational data, from data
   warehouses
  airline commission calculation
    example, 119–121
  credit scoring example, 123–125
  description, 117–118
  direct access, 118–119
  examples, 119–126
  indirect access, 119–126
  retail personalization example,
    121–123
operational data, to data
   warehouses
  format inconsistencies, 74
  integration, 72–74
  limiting, 75–77
  loading, 74–76

  semantic field transformation, 74
  transferring from legacy
    systems, 72
operational input keys, 109
process models, definition, 78–79
profile records
  definition, 114
  description, 114–115
  drawbacks, 116
  multiple, 117
redundant data, 96–97
reference data, 103–105
reference tables, 103–105
referential integrity, 99
renaming data elements, 110
requirements, 134–135
resequencing input files, 109
snapshots
  components of, 113
  definition, 100–101
  description, 100–102
  examples, 113
stability criteria, 114
star joins, 126–133
time-generated events, 112–113
transformation, 108–112
Zachman framework, 134–135
developing distributed warehouses
across distributed locations,
   218–219
coordinating development groups,
   226–231
corporate data models, 219–223
data passage problem, 234
leaving detailed data, 234
metadata, 223, 234–235
on multiple levels, 223–226
multiple platforms, common detail
   data, 235–236
multiple platforms, same data
   type, 232–234

redundancy, 228–231
related warehouses, 217–223
requirements, by level, 228–231
typical cases, 213–215
unrelated warehouses, 215–217
dimensions, database, 360–361
direct access storage device
(DASD), 4, 37. *See also* disk
storage; storage.
DIS (data item set), 84–88
discovery mode of inquiry, 276
disk storage. *See also* DASD;
storage.
access speed, 342–343
archival, 343–345
description, 340
media transparency, 345
near-line storage, 341
performance, 342–343
distributed warehouses. *See also*
data warehouses.
developing
across distributed locations,
218–219
coordinating development
groups, 226–231
corporate data models, 219–223
data passage problem, 234
leaving detailed data, 234
metadata, 223, 234–235
on multiple levels, 223–226
multiple platforms, common
detail data, 235–236
multiple platforms, same data
type, 232–234
redundancy, 228–231
related warehouses, 217–223
requirements, by level, 228–231
typical cases, 213–215
unrelated warehouses, 215–217

global
accessing, 207–211
assessing need for, 194–197
definition, 193–194
description, 198–201
mapping to local, 201–205
moving data into, 208–210
operational data, 210–211
redundancy, 206–207
independently evolving, 213
local
accessing, 207–211
assessing need for, 194–197
definition, 193–194
description, 197–198
mapping to global, 201–205
moving data to global, 208–210
technological distribution, 211–213
types of, 193–194
documents. *See also* unstructured
data.
in two-tiered data warehouses,
321–322, 322–323
as unstructured data, 307, 321–322,
322–323, 328–329
drill-down analysis
creating data for, 245–247
description, 243–245
performance indicators, 244
DSS (decision support systems). *See
also* data warehouses.
architected environment
architectural environment, 16–18
atomic environment, 16–18
CASE tools, 22
CLDS cycle, 21
data example, 17–18
data integration, 18–19
data warehouse environment,
16–18, 25–28

DSS (decision support systems)
(continued)
data warehouse users. *See* DSS
analysts.
departmental environment, 16–18
DSS analysts, 20
ETL (extract/transform/load),
18–19
individual environment, 16–18
levels of data, 16–18
migration from production
environment, 23–24
operational environment,
16–18, 22
patterns of hardware
utilization, 22
primitive *versus* derived data,
14–15
removing bulk data, 23–24
reporting, 64–65
SDLC (system development life
cycle), 20–22
spiral development, 21
transforming legacy systems,
23–24
waterfall development, 21
naturally evolving architecture
algorithmic differential of data, 8
converting data to information,
12–14
data credibility, 7–9
definition, 6
external data, 9
levels of extraction, 8–9
productivity, 9–12
resource requirements, 11
time basis of data, 7
DSS analysts
cost justification, 461
data types, 460–461
discovery mode, 276
explorers, 458
farmers, 458
feedback loop, 278–279
heuristic mode, 458
mindset of, 20
miners, 459
requirements for warehouses
data models, 378
relational foundation, 378–379
statistical processing, 379–380
Zachman framework, 134–135
ROI (return on investment), 461
tourists, 459
types of, 457–460
user community, 459–460
user view sessions, 83–84
dual level granularity, 46–50

E
EAI (enterprise application
integration), 403
eBusiness environment
clickstream data, 394–396
data granularity, 394–396
definition, 393
ODS (operational data store), 397
performance, 397
profile records, 396–397
warehouse interface to, 394
warehouse support for, 299–300,
302
editing data, 290, 291
EIS (executive information systems)
on data warehouses, 247–248
detailed data, 253–254
drill-down analysis
creating data for, 245–247
description, 243–245
performance indicators, 244
event mapping, 251–253

example, 240–243
retrieving data, 248–251
summary data only, 254–255
uses for, 240
e-mail data. *See also* unstructured
    data.
  auditing, 452–454
  context indexes, 454
  data volume, 453
  indexing, 453–454
  screening, 453–454
  simple indexes, 454
end users. *See* DSS analysts.
end-user requirements
  data models, 378
  relational foundation, 378–379
  statistical processing, 379–380
  Zachman framework, 134–135
enterprise application integration
    (EAI), 403
ERD (entity relationship diagram),
    81–84
ERP (enterprise resource planning),
    407–408
ETL (extract/transform/load)
    software, 18–19, 111–112, 402
event mapping, 251–253
events, 112–113
executive information systems (EIS).
    See EIS (executive information
    systems).
exploration, 50
exploration warehouses
  description, 380–382
  external data, 384
  freezing, 383
  refreshing, 383
explorers, 458
external data. *See also* data.
  archiving, 267
  capturing, 260

comparing to internal, 267–268
components of, 264–265
frequency of availability, 260
internal to corporations, 260
lack of discipline, 260
metadata, 261–263
modeling, 265
in naturally evolving
    architecture, 9
notification data, 261–263
problems with, 257–258, 260–261
secondary reports, 266
sources of, 259
storing, 263–264
types of, 258
unpredictability, 260
in warehouses, 260–261
extract programs, history of DSS, 5
extracting data, 108
extract/transform/load (ETL)
    software, 18–19, 111–112, 402

F
fact tables, 360–361, 361–362
farmers, 458
FASB (Financial Accounting
    Standards Board), 444
feedback loop, DSS analysts and
    data architects, 278–279
fiche, definition, 37
financial compliance
  activities governed by, 446
  auditing corporate
      communications, 452–454
  compliance data *versus* simple
      data, 448
  content, 448
  context indexes, 454
  contingent sales, 452–453
  data volume, 453

financial compliance *(continued)*
description, 446–447
indexing corporate
communications, 453–454
longevity of data, 449
past and present transactions,
446–447
prefinancial negotiations, 449–452
probability of access, 448
procedures, 446
reasons for, 449–452
response time, 448
screening data, 453–454
sensitivity of data, 448
simple indexes, 454
speed of queries, 448
transactions audited, 447–449
financial warehouses, 397–399
format conversion, 111
format inconsistencies, 74
4GLs (fourth generation
languages), 4
freespace, 174
freezing exploration warehouses,
383
frequency of availability, external
data, 260

G
GAAP (Generally Accepted
Accounting Practices), 444
GIF (government information
factory), 404–406
Girl/Boy Scout analogy, 286
global distributed warehouses
accessing, 207–211
assessing need for, 194–197
definition, 193–194
description, 198–201
mapping to local, 201–205
moving data into, 208–210

operational data, 210–211
redundancy, 206–207
GM (Granularity Manager), 290–291,
394–396
government information factory
(GIF), 404–406
granularity
benefits of, 42–43
clickstream (Web log) data, 149
for data marts, 42–43
definition, 41
dual levels, 46–50
eBusiness environment, 394–396
examples
banking environment, 150–151
insurance company environment,
155–156
level of detail, 43–46
manufacturing environment,
151–154
feedback loop techniques, 148–150
input to planning, 141–142
level, determining, 140–141,
147–148
manufacturing process control
data, 149
overflow data, 142–143
overflow storage, 144–147
raising, 149
record size and, 143
relational database model, 359
too low, 41, 149–150
and versatility, 41
Granularity Manager (GM), 290–291,
394–396

H
hardware utilization, patterns of, 22
heterogeneous data, 61–64
heuristic analysis, 52
heuristic mode, 458

historical data, 295, 425–426, 431–432
homogeneous data, 61–64

I

identifiers, unstructured data, 328
impact analysis, 282
independent data marts, 370–375.
    See also data marts.
independently evolving distributed
    warehouses, 213
index utilization, efficiency, 165
indexing
    corporate communications, 453–454
    data, 162
    DBMS, 174
index-only processing, 171
individual date organization, 38
industrially recognized themes,
    313–316
information overload, 422
Information Systems Architecture:
    Development in the 90s, 82
Inmon approach. *See* relational
    databases.
integrating data
    architected environment, 18–19
    cost justification for warehouses,
        424–426
    data models, 82
    designing warehouses, 108–112
    operational data to data
        warehouse, 18–19, 72–74
    scope of, 405
    warehouse environment, 30–31
    Web environment, 302
integrating data, unstructured with
    structured
    fundamental mismatches, 310
    matching all information, 312–313
    matching text across environments,
        310–311

probabilistic matching, 311–312
problems, 309
removing stop words, 310–311
text basis for, 308–311
themed matches
    industrially recognized themes,
        313–316
    linkage through abstraction,
        318–319
    linkage through metadata,
        318–319
    linkage through themes, 317–318
    naturally occurring themes,
        316–317
    raw match of data, 317
interfaces, designing and building,
    275–276
interpretive data, 295
inverting data warehouses, 350–351
IT architecture, history of
    adaptive data marts, 403
    atomic data, 402
    business intelligence, 402
    CIF (corporate information
        factory)
        analytics, 406–407
        CRM enhancement, 408
        data volume, 409
        description, 403
        ERP (enterprise resource
            planning), 407–408
        future of, 406–409
        SAP, 407–408
        standards compliance, 408
        unstructured data, 408
        visualization, 408
    EAI (enterprise application
        integration), 403
    ETL (extract/transform/load), 402
    GIF (government information
        factory), 404–406

IT architecture, history of *(continued)*
longevity of data, 405
9/11, effects of, 404
origins of IT, 402
scope of data sharing and
integration, 405
security of government data, 405
unstructured data, 403
unstructured visualization, 404
VODS (virtual operational data
store), 403
Iterations methodology, 282
iterative development, 91–94, 285
iterative migration, 277

J
JAD (Joint Application Design)
sessions, 83–84
judgment samples, 50–53
justifying the cost of warehouses.
See cost justification.

K
keys, two-tiered data warehouses,
321–322
Kimball approach. *See*
multidimensional databases;
relational databases.

L
language interface, 166
leaving detailed data, developing
distributed warehouses, 234
legacy data. *See also* migrating to the
architected environment;
operational data.
recovering, cost justification
building the warehouse, 420–421
cost of recovery, 419, 420
description, 418–419

value of historical data, 425–426
refreshing data warehouses,
188–190
transforming to data warehouse,
23–24
legal requirements. *See* standards
compliance.
levels of data
See atomic environment
See departmental environment
See individual environment
See operational environment
levels of extraction, in naturally
evolving architecture, 8–9
libraries, two-tiered data
warehouses, 321–322
life cycles
data
description, 386–387
mapping to warehouse
environment, 387–388
system development
architected environment, 20–22
data migration, 286
SDLC (system development life
cycle), 20–22
limiting migrated data, 75–77
living sample database, 50–53
load-and-access processing, 172
loading data
efficiency, 166–168
en masse, 168
with a language interface, 168
for migration, 74–76
staging, 168
with a utility, 168
local distributed warehouses
accessing, 207–211
assessing need for, 194–197
definition, 193–194

description, 197–198
mapping to global, 201–205
moving data to global, 208–210
lock management, 171
logs
clickstream, 149
granularity, 149
tapes, refreshing data warehouses, 190
transaction, 295
Web, 149, 290
longevity of data, financial compliance, 449

M
macro level cost justification, 414–415
magnetic tape, 37
Management Information System (MIS), history of DSS, 4
mapping
data life cycles to warehouse environment, 387–388
global distributed warehouses to local, 201–205
operational data to data warehouses, 183–184
matching unstructured data with structured data
fundamental mismatches, 310
matching all information, 312–313
matching text across environments, 310–311
probabilistic matching, 311–312
problems, 309
removing stop words, 310–311
text basis for, 308–311
themed matches
industrially recognized themes, 313–316

linkage through abstraction, 318–319
linkage through metadata, 318–319
linkage through themes, 317–318
naturally occurring themes, 316–317
raw match of data, 317
merging multiple inputs, 109
metadata. *See also* data.
business, 165
in data warehousing, 182–185
designing for, 102–105
developing distributed warehouses, 223, 234–235
external data, 261–263
linking unstructured data with structured data, 318–319
managing, 165
mapping operational data to data warehouses, 183–184
technical, 165
tracking structural changes, 184–185
micro level cost justification, 415–417
migrating to the architected environment. *See also* architected environment; legacy data.
agents of change, 281–282
cleansing operational data, 280–282
delta lists, 282
differences from the operational environment, 282
feedback loop, 278–279
impact analysis, 282
methodology
Boy/Girl Scout analogy, 286
data driven, 286
drawbacks, 283–285
iterative development, 285

migrating to the architected
environment *(continued)*
spiral development, 285
system development life cycles,
286
waterfall development, 285
motivation for, 281–282
planning
corporate data model, 270–271
data arrival rate, 275
data occurrences, 275
data refreshment frequency, 278
data volume, 273
defining the system of record,
272–273
designing and building
interfaces, 275–276
designing the data warehouse,
273–275
excluding derived data, 272
identifying the best data, 272–273
iterative migration, 277
populating subject areas, 276
resource requirements, 276
stability analysis, 275
starting point, 270
technological challenges, 273
typical subject areas, 275
from the production environment,
23–24
report to IS management, 282
resource estimation, 282
spiral development, 282
strategic considerations, 280–282
mindset
DSS analysts, 20
Web users, 290
miners, 459
MIS (Management Information
System), history of DSS, 4
modeling, external data, 265
modeling constructs, 84–88

monitoring
activity monitor, 146–147
data, 144, 146–147, 162, 348–349
data warehouse environment,
25–28
multidimensional databases. *See also*
relational databases.
description, 360–361
independent data marts, 370–375
versus relational
direct *versus* indirect data access,
364, 365–366
graceful change, 367–369
meeting future needs, 366–367
model shape, 363
overview, 362
reshaping relational data, 364–365
roots of differences, 363–364
serviceability, 363
multidimensional DBMS level. *See*
departmental environment.
multidimensional processing,
175–181

N

naturally evolving architecture
algorithmic differential of data, 8
converting data to information,
12–14
data credibility, 7–9
definition, 6
external data, 9
levels of extraction, 8–9
productivity, 9–12
resource requirements, 11
time basis of data, 7
near-line storage, 33, 341
9/11, effects on IT architecture, 404
nonkey data, 109
nonstandard input formats, 110
normalization, 94–102
notification data, 261–263

O

ODS (operational data store)
  classes of, 133–134, 434–435
  database design, 435–436
  designing support for, 133–134
  eBusiness environment, 397
  example, 440–441
  historical data, 431–432
  multiple, 439
  profile records, 432–433
  size, compared to warehouses,
      436–437
  time slicing, 438
  transaction integrity, 437–438
  updating, 430–431
  versus warehouses, 430–433
  Web environment, 293, 439–440
OLAP foundation, 177–178
OLAP level. *See* departmental
    environment; multidimensional
    processing.
OLTP (online transaction
    processing), history of DSS, 4
operational data. *See also* data.
  cleansing, 280–282
  from data warehouses
    airline commission calculation
        example, 119–121
    credit scoring example, 123–125
    description, 117–118
    direct access, 118–119
    examples, 119–126
    indirect access, 119–126
    retail personalization example,
        121–123
  to data warehouses
    format inconsistencies, 74
    integration, 72–74
    limiting, 75–77
    loading, 74–76

  semantic field transformation, 74
  transferring from legacy
      systems, 72
  description, 16–18
  global distributed warehouses,
      210–211
operational data store (ODS). *See*
    ODS (operational data store).
operational environment
  description, 16–18
  patterns of hardware utilization, 22
  time horizon, 66
  window of opportunity, 65–67
operational input keys, 109
optical disk, definition, 37
overflow storage
  active *versus* inactive data, 144
  activity monitor, 146–147
  alternative storage, 144, 145
  CMSM (cross-media storage
      manager), 144, 146
  definition, 33, 145
  dormant data, 144
  fat storage, 144
  infrequently used data, 144
  low-performance disk, 144
  magnetic tape, 144, 145
  media for, 145
  monitoring data usage, 144
  near-line storage, 144, 145
  performance implications, 146
  software requirements, 146–147

P

parallel storage, 164–165
partitioning data, 53–56
PC technology, history of DSS, 4
PDF files. *See* unstructured data.
performance
  data warehouse environment,
      25–28

disk storage, 342–343
drill-down analysis, 244
eBusiness environment, 397
Web environment, 302
petabytes, 349
physical model, 88–91
planning for migration
  corporate data model, 270–271
  data arrival rate, 275
  data occurrences, 275
  data refreshment frequency, 278
  data volume, 273
  defining the system of record,
    272–273
  designing and building interfaces,
    275–276
  designing the data warehouse,
    273–275
  excluding derived data, 272
  identifying the best data, 272–273
  iterative migration, 277
  populating subject areas, 276
  resource requirements, 276
  stability analysis, 275
  starting point, 270
  technological challenges, 273
  typical subject areas, 275
populating data warehouses,
  triggering event, 112–113
populating subject areas, 276
predictive analysis, 296–297
prefinancial negotiations, 449–452
primary data grouping, 84
primitive *versus* derived data, 14–15
probabilistic matching, 311–312
process models, definition, 78–79
productivity, in naturally evolving
  architecture, 9–12
profile records
 data warehouse
  definition, 114
  description, 114–115

drawbacks, 116
  multiple, 117
eBusiness environment, 396–397
ODS (operational data store),
  432–433
Web users, 295–297
pulling data, 393
purging data, 64
pushing data, 393

Q
quick-restore capability, 171–172

R
redundancy
  designing data warehouses, 96–97
  distributed warehouses, 206–207,
    228–231
  global distributed warehouses,
    206–207
  Web environment, 294
reference data, 103–105
reference tables, 103–105
referential integrity, 99
refreshing data warehouses
  CDC (changed data capture), 189
  data replication, 189
  description, 188–190
  log tapes, 190
  techniques, 189–190
refreshing exploration warehouses,
  383
regulations. *See* standards
  compliance.
relational databases. *See also*
  multidimensional databases.
  description, 357–359
  granularity, 359
  normalizing data, 359
relational tables, 88
renaming data elements, 110

requirements for warehouses
  data models, 378
  relational foundation, 378–379
  statistical processing, 379–380
  Zachman framework, 134–135
resequencing input files, 109
resource, requirements, naturally
  evolving architecture, 11
resource contention
  convenience fields, 381
  data mining warehouses, 382
  exploration warehouses
    description, 380–382
    external data, 384
    freezing, 383
    refreshing, 383
response time
  DSS environment, 26–27
  financial compliance, 448
  Web environment, 301
restoring data, quick-restore
  capability, 171–172
retail personalization example,
  121–123
review checklist, database design
  administering the review, 466
  agenda, 465
  description, 463–464
  example, 466–488
  participants in reviews, 465
  results, 465–466
  timing of reviews, 464
ROI (return on investment), 461
rolling summary data, 56–58

S
SAP, 407–408
Sarbanes Oxley standards
  activities governed by, 446
  auditing corporate
    communications, 452–454

compliance data *versus* simple
    data, 448
content, 448
context indexes, 454
contingent sales, 452–453
data volume, 453
description, 446–447
indexing corporate
    communications, 453–454
longevity of data, 449
past and present transactions,
    446–447
prefinancial negotiations, 449–452
probability of access, 448
procedures, 446
reasons for, 449–452
response time, 448
screening data, 453–454
sensitivity of data, 448
simple indexes, 454
speed of queries, 448
transactions audited, 447–449
screening data for financial
    compliance, 453–454
SDLC (system development life
    cycle), 20–22
secondary data grouping, 85
secondary reports, 266
security, government data, 405
selecting data for migration, 108
self-organizing map (SOM), 324–327
semantic field transformation, 74
sensitivity of data, financial
    compliance, 448
simple direct files, 58–59
simple indexes of corporate
    communications, 454
size of warehouses. *See* data,
    volume.
snapshots
  components of, 113
  definition, 100–101

snapshots *(continued)*
  description, 100–102
  examples, 113
snowflake structures, 361–362
SOM (self-organizing map), 324–327
speed of data, 423–424
spider webs
  example, 180
  history of DSS (decision support
    systems), 6
spiral development, 21, 282, 285
spreadsheet data. *See* unstructured
  data.
stability analysis, 80–81, 275
stability criteria, 114
staging data, 350–351
staging data for loading, 168
standards compliance
  basic activities, 445
  bridging structured and
    unstructured data, 408
  FASB (Financial Accounting
    Standards Board), 444
  financial compliance
    activities governed by, 446
    auditing corporate
      communications, 452–454
    compliance data *versus* simple
      data, 448
    content, 448
    context indexes, 454
    contingent sales, 452–453
    data volume, 453
    description, 446–447
    indexing corporate
      communications, 453–454
    longevity of data, 449
    past and present transactions,
      446–447
    prefinancial negotiations, 449–452
    probability of access, 448

    procedures, 446
    reasons for, 449–452
    response time, 448
    screening data, 453–454
    sensitivity of data, 448
    simple indexes, 454
    speed of queries, 448
    transactions audited, 447–449
  GAAP (Generally Accepted
    Accounting Practices), 444
  history of, 443–445
star joins, 126–133
statistical processing, requirements
  for warehouses, 379–380
stop words, removing, 310–311
storage
  across multiple media, 182
  offline. *See* overflow storage.
  rolling summary data, 56–58
storage devices
  DASD (direct access storage
    device), 37
  fiche, 37
  low-performance disk, 144
  magnetic tape, 37, 144, 145
  media for, 145, 409
  media transparency, 345
  optical disk, 37
  Web environment, 297–298
structured data. *See also* architected
  environment; data warehouses;
  unstructured data.
  business intelligence, 323–324
  components, 327–328
  compounded keys, 60
  continuous files, 58–60
  cumulative structure, 56–57
  simple direct files, 58–59
  sources of, 305–306
  storage of rolling summary data,
    56–58

visualizing, 323–324. *See also* business intelligence.
structured visualization, 323–324. *See also* business intelligence.
subject areas
  migration, 275
  populating, 276
  typical, 34–35, 275
subject orientation, 29–30, 34–38
summarizing data
  for migration, 110
  Web environment, 291
system development life cycles
  architected environment, 20–22
  data migration, 286
  SDLC (system development life cycle), 20–22
system of record
  current value, 400
  defining, 272–273
  definition, 399
  description, 399–401

T

technical metadata, 165
technological challenges, data migration, 273
technology, and data warehouses
  compound keys, 169
  cross-technology interfaces, 162–163
  data
    compacting, 169
    indexing, 162
    loading, efficiency, 166–168
    management, 164–165
    monitoring, 162
    placement, 163–164
    variable length, 169–170
    volume, managing, 159–161
  index utilization, efficiency, 165
  index-only processing, 171
  language interface, 166
  lock management, 171
  metadata management, 165
  multiple media, 161
  parallel storage, 164–165
  quick-restore capability, 171–172
testing data warehouses, 190–191, 388–390
text, matching unstructured data with structured, 308–311. *See also* themed matches.
themed matches
  industrially recognized themes, 313–316
  linkage through abstraction, 318–319
  linkage through metadata, 318–319
  linkage through themes, 317–318
  naturally occurring themes, 316–317
  raw match of data, 317
time basis of data, in naturally evolving architecture, 7
time horizon, 65–67
time horizons, 33
time slicing, ODS, 438
time value of data, 422–424
time variance, 32–33
time-generated events, 112–113
tortoise and hare, parable, 253–254
tourists, 459
tracing data flow, 390–393
tracking Web-user movement. *See* clickstream data.
transaction integrity, ODS, 437–438
transaction log, 295
transferring data from legacy systems. *See* migrating.
transformation, designing for, 108–112

trends, contextual data, 185–188
two-tiered warehouse
  definition, 320
  description, 320
  documents, 321–322, 322–323
  keys, 321–322
  libraries, 321–322
  structured tier *versus* unstructured,
    321–322
  unstructured communications,
    321–322
  visualizing unstructured data,
    323–324. *See also* business
    intelligence.
"Type of" data, 85, 87

U
unstructured data. *See also*
  structured data.
  categories of, 307
  CIF (corporate information
    factory), 408
  close identifiers, 328
  communications, 307, 328–329
  data volume, 326–327
  description, 306
  documents, 307, 321–322, 322–323,
    328–329
  history of IT, 403
  identifiers, 328
  SOM (self-organizing map),
    324–327
  sources of, 305
  two-tiered warehouse
    definition, 320
    description, 320
    documents, 321–322, 322–323
    keys, 321–322
    libraries, 321–322
    structured tier *versus*
      unstructured, 321–322

    unstructured communications,
      321–322
    visualizing unstructured data,
      323–324. *See also* business
      intelligence.
    visualizing, 323–324. *See also*
      business intelligence.
  warehouse structure, 325–326
unstructured data, integrating with
  structured. *See also* two-tiered
  warehouse.
  fundamental mismatches, 310
  matching all information, 312–313
  matching text across environments,
    310–311
  probabilistic matching, 311–312
  problems, 309
  removing stop words, 310–311
  text basis for, 308–311
  themed matches
    industrially recognized themes,
      313–316
    linkage through abstraction,
      318–319
    linkage through metadata,
      318–319
    linkage through themes, 317–318
    naturally occurring themes,
      316–317
    raw match of data, 317
unstructured visualization, 404
updating, ODS, 430–431
user requirements. *See* requirements
  for warehouses.
users, warehouses. *See* DSS analysts.
users, Web
  mindset, 290
  movements, tracking, 290–291
  profiles, 295–297
  tracking movements, 290–291

V

visualizing
  structured data, 323–324
  unstructured data, 323–324, 408.
      See also business intelligence.
VODS (virtual operational data
  store), 403
volume of data. *See* data, volume.

W

waterfall development, 21, 285
Web environment
  clickstream data, 290–291
  data
    aggregating, 291
    cleaning and converting, 300
    clickstream, 290–291
    converting, 290
    editing, 290, 291
    historical, 295
    integrating, 302
    interpretive, 295
    profile *versus* detailed transaction,
        294–295
    redundant, 294
    summarizing, 291
    user movements, 290–291
    volume, 298, 302
  data flow
    warehouse to Web, 291–293, 301
    Web to warehouse, 291, 300–310
  eBusiness, 299–300, 302
  GM (Granularity Manager), 290–291
  multiple site support, 298–299
  ODS (operational data store), 293,
      439–440
  performance, 302
  predictive analysis, 296–297
  profile records, 295–297
  response time, 301
  storing data in, 297–298
  tracking user movement. *See*
      clickstream data.
  transaction log, 295
  user mindset, 290
  user movements, tracking, 290–291
  user profiles, 295–297
  Web logs, 290
Web logs, 290
Welch, J D, 282

Z

Zachman, John, 134
Zachman framework, 134–135
Zeno's parable, 253–254